ADVANCE PRAISE FOR

HERE'S LOOKING AT YOU

"*Here's Looking at You* takes on at least two sizable tasks—exploring the relationship of politics *and* film as well as assessing political messages *in* film—no easy feat for a slim volume. Ernest Giglio's engaging analysis brings even the casual consumer of contemporary cinemaplex fare to a clearer understanding of how today's industry came to be, and brings into sharper focus both the potential of and the challenges facing film as a medium for the expression of political ideas. In short, Giglio's work is a great resource for introducing students to the longstanding, tempestuous relationship between Hollywood and American politics."

Staci Beavers, Associate Professor of Political Science,
California State University, San Marcos

"Ernest Giglio does a good job of surveying films with political content that were produced or distributed by Hollywood studios since the turn of the twenty-first century. ...I used *Here's Looking at You* in my undergraduate course on Politics and Film last semester.... I will be using it again next semester."

Jeffrey Hart, Professor of Political Science,
Indiana University, Bloomington

HERE'S LOOKING AT YOU

Politics,
Media &
Popular Culture

David A. Schultz, *General Editor*

Vol. 11

PETER LANG
New York • Washington, D.C./Baltimore • Bern
Frankfurt am Main • Berlin • Brussels • Vienna • Oxford

Ernest Giglio

HERE'S LOOKING AT YOU

Hollywood, Film & Politics

SECOND EDITION

PETER LANG
New York • Washington, D.C./Baltimore • Bern
Frankfurt am Main • Berlin • Brussels • Vienna • Oxford

Library of Congress Cataloging-in-Publication Data

Giglio, Ernest D.
Here's looking at you: Hollywood, film & politics / Ernest Giglio.— 2nd ed.
p. cm. — (Politics, media, and popular culture; v. 11)
Filmography: p.
Includes bibliographical references and index.
1. Motion pictures—Political aspects. 2. Politics in motion pictures.
I. Title: Here is looking at you. II. Title. III. Series: Politics, media & popular culture; v. 11.
PN1995.9.P6G56   791.43'658—dc22   2004022839
ISBN 13: 978-0-8204-7099-3
ISBN 10: 0-8204-7099-6
ISSN 1094-6225

Bibliographic information published by **Die Deutsche Bibliothek**.
Die Deutsche Bibliothek lists this publication in the "Deutsche
Nationalbibliografie"; detailed bibliographic data is available
on the Internet at http://dnb.ddb.de/.

Cover design by Lisa Barfield

The paper in this book meets the guidelines for permanence and durability
of the Committee on Production Guidelines for Book Longevity
of the Council of Library Resources.

To my colleagues in Politics & Film and their students,
who will come to both appreciate and fear the power of the medium.

CONTENTS

List of Illustrations ix
Preface xi
Acknowledgments xv

One   It's Showtime: The Hollywood-Washington Connection 1
Two   In Search of the Political Film: From Riefenstahl to the Three Stooges 27
Three   Nonfiction Film: Investigating the Real 43
Four   Kiss, Kiss, Bang, Bang: Or How I Came to Love Sex
        and Violence on the Big Screen 69
Five   HUAC and the Blacklist: The Red Scare Comes to Hollywood 95
Six   Reel Politicians: Idealists, Saviors and Villains 119
Seven   Picturing Justice: The Law and Lawyers in Hollywood Films 145
Eight   Hollywood Goes to War: From the Great War to the Good War 175
Nine   Picturing Vietnam on Film: Lessons Learned and Forgotten 201
Ten   Hollywood Confronts the Nuclear Holocaust 221
Eleven Does Political Film Have a Future in Hollywood? 243

        Notes 255
        Select Bibliography 283
        Select Filmography 291
        Index 313

 ILLUSTRATIONS

Permission to include movie stills and to reprint cartoons is acknowledged.

Figure One. Total Recall cartoon: 2003.
        Reprinted with permission, United Feature Syndicate, Inc. 5
Figure Two. Money and Politics cartoon: 2004.
        Reprinted with permission, *New Orleans Times-Picayune.* 10
Figure Three. Hollywood Stars and the Iraqi War cartoon: 2003.
        Reprinted with permission, *Omaha World-Herald.* 17
Figure Four. Birth of a Nation: 1915. 25
Figure Five. Michael Moore receives rifle. 54
        Bowling for Columbine: 2002. Reprinted with permission, Photofest.
Figure Six. Filmmaker Leni Riefenstahl: 1932–33.
        Reprinted with permission, Bavarian State Library Archives, Munich. 62
Figure Seven. McCarthy-Terrorist cartoon: 2003.
        Reprinted with permission, *Green Bay Press Gazette.* 100
Figure Eight. Salt of the Earth: 1953.
        Reprinted with permission of *Movie Stars News* and Jerry Ohlinger. 114
Figure Nine. Ford cartoon: 1995.
        Reprinted with permission, *Seattle Post-Intelligencer.* 135
Figure Ten. Actor Gene Kelly and local citizens of Williamsport, Pennsylvania: 1945.
        Reprinted with permission of Charlotte Gordon. 182

Figure Eleven. Jackie Cochran instructing WASPs during World War II: 1943.
　　　　Reprinted with permission, The Women's Collection,
　　　　Texas Woman's University. 187
Figure Twelve. Local Korean War parade, Williamsport, Pennsylvania: 1997
　　　　Reprinted with permission, *Williamsport Sun-Gazette*. 193
Figure Thirteen. Marilyn Monroe in Korea: 1954. Personal Collection. 194
Figure Fourteen. *Dr. Strangelove*: 1964.
　　　　Reprinted with permission, Columbia Pictures. 231
Figure Fifteen. Three Mile Island: 2004.
　　　　Reprinted with permission, *Williamsport Sun-Gazette*. 234

PREFACE

T his book began a long time ago in the fertile imagination of a small boy whose childhood was entwined with the movies. In the early stages of childhood his mother would take the boy and his sister to the neighborhood movie theater every Friday afternoon after school while his father worked the night shift at the Brooklyn Navy Yard. The world of work and the travails of war were remote events to youngsters compared to a good movie and games in the schoolyard.

The trip to the movies became a weekly ritual—a double feature at the theater followed by a stop at Fisher's Jewish bakery on the way home to pick up danish pastries and a loaf of rye. Of course, I must confess that often I failed to understand much of what I saw on the big screen, but I still found it fascinating, often funny, occasionally sad, and sometimes boring. The westerns were exciting, and I laughed heartily at the cartoons and the slapstick comedies. Sometimes my mother had to nudge me when I dozed off during the love scenes. But at my age, what did I know of such things!

When I reached twelve I was permitted to go to the movies with my friends. Now the weekly picture show involved Saturdays rather than Friday afternoons. I have no sense of what Saturday matinees were like elsewhere, but a kid in New York City during World War II could spend six hours in a dark movie theater and never see the same film twice. I remember the routine well: all the boys (girls were not part of the gang) would pack a lunch, hide it inside our knickers, enter the theater around 9:00 in the morning and emerge sometime after 3:00 in the afternoon with eyes that had to adjust to the light. Once several of us were caught with our lunch and had to eat it standing up in the theater lobby shortly after having had breakfast. But that was a small price to pay for more than six hours of entertainment.

During those hours in the theater we would see a double feature (the first film was usually a major Hollywood production and the second a shorter feature known as a B-film), the weekly serial and newsreel, cartoons, several short subjects, and occasionally play one or two give-away contests. Going to the movies was a social experience in those days. I even saw Babe Ruth once when the local theater was showing *Pride of the Yankees*. But mostly those Saturday matinees featured war movies in which actors like John Wayne, Humphrey Bogart, and Errol Flynn single-handedly took on the Nazis and the Japanese. For a youngster, they were larger-than-life heroes; reel characters that invaded our dreams and assured us that we would be victorious against the forces of fascism. For a change of pace, the theater would show an animated film from Walt Disney, a Lassie adventure story, a musical, or a Bing Crosby/Bob Hope road movie as those at home waited out the war.

But as a typical teenager, going to the movies was a way to escape from homework for a few hours or a diversion from a game of stickball in the schoolyard. Movies were not to be taken seriously, an attitude, I later learned, that I shared with the justices on the U. S. Supreme Court, who considered movies to be purely entertainment, much like us kids. It was not until the 1950s that the Court would reverse itself and bring movies under the protection of the First Amendment to the U. S. Constitution.

Similarly, I did not come to appreciate film as an art form or as a politicizing agent until, as an undergraduate student at Queens College (CUNY); I religiously took the subway into Manhattan every Wednesday afternoon to attend the newly opened Museum of Modern Art's film series. Now the weekly ritual took on substance as I became familiar with the great directors of the silent screen—D. W. Griffith, Fritz Lang, Erich von Stroheim—and with the films of Charlie Chaplin, Lillian Gish, John Barrymore, John Gilbert, and Rudolph Valentino. These weekly visits provided an opportunity to see some of the truly great film classics of the silent cinema, such as *Birth of a Nation, Intolerance*, and *Modern Times*, and to develop an interest in film as an expression of the political culture. Going to the movies was no longer a social diversion; it became serious business.

I was so smitten by the movies that as a graduate student at Syracuse University in the 1960s, I found it possible to combine my interest in constitutional law with my love affair with the movies. After completion of the academic course work, I had to decide on a topic for my doctoral dissertation. My interest in law and my fascination with film provided a perfect opportunity for a marriage of convenience. Doing the dissertation proved to be more exciting than any film script. Imagine the excitement when your research discovers that in the second half of the twentieth century, movies were subject to censorship by state agencies and local censor boards in addition to the internal rules and regulations of the industry's Production Code Administration. The history of film censorship also proved to be indicative of the revolution in social mores that had occurred during the century. For example, the earliest known instance of film censorship occurred in 1896 on the boardwalk in Atlantic City where the peep show *Dolorita's Passion Dance* was apparently too risqué for the local police, who proceeded to shut it down. If Dolorita's shaking and shimmering were too provocative for a Victorian public that covered itself in head-to-toe swimwear, it would strike contemporary audiences, comprised of individuals whose swimwear is just enough to cover the essential "private parts," to be downright silly. With virtually two-thirds of contemporary Hollywood films R-rated, it is a rare film indeed where the major characters keep their clothes on. At the beginning of the twenty-first century, motion pictures serve to document the changes that have occurred in social mores, gender and racial attitudes, and sexual values and practices.

As a college professor, the young boy who watched the movies grow up with him now had an opportunity to fuse his love for movies with his professional interests in an undergraduate course on *The Political Film*. To provide material for the course, I put together a custom-made in-house reader, which subsequently provided the impetus for this book. It has proven to be a long, but rewarding journey.

PREFACE TO THE SECOND EDITION

It is not often that authors receive a second chance to reexamine their work. Peter Lang has given me that opportunity and I want to thank the publisher for it.

The original *Here's Looking at You*, a title taken from that famous line in nearly everyone's favorite film, *Casablanca*, was a nostalgic and sentimental journey backwards into the past by a boy who grew up with the movies and came to love them. Since publication five years ago, reflection has turned that childhood affection into disappointment. The second edition, therefore, is a much more critical and acerbic book, reflecting the author's discontent with mainstream Hollywood. Three events are responsible for this transformation. Foremost were the revelations by the Federal Trade Commission that the industry used youngsters to test R-rated film material. What was even more dispiriting was the fact that few opposition voices outside of the industry were heard, including parents, who should have been outraged. On second thought, maybe this should not be so surprising because teenagers flock to see R-rated raunchy and vulgar comedies and mindless violent action films, either with their parents' consent or indifference. Hollywood seems to cater to teenagers, sophomoric humor, and formulaic action films. My personal guess is that there are only a handful of intelligent films intended for adults released by Hollywood each year. *Adult* here does not refer to sexually explicit films but rather mature stories of humans or institutions confronting the serious issues that challenge them.

Two other recent events are also troublesome. One has to do with the increasing entanglement of show business/pop culture celebrities with real-world politics. The line that once separated entertainment from politics has virtually disappeared. Politics is serious business; it should not be reduced to a popularity contest or serve as a source for public entertainment. Given the world situation, intelligence, knowledge, and public service should be required of our leaders, not appearances on the big screen or late-night television. To the best of my knowledge there is no automatic transfer effect from the cinematic world to the real one. The other disappointing news is the demise of the independent film movement since the potential promise first shown in the 1970s and 1980s. In the new Hollywood, the major studios continue to churn out blockbusters, action flicks, and teenage fare, but, unfortunately, it seems that they have turned their subsidiaries into clones. As "indie" budgets escalate upward, they will surely lose their most precious commodity—independence—and with it, the future hopes for the political film genre. Unfortunately, in Hollywood, success is not always a blessing.

 ACKNOWLEDGMENTS

T his book has been a labor of love, but even efforts of affection are enriched by external stimulation and assistance. Without a doubt, this project has benefited greatly from numerous contributors, many of whom remain unaware of the extent of their support and encouragement. However, there are colleagues, libraries, and organizations that have provided the kind of valuable assistance that demands recognition.

I am particularly indebted to Lycoming College for providing part of the research funding for this project and for allowing me to take a sabbatical leave at an opportune time in order to complete the manuscript. I also want to thank the librarians and staff at the University of Wisconsin Film & Television Archives, the Wisconsin State Historical Society, the British Film Institute in London, and especially the reference librarians at Lycoming College—Janet Hurlbert, Tasha Cooper, Margaret Murray, and Lisette Ormsbee—who provided the kind of services that researchers desperately require at a moment's notice. Additional support came from several colleagues: Alan and Meryl Aldridge at the University of Nottingham (UK) offered valuable suggestions during the early stages of the manuscript, Professor Christa Slaton of Auburn University made several helpful suggestions regarding the first two chapters, and Professor John Williams of Principia College read a good deal of the first draft and tested the manuscript in his political film course. His students' comments were immensely valuable during the subsequent rewrite. Equally important was the information collected during the documentary film program at the 1998 Robert Flaherty Film Seminar, particularly in writing chapter three. I would be remiss if I failed to mention the importance of the feedback received from the students in my Political Film course as well as the comments obtained from several Elderhostel groups. A number of student assistants helped with the library research, but Emily Hautala and Stephanie Wilkie deserve mention for putting the filmography together. Special recognition has to be given to Elisabeth Giglio whose editorial skills and insightful comments improved the quality of the writing and provided the text with structure and clarity. Without her invaluable suggestions, this book might have remained on computer disk rather than the printed page. Finally, Heidi Burns, senior editor at Peter Lang, read through the entire first draft with a keen eye for detail and a razor-sharp pencil to detect the mistakes. Hollywood, of course, has been a silent collaborator, providing the films that serve as the primary textual material. While many film studios were helpful, a few were uncooperative, refusing permission to use photo stills from their films.

Naturally I accept responsibility for any errors or omissions in the manuscript. As is usually the case in writing a book, the buck always stops at the author's desk.

Williamsport, PA

ACKNOWLEDGMENTS FOR THE SECOND EDITION

I would like to reiterate my appreciation for all those who assisted on the original book and take this opportunity to recognize those who have contributed to the second edition of *Here's Looking at You*. As usual, the Lycoming College library staff assisted in securing books from interlibrary loan and referencing research material. Two staff members were particularly helpful: Gail Spencer and Megan Maiolo. The Bavarian State Library provided a photo still of Leni Riefenstahl from its archives. Jack Schrems, a longtime colleague, read through the draft of the second edition and provided valuable advice, suggestions, and corrections. A political scientist by profession, Dr. Schrems demonstrated considerable skill in editing the first draft. The staff at Peter Lang was always available to answer questions, but I am particularly indebted to the series editor, David Schultz, for his support and encouragement along the way. I hope the second edition meets his expectations. I would be remiss in not recognizing the encouragement provided by my colleagues in the Conference on Politics & Film, a related group within the American Political Science Association. There are far too many members to mention individually but the following colleagues have used the book and provided valuable insights and feedback: Barbara Allen, Ron Briley, Richard Ostrom, Jay Parker, Jeffrey Sadow, Christa

Slaton, David Whiteman, John Williams, and Kevan Yenerall. Michael Haas, head of the Political Film Society, deserves a special word of gratitude for his assistance in the formation of the Politics & Film Group.

A closing note of thanks to the newspapers, cartoonists, film studios, and individuals who gave permission to reprint their work. In two cases, permission was unobtainable. After six months of effort, I failed to locate the rights holder of the blacklisted film, *Salt of the Earth*. On the other hand, while Michael Moore is quite visible, he also was uncooperative. All efforts to reach him or his staff to secure permission were unsuccessful. I was particularly irked because my mail to him was either ignored or answered with a generic response, usually promoting his latest book or film. In fact, Mr. Moore has been so successful at evading me that I am tempted to make a film on the subject and call it *Michael and Me*.

Williamsport, PA &
New York City

IT'S SHOWTIME

The Hollywood-Washington Connection

CHAPTER ONE

"It used to be that Washington admired Hollywood for its sex and Hollywood admired Washington for its power. These days, Washington admires Hollywood for its power and Hollywood admires Washington for its sex."

ROBERT LICHTER, CENTER FOR MEDIA & PUBLIC POLICY

Close your eyes! Imagine the following scene taking place in a Hollywood studio where two writers are brainstorming a script involving American politics:

FIRST SCREENWRITER: "Gee whiz. How did we get stuck with this project? Everybody knows there's no market for political films in this country."

SECOND SCREENWRITER: "Shut up and get to work. We need an outline by this afternoon. Got any brilliant ideas?"

FIRST SCREENWRITER: "Yeah, let's jump in the Jaguar and drive to Vegas."

SECOND SCREENWRITER: "Brilliant!"

FIRST SCREENWRITER: "Okay, how about this. The major character is a womanizing president who gets caught doing it with an intern in the Oval Office?"

SECOND SCREENWRITER: "Where have you been, lamebrain? That's been done already. We need something fresh, something different, even unusual."

FIRST SCREENWRITER: "Well, try this. We make the central character a professional athlete who's getting too old to play, so he decides to go into politics. Say, a former NFL Quarterback?"

SECOND SCREENWRITER: "Too conventional."

FIRST SCREENWRITER: "Okay, let's make him a professional wrestler, one of those costume guys that enters the ring in drag."

SECOND SCREENWRITER: "Are you brain dead? I know this is a movie but who's going to believe that the American people are so dumb as to elect a guy from the WWF into office?"

FIRST SCREENWRITER: "I got it! We'll make him an ex-NASCAR driver. Can't you just visualize it: helmet down, goggles on, behind the wheel."

SECOND SCREENWRITER: "Hmm. It has possibilities. I like the concept but I got a better idea. We'll make the major character an actor—an action adventure star—a macho guy whose film career is coming to an end. But he's still very popular so he goes into politics. In California. It would have to be California to be believable."

FIRST SCREENWRITER: "That's great. I'm beginning to see this guy now. He's the kind of guy who throws terrorists off Air Force One and can say 'Get off my plane' without everybody in the theater laughing."

SECOND SCREENWRITER: "Oh, this is good. We can convert those clichés into political slogans."

FIRST SCREENWRITER: "But wait. What about sex? Don't we need to put sex in this script if we want to market it to teenagers?"

SECOND SCREENWRITER: "That's true. But we're going against type here. Our guy likes women but he's a family man, complete with wife, kids, and dog."

FIRST SCREENWRITER: "I get it—he's a tough guy, but sensitive. He can kill with his bare hands but he also loves kids and animals."

SECOND SCREENWRITER: "Oh, this is good stuff. But what's his politics? Liberal? Conservative?"

FIRST SCREENWRITER: "Republican. He fits the new political image of compassionate conservatism. He speaks softly but carries an AK-47. He's that kind of guy."

SECOND SCREENWRITER: "Brilliant. You're a genius. Start writing your Oscar speech. Let's fill in the outline and take it to production."

How likely is it that this fictitious scenario will ever happen? Fifty years ago the basic premise would have been considered ludicrous, even by Hollywood standards. But today, this sort of storyline is likely to be sitting in your local city hall, state capital, or someday, possibly in the Oval Office.

THE RELATIONSHIP BETWEEN FILM AND POLITICS

The relationship between film and politics occurs in two contexts. One takes place in the real world of politics where the film industry and its members run for office, support candidates, raise and contribute money to political campaigns, lobby governments for special favors, and work as political activists for a host of causes. The other relationship occurs on the big screen where film content serves as an instrument for propaganda, as an agent for social change, and as a manipulator of public opinion. But sometimes these relationships intersect in an environment where fantasy and reality are so entangled that one cannot be separated from the other.

Hasta La Vista, Baby: I'm Back

Once upon a time in a small town near Graz, Austria, a boy was born to the Schwarzeneggers and christened Arnold. That's right, Arnold Schwarzenegger! Arnold was a sickly child, the kind of boy featured in the *Charles Atlas* magazine ads brushing the kicked sand off his face. Growing up he was bullied by both his father, a policeman and Nazi sympathizer, and his brother. As a consequence, Arnold retreated into the fantasy world of the movies, escaping into the kind of make-believe land characterized by anthropologist Hortense Powdermaker as "the dream factory."[1] At age fifteen he visualized a life of fame, fortune, and power, modeling himself after a noted bodybuilder. His father scoffed at his bodybuilding fantasy, but Arnold was undeterred. The first step in the realization of his dream came in 1968 when the owner of a worldwide fitness empire took him to America. The next step came at age twenty, when the once skinny Arnold, won the top amateur bodybuilder event and became Mr. Universe. The following year, the developed Arnold beat the professional bodybuilder champ and added the title of Mr. Olympia to his reputation. In the succeeding years, Arnold won thirteen such contests.

His first foray into movies occurred in the B-film *Hercules in New York* (1970), but it would take another five years for him to receive national recognition in the documentary *Pumping Iron* (1975). Schwarzenegger's main competition in the film came from another bodybuilder, Louis Ferrigno, who later played the Incredible Hulk in the movies. But Schwarzenegger dominated the documentary and impressed the Hollywood talent scouts. Seven years later, Schwarzenegger became a star playing the avenging hero *Conan the Barbarian* (1982). With the first of *The Terminator* (1984) films, he became a superstar, eventually making twenty-seven films that grossed $1.5 billion and earning him a salary of $25 to $30 million per picture.

By the mid eighties, little Arnie, the skinny kid who could hardly speak English when he came to America and who never lost his accent, had achieved fame and riches. The next step up in his dream fulfillment ladder occurs in 1986 when he marries Maria Shriver, the daughter of Sargent Shriver and Eunice Kennedy. Now he is a member of the Kennedy clan. Through marriage, Schwarzenegger has a political power base, although his politics are more conservative Republican than liberal Democrat. With his promising movie career he has little time for politics except for the occasional appointed position in his home state of California. Still, the elder George Bush appointed him to serve as chairman of the President's Counsel on Physical Fitness & Sports, a largely honorary national post. By the millennium, Schwarzenegger had worked in inner-city youth programs and in the national fitness program but had little political experience and had yet to run for public office.[2]

All that changed in 2003. The determined skinny kid who became an international bodybuilder capitalized on the political misfortunes of the incumbent Democratic governor of California, Gray Davis, to enter the political arena. Davis, elected in 1998 and reelected handily in 2002, became the object of a recall election as a consequence of the state's economic downturn, the 2001 energy crisis that resulted in high utility bills and rolling blackouts, and the voter perception that the governor was aloof and distant.[3] California is one of the American states that offer its citizens three forms of "direct democracy"—the initiative, referendum, and recall. The initiative provides an opportunity for citizens to propose legislation or an amendment to the state constitution while the referendum allows voters to approve or reject a specific project or piece of legislation. On the other hand, the recall is a procedure that permits voters to remove elected officials from office before their terms expire.

At the start of the recall process, almost 250 candidates had paid the required filing fee. The relatively easy filing requirements attracted both serious (the 2002 Republication gubernatorial candidate Bill Simon, State Senator Tom McClintock, Peter Ueberroth, former commissioner of major league baseball, and political commentator Arianna Huffington) and less serious (former child TV star Gary Coleman, pornography publisher Larry Flynt, and porno star Mary Carey) candidates. By the October 7 election date, only 135 names remained on the ballot, including several candidates who dropped out of the race after the ballots were printed.

Schwarzenegger announced his candidacy as a guest on Jay Leno's *Tonight Show*, hoping to follow in the political footsteps of another novice celebrity, pro-wrestler Jesse Ventura.[4] He immediately became the leading Republican candidate, with his chief opposition on the Democratic side coming from the incumbent Lt. Governor, Cruz Bustamante. Shwarzenegger quickly established a Web site to promote his candidacy and raise campaign funds. He elicited help from experienced Republicans like former California Governor Pete Wilson and former Secretary of State George Shultz. From the beginning, his campaign was dogged by accusations concerning political allegiances and his treatment of women. MoveOn,[5] an Internet-based political activist group intervened in the recall election, urging its Web readers not to vote for Arnold. Their anti-Schwarzenegger campaign focused on two reasons: his alleged Nazi sympathies and his sexual harassment of women. The Nazi charge failed for lack of specific evidence and the revelation that Schwarzenegger had been honored by the Simon Wiesenthal Center for supporting its Holocaust studies. The sexual harassment charges, based upon complaints by sixteen women, followed him throughout the campaign. Schwarzenegger's response was to deny the charge or to avoid the specific complaints while admitting to bad behavior in the past.

FIGURE 1. Total Recall cartoon: 2003. Reprinted with permission, United Feature Syndicate, Inc.

The California recall election escalated into a three-ring circus.[6] First, civil rights groups challenged the election ballot when it was discovered that six counties were scheduled to use a punch-card ballot similar to the one in Florida during the 2000 presidential election. The civil rights group noted that these particular counties contained heavy minority populations. The federal appeals court found the ballot confusing and ordered the election delayed until March in order to give the counties time to replace the ballots. On rehearing by the full court, however, the decision was reversed and the October 7 election date retained. Another criticism of the recall ballot concerned its design. Voters needed first to decide whether or not to recall Governor Davis by voting YES or NO. Voters who wanted Davis out of Sacramento would vote NO and proceed to vote for one of the 135 replacement candidates. Voters who favored retaining Davis would vote YES but they still had to vote for the governor's replacement. The ballot's two-segment construction placed the governor's supporters in the awkward position of voting simultaneously for him and his replacement. No Hollywood writer could have scripted a more convoluted ballot.

When the votes were counted, 55 percent favored the recall of the governor, only the second gubernatorial recall in American politics. On Davis's replacement, Schwarzenegger easily gained first place, receiving 48 percent of the votes, a considerable achievement in a state where registered Democrats outnumber Republicans. The recall campaign cost California taxpayers some $60 million. The various candidates spent an estimated $42 million, including $10 million from Schwarzenegger. Unlike most fairy tales, the end of this one has yet to be written. Despite his victory, Schwarzenegger's political future remains unclear. He is prevented from running for the presidency unless the U.S. Constitution is amended, an unlikely event. Nonetheless, he is eligible to run for reelection in 2006 or consider a race for the U.S. Senate.

Whatever his personal political ambitions, Schwarzenegger faces a daunting challenge. California has a substantial budget deficit that will require tax increases, spending cuts, or both. Moreover, the new governor needs to provide the kind of environment that better attracts business to the state and discourages businesses from leaving for tax-friendlier locations. Hollywood expects him to curb the movement of filming to Canada, Mexico, and overseas locations. Finally, Schwarzenegger will find that it is easier to "kick butt" on screen than work with a Democratic legislature, his Republican colleagues, and the voters (not just his fans) of California. Less than one year into office, the governor, upset over the failure to pass his budget, referred to the Democratically controlled legislature as "girlie men," and the political honeymoon was over. Did the Terminator take on one job too many?

INTO THE POLITICAL ARENA

Entertainment and reality sometimes coalesce into a hybrid existence where real players and their screen counterparts become virtually indistinguishable. For example, the plots of two films, *Wag the Dog* (1977) and *Primary Colors* (1998) during Bill Clinton's presidency center on an American president besieged by charges of improper sexual behavior. Both movies were in release during the time when Clinton faced charges of sexual misbehavior with Paula Jones and Monica Lewinsky. The reel president's political consultants in *Wag the Dog* wage a phony war against Albania as a diversion while president Clinton initiated a campaign of saber-rattling against Saddam Hussein, which had the temporary effect of taking the accusations off the front page. As the film's political consultant (played by Robert DeNiro) says: "You want to win this election, you better change the subject. You wanna change this subject, you better have a war."[7] Four days after Clinton admitted to the American people that he had an "inappropriate relationship" with

Lewinsky, he ordered cruise missile strikes against terrorist camps in Sudan and Afghanistan. Several months later, during his congressional impeachment hearings, Clinton ordered more air strikes against Iraq. Fortuitous timing or another effort by the president's spin doctors to divert attention away from the impeachment hearings? Meanwhile, in *Primary Colors*, John Travolta's Southern governor is mounting a campaign for the presidency. Travolta's character is an undisguised imitation of the real Bill Clinton, right down to his weakness for Krispy Kremes. Coincidental? Unlikely since the film was based on a book written by a member of Clinton's 1992 campaign staff. These two films provide contemporary evidence that seriously questions the accuracy of producer Samuel Goldwyn's alleged answer to an assistant who wanted to make a political film: "If you want to send a message, use Western Union."

Hollywood is foremost in the entertainment business, but the industry also delivers political messages in selected films. As an example, the cynical message of *Wag the Dog* seems to be that political spin-doctors easily manipulate the American people and are readily deceived by second-rate media talent. The film wants audiences to accept a gullible American public, one easily fooled by emotional appeals and false appeals to nationalism. This trait is usually associated with fascism rather than the reasoned discourse of democracy. Moreover, the wicked satire in *Wag the Dog* distorts the line between truth and virtual reality when it portrays an egotistical Hollywood director's successful creation of a studio war waged on television to save the president's political career, an act that ultimately costs the director his life.

Primary Colors, on the other hand, plays like an apology for sleazy and ruthless politicians. It expects audiences to love the womanizing and unscrupulous governor because his public policies are better than those of his opponent. Essentially the movie asks audiences to forgive the flaws of Travolta's character, a Clinton clone, because he will make a superior president. These may not be the civics lessons American parents want their children to learn. While it is undisputed that the vast majority of Hollywood fare is designed to attract audiences and make a profit, *Primary Colors* and *Wag the Dog* remind us that, occasionally, the film industry is also in the business of delivering political messages, both intentional and inadvertent.

As early as D. W. Griffith's *Birth of a Nation* (1915), a biased presentation of slavery, Reconstruction policies, and the Ku Klux Klan, filmmakers have viewed the medium as an instrument to communicate stories that express their personal beliefs about love, life, death, and politics. Had the film industry produced commercial entertainment exclusively, the history of Hollywood (and America too) would be quite different. As presented, the historical record of the Hollywood-Washington relationship includes: efforts by government to censor and regulate motion pictures; the film industry's anti-union activities, which erupted periodically into violent conflict between workers and the studios; the government's utilization of the film industry for propaganda purposes during both World Wars; and the sanctioned compliance, especially by the studios, with the methods of the House Un-American Activities Committee (HUAC) and the industry's imposition of the secret blacklist. Not even Orwell's Big Brother could rewrite this history to make the film industry a virtuous hero.

In the context of practical politics, the Hollywood-Washington relationship is best expressed in terms of political campaigns and elections, support for issue-oriented causes, ally and partner with government during national crises, and lobbyist for policies that directly affect the industry and its members.

In the past, entertainers usually did not seek political office. Entering politics is essentially a post-World War II development, although P. T. Barnum, the nineteenth-century showman, served two terms in the Connecticut state legislature. The recent successful candidates tended to be Republicans such as Shirley Temple, the child star, George Murphy, a 1930s to 1940s song and dance man in Hollywood musicals, Ronald Reagan, a B-actor for two decades until he was smitten with the political bug, and Sonny Bono, a singer and TV personality who shared the spotlight with his wife, Cher. Of this group, Reagan and Bono had previous political experience at the state or local level before entering the national scene. Temple failed in her bid for Congress but was rewarded with several appointed positions, including a post as delegate to the United Nations (UN). Murphy served one term in the U.S. Senate while Bono died while serving in Congress. His widow finished her husband's term and was reelected for another term. Reagan, of course, was the most notable Hollywood politician, serving two terms as governor of California and two terms as U.S. president.[8]

When not running for office, Hollywood activists are not averse to providing encouragement and support to their favorite candidates. What do candidates receive from their connection with Hollywood stars? Money, of course. Perhaps of equal importance is national exposure through association with Hollywood types that cannot be measured in dollars alone. Hobnobbing with prominent Hollywood figures brings a kind of celebrity status to politicians, particularly those who have yet to establish national reputations. The Kennedys did this in the 1950s and 1960s and Clinton in the 1990s. The question whether it is profitable for a politician to have friends in Hollywood is no longer raised in a celebrity-obsessed culture where announcements for public office are made on late-night television and where candidates appear on talk shows to raise money and promote their candidacy through indirect appeals. Schwarzenegger was not the only candidate to exploit his celebrity status. Former Attorney General Janet Reno also appeared on the *Tonight Show* with Jay Leno to gather support in her race against Jeb Bush for governor of Florida. How much longer will it be before Jay Leno appears before Congress to discuss policy matters?

Overall, members of the Hollywood community play their greatest political role and make their most significant contributions through their status as celebrities. Their celebrity standing and their money provide them with the kind of access and influence unavailable to the ordinary citizen. What other explanation can there be for the media conspiring with Warren Beatty as he contemplated over several months in 2000 whether he ought to consider a run for the Democratic presidential nomination. While that is Beatty's prerogative, it is doubtful that an ordinary citizen would be deemed worthy enough to be given three months of publicity, including front-page coverage in the *New York Times*.[9]

As a class, celebrities do not shy away from publicity. Usually, that publicity takes the form of film promotions, appearances at premieres, and charity events. However, at the 2004 Democratic National Convention in Boston there were so many celebrities involved that a TV watcher who tuned in during the middle of the convention proceedings could be forgiven if he mistakenly thought it was a Hollywood roast. During the convention week, the media pounced on celebrities like Ben Affleck for their opinions and for their interest in running for political office.

Money is the engine that drives election campaigns. Candidates for public office seek financial support for their increasingly expensive political races. Without financial resources, a campaign will be stillborn. The Hollywood-Washington connection plays an important role: first in providing the funding for outsiders to run, and second in permitting insiders with the financial base to contemplate a run for public office. There is nothing intrinsically wrong with Hollywood fulfilling these functions because it is not a crime for film personalities to run for elective office. Nor is it illegal for Hollywood to protect its economic self-interest by recruiting its leadership elite from the White House staff. Neither is there a law against Hollywood soliciting political assistance from its Washington friends. What is truly alarming, however, is that Hollywood money gains the industry an unequal amount of access and an inordinate amount of influence while it blurs the line between public office and celebrity status. The development and acceptance of a "culture of celebrity" has led one critic to observe that popular entertainment has replaced ideology in American politics. In this regard it seems that political candidates emulate movie stars, that primary campaigns resemble casting calls, that political campaigns are closer to auditions than to the articulation of substantive policy agendas, and that the electorate today behaves as if it were a film audience passively surveying the political performance.[10]

Is it profitable for a politician to have friends in Hollywood? Without question! Actor Warren Beatty, for example, reportedly raised one million dollars for the 1972 McGovern presidential campaign; singer Barbra Streisand raised $1.5 million for the Democratic Party in 1986 by hosting a $5000-a-plate dinner.[11] A decade later, Streisand exceeded even that amount by raising an estimated $3.5 million for the

FIGURE 2. Money and Politics cartoon: 2004. Reprinted with permission, *New Orleans Times-Picayune.*

Democratic Party with a posh affair for President Clinton at her Beverly Hills estate. Ticket prices ranged from $2500 to $12,500; the latter sum entitled the donor to a preferred seat close to the president.[12] In the 2000 presidential race, Streisand gave a concert for Al Gore's campaign, which raised several millions. However, she did not forget Bill Clinton, as the singer threw a luncheon party for the former president to raise funds for his presidential library. What makes celebrities like Streisand so valuable as campaign fund-raisers is their ability to attract enormous crowds, since small amounts from vast audiences raise considerable sums that future campaign finance laws would not find objectionable. Consider this fact: for the 2000 national elections, some $5.8 million was contributed to the Democratic National

Committee from supporters within the entertainment industry.[13] And if you want-ed to run for political office, whom better to have for a son than actor George Clooney? Clooney raised more than $200,000 for his father's 2004 congressional race by hosting two events in his father's hometown.[14] But due to the campaign finance restrictions of the McCain-Feingold law, contributing in 2004 became more difficult. Under the law, a donor is restricted to $2000 to each candidate in the election. The law prohibits a Hollywood "fat cat" from giving $100,000. But it is still possible for a celebrity to throw a party for fifty friends, who write $2000 checks.

Sometimes the contributions take on the appearance of gifts to friends. President Clinton's friendship with the formerly married acting team of Kim Basinger and Alec Baldwin helped him raise money for Democratic candidates. Hollywood stars like Tom Hanks helped to raise money for the president's legal defense fund to settle the Paula Jones lawsuit, a sum of more than $2 million.[15] In return, the president allowed Hanks and his wife to stay at the White House and Basinger and Baldwin to share photo opportunities with him. When Florida became the pivotal state in the close 2000 presidential election, money was neces-sary to offset expenses associated with the recount. Former actress Jane Fonda responded to the cause with a donation of $100,000, while screenwriter Stephen Bing gave $200,000 to Al Gore's recount committee.[16]

Occasionally, the president can do a favor or two for the stars, as when Clinton sent his national security adviser to explain the administration's position on Scientology to an interest group headed by actor John Travolta.[17] These activities only serve to reinforce the culture of celebrity and to cloud the line between enter-tainment and politics. Even so, sometimes the Hollywood association can backfire. Warren Beatty's close friendship with Gary Hart cost the senator politically as he fell under the spell of a Hollywood lifestyle that was at odds with public probity. As a consequence, Hart's promising political career came to a dramatic end.[18] Whether Senator Hart would have won the 1988 presidential race is conjecture, but at the time he was considered to be one of the brightest young candidates on the national political scene.

The relationship between film and politics dates back at least to the pre-World War I period when movie moguls like Sam Goldwyn, Louis Mayer, and Jack and Harry Warner dominated Hollywood but would never think of running for polit-ical office. Instead these "émigrés" were gamblers, taking a chance on a high-risk business while remaining loyal to their adopted country. At heart, they were entre-preneurs, poor but rising capitalists, who responded when their perception of the American dream appeared threatened. They cultivated favor with Washington politicians but kept vigil over candidates who might alter the status quo.[19] The moguls controlled their film studios with tight fists while they courted the

Washington power brokers. Louis B. Mayer of Metro-Goldwyn-Mayer (MGM) cultivated a close friendship with Herbert Hoover, first when Hoover served as secretary of commerce and later, as president. To gain support for Hoover's run for the presidency in 1928, Mayer intervened to persuade newspaper magnate William Randolph Hearst to put aside his personal aspiration for the White House to back Hoover's candidacy. This was the first of many personal Hollywood-Washington associations that developed into political support. Conversely, when the studio moguls felt threatened, as they did with Upton Sinclair's 1934 gubernatorial bid, they joined forces to defeat him. Sinclair, a socialist trying to win office during the Great Depression, ran his campaign on the slogan of "end poverty in California" (EPIC). Naturally his EPIC platform was designed to promote economic and social justice, an idea that frightened these budding Hollywood capitalists. Fearing Sinclair's possible election, MGM produced the first film shorts intended to destroy a political candidate. These five-minute shorts sought to discredit Sinclair and his EPIC campaign. Using a bogus news report, these shorts implied that tramps and hobos would spend winters basking in the Hollywood sun should Sinclair become governor. The studio moguls feared that Sinclair would impose a business tax on them to pay for his EPIC program.[20]

While the studio heads were political conservatives, many of the actors, writers, technicians, and workers were political liberals and leftists, who favored unionization for better wages and benefits. They signed petitions, participated in marches and demonstrations, and some joined the Communist Party because it was the only viable radical political movement at the time. Paul Buhle and Dave Wagner in their book *Radical Hollywood* estimate that the Hollywood left contained some of the best talent in the industry, including a number of Academy Award winners and a good number of films found on the American Film Institute's 100 Best film list.[21] The authors maintain that many of the gangster, western, and film noir movies of the thirties and forties provided a socially acceptable outlet, especially for the leftist screenwriters, to include social commentary in their work, including critiques of capitalism. The political irony here is that under the old studio system the moguls had virtually absolute power, which meant that the Mayers, Goldwyns, and Warners had to sign off on these pictures. When you consider the gangster movies of this era where the mobsters are usually poor boys who came from immigrant families and when you think about the westerns where the villains were often the local bankers and the railroad barons, it makes you wonder whether the studio moguls ever read their own production scripts.

The Hollywood-Washington relationship becomes more intense during wartime and periods of national crises. These were times when the film industry and the government needed each other. World War I presented the industry with an opportunity to enlarge its relationship and enhance its favor with the government.

When America finally entered the war in 1917 the government asked the film industry to volunteer its most important stars to aid in the war effort. The studios responded by sending Douglas Fairbanks, Charlie Chaplin, and America's sweetheart, Mary Pickford, on tour to sell Liberty war bonds. This scene was repeated during the Second World War when Washington again called on Hollywood to aid the war effort and the industry responded anew. In one 1942 bond drive, 337 stars participated in selling a staggering $850 million in war bonds. Singer Kate Smith reportedly sold $39 million in war bonds during a single radio marathon. Later in the war, news of the Nazi atrocities against the Jews led the studio heads to make financial contributions to support the creation of a Jewish Palestine.[22]

The cooperative relationship during World War II and its aftermath was nothing short of 100 percent and is treated fully in chapter eight. That same sort of spirit was resurrected again after the terrorist attack of September 11, 2001. First, Hollywood offered the government positive assistance. Eventually, the industry made a propaganda film that was aired on Middle East television. Then, the studios voluntarily postponed distribution of films with terrorist plots, such as *Bad Company* (2002) and *Collateral Damage* (2002). Both did poorly at the box office but to decide whether that was due to the postponement or the films themselves is problematic.

Sometimes the cooperation is insidious and unworthy of a democratic state. During the Cold War it was reported that the CIA worked closely with anticommunists in the film industry to spot potentially troubling movie content that portrayed a less than positive image of the United States. That meant Hollywood was not to dwell on labor problems, the plight of minorities, and social and economic inequality. According to British film producer and historian Frances Saunders,[23] the CIA planted agents inside Hollywood studios to monitor communist activities and leftist themes. One undercover agent filed a critical report on the film, *Giant* (1956) because the screenplay contained an unflattering portrayal of rich Texans who had gained their wealth at the expense of exploited Mexican labor.

Benefits flow from government cooperation; otherwise the assistance is withheld. For instance, actor John Wayne secured government assistance that made it possible for him to make his pro-Vietnam war film, *The Green Berets*. Generally, it would be very difficult to make a war film without some cooperation from the military. You want to make a film about space or astronauts and want it to be realistic? Whom do you call? NASA, naturally. The film, *The Right Stuff* (1983), could not have been made without the cooperation of the space agency. Nor could *Apollo 13* (1995), the story of the ill-fated moon mission, have been produced without their assistance. Reportedly, NASA offered film companies access to all its facilities—mission control, launch-pads, training services—a considerable savings—but on condition that the agency approve the script.[24]

However, what good is the cooperation and assistance if the film's distribution date is scheduled to please the military? Take the case of *Buffalo Soldiers* (2003), the film version of the Robert O'Connor book, which concerns the peacetime army in Germany before the fall of the Berlin Wall. The central character is a supply specialist who operates a black market business out of the supply depot and manufactures heroin on the side. In the mode of *M*A*S*H* (1970) and other irreverent military comedies, this satirical and cynical film was completed in the summer of 2001 and scheduled to open in mid September. Because of 9/11 the film was pushed back to the following summer, but the beginning of the Afghanistan offensive interfered. The film was then rescheduled for early 2003 but delayed again due to the opening of the Iraqi War. Finally released during the summer of 2003, the film flopped at the box office due to mixed reviews and the two-year delay. Would a more positive military portrayal have allowed the film to open on schedule? Probably, because like all bureaucracies the military is sensitive about its public image, and Hollywood is responsive to offending institutions that it relies on to produce films. That is the normal *quid pro quo* of doing business; you reward your friends. But the largess that the government bestows on friends should not come at taxpayer expense as it did when the Pentagon honored Jack Valenti, former president of the Motion Picture Association, with a dinner that cost an estimated $350,000. Valenti received a citizenship award from Secretary of Defense William Cohen for promoting the military in Hollywood films. Naturally, the award was bestowed on Valenti for the positive depiction of the military on the big screen.[25] Meanwhile, *Buffalo Soldiers*, distributed by Miramax, contains over 100 "fuck" words and a totally negative view of the military, and obviously would not appear on the Pentagon's "best films" list anytime soon.

The symbiotic relationship between government and film industry has ramifications beyond political campaigns and public relations gambits. Government and special interest groups exploit the reputation and popularity of film stars while Hollywood keeps one eye on state policies that might impact the industry. Its primary focus, however, is on national and international policies as its films gain worldwide acceptance. The popularity of Hollywood films abroad, shown in venues as diverse as makeshift theaters inside Chinese factories to glamorous movie palaces installed with stereophonic sound, reinforces the industry's concern with its global image. Back in the thirties the studios worried about the response to its films in countries like Nazi Germany and Fascist Italy. Today, it frets over China's response to two 1997 films on the life of the Dalai Lama, *Seven Years in Tibet*, and *Kundun*. Due to its sympathetic portrayal of the Dalai Lama and the Tibetan people, neither film has been shown in China. Moreover, the Chinese government denied permission for location shooting and threatened economic reprisals against the studios that produced the films. The Disney Company, which made *Kundun*, became so alarmed at the damage the film might do to its other financial investments in China (Disney stores and merchandise) that it hired Henry Kissinger, former secretary of state in the Nixon administration, to represent their interests.

Occasionally the impetus for political intervention emanates from the American side. In 1997 news reports said that President Clinton had asked MGM to delay the release of its movie *Red Corner* (1997), starring Richard Gere, until after the official visit of Chinese president Jiang Zemen. Instead this film about an American lawyer falsely accused of murder, originally scheduled to open in November, was moved up to coincide with Jiang's October visit. It is unclear whether the change in the theatrical release date was politically motivated, given Richard Gere's support for the Dalai Lama, or a marketing ploy by MGM to capitalize on the additional publicity surrounding Jiang's visit. In either event, this incident supports the financial importance of global interests to the film industry. Just fifty years ago, the film studios worried how their pictures would "play in Peoria"; today the industry's concern is how their films will be received in Beijing. This is precisely the reason why the film industry lobbies Washington. Motion pictures represent a significant global economic power, a far cry from its humble beginnings in penny arcades and urban nickelodeons. Hollywood films have become the second largest American export after military hardware, and receipts from foreign distribution contribute more than half of a film's revenue.[26] Often, foreign receipts mean the difference between a film's profit or loss.

A strong showing in foreign markets usually determines the fiscal fate of a film. Take the case of the Academy Award-winning film, *Titanic* (1997). The film did not have to rely on foreign distribution to make a profit, yet its universal popularity enabled it to become a box office blockbuster. After being in release for six months, *Titanic* already had earned a hefty $585 million at home, with an additional two billion abroad.[27] Financial receipts of this magnitude explain why the film industry turned to Washington to recruit Jack Valenti, former aide to President Lyndon Johnson (LBJ), as its leader. It also explains why the Motion Picture Association of America (MPAA) has an office in Washington while its film production and auxiliary services operate out of Los Angeles. This arrangement allows the leadership to oversee the interests of the film industry close to the seat of government in the nation's capital. The universal appeal of Hollywood movies also reveals why the MPAA president's voice is heard in the halls of government. Comparable to Coke and McDonald's, Hollywood is symbolic of the economic rewards under corporate capitalism. For better or worse, Hollywood movies have dominated the world market since the 1920s, overpowering the production capacity and the film budgets of other countries. By the middle of the nineties, American films accounted for 80 percent of the European box office. While American films glutted global markets, European films failed to receive worldwide distribution. The situation reached a crisis during the GATT negotiations when Hollywood lobbied the Clinton administration to include its films under the terms of the agreement so that the industry could trade freely throughout the world. On the other hand, the European Union (EU) demanded quotas be placed on American films to protect their respective film industries. The stalemate was broken by Clinton's intervention after the president consulted with Lew Wasserman, chairman of MCA-Universal, the mega-entertainment corporation.[28]

In addition to its politicking and lobbying, members from the Hollywood community are active in promoting various political, social, and environmental causes. As citizens, Hollywood personalities have every right to engage in supporting political and social causes. Robert Redford, among others, has long been associated with environmental causes. He has been a recruiter and fundraiser for the National Resources Defense Council, an environmental lobby group. Academy Award actress Meryl Streep also has lobbied hard on environmental issues. As cofounder of Mothers and Others, she worked to convince the Environmental Protection Agency to alter the ways pesticides are regulated.

No one in the government or the film industry is terribly upset if Richard Gere wants to raise funds for the Dalai Lama or deliver a public plea to free Tibet during the Academy Award ceremonies. Similarly, the Oscar show went on despite the refusal of Marlon Brando to accept his best actor award for his performance in *The Godfather* (1972). Brando decided not to attend the ceremony because of America's mistreatment of Native Americans. Instead the actor dispatched Sacheen Littlefeather to read Brando's speech and pick up the Oscar. Littlefeather showed up dressed in Native American costume, but she later turned out to be a B-actress rather than a political activist. Show business always has its silly side, and occasionally the government makes the mistake of joining in the fun. This bit of Oscar history happened at the 1973 Awards when Groucho Marx, in accepting his Honorary Achievement Award, made some comments about communism that put him on an FBI watch list.[29]

In the sixties, Hollywood activists joined the civil rights movement, and they were also outspoken against the Vietnam War. Actress Jane Fonda took a trip to Hanoi as an expression of her anti war sentiments. In the seventies, the Hollywood crowd was anti-nukes and pro-environment. AIDS was the cause to support in the eighties. The point is that as long as there is a Hollywood, there will always be some cause to advocate or support. Usually such public demonstrations are accepted as expressions of genuine humanitarian and social concern or else as publicity promotions. When the country is at war or when it suffers from a human disaster such as the 9/11 terrorist attacks, the tolerance level for criticism and public dissent is close to zero. Once the Bush administration decided to connect Saddam Hussein with the destruction of the Twin Towers and target Iraq for military action, a sig-

FIGURE 3. Hollywood Stars and the Iraqi War cartoon: 2003. Reprinted with permission, *Omaha World-Herald*.

nificant number of Hollywood stars such as Tim Robbins, his wife Susan Sarandon, and Jane Fonda (again) openly joined the global antiwar opposition. Early in 2002, a letter signed by 104 film and television actors was sent to President Bush asking him to pursue a course of diplomacy through the United Nations to resolve the Iraqi crisis. The White House responded through its press secretary that: "The president agrees violence is not the answer in Iraq and that's why he hopes Saddam Hussein will disarm."[30] As the United States moved closer to taking military action against Iraq, the number of worldwide antiwar protests increased accordingly. On January 19, 2003, Hollywood stars such as Martin Sheen of television's *The West Wing* joined massive domestic protests in San Francisco and Washington. On this particular day, it seemed as if the Vietnam era had returned to America. The next month, more Hollywood actors, e.g., George Clooney, Sean Penn, Ed Harris, and singer Madonna, spoke out against the war on German television. Documentary filmmaker Michael Moore took the opportunity during his 2003 Oscar speech, to a chorus of cheers and jeers, to rail against the president, proclaiming: "We are against this war, Mr. Bush. Shame on you. Shame on you." By mid March, several Hollywood stars delivered an antiwar petition signed by one million people to the U.S. mission at the UN. The actors were part of an antiwar lobby known as "Artists United to Win Without War."[31] Two weeks later, the United States launched a preemptive strike against Iraq and the war was on. However, in contrast to the black-listing of the 1950s, these actors apparently have not suffered from their political activities. None has been blackballed by the industry nor prevented from working at his or her craft. At the 2004 Academy Awards, both Tim Robbins and Sean Penn won Oscars for their film performances in *Mystic River* (2003). Is it possible that Hollywood has learned a lesson from the wrongs it committed during the Red Scare?

FILM CONTENT

Hollywood releases some 400 films annually. The overwhelming majority are pure-ly commercial ventures. However, there exists a small minority of films, ranging in any given year from 5 to 10 percent that present explicit and latent political mes-sages. The place where the film-politics connection is most obviously displayed is in the movies themselves, yet Hollywood seldom takes advantage of this power. Why does Hollywood avoid the dogmatic political film, the critical political biography, or the ideological political drama? The reason is quite simple: overtly political movies are box office poison.[32] To admit that 90 percent of Hollywood films are intended strictly for entertainment ignores the political content of the remaining 10 percent. These include films that are ideological, propagandistic, historically deceptive, and politically motivated.

Film as Ideology

For all their global popularity and financial prosperity, there remains a reluctance within the industry to acknowledge a symbiotic relationship between the world of film and the world of politics. The industry's leadership periodically reinforces the denial. Will Hays, former postmaster general, recruited by the film industry to be its chief censor and production czar in the 1920s, announced the denial when he said "American motion pictures continue to be free from any but the highest pos-sible entertainment purpose."[33] It is not surprising, therefore, that as a mainstream industry, Hollywood steers clear of controversy. That admission, however, is a far cry from perpetuating the myth of political abstention. Notable exceptions are found in the films of contemporary "auteurs," directors such as Costas-Gavras, Oliver Stone, Spike Lee, and independents such as David O. Russell, who exercise a greater degree of total control over their productions than normally permitted under the old studio system. Actor-turned-director John Cassavetes' films of the six-ties and seventies were highly original examinations of American society; they encompassed personal statements the studios were reluctant to support. Cassavetes made his films using his own resources and borrowing from friends. This kind of artistic freedom enables directors to select their subject matter and present events to suit their personal interpretations, whether that agenda includes government cover-up in Latin America (*Missing*), a challenge to the historical record on the assassination of President Kennedy (*JFK*), the depiction of contemporary race relations (*Do the Right Thing* and *Jungle Fever*), or early skirmishes in the gender wars (*A Woman under the Influence*). What differentiates these directors from their peers is their control over the creative process, from initial script idea to final editing, stamping the film with their imprint in a way that cannot be duplicated by another filmmaker.

Traditional Hollywood, on the other hand, hedges its bets by producing films that contain a conservative political orientation (*Green Berets, Death Wish,* and the *Dirty Harry* series), as well as those that advance a liberal policy perspective or examine flaws in the existing system (*Modern Times, The Grapes of Wrath, The China Syndrome,* and *Norma Rae*). Always conscious of the high risk factor inherent in the entertainment business, mainstream Hollywood generally avoids controversial subjects and ideological treatment. It is a rather different story for a multimillionaire such as Mel Gibson to put up $25 to $30 million of his own money to make a film like *The Passion of the Christ* (2004) because no Hollywood studio would produce it. The film created quite a stir before its release, but despite the controversy, it became a box office hit. Had the film flopped, however, Gibson would not be a candidate for welfare. Gibson is so financially secure that he could take a chance on a "religious film" that was accused of being anti-Semitic. It is not surprising that the Hollywood establishment would pass on it as they did subsequently with Michael Moore's *Fahrenheit 9/11.*

Gibson had the financial means to successfully defy the conventional wisdom within the industry. There also are a few auteurs that have the clout to convince the major studios to risk box office failure by exploiting the medium for political purposes. Oliver Stone, for one, is such an auteur. His films (*Platoon, Salvador, JFK,* and *Nixon*) certainly put the neutrality-entertainment myth to the test. If Stone's films are pure fictional creations, why did the Justice Department declassify the Kennedy assassination files after the release of JFK (1991)?[34] Was this a case of mere coincidence or reaction by the government to defuse the controversy caused by the film? Also why did Stone's portrayal of Nixon raise such criticism and cries of inaccuracies from the former president's family and members of his administration[35] when the film was advertised and marketed as commercial entertainment and not as a political documentary? Why should Nixon supporters worry about the screen representation if the film is intended primarily for entertainment? Furthermore, in the Reagan era of the 1980s, Stone took a risk in distributing *Salvador* (1985); a stinging indictment of American policy in Central America that was advertised to suggest that the film represented political reality in El Salvador, a marketing strategy also utilized by Stone to maximum effect with *JFK*. Filmmakers such as Stone, however, are the exception, not the rule in Hollywood.

Contemporary auteurs have no monopoly on sending messages to American audiences. Charlie Chaplin's *The Great Dictator* (1940), for instance, was a devastating satire on Hitler and Mussolini that also served as a warning to the world of the dangers of fascism. Because Chaplin's film was released at a time when the United States officially declared a neutral policy toward the European war, its ideological stance against fascism was financially risky and politically controversial. In the 1990s, actor-turned-director Kevin Costner presented a revisionist view of Native Americans in his *Dances with Wolves* (1990) while Oliver Stone's *JFK* promoted his version of the conspiracy behind the Kennedy assassination. Stone's *Nixon* provided the director with an opportunity to portray the former president in psychological terms as a tormented individual. Despite being marketed as commercial entertainment, these films nonetheless qualify as ideological because they represent deliberate, conscious attempts to create works with a definite political perspective, narrated within a particular historical setting, and featuring characters who are readily recognizable or representational.[36]

Film as Propaganda

In 1936, the German-Jewish literary critic Walter Benjamin wrote that the film medium had emerged as a significant propaganda tool because of its ability to lend support to, and provide a rationale for, mass movements.[37] Benjamin, naturally, had Nazi Germany and Fascist Italy in mind. He warned that even the weekly newsreel, with its ability to engage the individual in the presentation of big parades and political rallies, has the potential to become an unwitting ally of fascism. Benjamin's essay was published the year after the completion of *Triumph of the Will* (1936), Leni Riefenstahl's homage to Hitler and the Nazi Party. Riefenstahl admitted that the filming of the 1934 Nuremberg Party Convention was more than a straightforward recreation of a historical event but denied that it was politically motivated. Commissioned by Hitler himself and approved by Goebbels, the film employed deft camera work, sound, lighting, and editing, to create a testimonial to the glory of Nazism.

Similarly, during World War II, the American government asked Frank Capra, the director of *Mr. Smith Goes to Washington* (1939), to produce a series of films on *Why We Fight* (1942–45) scheduled for showing to military personnel. These films were produced under the auspices of the Army Signal Corps, and like *Triumph of the Will*, presented a distorted image of American society in the early forties. Intended by the government to serve as morale boosters for the American G.I., the films made no reference to segregation, discrimination, poverty, labor strife, or class antagonism. The *Why We Fight* series portrayed a nation so unspoiled and uncorrupted that it led actor-director John Cassavetes to comment that America might have been the invention of Frank Capra rather than a real place.[38] Cassavetes' quip referred to Hollywood's perpetuation of the cherished myths of an unblemished America. Whether genuine or fake, Capra's representation of America was an idealization of a place that a majority of the public either believed or wished to believe, was real. Certainly the series portrayed a country where the people regarded government as decent and honest, where right would triumph over force, where the average American's faith and wisdom would overcome adversity, and where capitalism delivers the American dream to all people.

Not all political propaganda is overt and government sponsored. Besides the kind of overt propaganda distributed by governments, Dan Nimmo in a typology of political movies also includes examples of covert propaganda in commercial films.[39] One example is the western, *High Noon* (1952), released during the Red Scare. On the surface, the film is a standard western with a plot that pits the good sheriff (Gary Cooper), standing alone, against a gang of outlaws he once sent to prison. However, Nimmo insists that a viewer knowledgeable about the HUAC hearings and the subsequent blacklisting could interpret the film as an answer to those friendly witnesses who abandoned their colleagues before the committee. Such an interpretation would stamp covert political propaganda on a film that many viewed at the time as a lean and tough western rather than an attack on the HUAC inquisition. Naturally, it could be interpreted in both ways, but its true intention remains in the hearts of those involved in the film.

Nimmo treats commercial films that are covered with a slight indoctrination veneer as "thinly veiled propaganda."[40] Within this category, Nimmo places such films about American politicians as *Mr. Smith Goes to Washington* and *The Seduction of Joe Tynan* (1979), which are produced primarily for entertainment purposes but also deliver some propaganda in the process. For example, *Mr. Smith* preaches the message that grassroots democracy can work so that the ordinary citizen has the ability to overcome evil. *Joe Tynan*, on the other hand, portrays Washington politics in romantic terms as a game of legislative trade-offs between lobbyists and politicians, especially when Meryl Streep plays the lobbyist. Senator Joe Tynan's (Alan Alda) personal ambition to occupy the White House someday may be attainable, but the film hints that if he becomes president, his soul will not be intact.

Film as History

After seeing *Birth of a Nation*, President Wilson reportedly described the movies as "history written in lightening."[41] The President could just as readily have characterized the medium in class terms because, historians remind us, movies had humble roots, serving as entertainment for the masses in the inner cities of industrial America. Is there a better way for future generations to experience the misery and poverty of the Great Depression than through a systematic viewing of 1930s Hollywood fare? Workers crowded into movie theaters during the Depression years to escape from their economic misery and be transported temporarily into the fantasy world of the Busby Berkeley musical and the wholesome comedies and dramas distributed under the film industry's production code. Occasionally Hollywood deviated from its usual assembly-line films with movies that reminded the working class of their disadvantaged socioeconomic status. Warner Brothers, in particular, exposed the evils of slum living, delinquency, and urban crime in a series of thirties films such as *Crime School* (1938), *Angels with Dirty Faces* (1938), and *Hell's Kitchen* (1939); the last featured a young Midwestern actor named Ronald Reagan. These films served as deterministic indictments of the economic condition of the American underclass in the political context of Depression America.

On other occasions, studios produced films on a specific political figure, usually biographies of presidents. Such was the case in *Abe Lincoln in Illinois* (1940), *Wilson* (1944), *Sunrise at Campobello* (Franklin Roosevelt) (1960), and *Nixon*. Whether these films accurately portrayed reality or respected the historical record remains a matter of debate.[42] In the films cited above, only Stone's *Nixon* comes off as a flawed figure; all the others are romantic dramas that distort history.

Nonetheless, historians have come to extol the virtues of studying film because the camera is capable of recording an event for posterity at a particular time and place, subject to the major caveat of reconstructing the past from a contemporary viewpoint. Hollywood often takes liberties with the historical record, justifying its necessity on dramatic grounds. However, where dramatic license distorts the facts, film does a disservice to the larger historical record. Who, then, is left with the responsibility to correct the errors of commission or omission? There are enough recent illustrations to fill several pages, but a few examples will suffice. Audiences that view Alan Parker's film, *Mississippi Burning* (1988) without sufficient knowledge would conclude that only whites were involved in the civil rights movement. In Parker's film, southern blacks are mere spectators to the struggle, an impression that would be incredulous to Martin Luther King and his Southern Christian Leadership Conference. Similarly, those who lived through the Cuban Missile Crisis may want to check their recollections after watching the film version, *Thirteen Days* (2001). The film is seen through the perspective of its star, Kevin Costner, who plays Kenneth O'Donnell, a political advisor to the Kennedys. The film misrepresents the importance of O'Donnell in the decision-making process that resolved the conflict with the Soviet Union. The greater distortion lies in the inaccurate portrayals of the major participants like McGeorge Bundy, Dean Acheson, and Robert McNamara and in the positions taken by the military during the crisis.[43]

Three recent World War II pictures raised issues of historical accuracy.[44] In *Saving Private Ryan* (1998) director Steven Spielberg substituted Tom Hanks's officer for the real-life priest sent to remove the remaining Ryan son from harm's way after the deaths of his other brothers. In this particular case, the substitution does not alter the film's realistic portrayal of the horrors of combat during the Omaha Beach invasion. Here the dramatic license changes the individual responsible for saving the boy's life but leaves intact the powerful thematic message that war is hell. In another case, the prevailing perspective in the bloated blockbuster, *Pearl Harbor* (2001) implies that Japan was deliberately forced into taking steps against the United States because of the American oil embargo and other provocative actions.[45] Historians generally agree that President Roosevelt believed war with Japan was inevitable and if it did happen, it would be better if the Japanese were the aggressors. However, this is a far cry from a conspiracy theory that FDR purposely set up Pearl Harbor as an attractive target for the Japanese to attack. The film also implied that Japan was unfairly victimized by the atomic bomb. Moreover, because the naval base of Pearl Harbor is located in Hawaii, the absence of Hawaiians in the film was curious. Were there no Hawaiians in Hawaii at the time of Pearl Harbor? What was director Michael Bay thinking?

Still another WWII example is the film, *U-571* (2000), which chronicles the Allies' ability to decipher the German enigma code and prevent German submarines from sinking merchant ships and other Allied naval vessels. The plot revolves around an American submarine crew that boards a damaged German U-boat to remove the enigma code machine. The ability to decipher enemy messages was crucial for Allied success in the Atlantic theater of war. The film, however, mistakenly left the impression that it was the Americans who were solely responsible for the successful mission to capture the code machine. In fact, the British Navy had accomplished the feat before the U.S. entered the war. The substitution of the American Navy for the British Navy cannot be attributed to dramatic license alone but rather to a misplaced spirit of nationalism. *U-571* shouts, "America won the war." That would be news to our allies who suffered deaths and casualties in the millions. A final example is the fifth Hollywood version of *The Alamo* (2004), a bragging rights event for the state of Texas. The 1960 version, directed by John Wayne, served as a metaphor for American determination during the Cold War. The latest version, directed by a Texan, distorts historical fact to the extent that the film becomes a blatant propaganda piece. Facts are rearranged, resulting in a slanted view of history. Even more serious is the charge by one film scholar that "the film seeks to legitimate the use of military force to avenge a massacre without regard to principles of international law."[46]

The educational value of these films diminishes proportionally to the distortions with historical fact. Good intentions are deceptive when filmmakers tamper with history, converting historical events into historical fiction. Educators who utilize film need to provide explanations and guidance lest their students learn the wrong lessons.

Film as Politicizing Agent

The process by which young people acquire their political values and beliefs is known as "political socialization." Naturally, youngsters are most influenced by their family heritage and political environment, by the strength of their ethnic group affiliation, and their socioeconomic class. Hence, a youngster raised in a Republican family that votes consistently and that discusses politics on a regular basis, is white and middle to upper-middle class is very likely to become a Republican voter and share the values of the party. The mass media play a role in this process too, but it is ill-defined. For example, it is unclear whether audiences that view a specific political film will be so impressed as to alter their political values, change their party allegiance, or engage in some act of civil disobedience. Thus describing political film as an agent of political or social change is problematic because the empirical evidence that would indicate a causal relationship between the two variables has yet to be established. In situations where social scientists are able to establish a connection between two variables, the empirical evidence is usually insufficient to establish causality. Still Stephen Vaughn,[47] in his book on Reagan's Hollywood tenure, presents a convincing argument for adopting a "preponderance of the evidence" approach when the methodology is applied to political figures. Vaughn's analysis of Reagan's film career furnishes clues toward understanding his shifting position on social and political issues while in the White House. Vaughn's research is crucial to understanding Reagan's transformation from a liberal New Deal Democrat to a conservative Cold War warrior.

Speculating on the factors that motivate the politics of political leaders is far different from documenting the influence of films on social and political behavior. This issue arose as early as the beginning of the last century when lynching of blacks increased after showings of *The Birth of a Nation*. Did the film's release incite mob violence? Did the film help to recruit members for the Ku Klux Klan? The findings suggest a relationship but not enough to prove causality. This issue of cause-effect persisted into the thirties when publication of the *Payne Fund Studies*, which linked juvenile delinquency to the Hollywood crime and gangster films of that era, served as a catalyst for establishing tougher regulations over motion pictures. Although methodologically flawed, the film industry and the government interpret-

FIGURE 4. Birth of a Nation: 1915.

ed the results as proof of a causal connection between film content and criminal and delinquent behavior. These studies lent "scientific respectability" to the industry's establishment of the production code, a content-based guideline for the making of movies. The code served as the basis for the industry's regulation over film content for more than thirty years.[48]

In the nineties, politicians revived the cause-effect relationship when in seeking votes, they blamed Hollywood and the entertainment industry for criminal behavior, particularly that of juveniles and teenagers, and for the loss of moral values. The subject became a campaign issue during the 1996 presidential race when the Republican candidate, Senator Bob Dole, condemned the entertainment industry for depicting "mindless violence and loveless sex," which he cited as the cause for the erosion of the nation's standards of morality and civility.[49]

Dole lost the election and Hollywood was unfazed by the criticism. Gratuitous violence continues to appear in many Hollywood action films. One illustration is *Money Train* (1995). When a New York City token clerk died as a result of the fire-bombing of his subway booth, police and politicians blamed the film because it contained a similar scene and because it had opened in theaters four days earlier. However, whether the young men responsible for the crime indeed saw the film and were stimulated to copycat the crime is virtually impossible to answer empirically.[50] The incident, however, raised anew the fundamental behavioral question: Does life imitate art or does art merely mirror life?

Failure by social science to document the nexus between film representations and antisocial behavior does not negate the possibility that specific films play a limited, but influential, role in the formation of individual beliefs and values. Research on the subject continues. Two attitudinal studies sought to measure the influence of a specific film on attitudes rather than exposure to a particular group of films identified as a genre. One study focused on the impact of the Watergate scandal by collecting data from the viewing of *All the President's Men* (1976).[51] The study found that a substantial attitudinal change occurred, with the students who viewed the film exhibiting a marked increase in political alienation while simultaneously displaying a more positive attitude toward the press. While the result could be expected, the authors, nonetheless, concluded that exposure to a clearly delivered political message in a well-crafted film can have a short-term influence on a particular attitude, in this case, judgments on politicians and the press. The long-term impact, however, is still unknown.

In the other study,[52] involving Michael Moore's film, *Roger and Me* (1989), the researchers discovered similar findings in both an American sample and a Japanese comparison group. *Roger and Me* concerns the unsuccessful attempt by filmmaker Michael Moore to locate and interview Roger Smith, the CEO of General Motors (GM), to explain on camera why GM was closing plants in Moore's native city of Flint, Michigan. Despite some controversy over whether the film was a documentary or a comedic fable, the study results suggest that the American sample that viewed the film had substantially more negative feelings toward American corporations than the control group, who had not seen the film. Similarly, the Japanese sample group of university students duplicated the American findings except that, in addition to the negative attitudes displayed toward business, the Japanese also expressed more positive feelings toward their home companies.

While these studies are unlikely to end the debate over the power of the film industry to shape public opinion, their findings add to the body of existing evidence that suggests that films that contain political messages are capable of providing audiences with more than harmless diversions. As imaging and media manipulation play a larger role in the American political culture, the presentation and the context of political messages take on greater significance. Moreover, as the mediated images proliferate, the desire to strengthen the bond between the image makers (Hollywood) and the policymakers (Washington) becomes stronger.

IN SEARCH OF THE POLITICAL FILM

CHAPTER TWO

From Riefenstahl to the Three Stooges

I n a scene from the film *Casablanca*, Claude Rains, who plays the corrupt Vichy French police chief Captain Renault, warns Humphrey Bogart, the cynical American owner of Rick's Café:

RENAULT: "We're going to make an arrest in your cafe."
RICK: "Again."
RENAULT: "This is no ordinary arrest, a murderer no less. If you're thinking of warning him, don't put yourself out. He cannot possibly escape."
RICK: "I stick my neck out for nobody."
RENAULT: "A wise foreign policy."

WHAT MAKES A FILM "POLITICAL"?

Does this scene at the beginning of *Casablanca* set up the audience to expect an anti-Nazi, pro-Allies political film? Released to theaters in 1942 to take advantage of the Allied invasion of North Africa, this classic film has earned high praise from screen critics and film buffs alike. Considered by Warner Bros. a B-list production with a script worked on by four different writers, often on the day of filming, *Casablanca* has become a Hollywood legend. Ranked second only to *Citizen Kane* on the American Film Institute's best 100 films list, *Casablanca* has been the source for numerous books and articles over the past half-century.[1] Even so, no consensus exists on the question of whether *Casablanca* is essentially a romantic drama, a political film, or both.

What makes a film political? There is no empirical answer to the question despite years of effort. The question has been debated since the 1970s when the American Political Science Association published a series of articles on teaching methodologies in courses that integrated film as part of the curriculum. Students challenge their professors to justify the films they include, that is, they want to know why *Casablanca* is selected but not *Bulworth* (1998). It is a legitimate line of inquiry.

The question about film in the subject content of a course requires a reasoned response. What characteristics make a film such as *Casablanca* a legitimate contender but a film like *Bulworth*, which after all had a U.S. senator as its major character, fail to qualify? The question leads naturally to attempts to define political film and to consideration of a separate film genre. The effort to identify a distinct political film genre, however, is so fraught with traps and tricks that scholars and practitioners ought to heed the warning by anthropologist Clifford Geertz,[2] who reminded his colleagues of their scholarly obligation to more precisely identify the object of their studies by recounting a Javanese folktale of a legendary figure, "Stupid Boy," who having been counseled by his mother to seek a quiet wife, returns to his village with a corpse.

Similarly, political scientists and film scholars searching for the political film have to provide satisfactory answers to the following questions. What distinguishes a political film from other genres? How does the viewer know when a film contains a political agenda or seeks to promote a particular political ideology? These questions are vital to the classification process. Unfortunately they are easier to ask than to answer.

What has emerged from the scholarly efforts of political scientists, film scholars and critics, and filmmakers is the emergence of three schools of thought on the subject. At the extremes are the inclusives and the exclusives. The inclusives are those who consider all films to contain some level of political meaning, however silly or simple-minded. The exclusives are those who deny even the possibility of a political film genre, especially in profit-driven Hollywood.

The first group points to a wide range of films that contain a variety of political ideas and concepts. They include thematic messages that express the ideas and values that reflect the spirit of the government in power, mirror the national mood at the time, or provide support and reinforcement for the status quo.[3] For example, this category would include films of the 1980s that reflected both the new populism and the renascent nationalism of the Reagan administration. Movies such as *Country* (1984), which portrayed ordinary farmers struggling to retain their property despite the policies of the federal bureaucracy, and films that rewrote American foreign policy such as *Rambo: First Blood Part II* (1985), *Red Dawn* (1984), and *Uncommon Valor* (1983). These films take on the appearance of jingoistic fables, leading audiences to believe that America remained a potent military power after the defeat in Vietnam.[4]

For the inclusives, all films contain messages, even if conveyed unintentionally by Hollywood, because their creators express the underlying values of the larger society. A Hollywood film that displays and even flaunts the material goods of American society to the Third World conveys the message, however unintended, that capitalism produces the affluent society. Though the intention is to provide mass entertainment, nations are delivered a mostly positive image of the United States through a steady diet of commercial films that reinforce the values of a corporate capitalist economy. Even in films such as *American Beauty* (2000) and *Ice Storm* (1997) that are critical of middle-class affluence and suburban life, the characters inhabit a lifestyle that is way beyond the means of the rest of the world.

At the opposite end of the spectrum, the exclusives, comprised mostly of film critics and cinema society members, consider the very phrase "political film genre" an oxymoron. To these cinema purists a political film is simply a piece of propaganda. This group argues that filmmaking is essentially a collaborative process, from the banks that provide the studios with the finances to support film projects to the editing process that completes the film's final form. With so many participants in financing, distribution, and production, it is unlikely for the process to produce ideological or political message films. It is more probable that Hollywood's intention is to promote traditional plots and recycled formulas rather than explore fresh ideas and innovative filmmaking.

The film industry is generally sensitive to audience response, and so Hollywood shuns controversy. The major studios avoid ideological films for the same reason it abstains from making pornography—fear of public reaction as measured at the box office. If Hollywood films are intended as political tracts, why do the studios bother with research on alternative film endings?[5] These audience reaction surveys ("sneak previews") are designed to elicit viewer feedback to permit producers to alter their films before national distribution. Furthermore, whenever Hollywood tackles an obvious political subject, such as election campaigning, the industry dilutes the political message with comedy, romance, or action. Warren Beatty's *Bulworth* is a recent example of diffusing a political message—the need for campaign finance reform—within the parameters of farce. The film also is brutally honest about racism in America. Unfortunately, it is dubious whether audiences understood that message diffused through rap music.

The exclusives maintain that past Hollywood ventures into the political arena have resulted in disappointing box office profits. The old adage that political films are "box office poison" is supported by the financial returns of four recent Hollywood films that, although flawed, nonetheless explore contemporary political issues. While two of those films, *Wag the Dog* and *Primary Colors,* had respectable domestic grosses, $43 million and $39 million, respectively, the results were less than expected. Both *Bulworth*, about a depressed U.S. senator who falls in love and discovers new reasons for remaining in politics, and *The Contender* (2000), about a woman senator nominated for vice president, were considered box office flops. Contrast these poor returns against the earnings of blockbuster films such as *Jurassic Park* (1993), *Titanic* (1997), *The Lord of the Rings: The Fellowship of the Ring* (2001), and *Spiderman* (2002), which individually earned twice as much as all four of those political films combined! The feeble box office showing for political films reinforces the exclusives' position that Hollywood cannot make commercially successful political films because

> the issues are complex and, to some extent, abstract, and have to be embodied in human antagonists to make them come alive. But then in order to make the characters both dramatic and human in a 90 or 100 minute context, the issues usually have to be foreshortened and oversimplified. In effect, the filmmaker is caught between the Scylla of depersonalization and the charybdis of oversimplification.[6]

Finally, the exclusives are skeptical that Hollywood is capable of producing a film with a political theme because the industry reduces the subject to easily recognizable clichés and stereotypes. In Hollywood, that means appealing to non-discriminating mainstream viewers with a plot that arouses emotions rather than provokes logical reasoning. Hollywood thus reduces the complexities of political life to personal stories that are most likely to attract the masses. This tendency to dilute political ideas led film critic John Simon, relying on classical music as a reference point, to remind us "Beethoven will not sound like Beethoven if played on a kazoo."[7]

Whether a film scholar or an ordinary moviegoer, it is difficult to defend either viewpoint. The first group is much too inclusive. If every Hollywood film delivered a political message, the studios would have had to file for bankruptcy given their usual weak showing at the box office. Furthermore, to maintain that all films contain messages of social, economic, or political import relieves researchers of the task of classifying thousands of Hollywood-made films because all films are political. This absolutist posture discourages anyone, scholar or moviegoer, from attempting to narrow the frame of reference.

Meanwhile, the argument that the film medium is an inadequate venue to deliver political messages or the kind of industry unlikely to produce films that are ideological ignores the historical record. For instance, how would this group explain such commercial propaganda pieces as *The Birth of a Nation* and *The Great Dictator*? Both films were produced before World War II, when the major studios dominated film output and controlled their distribution. Subsequent legal decisions and the success of independent producers today eroded the studios' monopoly over quality productions, permitting greater freedom to filmmakers. To cite but one example, four of the five films nominated for best picture in 1996 came from independents. It is much easier today for young filmmakers like Quentin Tarantino (*Reservoir Dogs*, *Pulp Fiction*) and Steven Soderbergh (*sex, lies, and videotape*) to secure financial backing for their projects. These independents are more likely to tackle controversial subjects and assume more risk than the major film studios. Once these filmmakers acquire an audience, the prospects for exploring subjects once held to be taboo from a business or socially acceptable viewpoint is likely to expand over time.

To argue that Hollywood is a business "pure and simple" overlooks a small group of Hollywood films, possibly 5 to 10 percent of the annual production, that probe serious public policy issues. The argument that film cannot serve as a useful medium for the dissemination of ideas conveys a rejection of popular culture as a contributor to social life. To disregard a political film because it is imperfect rejects the inquisitive intellect. The fundamental question is not whether political films are first-rate or awful, which is the venue of the film critic, but whether they exist, in what context, and with what effect.

IDENTIFYING THE POLITICAL FILM

A group of political scientists emerged in the 1980s with an alternative to the absolutist positions. These political scientists drew on the earlier work of the Cineaste Circle, a group of film writers and critics, who define the political film through analyzing the work of European filmmakers such as Bernardo Bertolucci, Costa-Gavras, Bertrand Tavernier, Andrzej Wajda, and Lina Wertmuller.[8] The Cineaste circle represents a middle ground between the two viewpoints of inclusivity and exclusivity by defining film genres through their directors instead of their content. Similarly, American political scientists like Terry Christensen and Michael Genovese accept the realities of film as an essentially commercial enterprise while maintaining that there exists a select but limited category of films with political overtones.[9] Even though the political ideas contained in these films may be presented in a simplistic manner or hidden within the subtext, their presence is sufficient to warrant a separate and distinct genre described as the political film. While the colleagues in this group have grown to include others who share in the belief of a distinct political film genre, they disagree on the characteristics necessary for inclusion.

In *Reel Politics*, Christensen expressed the inclusives' position because good films contain multilayered levels of meaning, even political in nature, however subtle or unintended. In his filmography he identified 261 Hollywood films that were so clearly political in content that few would disagree with his choices. Unfortunately, Christensen simply assumed the existence of a political film genre without bothering to define it.

It was left to Michael Genovese to place parameters around a political film genre and to set criteria for selection into the category. Deviating from the Cineaste Circle's emphasis on the film's director, Genovese's taxonomy requires that a film satisfy at least *one* of the following criteria:

1. the film serves as a vehicle for international propaganda;
2. the film's major intention is to bring about political change; or
3. the film is designed to support the existing economic, political, and social systems.[10]

The value of Genovese's classification lies in the acceptance of a limited category with specific conditions for inclusion. Despite noble intentions, Genovese's effort to categorize political film falls somewhat short. Admittedly, all definitions are inherently incomplete and subjective, but Genovese's criteria raise concerns. First, films produced by or at the request of those in power undoubtedly serve propaganda objectives. Even so, is it absolutely necessary that films advocate political change as required in the second criterion? Why would an exposé of the political system without an explicit mandate for change disqualify a film from the political category? Suppose a film scrutinizes the government of the day or the fundamental principles supporting the political system, the unequal distribution of justice within the legal system, the social class structure, or the prevailing power relationships without offering a prescription for change? Why should such a film be excluded from the political genre because it merely discloses wrongs without advocating a political solution? To demonstrate the problems, take the 1979 film *The China Syndrome* as an example. It does not preach against the use of nuclear power *per se*, but it nonetheless demonstrates the capability for disaster should a nuclear accident occur, while it alerts the audience to expect a possible government cover-up should such a catastrophe befall the country. In light of the Three Mile Island nuclear accident outside of Harrisburg, Pennsylvania, which coincidentally happened a few weeks after the film's release, why is it not legitimate to state that the film served a political function by informing the public about the negative side of nuclear power as an energy source, a viewpoint unlikely to be publicized by the nuclear power industry or the U.S. government?

Genovese's third criterion includes films that support the status quo. His contention is that any film that justifies the government in power or supports the existing legal/justice system or the socioeconomic class structure is inherently political because it works against institutional reform and social change. However, it is naive to think that Hollywood will attack an economic system that has made entertainment a profitable business. Why would we expect Hollywood to attack corporate capitalism? We do not expect the Ford Motor Company to continue to manufacture automobiles like the failed Edsel, which the public refused to buy. Then why would the film industry produce films that the public refuses to spend their entertainment dollars to see? Because the film industry seeks to attract a mass audience, its product usually follows consumer tastes. Again, should Genovese not have expected a film like *The Man in the Gray Flannel Suit* (1956) to support business conformity during the 1950s while touting the virtues of corporate capitalism? Is the expected support of the status quo sufficient to warrant inclusion in the political film genre? Instead it might have been preferable for Genovese to qualify the status quo criterion to restrict it to films that support the existing political and socioeconomic systems at *the expense of disadvantaged and deprived groups*. This definitional adjustment would exclude *The Man in the Gray Flannel Suit* from consideration in Genovese's political film genre but include movies such as *The Grapes of Wrath* (1940), *Salt of the Earth* (1953), and *Alamo Bay* (1985)—films that attack the uneven distribution of goods and rewards while addressing issues of regional poverty, labor exploitation, and racial and ethnic discrimination. In this way, inclusion of the status quo qualification would have narrowed Genovese's definition while adhering to its intent.

Peter Haas, another political scientist who teaches a politics and film course, accepts the existence of a distinct film genre. Like Christensen, Haas recognizes that political content films have yet to be accepted as a separate genre for several reasons. One has already been mentioned, namely, the labeling of a film as "political" usually results in negative results at the box office and few, if any, achievement awards. This is not to dispute the fact that certain political content films make money but rather that the conventional wisdom urges caution. The Political Film Society, a Los Angeles-based group of academics, scholars, and film buffs, makes annual awards to films in several categories: expose, democracy, human rights. The Society reports that between 1986 and 2000, twenty-five political films received Oscar nominations for best picture or direction. The Society recognized two-fifths of these with awards. Even so, Hollywood awarded Oscars to only 12 percent. The point taken is that while Hollywood may recognize the achievement of political films through Academy nominations, they seldom honor them with their highest award-the Oscar.[11] Is this a coincidence or just another indication that the industry treats serious political films with faint praise?

A second reason is that political films lack the internal consistency of other film genres. They vary so widely in content and structure that defining becomes more problematic. After all, political film content occurs in narratives that can be dramatic or even funny. The antifascist statement conveyed by *The Great Dictator* may be diluted by the comedy but this does mean that it is any less effective than the same message expressed within the dramatic context of a *Casablanca*. Also, political films often are devoid of the conventions of plot and character existent in other film genres. In that sense, they look different from westerns or science fiction films. Westerns, for example, have standard polarized plots of good cowboys versus bad, of shootouts and posse chases, of larger-than-life heroes and one-dimensional villains. Political films, on the other hand, often lack this simplified narrative and are peopled with more ambiguous characters. For all these reasons, there is reluctance on the part of film critics, writers, and those who dominate the labeling process, to recognize a political film category distinct from all the others.

Haas mentions another reason for the lack of acceptance of a separate genre that is particularly relevant to political science. If a closed category of political films were to be commonly accepted, it might rule out those films that exist on the margins of categorization, denying attention to the political aspects of nonpolitical films. Hence, rather than attempt to define what makes a film political, Haas[12] instead develops a typology to help us identify different kinds of political films:

Politically Reflective Films	Pure Political Films
Socially Reflective Films	Auteur Political Films

In Haas's scheme, the "pure" political film is also the most obvious; namely, political films are those produced by governments and select commercial features with unmistakable political content, like *Mr. Smith Goes to Washington* (1939), *The Candidate* (1972), and *Thirteen Days* (2000). There is little debate about the political content of these films. Because audiences are more likely to grasp the political nature of such features, they are also more likely to suffer at the box office. What Haas identifies, as "politically reflective" films are those where the political content is used as a plot device but is secondary to the development of the major theme. Films like *Independence Day* (1996) and *Air Force One* (1997) use the institution of the presidency as a contrivance for action thrillers in which Americans fantasize that their political leaders are Bill Pullman and Harrison Ford. The third category of "auteur" political films includes a small group of directors whose films impart political meaning but without the requisite political references. Francis Ford Coppola's *Godfather* films fit in here because the American-based Mafia is run like an efficient political machine, dispensing rewards and administering punishment. The last category in Haas's typology, "socially reflective" films, is the depository for the vast majority of Hollywood films that are produced and marketed as entertainment, pure and simple. These films have no political intentions, characters, or events, although, in some cases, they may suggest or infer slight political meanings. The popular classic, *Gone with the Wind* (1939), a romantic drama that takes place during the American Civil War, would be a prime example.

REDEFINING THE POLITICAL FILM

Christensen assumed a political film genre, Genovese tried to define it, and Haas created a typology to help place individual films in their appropriate category. All acknowledge the existence of political content in films but depart over selection criteria. Another approach is to require two factors—intention and effect—be taken into account in identifying the political film. Following constitutional law scholar Cass Sunstein, who defined political speech as speech that is "both intended and received as a contribution to public deliberation about some issue,"[13] this approach necessitates that *both* criteria be satisfied for inclusion. Consider what happens when the intent-effect test is applied in practice.

Intent

At the production level, the definition requires that those involved in the filmmaking process—producer, director, film studio—either intend to deliver a political statement or such intention is reasonably implied from media interviews, commercial advertisements, and the consensus of film scholars and reviewers. An unmistakable example of an intended political film is the propaganda film typified by Leni Riefenstahl's *Triumph of the Will* or Frank Capra's *Why We Fight* series. These nonfiction propaganda films were made with the support of their respective governments to further state interests. Similarly, commercial features under the creative direction of auteurs occasionally are utilized to critique government actions taken at home or abroad. For instance, Oliver Stone disputed the "lone gunman" theory of the Warren Report in his film, *JFK*, while another of his films, *Salvador*, was highly critical of American support to Latin American dictators. Both films express the director's personal opinion, which differed from the official explanations.

Many directors, however, have to fulfill contractual obligations under which the studios exercise final judgment over their films. Under such conditions, filmmakers first must satisfy the demands of the studio before personalizing the film with any political messages. One relevant example from the 1950s is Carl Foreman's script for the western *High Noon*. Was the film a tribute to rugged individualism and personal courage or an intended attack on the friendly witnesses, which included the major studio heads, who testified before HUAC during the post–World War II Hollywood hearings into communism?[14] Foreman claimed afterward that his original script was a parable on individual decency (Marshall Will Kane) versus the forces of evil (Frank Miller's gang) and an indifferent community. Once HUAC subpoenaed Foreman, the script began to reflect his personal situation, that is, his opposition to the committee hearings and his anger at the capitulation of the studios.

High Noon then became a parable on Hollywood cowardice. Had the studio heads understood it as an attack on them and on the HUAC hearings, the film probably would have been shelved.

On other occasions, the initial intention behind a film may change during the course of production. This is what happened to *Force of Evil* (1949),[15] a film about two Jewish brothers coming to terms with crime and greed in a New York City ethnic ghetto. Director Abraham Polonsky, whose name would subsequently be placed on the blacklist, wanted to make a traditional gangster film, but was asked to deliver a popular movie that had liberal overtones. During the shooting, the content became more radical as the film reached its conclusion, resulting in a film that challenged the acquisitive and materialistic values under capitalism. Films like *High Noon* and *Force of Evil* are capable of delivering multiple messages to an audience. Which message the audience receives is unknown.

Complicating matters further in determining a film's intent is the nature of the film business as a collective enterprise, particularly when a film is made under contract for a major studio. Peter Biskind explains the problem inherent in the making of any political film:

> A conservative director may work with a liberal writer, or vice versa, and both, even if they are trying to impose their politics on their films . . . may be overruled by the producer who is only trying to make a buck and thus expresses ideology in a different way, not as a personal preference or artistic vision, but as mediated by mainstream institutions like banks and studios, which transmit ideology in the guise of market decisions. . . . [16]

Under these conditions only established auteurs and independent filmmakers have an opportunity to make a political film with few, if any, strings attached. Another necessary consideration is the required capital to finance film projects. The studios borrow millions from banks to finance their projects, and banks are notoriously conservative institutions that minimize risks and maximize profits. Even the independents require national distribution if their films are to compete with the studios at the box office. Hence, it remains highly unlikely that a political film, even one that supports the government in power and the socioeconomic system, will materialize without the necessary financial support.

Effect

If a film's intent is not always discernable to the casual viewer, its impact on a viewing audience is even more problematic. How to measure the reception of a film's political text raises additional obstacles to defining the genre. An appropriate measuring instrument would gauge an audience's understanding of the film's political text, that is, whether the primary story depicts some aspect of political history, promotes a particular ideology, serves as propaganda, supports capitalism in situations where workers and people are exploited or disadvantaged by the socioeconomic class system, or advocates political change or reform. Audiences that saw Neil Jordan's film *Michael Collins* (1996) or Richard Attenborough's *Gandhi* (1982), to cite but two examples, are unlikely to mistake these films for something other than political biographies. Nor will audiences misconstrue the intent of a film like *Welcome to Sarajevo* (1997). Shot in Bosnia, the film depicts the plight of two reporters, one American, the other British, caught up in wartime perils. The political nature of the film *Sarajevo* is reinforced by news reports from Kosovo province on the fighting and the killings.

Films that examine American institutions and find them deficient mark the history of Hollywood. The industry had no problem in conveying the intent-effect criteria to audiences in the thirties in a number of social-message films. For example, audiences empathized with the plight of the Okies during the Great Depression as depicted in John Ford's *The Grapes of Wrath* (1940), a sympathetic story of poor farmers struggling to hold on to their land despite adverse weather conditions, callous banks, and an indifferent federal bureaucracy. Reform of the prison system was the message of *I Am a Fugitive from a Chain Gang* (1932) while prejudice against outsiders and minorities depicted in films like *Fury* (1936) and *They Won't Forget* (1937) cautioned against the injustices of mob violence. Meanwhile, in the post–World War II era, films like *Crossfire* (1947) and *Gentleman's Agreement* (1947), spoke out against anti-Semitism, while a cycle of 1949 and 1950 movies dealt with the issue of racial prejudice and discrimination: *Home of the Brave*, *Lost Boundaries*, *Pinky*, *Intruder in the Dust*, and *No Way Out*. Audiences living in America when segregation was the law of the land could hardly misinterpret the message these films conveyed.

Audiences experienced little difficulty in deciphering the message of these films as pleas for religious and racial tolerance. The problem, however, is that film audiences do not always accept the intended political message. Filmgoers, for a variety of reasons, including the desire of viewers to be entertained, may fail to notice the political content of a film altogether. Other film messages are subject to audience interpretation and categorical assignment by critics and reviewers. Take the case of *Forrest Gump* (1994). Audiences who saw this sentimental film could root for its dim-witted hero as he overcame adversity, or viewers might have been offended by its celebration of ignorance over intellectualism.

Forrest Gump is the kind of film Hollywood loves to make because its ambiguous message is encased within a slick entertainment production. Another film with an enigmatic message was liberal director Stanley Kramer's, *Guess Who's Coming to Dinner?* (1967). The plot revolves around the romance and intended marriage of black actor Sidney Poitier to the daughter of two white liberals, a judge (Spencer Tracy) and his wife (Katharine Hepburn). Audiences that viewed the film at face value accepted *Guess Who's Coming to Dinner?* as just another romantic comedy by the popular Hepburn-Tracy team. However, viewers who came to the theater with relevant background information discovered that the film also was a plea for racial harmony and integration. However, in order to reach that level of understanding, viewers in 1967 had to be aware that interracial cohabitation and marriage were illegal in sixteen American states at the time of the film's theatrical release. Armed with that knowledge, viewers could interpret the Kramer film as a political statement against these state antimiscegenation laws, albeit packaged in a highly entertaining movie.[17]

The same could be said about the film classic, *Casablanca*. Viewed by millions worldwide during its fifty-plus years in circulation, *Casablanca* is another film subject to different interpretations depending on the knowledge of the audience. For many viewers, the Rick-Ilsa (Humphrey Bogart-Ingrid Bergman) romance remains the quintessential love story. However, there are individual scenes and dialogue that would lead viewers cognizant of the pre-World War II political climate to accept the film's anti-isolationist, pro-democracy message. In this scenario, Rick's neutrality is transformed by his love for Ilsa, a passion so strong it overcomes his worldly cynicism and persuades him to assist Ilsa and her husband, Victor Laszlo, Czech patriot and resistance leader, escape Nazi-occupied Morocco. However, if *Casablanca* is really about world politics, why is it that the Victor Laszlo anti-Nazi character is secondary to the Bogart-Bergman love story? Furthermore, if Warner Brothers intended the film to deliver a pro-interventionist message, why was it not made and released a few years earlier, before Pearl Harbor? Then the timing of the film's national distribution, together with Warner Brothers' antifascist stand, would have lent credibility to the film's pro-intervention message. Without the presence of these factors, though, *Casablanca* remains an enigma.

Audiences that went to see the film *Destination Tokyo* (1944) during World War II could view it as one of many action/adventure war movies. However, because the U.S. Navy also showed the film to military personnel for training purposes, it took on another dimension for viewers with the additional knowledge. Audiences who want to understand film as propaganda need to be more than passive viewers. Such an audience would have to be knowledgeable about movies and filmmakers; this, though, is likely to be considered a burden for American filmgoers who patronize movies to be entertained. Chaplin's *The Great Dictator* and his later film, *A King in New York* (1957), both provide good illustrations about the duality of film content. As mentioned previously, viewers can appreciate *The Great Dictator* as vintage comedy or as an antifascist statement. Similarly, *A King in New York* also can be viewed at face value as one of Chaplin's lesser comedies or as political drama, a satiric attack on HUAC and McCarthyism. A viewer seeing the film without the relevant background information is likely to consider it comedy. However, the viewer who brings factual knowledge to the film surely will view it differently. English-born, Chaplin never became an American citizen. When his loyalty was questioned during the 1950s, Chaplin left the country, eventually residing in Switzerland. Later when he wanted to return to the States, he discovered that he was *persona non grata* and refused reentry by the Immigration and Naturalization Service. *A King in New York*, therefore, was produced in London but not exhibited in the states for two decades.[18] As scriptwriter, director, and star of *A King in New York*, Chaplin exercised complete control over the film, lending support to the view that he sought to critique America because it questioned his loyalty while it embraced mindless conformity and vacuous cultural values. On the other hand, was *A King in New York* second-rate Chaplin at best? Of more recent vintage, is there a film with greater ambiguity of meaning than *Seabiscuit* (2003)? This story of an undersized racehorse, which is given little chance of outrunning War Admiral, can be viewed as a tribute to a horse with a bigger heart and spirit than the reigning champion. It is a story that applauds the underdog. However, is it not also a film that recognizes the spirit of the American people and their president, Franklin Roosevelt, in their desire to overcome the hardships of the Great Depression? The film strategically interrupts the Seabiscuit story with newsreel footage of hard times in America. For the common man in the 1930s, Seabiscuit represented a symbol of resilience and courage, the very qualities the president said were necessary to restart the engine of American capitalism.

The duality of meaning in film content took an unexpected turn with the publication of film scholar Don Morlan's thesis that the popular shorts of the *Three Stooges* were more than exercises in mindless slapstick; they were films of social criticism and pro-World War II interventionism.[19] Morlan's research discovered that during the period from 1934 to 1958 the Stooges made a total of 190 shorts for Columbia Pictures in which thirty-four films portrayed conflicts between the upper and lower classes. These included their signature pie-in-the-face routine. The recipients of these pies were the wealthy and snobbish upper classes who were victimized by the Stooges in their film capacity as domestic servants or manual workers. Morlan contends that these shorts helped to uplift the morale of working Americans during hard economic times. He also insists that the Stooges contributed to pro-World War II propaganda in several shorts released between 1935 and 1941. One short in particular, *You Nazty Spy* (1940), was released to theaters nine months before Chaplin's *The Great Dictator*, leading Morlan to conclude that the Stooges were turning out shorts that, in their slapstick style, warned Americans of the evils of Nazism and Fascism before Chaplin's film. For Morlan's thesis to be more than mere speculation, tangible evidence of intent and viewer perception is required. Even if we concede that Jules White, the head of Columbia Pictures Short Subjects division, was an admitted interventionist and even if Curly, Larry, and Moe

were Popular Front activists (no evidence exists to support the truth of this assertion) who abhorred fascism and deliberately poked fun at Hitler and Mussolini in
their films, these assumptions would merely satisfy the first requirement of intent.
However, in the proposed two-tier definition, political intention alone is not
enough. The affective requirement must also be met, and this is where the Morlan
thesis about the Three Stooges breaks down. What did the audience at the time
think of the Three Stooges and what did the masses make of their films? Were
Curly, Larry, and Moe recognizable political activists? Did they appear at public pro-
war rallies? Were they outspoken members of the Popular Front movement? The
basic question here, which neither Morlan nor this author can answer with authority, is whether audiences who viewed the Stooges in the thirties and early forties
accepted their films as social criticism and pro-war interventionism. To state the
question differently, did a consensus exist among critics, film scholars, and the
movie audiences that their short films preached revolution, the overthrow of the government, or reform of the political or socioeconomic class system? Unless such a perception existed at the time, it remains problematic what messages, if any, the Three
Stooges were communicating in their slapstick routines.[20] Unlike *The Great Dictator*,
which made a statement against anti-Semitism and fascism that angered Hitler and
Mussolini, the shorts made by the *Three Stooges* were generally conceived to be
mindless slapstick routines from beginning to end, recycling the same plot in different contexts. If dictators were the patsies in one film, the victims in others were
employers, the rich, and the military. In sum, the Stooges' shorts were no more than
mass produced "fillers" to accompany the main feature or to round out a double bill
at a Saturday matinee.

In theory, the two-tier requirement to determine whether a film's content
qualifies for inclusion as a political film postulates the kind of empirical proof that
satisfies academic scholars. However, as the above discussion demonstrates, the two-
tier definition represents the ideal, yet serious practical problems arise in the application. In those instances when the intent requirement is met, documentation of the
second criterion involving audience perception is close to impossible to achieve.
Naturally it is easier to identify intentions in films like *Wag the Dog, Primary Colors,
Bulworth,* and *The Contender* because these movies feature a political subject, place
the action in Washington, and include representational political characters. When
these factors are joined in one narrative text, there is a greater likelihood that an audience will perceive the film as political.

Even proof of a single political factor is insufficient evidence on which to
make a valid judgment. For example, take the Geena Davis-Michael Keaton film,
Speechless (1994), about two speechwriters for opposition candidates in a U.S. senatorial race in New Mexico. The political subject is electioneering, with the story's
inspiration coming from the real-life romance of two speechwriters in the 1992

Clinton-Bush presidential campaign. That is where the similarities end because if the actual speechwriters acted as the two stars do in the film, both would have quickly been unemployed. While politics provides the background in *Speechless*, the film's focus is on romance. Except for a few brief scenes of campaigning, *Speechless* could have been about two sportswriters who meet, fall in love, have a misunderstanding, and yet end happily in a romantic embrace. The Davis and Keaton characters struggle to imitate the romantic comedy team of Tracy and Hepburn in a 1990s film that has love, not politics, on its mind. The audience, meanwhile, learns no more about running a U.S. senatorial campaign than if it had stayed at home.

Placing the action in a governmental location, such as the nation's capital, may add local color to the narrative, but the locale alone does not guarantee that a film will be political. Although the Kevin Costner film *No Way Out* (1987) is set in the Washington area, particularly in and around the Pentagon, and has the secretary of defense as a major character, its narrative focus is on romance and suspenseful action. Similarly, four other 1990s films center around sitting presidents: *Dave* (1993), *The American President* (1995), *My Fellow Americans* (1996), and *Air Force One* (1997), and are played strictly for laughs or thrills. Despite the inclusion of actual politicians and background shots of the Capitol building and the White House, the real world of politics is definitely not the major preoccupation of these film presidents.

On the other hand, a successful political film takes advantage of location and integrates it into the context of the film. Contrast the above films with *City Hall* (1996), shot on location in New York City, with a plot that involves a besieged mayor (Al Pacino) actively engaged in trying to keep racial peace after a black boy is shot. Pacino's mayor is occupied by politics in virtually every frame. The audience learns little about this mayor's personal life because the focus of the narrative is on his public activities. Pacino's mayor is a political animal while Kevin Kline's stand-in president, *Dave,* and Michael Douglas's widower president (*The American President*) are cardboard political characters that audiences are unlikely to take seriously.

Finally, the question remains: how to measure audience reaction? While it is theoretically feasible to measure audience feedback, it is also impractical. To gauge a film's affective impact requires exit-polling strategies to survey viewers immediately upon leaving the theater after a film's showing. Such a methodology would not guarantee a representative sample. On the other hand, cluster sampling of viewers in selected locations throughout the county would be more representative, but its applicability would be even more uncertain. There also is the question of the expense involved and whether the benefits are worth the cost. Besides, what government agency or private organization would be willing to commit the time and resources to collect the data? Hollywood could do it in conjunction with its "sneak previews" by inclusion of directed questions on the film's message. Yet while

Hollywood and the government have the resources, neither has the motivation or the interest.

Even assuming that funding is available and sampling problems satisfied, the results of an audience feedback survey still could prove ambiguous. To illustrate this point, take the case of the film, *Romero* (1989), about the Catholic Archbishop of El Salvador who was assassinated in 1980 by members of the military government. On its face, *Romero* can be understood in terms of rights and liberties; a repressive government denies human rights to its citizens and seeks to silence those clergy who support political and economic reform. Because a good deal of the financial resources to make the film came from the Catholic Church and because the film adheres closely to actual events in the life of the Catholic Archbishop, the Church might have produced the film for alternative motives. Therefore, was the intention behind the film to portray a human-interest story about an ordinary religious man thrust by history into becoming a spokesperson against injustice in Central America? Or was its real motive to show the schism in the Catholic Church between the adherents of liberal theology and those who unwittingly support ruthless governments in Third World countries as long as these governments do not interfere with Church practices? It is highly unlikely that even a methodologically sound survey will provide a definitive answer.

The truth of the matter is that to require both production intention and audience effect as essential characteristics of the political film is no more likely to be empirically possible than past definitions. For the overwhelming majority of Hollywood films, delivering entertainment is the message; profit is the goal. But for that small minority of films: some made by auteurs, some by independents, some produced by the studios, the political message is paramount and takes precedence over commercial success. For every acknowledged political film, there exist hundreds more for which the search for consensus among film and politics analysts remains elusive.

Can it be that the task of defining the political film is similar to the law's efforts to define obscenity? To substitute former Justice Potter Stewart's remark on obscenity[21] to defining political film: "we know it when we see it but we cannot explain the indispensable characteristics of its content." That describes the "pure" political film, but it is less helpful in developing a consensus concerning the "politically reflective" and the "auteur political" films. What is known for certain, however, is that the vast majority of Hollywood films are intentionally apolitical. It is that small remaining minority of films that occupy the realm of controversy.

Possibly in the final analysis both the obscene and the political character of a film may lie in the eye of the beholder rather than any textbook definition. Clearly the intention of the nonfiction film is less ambiguous than the entertainment purpose of many commercial features, even if their effect on audiences remains in doubt.

NONFICTION FILM

CHAPTER THREE

Investigating the Real

"Sometimes you have to lie. One often has to distort a thing to catch its true spirit."

ROBERT FLAHERTY

"Documentaries, like theatre pieces, novels or poems are forms of fiction . . ."

FREDERICK WISEMAN

"The easiest way to inject a propaganda idea into most people's minds is to let it go in through the medium of an entertainment picture when they do not realize that they are being propagandized."

ELMER DAVIS, DIRECTOR OF OWI DURING WWII

The opening scene in Leni Riefenstahl's documentary *Triumph of the Will*, about the 1934 Nuremberg Party conference, pans the sky as the camera tracks the landing of a small twin-engine plane. When the plane lands, the door opens and Adolph Hitler emerges triumphant, greeting the crowd of worshiping faces, waving flags, and offering party salutes. It is a dramatic introduction to one of the greatest propaganda films on record, a film in which Hitler is portrayed as the benevolent leader, *der Führer*, who has descended, God-like from Heaven, to restore the German people to their rightful place in history.

The film is wonderful theater, but also a blatant piece of Nazi propaganda. Propaganda is one film type under the more comprehensive genre known as "nonfiction" film—a category that includes everything from newsreels to propaganda tracts. A relative newcomer is the docudrama, a hybrid blend of fact and fiction.

This chapter, therefore, examines the effort by filmmakers to investigate aspects of reality and to transfer that reality onto film. Whatever the intention, the evidence indicates that few nonfiction films depict the world as it really is.

NONFICTION FILM

It would simplify matters if a consensus existed on an accepted definition of the nonfiction film. Similar to most attempts at classification, the nonfiction film defies simplistic explanation. This is not surprising because the genre encompasses visual images from newsreels and travelogues to rock concerts and Nazi Party rallies. One effort to distinguish the nonfiction film from the commercial feature describes the former as "discourses of sobriety,"[1] films that depict an unedited truth. Critics insist, however, that such films straddle fact and fiction, information and entertainment. Consequently, as a film category, works of nonfiction are tainted, because the term implies that the events depicted are true.[2]

If an acceptable definition of nonfiction film cannot marshal a critical consensus, nonetheless Richard Barsam has identified a half-dozen characteristics essential for inclusion in the genre.[3] These include the following: (1) a focus on a particular event, person, group, or social problem; (2) the film is shot on location with the actual participants and without costumes, stage sets, or sound effects; (3) the film has a structured narrative with a beginning and an ending; (4) the film is usually photographed in black and white, although color is becoming more popular; (5) the work typically is filmed without spoken narration, relying on the words of the actual participants; and (6) the film is customarily not intended for commercial distribution. There are exceptions to the last characteristic, notably in the films of Michael Moore, *Roger and Me, The Big One* (1998), *Bowling for Columbine* (2002), and *Fahrenheit 9/11* (2004), which broke the box office record for documentaries.

THE DEVELOPMENT OF THE NONFICTION FILM

Although film historians are likely to associate the development of the documentary with Robert Flaherty's 1922 recording of the life of Inuit Eskimos, *Nanook of the North*, or with the work of John Grierson in England, the cinematic effort to capture reality began decades earlier when European colonial companies engaged photographers to take pictures of their economic holdings to impress their home governments. By the first decade of the twentieth century, all the great European colonial powers employed cameramen to record activities in their African colonies and to show these films to private investors and the general public in commercial theaters.[4] Meanwhile, the desire for pictorial news footage, particularly of military battles, encouraged filmmakers to take desperate measures. Filmmaker Edward Amet depicted the destruction of Admiral Cervera's fleet at Santiago de Cuba during the Spanish-American war by filming richly detailed models floating around a bathtub.[5] Such fake battle footage was commonplace during these early years of filmmaking. American filmmakers produced some sixty-eight films of the Spanish-American war and the subsequent Philippine Insurrection for national distribution, making it the first war in American history to employ the camera as recorder.[6] But how much of this footage was real or staged for propaganda purposes is unclear.

World War I Era

In the years before the First World War when labor unions were struggling to organize and gain public acceptance, the American labor movement decided to use the new medium to educate and politicize the working class and to counter the negative images presented in the silent films distributed by Hollywood. The American Federation of Labor (AFL) made *A Martyr to His Cause* (1911), a film about the trial of the McNamara brothers accused of bombing the *Los Angeles Times*. Two years later the labor movement produced *From Dusk to Dawn* (1913), using professional actors to depict a story about labor strife that eventually ends in a Socialist Party election victory.[7] These silent films were important recruiting tools as the labor movement sought to organize unskilled immigrant workers, many unable to understand English. For these workers, a picture was worth a thousand words.

The nonfiction film came of age during World War I because, for the first time, film became an instrument of modern warfare, providing valuable information to the warring nations and a source of propaganda to use against their enemies. The British government, for instance, screened its 1915 film *Britain Prepared* to President Wilson and the Congress in an attempt to persuade the United States. to enter the war. Germany, meanwhile, put its film industry under state control to counter the Allied propaganda.[8] Both Germany and Britain were in competition for American support, but before 1917 few Hollywood films about the war treated the conflict in a way that would offend either side. However, once the United States officially entered the hostilities, all films that dealt with the war came under the control of the government's Committee on Public Information (CPI). Furthermore, World War I marked the first official effort by the United States to produce its own films when the government created a film section inside the Signal Corps with responsibility for turning out films that would aid the war effort.

Between the Wars

When the First World War ended, the factual film returned to recording other subjects. Filmmakers like Pare Lorentz, founder and head of the U.S. Film Service, made documentaries about the resettlement of the Dust Bowl's dispossessed in *The Plow That Broke the Plains* (1936) and the benefits of the Tennessee Valley Authority in *The River* (1937), both documentaries were underwritten by the government. Actually, the Department of Agriculture had been making films since the beginning of the century as part of its educational mission. By the thirties, the government had built its own sound stage in the nation's capital to facilitate film production.[9] Documentary film flourished at this time and led to efforts to improve production and national distribution. To consolidate filmmaking during this period, the labor movement advocated east and west coast production and distribution facilities. Subsequently, the Labor Film Services was based in New York while the Federated Film Corporation was set in Seattle. However, the federal government considered labor's efforts suspicious; the FBI monitored their activities and attended their films while the postal service denied mailing permits to labor film groups that sought to advertise films in their own magazines. Additionally, both liberal and leftist films were made of the Spanish Civil War and of the tragic effects of the economic depression. One leftist group, Frontier Films, included among its members such directors and screenwriters as Elia Kazan, John Howard Lawson, and Albert Maltz, all of whom joined the Communist Party and were called to appear before HUAC in the 1950s. To combat labor's earliest efforts, the corporate sector countered with a stream of its own films designed to portray labor organizers as Bolsheviks and anti-American radicals. This antilabor viewpoint was portrayed in *Courage of the Commonplace* (1917), *Bolshevism on Trial* (1919), and *Dangerous Hours* (1920). These films depicted union leaders as corrupt Bolshevik agents intent on generating discontent and subverting American industry.[10] During the twenties and thirties documentaries and feature films produced by Hollywood studios were used as propaganda weapons in the struggle between employers and the working classes.

World War II Era

Nonfiction films were never intended as popular entertainment. Initially, these travelogues, newsreels and short documentaries were used by theater owners to supplement the main feature. However, in the 1930s, the studios forced theater distributors to rent a "film package" for commercial showing, which generally included a major feature, a shorter minor film that usually ran about an hour, cartoons, and short subjects. As a consequence, the market for documentaries plummeted.

The German invasion of Poland in 1939 revived interest in documentary film. The U.S. government, although proclaiming neutrality, gave military and economic support to the Allies. The government also was not above propagandizing the war to the American people. For example, Louis de Rochemont's documentary *The Ramparts We Watch* (1940) conveyed the message that the democratic ideals of freedom and justice were not confined to the European conflict alone but affected Americans as well. Once America entered the war, the government encouraged the making of films that explicitly served the war effort. Subsequently, a wide range of government films were produced, covering subjects as varied as military training pictures and venereal disease educational films for service personnel to propaganda pieces like Frank Capra's *Why We Fight* series. But unlike the First World War, the government was better prepared to initiate the propaganda war the second time around. The Office of War Information (OWI) modeled itself on its World War I predecessor. After the war, the duties of the OWI were assigned to the Division of International Information, which later became the U.S. Information Agency (USIA), housed within the State Department.[11]

Post-World War II Developments

Nonfiction films flourished in the post-World War II period as a new breed of filmmaker saw the medium as an instrument for journalistic exposés and social reform. Their cameras viewed America with a fresh and often critical eye. Their subjects ranged from contemporary politics (*The War Room* 1993, *The Weather Underground* 2003) to social problems like the urban homeless (*Dark Days* 2000) to union organizing (*Live Nude Girls, Unite!* 2000).

Some, like Frederick Wiseman, remain prolific creators, working almost continuously on film projects. Others like Barbara Kopple produced a handful of films over two decades of which two, *Harlan County, USA* (1976) and *American Dream* (1989), won Academy Awards for Best Documentary Feature.[12] A third group of documentarists ventured into commercial features with varying degrees of success. The popular Michael Moore moved from the documentary style of *Roger and Me* to his second film, *Canadian Bacon* (1995), a commercial feature about an attempt by an inept president to begin a war with Canada to increase his popularity and reelection chances. Moore returned to the documentary form after *Canadian Bacon* flopped at the box office. Several documentary filmmakers find steady work in television; others discover an outlet for their talent in state-funded assignments and in projects for educational institutions. Few retain box office power; many produce one or two films and fade out of sight.

THE DOCUMENTARY FILM

The origins of the documentary film are related to the development of filmmaking in Europe a hundred years ago. The documentary film style arose in response to the oversimplified and romantic representation of reality in fiction films, even though both forms include a narrative and a dramatic structure. The documentary differs from fiction in several ways. First, it seeks to present the world the way it actually is rather than through an imaginary representation. Second, if the subject is historical, the documentary tries to recreate an era or a specific factual event without embellishment. Third, the emphasis in the documentary is on fashioning an argument or a point of view through the presentation of visible images or through the testimony of experts or witnesses. Finally, because the documentary represents people directly rather than through intermediary actors, the film engages the viewer more than even the most explicit fiction film since the viewer knows the event is real rather than simulated.

Frederick Wiseman and "Reality Fictions"

In the United States documentary film dates from the amateurish newsreels at the end of the nineteenth century to the sophisticated *cinema verite* style of contemporary filmmaker, Frederick Wiseman. Wiseman deserves credit for popularizing the form, as his documentaries appear regularly on public television and are made available to educational institutions. Of all the contemporary documentarists, it is Wiseman who has the best track record and has sustained the most interest.

Born in 1930 in Boston to professional parents, Wiseman followed his father's career path. After graduation from Yale Law School, Wiseman taught at Boston University before embarking on a film career. His first venture into filmmaking was in 1963 as a producer for the feature film, *The Cool World*, an examination into the lives of Harlem teenagers. Wiseman returned to fictional filmmaking twice more during his career. In 1982 Wiseman produced, directed, edited, and adapted *Seraphita's Diary* about a fashion model unable to cope with the demands of her profession and who escapes from these pressures by disappearing. Twenty years later, Wiseman adapted a chapter from a Russian novel into a short film, *The Last Letter* (2003), depicting a Jewish woman's letter to her son describing the destruction of her small Ukrainian town by the Nazis.

Wiseman's major work, however, remains his documentaries. His prolific filmmaking career spans three decades and more than thirty films.[13] His reputation was established in his first documentary, *Titicut Follies* (1967), where Wiseman took his camera inside the Bridgewater, Massachusetts, State Institution for the Criminally Insane. The idea for the film came to Wiseman on one of his student class visits to the institution, where he became outraged at the conditions within the prison walls. What he witnessed made him abandon his law books in favor of the camera. His stark depiction of institutional life entangled his film in a controversy with state authorities. Although Wiseman had received permission from state officials, the completed film did not please them, and they went to court to prevent its distribution.[14] The state contended that the film violated the privacy rights of the inmates since several were filmed nude, that Wiseman had not received knowledgeable consent from inmates, and that the filmmaker had violated the terms of their oral understanding over editorial rights. Wiseman denied the later charge and rested his case on the First Amendment ground that the public had a right to know conditions inside state institutions. After a series of legal decisions, a compromise was reached whereby the film was barred from public release but made available for educational usage. It was under this "limited use" restriction that the author secured the film for showing to his American Institutions television course at the University of Akron during the 1970–71 academic year. This restriction remained in effect for twenty-four years and was not removed by the court until 1991.[15]

Wiseman's documentaries often engage viewers in the emotional plight of their subjects even when the films lack the necessary historical context to make sense of their feelings. Still, there is no denying the power of his films, characterized as social tracts where the emphasis is on powerful institutions rather than the individuals entrapped within.[16] Wiseman's films often remind audiences of the early-twentieth-century muckrakers of print fame. For instance, *Meat* (1976) exposes the details of the slaughtering process that is favorably compared to Upton Sinclair's novel, *The Jungle*. In films such as *Titicut Follies* (1967), *High School I* (1968) and *II* (1994), *Hospital* (1970), and *Juvenile Court* (1973), Wiseman's camera often captures public institutions in ways that encourage viewers to question their practices and procedures. One good example occurs in *Public Housing* (1997), where Wiseman depicts the despair of the Chicago housing projects and the failure of public housing policy in the United States. His film does not require commentary because the camera substitutes for the spoken word.

Beyond the institutions, Wiseman is sensitive to everyday human drama. In his six-hour film, *Near Death* (1989) he explores the choices made by doctors, patients, and families during end-of-life medical crises. Although his camera is intrusive, Wiseman the filmmaker is not, because he is content to let the audience reach its own judgments. At one point in the film, his camera joins a group of doctors deep into conversation. What the audience overhears is quite different from the kind of advice doctors often provide to their patients.

It is too simplistic to label Wiseman a social reformer even though his films are often critical of institutions, their employees, clients, and their social and economic consequences. His films record the power underneath the façade of even benign institutions. Rather than draw judgments about the events he records, Wiseman prefers that his audiences come to their own conclusions. A recent illustration of Wiseman's filmic style is his four-hour documentary about a small New England town, *Belfast, Maine* (2000). On the surface, Belfast is a community of 6,000 farmers and fishermen who live and work in an idyllic environment. What his film captures, in addition to the happiness and congenial spirit, is a community where people experience pain and suffering as well.

In addition to *Meat* and *Titicut Follies*, Wiseman, as part of his direct cinema, has dealt with retail sales in *The Store*. In this film, Wiseman takes his camera into Neiman-Marcus's Dallas department store, where wealthy customers are shown buying expensive dresses and fur coats. His films bear the stamp of his personality and his cinematic technique identifies Wiseman as the American filmmaker who comes closest to being an "auteur" among contemporary documentarists. Wiseman's films should be viewed as empty canvases on which the filmmaker records images, leaving it to the imagination of the audience to complete the painting. For instance, in *The Store* (1983), Wiseman brought his camera into the very exclusive Neiman-Marcus department store to record fashion shows where champagne is served, marketing sessions where employees are almost as well dressed as the customers, and sales transactions involving $37,000 for a sable jacket and $45,000 for a diamond bracelet. Wiseman then takes his camera outside, showing scenes of ordinary people walking the streets and riding the buses downtown and commentary is unnecessary to illustrate the contrast between the elites, who can afford to spend lavishly on luxuries at Neiman-Marcus, and the people outside, who look like they barely have enough money to make ends meet.

Wiseman's work is characterized by most of the attributes of *cinema verite*: using lightweight, portable camera and sound equipment, hand-held filming, working without a script or narration, recording events as they develop and focusing the camera on hand gestures and body language that accompanies the dialogue.[17] He usually works with a three-person crew: a cameraman and an assistant, with himself as the sound recorder. Typically he spends twelve to fifteen hours filming and, on any given documentary, Wiseman will record fifty to sixty hours of film, which he edits down to a length of ninety minutes to three hours. The entire editing process might take up to one year.[18] While Wiseman's films are never staged or rehearsed; the filmmaker's stamp is put on the film during the editing process when he imposes a structure on the film footage.

Wiseman is the rare documentarist who is willing to admit the subjectivity of his work in the sense that the notion of objectivity in capturing reality is often lost in the editing process. That is why Wiseman refers to his work as "reality fictions," since he emphasizes the "constructive nature of documentary."[19] In short, the meaning in his films is created during the editing process and conveyed to viewers who try to make sense out of what they experience. Wiseman's contempt for his colleagues who maintain that their work is factual—that the camera never lies despite evidence to the contrary—is reflected in the term, "reality fictions."

In contrast to Wiseman, other documentary filmmakers conveniently omit from mention a film trail of work that contains staged scenes, misidentified footage, events arranged to misrepresent chronology, and stock film incorporated into authentic footage. Even the father of American documentary, Robert Flaherty, manipulated the actual for dramatic effect. As early as the silent newsreels, sound effects were added for dramatic effect during the editing process. The *March of Time* newsreels, for instance, contained staged events and studio reconstructions if genuine footage was unobtainable. Perhaps the worst case of reconstruction occurred in the pre-World War II era when a newsreel made a film that depicted life inside Nazi Germany but shot it in the New Jersey farmlands.[20] Frank Capra's *Why We Fight* series also included staged footage and scenes inserted from commercial features.

Michael Moore: Populist Filmmaker or Self-Promoter?

Another contemporary documentarist, whose work and personality is 180 degrees from Wiseman, is Michael Moore. Whereas Wiseman is a very private person and quiet by nature, Moore is brash, irreverent, outspoken, and opinionated. In contrast to Wiseman, whose films are often grim, Moore's films contain humorous sequences. Born in Flint, Michigan, in the 1950s, Moore is the author of three best-selling books, and the director of four documentaries, including *Bowling for Columbine*, which won an Oscar, and one commercial feature. While his productivity cannot match Wiseman's prolific output, Moore's documentaries and books have gained wider popularity with audiences.

His three nonfiction books are political and social exposés that are often quite amusing. However, if Moore were a college student, his written work would be unlikely to receive a passing grade. Written in a colloquial style without much attention to grammar or sentence structure, Moore prefers to make broad unsubstantiated generalizations while also trying to get a few chuckles. In *Downsize This!* Moore's attack on corporate greed and the role money plays in our elections, the filmmaker has his staff mail campaign contributions to presidential candidates Buchanan, Dole, and Perot from fake organizations named "Abortionists for Buchanan," "Satan Worshippers for Dole," and "John Wayne Gacey Fan Club" to Perot. In *Stupid White Men*, Moore takes on the political establishment, especially George W. Bush, whom he characterizes as an illiterate, alcoholic felon. Finally, in his latest book, *Dude, Where's My Country?* Moore calls for regime change in the United States as he challenges President Bush to answer seven questions. Should the president fail to answer these questions correctly, Moore insists that he should resign. While the questions are serious, Moore treats them in a facetious manner. It makes the reader wonder whether Moore is more interested in being humorous than in providing alternative policies.

However, is Moore a true twenty-first-century populist and muckraker or a social satirist more adept at self-promotion than political or social analysis? Strange how Moore and Wiseman, who share little in common, both received public notice through early works that gave rise to controversy. Moore drew national attention with his first film, *Roger and Me*, in which he attempts to interview the CEO of General Motors (GM) Roger Smith. The young filmmaker's first project became a popular success when it was released in 1989. Advertised as a documentary about the woes of Moore's hometown of Flint, Michigan, the film became something of a *cause célèbre*. When GM shut down its auto plant in Flint, thousands of workers lost their jobs. At the heart of Moore's film is his unsuccessful attempt to track down GM's CEO, Roger Smith, in the company's Detroit headquarters and query him about plant closings. However, the interview never takes place because Smith avoids the confrontation. The elusive CEO is the real star of *Roger and Me*.

Roger and Me cost $260,000, a sum befitting a struggling documentarist. However, it was later learned that Warner Brothers gave Moore $3,000,000 for the rights to distribute the film, an amount that expressed confidence in its commercial value. However, when the Motion Picture Academy listed its Oscar nominees for best documentary, Moore's film was omitted because its commercial distribution qualified it for the feature film category. Even so, when the film was released on video, it was reclassified as a documentary. In some ways, this fable of *Roger and Me* is more interesting than the film itself because it questions the social construction of categories. Who decides whether Moore's film is a documentary or a commercial venture? The film studio? The Motion Picture Academy? The film critics? Moore himself? What *Roger and Me* demonstrates is the arbitrary classification of documentary films as authentic depictions of reality.

Ironically, it was the commercial success of *Roger and Me* that led movie critics and film scholars to more closely examine Moore's film. Moore considered his film a documentary,[21] but eventually it was revealed that he had taken liberties even beyond editing and the rearranging of scenes. For example, Moore charged that the plant closings resulted in 30,000 workers being laid off, but the actual figure for the Flint plant was a more modest 5,000. The 30,000 statistic actually referred to jobs lost in plant closings in four states over a twelve-year period. Furthermore, Moore insinuated that while GM was closing its plant, Flint was wasting millions on city projects that eventually failed. The implication is that the city could have saved some of these jobs by providing incentives to GM. In fact, the three city projects that failed were underway *before*, rather than after, the 1986 shutdowns. There were other minor discrepancies as well. One scene showed President Reagan touring Flint, leaving the viewer with the impression that all the hoopla surrounding the president's visit contrasted sharply with the image of a dying city. In actuality, Reagan visited Flint in 1980 as a presidential candidate rather than as president six years later.[22] These discrepancies led one film critic to comment that the problem with the film was not that it expressed a personal viewpoint, but rather that it was unfair.[23] While the film left the audience with a negative impression of corporate capitalism, Moore resorted to misrepresentation and dramatic reconstruction to demonstrate it.

Moore's film can be contrasted with Barbara Koppel's documentary, *American Dream* (1989), which was released in the same year as *Roger and Me*. *American Dream* concerned the 1985 strike by the meatpackers' union at the Hormel plant in Austin, Minnesota. Whereas Koppel's film is a traditional documentary, complete with exposition, detailed observation, and support for the strikers' cause, Moore's film, while sympathetic to the plight of his home town, uses humor and sarcasm as social commentary. What these films share in common is that neither filmmaker was successful in gaining access to the power brokers—the corporate leaders—demonstrating the powerlessness of ordinary workers who challenge the authority of the modern corporation.[24] Unlike Moore, however, Koppel was not criticized for her failure to include the strike from the corporate viewpoint.

Moore's ego was bruised by the criticism his film received, but his next documentaries were highly regarded by critics and audiences. *The Big One* is a film record of Moore's national tour to promote his book, *Downsize This!*, a critique of corporate capitalism. The camera follows Moore from book signings to plant closings to union organizing strikes. Moore's film criticizes American companies that close their factories, throwing thousands out of work, but then open plants in Mexico and other underdeveloped nations. As in his written work, Moore offers no solutions except to visit one of these companies and, on camera, present the company representative with a check for eighty cents to cover the first hour of wages to its Mexican workers. It's good for a quick laugh but resolves nothing. However, Moore is successful in persuading the CEO of the Nike plant in Portland, Maine, to make a contribution of $10,000 to relieve his guilty conscience for paying Indonesian workers forty cents an hour to construct the sneakers. What Moore fails to mention is the millions Nike pays Michael Jordan to promote the company's sneakers to youngsters throughout America and the underdeveloped world.

In his subsequent documentary, *Bowling for Columbine*, Moore uses the massacre at Columbine High School in Littleton, Colorado, to raise issues related to violence and gun ownership. His film is a devastating indictment of the gun culture in America, including statistics on shootings in the United States compared to other nations, in addition to film footage of the Columbine shootings, that explores the nature of American violence and the country's love affair with guns. Once again, however, Moore's tendency to make light of a serious subject is evident. For example, he opens a checking account in a Michigan bank because it advertises that each customer who signs up for a new account receives a free gun. So after a quick background check, Moore walks out of the bank with a rifle. The point that it is as easy in some states to get a gun as a set of dishes is not lost on the viewer, but the muckrakers of old would have tried to connect the availability of guns to the more than 11,000 gun deaths in America each year. To be fair to Moore, he was success-ful in getting Kmart to stop selling gun ammunition in their stores, a modest change in policy. His talent was finally recognized by the Motion Picture Academy when *Bowling for Columbine* received an Oscar for best documentary.

FIGURE 5. Michael Moore receives rifle for opening a bank account in *Bowling for Columbine.* Reprinted by permission, *Photofest.*

Moore's latest documentary, *Fahrenheit 9/11* (2004), caused a storm of contro-versy before it reached the theaters. Winner of the coveted Palme d'Or, top prize at the Cannes film festival, *Fahrenheit 9/11* is a stinging indictment of the Bush fam-ily's relationship with the Saudis, including the bin Laden family, before the terror-ist attack on the Twin Towers. Disney held the distribution rights to the film but refused to permit its subsidiary, Miramax, to distribute it. Moore labeled the action "censorship," and it looked as if the film might not get released. However, the Weinstein brothers, film producers, came to the rescue by buying the distribution rights for $6 million and distributing the film through independents Lions Gate Films and IFC Films. Once released, the film ran into a ratings snafu as its ads wrongly identified the rating as NC-17, a rating that would have prevented teenagers from viewing the film. After a few days, the correct R-rating replaced NC-

17 in the advertisements. Also, the film's ads were challenged as being in violation of the campaign finance laws. Whether any of these mishaps were by design or inadvertent, the film earned $24 million its opening weekend and a healthy $61 million during its first two weeks.

Fahrenheit 9/11 is really two films spliced together. During its first half, Moore is at his best in exposing the Bush family's business dealings with the Saudis, covering the disputed 2000 presidential election and the terrorist attack on September 11, 2001. The first half climax is reached as Moore shows footage of a dazed and confused President Bush sitting in an elementary school reading stories to young children after being informed of the terrorist attack on New York. The early muckrakers such as Upton Sinclair and Frank Norris would have been proud of Moore's depiction up to this point. For some unexplainable reason, Moore turns his attention to Iraq during the film's second hour and Moore, the filmmaker, becomes Moore, the partisan ideologue. The film disputes the Bush administration's decision to invade Iraq and questions its continued presence in the country. By releasing the film four months before the November presidential election and by openly advocating Bush's defeat, Moore entered the 2004 campaign. The documentarist became the propagandist. These comments are not meant to disparage the film's intentions or to rebuff its humorous barbs directed against the Bush administration, the Congress, and the USA Patriot Act—all deserving targets for political satire. However, there are too many moments in the film where Moore seems more interested in the cheap laugh than in recording how and why the United States went to war against Iraq.

The financial success of *Fahrenheit 9/11* (a domestic box office gross of over $100 million) raises an interesting question about the future role of political documentary. Is the movie a model for future filmmakers to emulate or is it nothing more than an aberration, a peculiarity that occasionally happens in the film industry? *Fahrenheit 9/11* is a left-leaning contemporary piece of visual muckraking that simultaneously exposes political events and advocates political change, the kind of public affairs reporting avoided by mainstream media. The question is whether it will serve as the model for the twenty-first-century documentary and eclipse the more traditional documentaries aired on public broadcasting and the cable networks. Whether deliberate or coincidental, the fact remains that over the past few years documentaries intended for the movie theaters have questioned America's intervention in Vietnam, criticized the fast-food industry, sympathized with 1960s' radicals and cast doubt on the wisdom of going to war with Iraq. What are most impressive about *Fahrenheit 9/11*, however, are the scope of its audience appeal and the sweep of its national publicity. Its popularity has elevated Michael Moore to national status sufficient to permit him to attend the 2004 Republican National

Convention, much to the chagrin of conservatives. It also represents the first time that a documentary filmmaker has entered a presidential election with the intention of influencing the outcome.

It is much too early to gauge the long-term effects of *Fahrenheit 9/11* on the documentary form. For the present, the film is a commercial success that has elevated Moore to celebrity status and added to the marketing acumen of the Weinstein brothers. It remains to be seen whether the film will influence the direction political documentary will take in the future.

There is a tendency in Moore's films to set people up to embarrass them on camera. It is a staple of his documentaries. He does it to a CEO in Milwaukee in *The Big One*, Charlton Heston in *Bowling for Columbine*, and Roger Smith in *Roger and Me*. Moore loves to make fun of people who avoid him or who refuse to answer his questions. Unlike Wiseman and Koppel, Moore is not a neutral filmmaker but rather a partisan ideologue. His political criticism and acerbic style raised considerable controversy when *Fahrenheit 9/11* hit the theaters.

Moore is such a genial fellow that it is hard to dislike him. His barbs, however, can be deadly on target and he can make his interviewees appear foolish. Occasionally, Moore's questions go unanswered and sometimes he and his camera are asked to leave the premises. Comparable to other investigative journalists, Moore is also subject to legal action by a disgruntled participant in one of his films. These are all hazards of the profession. However, there are more serious consequences to filming documentaries than being sued or asked to move on. For instance, while filming *Harlan County, USA* Barbara Koppel was harassed and even shot at.[25] Another filmmaker, Hugh O'Connor, was shot dead while working on a documentary about Appalachia in the 1960s. There are repercussions for the participants as well. To cite one example, the Louds agreed to be the subjects of a twelve-part television series on the American family in the seventies. The TV series required that a camera crew invade their home and film their daily movements and activities. Shortly after the series was aired on television, the Louds divorced. The family charged that the filmmakers selected for inclusion all the negative portrayals, shouting matches, and bad times that had happened during the filming schedule and ignored all the positive details and the good times. Wiseman ran into a different problem with his *Titicut Follies*. Although Wiseman received legal consent from the patients before filming, his critics questioned whether mental patients could give informed consent. The most discouraging fact, however, about *Titicut* and the others is that, with one or two exceptions, they led to no change in institutional policies. The documentarist might rejoin that the filmmaker is an artist first rather than a political activist. Unfortunately, what these examples indicate is that public exposure alone is insufficient to generate social action.

THE DOCUDRAMA

Somewhere between fact and fiction in the film lexicon is the docudrama, a hybrid form whose description reflects the dividing line between documentary (reality) and drama (fiction). Of the several definitions of the genre, the following is a fairly comprehensive characterization:

> A unique blend of fact and fiction, which dramatizes events and historic personages from our recent memory. . . . It is a TV recreation based on fact though it relies on actors, dialogue, sets and costumes to recreate an earlier event. The accuracy and comprehensiveness of such a recreation . . . can vary widely and is conditioned not only by intent but also by factors such as budget and production time.[26]

A common misperception is that the docudrama originated in the 1970s with the televised "movie of the week" programming. The form actually dates back to the old newsreels that restaged historic events such as the Spanish-American War and the First World War for American audiences. In the thirties, the Hollywood studios turned to historic events as the source for epic films like the *Sign of the Cross* (1932) and *The Crusades* (1935), two Cecil B. De Mille stagy productions. Hollywood also found the lives of famous people a good source for recreation. Warner Brothers, in particular, became identified with film biographies as the studio reconstructed the lives of such historic figures as Emile Zola, Louis Pasteur, and Benito Juarez. Film biographies were so popular with audiences that for more than thirty years, 4 percent of the studios' annual releases included them.[27] Hollywood continues to utilize the genre, especially in contemporary biographies such as the ones on presidents Kennedy and Nixon and in investigative-exposé type films such as *Silkwood* (1983) and *Missing* (1982).

A significant expansion of the genre occurred in the seventies as the television networks sought to compete with Hollywood for the entertainment dollar. Television, which had been buying Hollywood films to show in primetime, discovered that it was less expensive and a better marketing strategy to produce original films for the networks. Thus was born the "TV Movie of the Week," with plots that were "ripped from the headlines." The networks competed aggressively for first televising rights to contemporary events that included stories based on real events or programs that used historical themes or persons. Within this broad category, the networks filmed a story of the friendship between two football players on the Chicago Bears (*Brian's Song*, 1971*)*, a miniseries on slavery (*Roots*, 1976–77), and an account of the Supreme Court abortion decision, (*Roe v. Wade*, 1989). More often, the networks turned to personal stories of cowardice and heroism, joy and suffering, criminals and sordid affairs; the latter included three versions of the sleazy affair between teenager Amy Fisher and her married, middle-aged lover, Joey Buttafuoco.[28]

Critics of the docudrama are quick to mention its weaknesses and faults. Because docudramas often rely upon events in recent memory, the networks rush to televise their version first. Sometimes this rush to judgment raises serious questions about the validity of the form. USA network, for example, televised, *D.C. Sniper: 23 Days of Fear* (2003), its docudrama about the crime wave in the metropolitan Washington, D.C., area when two snipers shot thirteen people, ten of whom died. The broadcast occurred around the time of the trial of one of the two suspects. In its haste to beat the competition, the network's film preceded the trial verdict. As a result, the film was neither informative nor particularly interesting. It also raised concerns about interference with the course of justice. Similarly, the same network rushed to film a highly publicized California murder case about a pregnant wife, Laci Peterson, who disappears and is later found dead. Subsequently, her husband Scott is arrested and charged with her murder and that of their unborn son. While the state was in the process of jury selection, the USA network televised the docudrama, *The Perfect Husband* (2004). Though the film ends with Scott in jail awaiting trial, the movie provides him with an opportunity to deny his guilt and to lay down a defense. The film was a pointless exercise with the possible danger of polluting the potential jury pool. Both these exploitation dramas raise questions about the intrinsic value of television docudramas.

Because the docudrama is a fictionalized version of real people and events, dramatic license is to be expected. However, when the liberties taken involve important public figures that are still alive, the docudrama becomes a subject of controversy. This happened when the CBS network produced a miniseries on *The Reagans* to be televised during the semiannual network competition. Advanced previews of the miniseries raised considerable criticism from conservatives and several important Republican leaders because the portrait of the former president and his wife was not flattering. It was particularly upsetting because Mr. Reagan was suffering from Alzheimer's disease at the time. The controversy caused CBS to cancel the miniseries. Assuming the viewing audience is capable of distinguishing fact from fiction, why is censorship necessary? One possible answer is that when you broadcast entertainment and news over the same medium, the opportunity to blur truth and fiction is constantly present.

Regrettably, the form encourages misrepresentation because producers are free to engage in dramatic license given the claimed fictionalized treatment. A prime example occurred in NBC's docudrama, *Saving Jessica Lynch* (2003), the story of the American soldier captured during the Iraq War. Because the network failed to receive authorization from Pfc. Lynch, the film avoided recreating the various versions of her capture, imprisonment, and rescue. Instead, NBC focused its story on Mohammed Al-Rehaief, the Iraqi who led American forces to Jessica's location. Because the network wanted to be first to televise her story in primetime and because it could not receive her authorization, the story it told relied on secondary sources. Several days later, Pfc. Lynch told her story on television and in a ghost-written book, *I am a Soldier, Too.* Eleven American soldiers died in the ambush that led to her capture. The film never made it clear to viewers why her story became newsworthy and required special attention. One suggested answer is that the media bought the Rambo-Pentagon version of her capture and rescue, which promoted support for the war. This observation, revealed in the authorized biography, was omitted from the television film. In short, the mythology surrounding Pfc. Lynch's exaggerated story served as a propaganda tool for the military. In propaganda the filmmaker always manipulates an audience to accept the message delivered.

THE PROPAGANDA FILM

Propaganda films come in several configurations. One is the documentary, a sup-posedly objective recording of an actual event, a political movement such as Nazi Socialism, or the depiction of a culture portrayed through its inhabitants. The pro-paganda in these films often is deceptive because their creators claim neutrality, as if their films were unedited newsreels. Riefenstahl's *Triumph of the Will*, mentioned earlier, is an example. Another form of propaganda occurs in commercial films where the message frequently is surreptitiously hidden in the subtext, usually evident only to the scholar or trained viewer.

What exactly is propaganda and why does the term invoke such disdain? It is a term that defies classification since one person's truth is another's falsehood. No one definition is universally accepted, yet there is general agreement that the term has come to include the twin elements of premeditation and manipulation. Hence, David Culbert says that propaganda is "the controlled dissemination of deliberate-ly distorted notions in an effort to induce action favorable to predetermined ends of special interest groups."[29] His definition is broad enough to encompass the out-put from state-controlled film industries, political campaign broadcasts, and docudramas.

Propaganda differs from both fact and opinion in that its goal is primarily to present information in such a manner as to influence or persuade an intended audience in a particular way. On the other hand, facts are statements whose authen-ticity is observable by the senses or verifiable by research. In the film world, the title credits, listing the film's players, writers, technicians, and director represent factu-al information about the movie. In *Casablanca*, for instance, the names of Humphrey Bogart and Ingrid Bergman in the title credits provide us with the major players while Michael Curtiz's name indicates that he served as its director. All these "facts" are subject to corroboration from other, external sources. However, to insist that *Casablanca* is a political film is to render an opinion about it, that is, to express a personal feeling or intuition concerning the film that may actually make good sense and prove to be correct, but that still requires factual evidence for verification. Sometimes fact and opinion are blended into one statement, and it is necessary to extract and distinguish one from the other. Staying with the film *Casablanca*, suppose a film critic described the film in the following manner:

> *Casablanca* takes place in Nazi-occupied Morocco where Humphrey Bogart, as the American owner of Rick's Place, helps two European refugees, including Ingrid Bergman, his former lover, escape to freedom. Bogart's character represents the American position favoring intervention in the European war before the Japanese attack on Pearl Harbor.

In this hypothetical review, the first sentence includes information that can be confirmed from the film itself. However, the last sentence states an opinion rather than historical fact.

The term propaganda is a neutral label that acquired a pejorative meaning. Its origin is in Pope Gregory XV's establishment of the Congregation for the Propagation of the Faith in 1622 to counter the Protestant Reformation.[30] Thus in the seventeenth century propaganda meant the spreading of theological dogma or religious doctrine. By the nineteenth century the technique came to be identified with the efforts of governments to manipulate public opinion.

In the twentieth century, the term became associated with Nazi Germany. Though it is true that Hitler came to power in 1933 by democratic means, he resorted to force and mass manipulation to consolidate that power. The Nazis systemically eliminated their opponents via assassinations, cold-blooded murders, and terrorist threats so that when Hitler became chancellor, the Nazis had already eliminated or frightened most of the political opposition. Once in command, the Nazis sought to mobilize the German people via a campaign of emotional and patriotic appeals. These were coupled with the manipulation of public opinion through the selection of "ethnic and racial scapegoats," which required elimination in order for Germany to fulfill its historical destiny. This campaign to capture the hearts and minds of the German people was entrusted to the propagandists. Hitler understood the value of film as a tactical weapon in his goal to "purify" Germany and resurrect Germany to its former glory in the form of the Third Reich. While documentarists acknowledge that film is an ideal method for portraying reality, it also can distort reality by strategic editing and cutting. In that sense, it is the perfect propaganda weapon by which to rearrange ideas and phenomena in such a way as to make them appear to be true. To cite one example, Hitler ordered a "film hour for the young" as part of the official school curriculum. By 1934, every German school was required to show Nazi-produced films during this one-hour period. Hitler had discovered in the film medium the ideal medium to indoctrinate the young, excite street bullies, convert the apathetic, and persuade the indecisive. Historians mark the 1933 book burning or the "Kristallnacht" in 1938 as symbolic of the Nazis rise to power. However, the underlying explanation for their rise and their ability to retain control rests on their utilization of propaganda to forge a mass psychology that supported their physical show of power.

Nazi propaganda had two national objectives. One was to enlist internal support for Hitler's global plans for a Third Reich that "would last a thousand years" and the other goal sought to weaken the morale and the resistance of the enemy. The first goal is demonstrated in the film, *Baptism of Fire* (1940), which trumpeted the superiority of German air power; the second goal is best illustrated by another 1940 film, *The External/Wandering Jew*, which portrayed the Nazi ideal of a master race.[31] As Minister of Propaganda, Goebbels's efforts were directed at solidifying support at home. His intention was to create a competitive German film industry, with Berlin as a pseudo-Hollywood. Contrary to much of the popular mythology found in American World War II movies, Goebbels disdained the overtly propaganda film replete with swastikas, SS uniforms, and "Heil Hitler" salutes—characteristics more common to American-made movies during this period than anything found in German films. Of the 1,097 feature films produced under Goebbels's orders between 1933 and 1945, only 183 or one-sixth, were overtly propagandistic.[32] This figure shows that the Nazis produced fewer wartime propaganda films than the Americans or the British.

Goebbels preferred historical dramas that contained mythic heroes rather than the blatantly propagandist *Triumph of the Will*. Despite Riefenstahl's plea that the film was merely a recording of a historic event by an artist rather than a piece of Nazi propaganda, she failed to satisfactorily explain why her film contained restaged scenes, some reshot without Hitler present.[33] Other scenes were arranged so as to give coherence to the series of events, thus "dramatizing" the film footage. *Triumph* took months of planning, shooting, and editing in order for Riefenstahl to present a view of a united Nazi Party when, in truth, Hitler had ordered the assassination of a rival faction the night before the Nuremberg Party Congress scene depicted in the film.

Riefenstahl was a fiercely independent child but with a need to be the center of attention. Acting came very naturally to her and she moved quickly from actress to director. At age twenty-nine she had formed her own film company. While touring Germany to promote her film, she attended a Nazi rally and was so impressed with Hitler that she wrote him afterward. In return, Hitler met her and took an interest in her work. Leni attended Nazi parties where she met Hitler again. After one party, Goebbels noted that Leni was " . . . the only one of all the stars who under-

FIGURE 6. Filmmaker Leni Riefenstahl walking in her Berlin garden with Hitler and Goebbels. Reprinted with permission, Bavarian State Library Archives, Munich.

stands us."[34] In 1933 she made her first film for the Nazi Party. When Hitler saw it he commissioned her to make a film of the upcoming Nuremberg party rally, which turned out to be *Triumph of the Will*.

Riefenstahl insisted that she was an artist, not a political figure. Nonetheless she sounded very political in this congratulatory telegram sent to Hitler when France surrendered:

> Adolf Hitler—Fuehrer Headquarters. With indescribable joy, deeply moved and full of gratitude, we now bear witness to your, my Fuehrer, and the Germans' great victory—the entry of German troops into Paris. You achieve feats that have been unimaginable so far, unprecedented in the history of mankind. How can I thank you? Expressing congratulations is much too little to show you the emotions that move me. Leni Riefenstahl"[35]

True, Leni did not join the party, nor was she anti-Semitic. Even so, she was a favorite of Hitler, and so one would assume that she supported the cause as well. Apparently, she had unlimited budgets for her films and she was granted unrestricted access to the elite corps within the Nazi command bureaucracy.[36] Given the structure of the Nazi Party with its emphasis on loyalty and submission, an intelligent woman like Riefenstahl, who had access to the top echelon of party leadership, presumably did not have to become an official party member to know what was happening. Riefenstahl could hardly claim independence as a filmmaker because under Goebbels's command all film producers and artists had to register with the propaganda ministry and all scripts were subject to review and party clearance. Working within this hierarchical structure, Riefenstahl was as much a civil servant as Lorentz was in depression-era America.

Riefenstahl, who died at the age of 101 in 2003, spent the years after World War II reinventing herself as a photographer. Arrested and held by the Allies for three years, Riefenstahl subsequently was cleared of any wrongdoing during the de-Nazification process. However, her film career was finished. She remained defiant until her death that she was merely an artist rather than a political ideologue. Still, her life and work resurrect the eternal question of whether it is possible to separate art and politics.

World War II Propaganda

The Nazis were not alone in manufacturing propaganda during the Second World War. The United States had cranked up its own propaganda machine under the auspices of the OWI to coordinate film activities with Hollywood. Actually, however, there was an existing propaganda campaign at work in Hollywood long before Pearl Harbor. Morlan notes that in the five years leading up to America's entrance into World War II, the industry was busy producing both anti-Nazi and war preparedness films.[37] The anti-Nazi films included *Blockade* (1938), *Confessions of a Nazi Spy* (1939), *The Mortal Storm* (1940), and *Man Hunt* (1941). Four films released between 1940 and 1941, *Flight Command, Dive Bomber, A Yank in the RAF,* and *Sergeant York,* promoted the advantages of military readiness. If the United States was going to enter the war, these films suggested that it would not be on the German side. Morlan also insists that a number of the early Three Stooges' comedy shorts, such as *You Nazty Spy,* were really directed at the fascists.

Whether the Three Stooges shorts were intended to help the Allied war effort is problematic, but there is no doubt that the film studios were anxious to cooperate with the government once the United States officially entered the war. Animation studios like Walt Disney especially welcomed government business because the war had cut off part of the foreign market. Hence, the studios recruited cartoon makers to produce training films for U.S. soldiers in addition to churning out propaganda shorts. Warner Brothers proved to be the busiest studio, using the Bugs Bunny cartoon character to sell war bonds and introducing a new character, Private Snafu, to star in a series of military training films. Warner's produced twenty-five Private Snafu films between 1942 and 1945 in which the hapless private would be lectured on subjects ranging from malaria to venereal disease. Also a number of Bugs Bunny cartoons made fun of the Japanese in a manner that would be considered racist slander today; Daffy Duck cartoons sent a similar message to Hitler and the Nazis. Walt Disney studios, meanwhile, lent its Donald Duck character to the war effort by placing him in patriotic cartoons. One Donald Duck episode, *Der Fuehrer's Face* (1942), had the duck waking up in a world conquered by the Nazis to illustrate what life would be like living under a totalitarian regime.[38]

Like cartoons and short subjects, feature films also had to make a wartime adjustment. Hollywood no longer could portray the Axis Powers in a positive light. The most significant attitude conversion was reserved for the Russians. Before the signing of the Nazi-Soviet Non-Aggression pact in June, 1941, Hollywood either ignored or poked gentle fun at the Russians in films like *Ninotchka* (1940) and *Comrade X* (1940). After the Nazi invasion of Russia, Hollywood supported the Allies' newest member in the most praiseworthy terms. At least four features released in 1943 and 1944 glorified Stalin, the military, and the courage of the Russian people. Two war films, *The North Star* (1943) and *Days of Glory* (1944) paid tribute to the heroism of partisans and guerrillas in their fight against overwhelming German forces. Reportedly, the Russians loved *The North Star*, a big hit in Siberia where it played to 50,000 people.[39] Meanwhile, MGM's *Song of Russia* primarily portrayed a love affair between an American conductor (Robert Taylor) and a Russian concert pianist (Susan Peters), two unlikely combatants. However, when the Germans invade Russia, the lovers exchange their musical talents for military weapons and join the partisans in their fight against the invading Nazis. Although a love story set against a war background, *Song of Russia* abounds with praise for collectivism, comparing, for example, the Soviet collective farms with those in Midwestern America. Its pro-Soviet ideology put the film on HUAC's subversive list, even though Taylor's patriotism was never questioned during his appearance before the committee.

Resonant complaints were saved for the film, *Mission to Moscow* (1943), a box office fiasco released after the Battle of Stalingrad to drum up American support for the Russians. *Mission to Moscow* purported to be a factual record of Ambassador Joseph Davies's three years of service (1936–38) in the Soviet Union. It proved to be such an exaggerated glorification of Stalinist Russia that its credibility was seriously damaged.[40] For example, condensing the four Stalinist purge trials into one may be forgiven, but not at the expense of historical accuracy. For the film to present the Moscow trials as justification for Stalin to remove traitors plotting against him is pure fiction and content manipulation to serve political ends. Historians accept the fact that during the party purges of 1933 and 1938, Stalin removed an estimated 850,000 members from the party, ordered one million put to death, and another twelve million political enemies (real or imagined) shipped to Siberian labor camps. For *Mission to Moscow* to portray Stalin as a friendly, smiling "Uncle Joe" character to the American people is equivalent to Riefenstahl showing Hitler in *Triumph of the Will* as a kindly grandfather figure rather than a monster directly responsible for eleven million deaths. After the war, HUAC considered these four pro-Soviet films "un-American." But during its hearings, HUAC never questioned the loyalty of Warner Brothers, which produced and distributed *Mission to Moscow*, even though final approval rested with the studio. In Cold War America, the issue of individual loyalty proved to be highly selective.

Post-World War II Propaganda

After 1945, only a select few films dealt frankly with pressing social issues such as intolerance, racial injustice, anti-Semitism, and discrimination. These had to contend for audience attention with a slew of anticommunism films, which warned against communist infiltration and subversion and recruitment of disillusioned Americans as spies, traitors, and dupes for the Soviet Union. These films featured respected Hollywood stars like John Wayne, Robert Taylor, Helen Hayes, and Elizabeth Taylor, whose appearance lent credibility to the anticommunist message. The most blatant piece of anticommunist propaganda was a low-budget B-film called *The Red Menace* (1949), intended as a warning to dissatisfied Americans considering membership in a communist cell. The amateurish plot relates the story of a war veteran duped by the communists. The irony is that the communists in the film are portrayed as much smarter than the decent, but weak and naive, American followers. *Red Menace* is the classic, although sophomoric, propaganda film of the postwar era. Fourteen years later, Warner Brothers (perhaps as self-imposed penance for producing *Mission to Moscow*) made a film entitled *Red Nightmare* following the Cuban Missile Crisis. Told in flashback as in a dream, the plot has communists taking over an entire community, thereby depicting what life would be like under Soviet domination. Salvation comes from this dreadful fate only when the major character wakes up from his dream. Despite the anticommunist theme, the film was an embarrassment and never was released to theaters. Thus, the reputation of *The Red Menace* as the most overt piece of Cold War propaganda remained intact.

Another propaganda film from that era, but from an entirely different perspective, is *Salt of the Earth*. This fictional recreation of a successful strike in the zinc mines of the American Southwest of the early 1950s was denied commercial distribution in the United States.[41] Dismissed as a piece of "communist propaganda" by film critic Pauline Kael and blacklisted nationally, the film remained a source of controversy for many years. The movie starred a few professional actors and was produced, written, and directed by blacklisted filmmakers. The real union organizer actually was a member of the Communist Party. The film nonetheless depicted, in gritty black and white, corporate violence and a disregard for the health and safety of the mostly Chicano mine workers. When the mine owners succeed in securing an injunction to stop the workers from picketing, wives and mothers take their places on the picket line. Indeed, as described in a later chapter, the film underrepresents the real amount of violence that occurred during the actual strike when sixty-two women were arrested and several shot by company guards and local police. In addition to the threat to life, the cast of professional actors and local citizens and members of the crew were subjected to physical abuse and death threats in the wake of the Red Scare hysteria. Furthermore, the filmmakers were denied technical facilities and the lead actress was deported, requiring that the film be finished in Mexico. Looking back, the movie can be perceived as a piece of anticapitalist propaganda, but it also can be viewed as a piece of social muckraking and as an early feminist tract since the strongest characters in the film are women. *Salt of the Earth* is a good illustration of a film that is multilayered: a piece of "communist propaganda," a promotional for the trade-union movement, an argument against laissez-faire capitalism, a consciousness-raising tract as a precursor to the women's movement.

Salt of the Earth is hardly the traditional Hollywood film fare. While the vast majority of Hollywood films provide straight entertainment, a small fraction every year are intended by their creators to deliver a political message.[42] Some are subtle, containing political messages in the subtext, which must be ferreted out. For instance, Oliver Stone's films *JFK* and *Nixon* are good examples of historical fiction, promoted by the filmmaker as though grounded in indisputable facts. In *JFK*, Stone interpreted past events not as straightforward historical facts such as "Oswald shot Kennedy" but as a series of conditional theories such as "Oswald might have been part of a conspiracy to assassinate Kennedy." In this sense, Stone's film lends cinematic support to the fascist conspiracy theory surrounding the president's death.[43]

Categories of Propaganda

Nimmo contends that there are four distinct forms of film propaganda. The first category is that of the overtly propagandistic movie such as Frank Capra's *Why We Fight* series and *Triumph of the Will*. A second category includes commercial films loosely based on actual political figures and real events such as *Mission to Moscow* and *Salt of the Earth;* these are transparent propaganda efforts. A third category consists of covert propaganda films that require audiences to possess relevant factual knowledge if they are to understand the film's hidden message. Such would be the case for the 1950s western, *High Noon.* The last category, Nimmo reserves for films that contain what he identifies as "potential propaganda"; in other words, these are selected films with nonpolitical subjects that are produced for entertainment purposes, yet have the potential to carry propaganda messages. To illustrate his point, Nimmo maintains that the 1948 John Wayne western, *Red River*, which deals with a cattle drive over the Chisholm Trail, also can be viewed as a vindication for empire building (accumulation of territory) and capitalism (the search for a cattle market in the old West).[44]

Few would differ with Nimmo about the overt propaganda films within his classification scheme because these are films of political advocacy promoted by the state. But both second and third categories require the viewer to integrate previous knowledge with the action on screen. Without this prior information, both *Mission to Moscow* and *High Noon* can be accepted at face value. In the case of *Mission to Moscow*, much of the negative material on Stalin is excluded; hence the film became an apologia for the party purges, a strictly Stalinist view of historic events. Also important to note is the film's timing; the factual material on Stalin was not available to the filmmakers or the American people when the film was released in 1943.

More questions arise when a film like *The Birth of a Nation* has to be categorized. The government did not sponsor the film, although President Wilson did contribute some scholarly footnotes to the text. Based on the novel *The Clansman*, and written by a Southern evangelist, the film presents a particularly nasty portrayal of the black population. Not only are they shown as undisciplined beasts, lusting after white women, but also the rise of the Ku Klux Klan is justified as a necessary measure to protect white society and keep blacks in a subservient place within the social structure. The film enjoyed a successful showing around the world, but it is difficult to gauge just how much damage it caused to black Americans in its reinforcement of racial stereotypes. The film added the characteristics of meanness and violence to the cliché of the shuffling, befuddled, and easy-going Afro-American. To add insult to injury, white actors played all the major parts, including the principal black characters. Griffith restricted the participation of blacks to the crowd scenes.[45] *The Birth of a Nation*, therefore, should be understood as a piece of overt propaganda thinly disguised as Reconstruction history.

The fourth category, "potential propaganda" deserves little serious consideration. To cite just one example, Nimmo would have us believe that *Red River* is really an endorsement of American capitalism rather than a critically acclaimed Howard Hawks western. Still, several different interpretations have been offered about the film, including a story about male bonding (cowboys on the trail), intergenerational strife, (father Wayne versus foster son Montgomery Clift), and a remake of *Mutiny on the Bounty* (1935) (with Wayne as the tyrannical Captain Bligh). Which interpretation should an audience accept as authentic? This is one example of why latent political messages, such as those Nimmo attributes to *Red River*, require detailed documentation, rather than a few conjectures.

There is enough overt political propaganda around that it is unnecessary to deconstruct the texts to further personal agendas. Recent documentaries on political campaigns present another arena for propagandists to portray both negative and positive images of politics. Take the contrasting portrayals depicted in the documentaries, *The War Room* (1993) and *A Perfect Candidate* (1996). The first is an optimistic presentation of the successful 1992 Clinton campaign for the presidency; the other paints a dark picture of the electoral process as depicted in Oliver North's 1994 unsuccessful bid for a seat in the U.S. Senate. Which film more accurately depicts American politics may ultimately defy personal analysis or textual deconstruction.

KISS, KISS, BANG, BANG

CHAPTER FOUR

Or How I Came to Love Sex and Violence on the Big Screen

"My constituents can't read but they can understand pictures."

BOSS TWEED OF TAMMANY HALL

"Censorship made me."

MAE WEST

"We went back four times before we got an R ... We had to get rid of a few thrusts when he's having sex with the apple pie. The MPAA was like 'Can he thrust two times instead of four?'"

WARREN ZIDE, PRODUCER OF *AMERICAN PIE*.

In the 1940s and 1950s, parents sent their children to the local movie theater with little, if any, anxiety. Saturday matinees were reserved especially for youngsters and attendants were present in the theater. Parents relied, more or less, on appropriate film content since movies in those days were under the supervision of the Production Code, an industry-wide set of guidelines that controlled the making of Hollywood films. Parents were secure that their youngsters were not going to see films with sexual and violent content like *American Pie* (1999) or *American Psycho* (1999). Moreover, local theaters then had one screen, unlike modern movie multiplexes. There was little chance, therefore, that unaccompanied children would see a film other than the one they were meant to see.

All that changed with the demise of the Production Code and the creation of the industry-administered film rating system, together with the growth of multiplex theaters. Selecting an appropriate movie for children, especially teenagers, has become a more serious parental concern. How that change occurred, its detrimental effect on film content, and what Hollywood can do to restore parental confidence in the film industry is the subject of this chapter.

THE FILM INDUSTRY: FROM CENSORSHIP TO REGULATION

Virtually every new form of popular entertainment has been a target of public criticism; movies were no exception.[1] Efforts to control film content evolved through three often overlapping stages in cinema history; in its formative years, federal, state, and local governments censored movies, permissible until the 1952 U.S. Supreme Court decision in *Burstyn v. Wilson*[2] brought movies under the protection of the First Amendment and led to the end of government film censorship. In the next stage, beginning in the thirties, Hollywood instituted a form of self-regulation, first with the Production Code and later, through adoption of a film rating system, which had the affect of shifting the burden of censorship from the industry to parents and adult guardians. In the latest stage, pressure groups, which formerly negotiated with the industry over film content under the Production Code, have had to resort to the use of economic boycotts and threatened sanctions against the showing of specific films that offend their particular religious, racial, or sexual/gender sensibilities.[3]

Historically, pressure group activity and government intervention during the film industry's early years led to the passage of city censorship ordinances, state censorship statutes, and the creation of state and local censor boards. By the 1920s, seven states and more than a dozen cities had placed motion pictures under government regulation, requiring a permit or license from the censors prior to public exhibition.

Whether the silent films and early talkies were so immoral and socially dangerous as to warrant such regulation is open to question. The negative influence and social harm attributed to these early films were grossly exaggerated as they were charged with everything from causing juvenile crime to corrupting public morals since the lurid and sensational titles promised, but often failed to deliver, what was advertised. Nonetheless, this did not prevent state and local governments from enacting regulatory legislation.

It would be a mistake, however, to think that pre-Code Hollywood was entirely innocent. Some films of the early thirties,[4] for example, were often suggestive, provocative, and violent, complete with double entendres, fallen women, and vicious criminals. Moviegoers during these early depression years viewed James Cagney smash a grapefruit in Mae Clarke's face (*The Public Enemy*, 1931), and saw Edward G. Robinson (*Little Caesar*, 1930) and Paul Muni (*Scarface* 1930) shoot and maim their way up the crime ladder. Nor did these early films spare women, as audiences watched Barbara Stanwyck sleep her way to the top of the New York business community (*Baby Face*, 1933) while Jean Harlow's completely amoral character in *Red-Headed Woman* (1932) exploited her sex to gain entrance into the world of the rich and famous. Criticism against such screen content was reinforced by media reports of Hollywood as "sin city," a place of wild sexual orgies, bootleg whiskey, studio call girls, and drug abuse. Hollywood was beset with negative publicity about its stars' depraved conduct, drug usage, and, in the case of comedian Fatty Arbuckle, criminal charges of manslaughter and possible rape. Such stories, coupled with public complaints, led U.S. Senator Henry Myers of Montana to indict Hollywood as a place " . . . where debauchery, riotous living, drunkenness, ribaldry, dissipation, free love, seem to be conspicuous."[5]

To discourage government censorship and quiet public criticism, the film studios hired former U.S. Postmaster General Will Hays in 1922 to be their new industry leader. Hays saw his job as twofold: clean up film content and polish the industry's tarnished image. To achieve these goals, Hays sought to screen out undesirables from the film industry, to discourage migration of young people to Hollywood in pursuit of a film career, and to persuade the major film studios to make the kind of movies acceptable to civic and religious leaders. He also took a step towards self-regulation by encouraging the studios to permit his staff to review scripts for objectionable material. Later, he sought to control screen content by convincing producers to accept his list of "Don'ts" and "Be Carefuls," in the making of their films. This was to be accomplished, first, through avoidance of certain subjects and second, by treating particular topics with special care. For example, under Hays's direction even married screen couples were prevented from sharing the same bed. Profanity, nudity, white slavery, miscegenation, and ridicule of the clergy were to be avoided at all cost. Traditional social institutions like marriage and family were to be properly presented, while religion and symbols of authority, such as the police, were to be respected at all times. But Hays soon learned that verbal acceptance of the guidelines by studio executives did not guarantee compliance. By 1930, Hays had become disenchanted with efforts to improve screen morality.

Discouraged by the ineffectiveness of his office to control film content and apprehensive about the Catholic Church's formation of a National Legion of Decency to monitor movies, Hays convinced the major studios that a code of moral principles, enforced by his office, was necessary to insure the making of respectable motion pictures. Consequently, a set of guidelines based on moral principles, developed by a Catholic priest and a trade paper journalist, and strongly supported by the Catholic Church was instituted to guide the studios in the production of their films. Identified by the film industry as the Production Code,[6] it served as the internal regulating mechanism for more than three decades.

The Production Code

Making movies under the code was a game of barter and exchange between three participants: the major film studios, the Production Code Administration (PCA) headed by Catholic Joseph Breen, and the Legion of Decency. Not only did the code contain a list of prohibited subjects, but it also defined basic moral principles and applied these to specific plots portraying crime, sex, and religion or to situations and dialogue that included vulgarity, obscenity, and scantily-clad characters or that were offensive to national feelings. A separate section dealt with the treatment of special subjects such as: bedroom scenes, surgeries and childbirth, alcohol and drinking, and hangings and electrocutions. Strict application of the code often made the honest treatment of some adult material on the screen virtually impossible.

When box office receipts were good, the studios were more likely to faithfully abide by the code. But as the depression deepened and receipts declined, the studios were more interested in filling theater seats than promoting public virtue. For example, gangster films were popular with depression audiences. The box office success of *Little Caesar, Public Enemy, and Scarface* encouraged the studios to promote screen violence so long as the criminals were punished at the end. The criminals in the above films all paid with their lives for their crimes but not before they did their share of killing. What thirties' moviegoer could forget the last scene in *Little Caesar* where Edward G. Robinson's gangster character, Rico Bandello, riddled with bullets as he lies dying in the street, utters his final words: "Mother of Mercy, is this the end of Rico?" It was!

Nor could adultery be presented without redemption or punishment. A contemporary film, such as *Unfaithful* (2002), contains a story line where a married woman has a torrid love affair with a younger man. When her husband discovers the affair, he confronts his wife's lover and then kills him. But instead of apprehension and punishment, the film's final scene provides moral ambiguity as husband and wife flee to safety in Mexico. A film with this ending could not have been made under the code. Some scholars, in fact, have suggested that the code was enforced more strictly against sexual conduct than violence.[7]

Evidence for this assertion of differentiated enforcement is typified by the PCA's treatment of Mae West. Mae's films, with their suggestive dialogue and implied immorality, proved very popular at the box office and posed a challenge to local censors, and later to code administrators because even her most innocent line of dialogue could be interpreted as a sexual innuendo. Born in Brooklyn to immigrant parents, Mae's stage career began at age seven. For two decades she performed in vaudeville, burlesque, and legitimate theater before reaching stardom in 1930s Hollywood. Mae was no dummy; she wrote most of her material and learned to exploit her sexuality to further her career. Her first two starring films, *She Done Him*

Wrong and *I'm No Angel*, both released in 1933 before implementation of the code, tested the resolve of the Hays Office and the local censors. For instance, in *She Done Him Wrong*, Mae plays Lady Lou, a barroom entertainer who tries to seduce the leader of the Salvation Army. In one scene Mae invites him to "come up sometime and see me," and in another scene she flaunts her sexuality in a song about liking "A Guy What Takes His Time." Then in a scene from *I'm No Angel*, Mae is dressed in a low-cut form-fitting sequin gown. In her usual style, she rubs up against her male co-star, who, naively praises her good behavior, to which she replies: "When I'm good, I'm very good, but when I'm bad, I'm better."[8] Everyone in the audience howled, the censors seethed, and Mae took the money to the bank because she understood that sexuality is in the delivery and the context.

Besides the treatment of sex and violence, film historian Gregory Black[9] maintains, with some justification, that the code served a conservative political agenda. It did this in guidelines that required studio movies to show respect for government and all authority figures, present only acceptable social behavior, and adhere to Judaic-Christian morality before they could receive a certificate for public distribution. Whether Hollywood adopted the code because it believed in its moral precepts or because it proved a useful instrument to fend off government regulation and economic boycotts is problematic. More likely, adherence to the code was sound economics and good business practice. It provided a uniform system for censorship, often preventing individual state and local censors from making their own deletions while also preempting a potential boycott by the Catholic Legion of Decency and other pressure groups. Therefore, the Production Code bought the film industry some much-needed public good will, staved off any threat of federal intervention, and provided an economic benefit as well.

Much has been made of the economic clout wielded by the Legion of Decency as a moral player in content negotiations with the PCA. Created by the Catholic hierarchy and armed with its concomitant threat of a boycott, the Legion supported the code's moral principles with an economic hammer. The power of the Legion lay in the pledge that Catholics took to boycott films condemned by the Church. Black contends, however, that the Church was more bluff than performance because it failed to deliver the boycotts in any consistent and systematic way. Where there was a strong Catholic presence as in such cities as Cincinnati, Philadelphia, St. Louis, and San Francisco, the Church's tactics were effective. But where Catholics were few in number, the Church's censorship directives had little impact.[10] There are two logical explanations for the inconsistency. The first reason is found in the population demographics. Where the Church had a large and faithful following, its pulpit commands naturally had the greatest influence. For instance, when Elia Kazan's *Baby Doll* opened in the heavily Catholic city of Albany, New York, the Bishop for the Diocese condemned the film and warned Catholics to avoid both the film and the theater that had booked it. When the Albany newspapers refused to advertise the film, that action combined with the bishop's condemnation, virtually guaranteed that *Baby Doll* would have a limited playing engagement.

But even when the Church could not deliver an effective boycott on every film it condemned, the Legion still could exert pressure on the industry to make cuts and alter scenes, especially since it had an ally in Joseph Breen, the Catholic leader of the PCA. The effectiveness of the relationship between the Legion and the PCA resulted in the startling statistic that only five films out of the more than 5,000 released with a PCA seal during the period, 1934–68, were condemned by the Catholic Church.[11] Most contemporary interest groups would consider what the Legion achieved as a model in effective lobbying. However, contrary to popular opinion, the Catholic Church is not a monolithic institution in practice. Divisions exist among the clergy as well as the laity. Catholic bishops occasionally disagreed with the Legion over the ratings assigned to specific films and over the action that should be taken against condemned films. Still, a combination of economic forces, state and local censors, and Catholic pressure led Hollywood to produce more musical comedies, children's pictures, and family movies in the decades prior to World War II.

Movies Under the Code

The major problem with the code, as with any content-restrictive set of guidelines, depended on its application by Breen and the PCA staff since Breen had been given virtually dictatorial power. In the initial stages of production, his office had approval over all scripts and musical lyrics. Once completed, the film had to receive authorization in the form of a certificate seal from his office before it could be shown in theaters. Since the major studios controlled a majority of the theaters at that time, a film released without a seal was unlikely to find a distributor.[12]

Breen's staff, meanwhile, often applied the narrowest interpretation possible to code guidelines, turning film production into a series of obstacles to overcome through negotiation and circumvention. First, Breen applied the code strictly to prohibit the filming of certain subjects, whether written by established authors such as Leo Tolstoy, William Faulkner, and Sinclair Lewis or by commercial hacks. Lewis's novel, *It Can't Happen Here*, was prevented from reaching the screen because of PCA objections. In addition, the code requirements strictly enforced could lead to absurd results. For example, the code permitted the treatment of sex on screen as long as the participants were punished for it. Divorce, however, was a taboo subject *per se* under the "sanctity of marriage" provision in the code. Therefore, it was impossible for a screenwriter to get rid of a spouse except through death by accident or natural causes, through annulment, or by murder.[13] Breen also had the authority to demand cuts and eliminate or edit dialogue. Possibly the silliest example of code application occurred during the filming of *Gone With the Wind* (1939) when Breen's staff wanted to rewrite the following dialogue between Scarlett O'Hara and Rhett Butler:

> Scarlett: "Oh, my darling, if you go, what shall I do?"
> Rhett: "Frankly, my dear, I don't give a damn."[14]

The code administrators wanted to change the line to "My dear, I don't care." Only the persuasion of the producer, David O. Selznick, preserved what eventually became one of the classic lines in screen history, along with Bogart's "Here's looking at You, Kid" from *Casablanca*. While the original intention of the code to place sensible restraints on screen material may have been laudable, its implementation was often arbitrary and unreasonable.

As the film industry recovered from World War II, Breen and his office became involved in numerous censorship controversies. At least half-a-dozen major films in the 1950s challenged the authority of the PCA. In rapid succession, Breen's office was confronted with films that violated the code in terms of subject matter and treatment. The film adaptation of the successful Broadway play, *The Moon Is Blue* (1953), was considered too risqué and the drug use and addiction in *The Man with the Golden Arm* (1956) too explicit; both were released without a PCA certificate. Cuts and dialogue changes had to be made in two 1954 films: *The Wild One* starring Marlon Brando as the leader of a motorcycle gang and *From Here to Eternity*, the film version of James Jones's novel of army life in Hawaii before Pearl Harbor. Other major productions that ran into trouble with the Breen office included *A Streetcar Named Desire* (1951) and *Baby Doll* (1956), two films based on the plays of Tennessee Williams. To Hollywood insiders, the Breen Office appeared under siege.

The constant squabbling over code violations, together with the growth of independent producers, the divorce of the film studios from theater ownership,[15] and the Supreme Court's decision in *Burstyn v. Wilson*, led ultimately to the code's demise.[16] The seeds of decades of discontent reached its climax in the 1960s. The catalyst was the selection in 1966 of Jack Valenti,[17] former administrative aide to President Lyndon Johnson, to head the Motion Picture Association. After a few weeks on the job, Valenti was faced with several major challenges to the code that would finally determine its fate.[18] The first dispute involved the film version of Edward Albee's play, *Who's Afraid of Virginia Woolf* (1966), where the words "screw" and "hump the hostess" were retained from the stage production. Both raised problems under the code, and the resolution, worked out after hours of negotiation, resulted in the exclusion of the word "screw" but retention of the phrase, "hump the hostess," even though both represent similar sexual activity. The second incident proved more serious. Director Michael Antonioni's British-Italian production, *Blow-Up* (1966), contained scenes of nudity, strictly prohibited under the code. The PCA denied the film an exhibition certificate. However, MGM defied the code by distributing the film through a subsidiary company, making it the first time that a major studio exhibited a film without a PCA certificate. Encouraged by MGM's rebelliousness, other producers followed suit and within two years, Valenti replaced the code with a film rating system that classifies films according to audience suitability. Thus as the decade of the sixties came to a close, Hollywood had transferred major responsibility for film content from the industry to parents and individual viewers. Political commentators note 1968 as a benchmark year for the Tet offensive in Vietnam and Nixon's election to the presidency, while film historians mark it as the year Hollywood exchanged a system of negotiations over screen content under the production code for a system of negotiations over assigned film ratings.

The Hollywood Movie Rating System

The rating system that Valenti persuaded the Hollywood moguls to adopt in 1968 was a stroke of administrative genius. The old production code clearly was dysfunctional, yet the prospect of external censorship by government or capitulation to the economic threats of pressure groups was totally unacceptable to the industry. Hence, Valenti was able to sell the new rating system to the studios as a reasonable compromise. The film classification system adopted by the industry is age-based and intended for parents; its sole purpose, according to Valenti, is in "giving advance cautionary warnings to parents so that parents could make the decision about the moviegoing of their young children."[19] In its application, the rating system is designed for film patrons seventeen and younger since adults are able to see any movie.

The Hollywood classification system has undergone several revisions over the years. New categories have been added and the former X category has been replaced by NC-17. The current rating system requires films to be placed in one of five categories based upon audience suitability:

G: General Audiences
PG: Parental Guidance Suggested; some material may not be suitable for children
PG-13: Parents Strongly Cautioned; some material may be inappropriate for children under 13
R: Restricted; under 17 requires accompanying parent or adult guardian
NC-17: No one 17 and under admitted

The ratings applied to Hollywood films are the result of the deliberations of a Los Angeles-based group of reviewers who work in the Code and Rating

Administration (CARA) under the supervision of a chairman appointed by the MPAA president. The rating process begins with a producer submitting his/her film, together with a fee, to CARA to be reviewed prior to national exhibition. The producer voluntarily submits to the rating process because as a matter of policy, non-rated films, along with NC-17 rated films, are not booked to play in the large theater chains like United Artists, Cineplex Odeon, Sony, AMC, and National Amusements. To receive a satisfactory rating (PG-13 and above preferred, R accepted) from CARA is a sound business decision by the studios and distributors because certain studios require at least an R rating in the director's contract.

After CARA reviews a film, each staff member assigns an appropriate rating accompanied by a justification. The staff then meets to discuss the initial ratings. The final rating is the result of a majority vote. There are options for the producer who is unhappy with the assigned rating, namely, to edit the film and resubmit it to receive a less severe classification or appeal the decision to the Rating Appeals Board, a group of reviewers from within the film industry. After listening to arguments to overturn the initial rating, the appeals group decides by a two-thirds vote either to uphold the assigned rating or overturn it. Their decision is final and not subject to further appeal. In order to render some semblance of objectivity, the MPAA president is not involved in the rating process at any stage of the proceedings. While fairness is an important attribute for any classification system, the real test is whether the Hollywood rating system actually achieves its stated objective and performs a vital service to parents. Since government also is concerned with the public interest and since Hollywood provides entertainment for the general population, the rating system should be judged on the effect it has on the larger society as well.

PUTTING HOLLYWOOD TO THE TEST: THE RATING SYSTEM ASSESSED

In theory, Hollywood's voluntary classification system neither acts as a censorship agent nor as a guide to recommended films. Its acknowledged purpose is to assist parents in selecting appropriate movies for their children's viewing. One question for assessment, therefore, is whether the rating system achieves its stated objective. Another, and possibly more important question, is whether the film industry has a social responsibility to promote the public good in providing commercial entertainment.

Film Content

Although the classification system is voluntary, it represents an agreement within the film industry (studios, distributors, and theater owners) to submit films for classification and to abide by the assigned ratings. CARA acts as a broker, approving or suggesting changes in film content, which the filmmakers and the studios may accept or reject. The rating process, however, favors CARA because there are economic consequences attached to an assigned rating; the most restrictive, NC-17, rating as compared to a less restrictive one, may significantly affect the number of theater bookings and, consequently, box office receipts. That is why the studios often make it a contractual obligation for a filmmaker to deliver a movie with a specific rating. For instance, director Paul Verhoeven was required by TriStar to secure at least an R rating for his sex-violence thriller, *Basic Instinct* (1992).[20] Verhoeven was upset with the required cuts but, in the end, the studio and CARA exercised the necessary leverage. The economic factor is so important that even highly respected directors such as Stanley Kubrick (*Eyes Wide Shut* 1999) and Brian DePalma (*Dressed to Kill* 1980) made the required cuts to avoid an NC-17 rating.

While CARA wields significant economic power to pressure the studios to tone down film violence, bad language, and explicit sex, MPAA statistics reveal that the R rating has evolved into the most popular classification. Between 1968 and 1996, CARA assigned ratings to more than 13,000 films, with 54 percent receiving an R rating.[21] But what is more significant is that the number of R-rated films, which requires those under seventeen be accompanied by a parent or guardian, has steadily increased over each decade. Thus, in the seventies, 42 percent of the films distributed by the MPAA were R-rated. This percentage increased to 59 percent in the eighties and to 63 percent in the nineties so that by 1995 two-thirds of the films released for distribution were R-restricted.

How can the popularity of the R rating within the industry be explained? The ordinary filmgoer might respond by making reference to their profitability. After all, the film industry is a commercial business whose primary purpose is to market films to audiences. But a recent study[22] by two California economists revealed that R-rated films were often a bad business investment. Using data of films released between 1985 and 1996, the authors concluded that during this period, G, PG, and PG-13 films were more financially successful than R-rated films, based on box office revenues and return on investment. Yet Hollywood continued to increase the number of R-rated films distributed in subsequent decades. The economists explained this counterproductive trend with two plausible, but speculative, explanations. One they attributed to human error, that is, the studios miscalculated and production costs exceeded estimated budgets while ticket sales were less than projected. Michael Cimino's 1980 disaster, *Heaven's Gate*, is a perfect example. Since filmmaking is a high-risk venture and since it is difficult to predict audience response, occasional mistakes are likely to occur. Still, all Hollywood financial disasters cannot be attributed to the R rating. A second explanation advanced by the economists is that the studio CEOs, while seeking maximum profits, also desire respectability and status among their peers. Hence, they are vulnerable to approving R-rated projects because Julia Roberts wants to play a particular character or Steven Spielberg is anxious to confront the challenge of a particular script or because the film project has "artistic" written all over it. In other words, some R-rated film projects are approved on the basis of vanity and ego enhancement rather than sound economics.

There is a third explanation that the researchers failed to consider, possibly because conclusive evidence is weak. Anecdotal evidence, however, suggests that the industry is aware, but refuses to acknowledge publicly, that low enforcement at the box office means that the under-17 teenage audience gets in to see restricted films. Of course, no empirical evidence exists for this assertion, but the dominance of violent and sexually explicit content in Hollywood films could be because the studio heads approve such projects, expecting that negotiations with CARA will result in the inclusion of enough of the questionable material to entice teenagers into the theaters. Furthermore, the studios are aware that the deleted material is often included in the overseas version and in the "director's cut" when the film is transferred to VHS or DVD. In that sense, the studios attempt to persuade viewers to see the film twice. The *American Pie* video, for example, advertised footage that had been cut from the theater version. Although the economic study excluded world revenues and video sales and rentals from its calculations, it is important to realize that the overseas ticket sales for *American Pie* virtually equaled the domestic box office, thereby doubling the film's gross. Money, therefore, helps to explain much about the industry's self-regulatory policy.

Hollywood always has insisted that audiences determine the kind of films that the industry produces because, at its core, CARA's ratings emulate public opinion and conform to public tastes. While older adults may shudder at what is being shown on the screen, teenagers and young adults seem indifferent to the excessive depiction of sex and violence in films. Hence, the official MPAA line is that in a free economy, market forces determine production. If audiences disapprove of such films, Hollywood reasons, they have the option of staying away, or in cases where opposition to a film is particularly robust, to picket the theaters. Ultimately, the film industry maintains, the choice rests with the American public.

Theoretically, the public has the capability to exert tremendous economic clout by boycotting films. But Hollywood recognizes that the movie audience is decentralized and lacks national leadership. Furthermore, any organized individual and small group protests would have minimal, if any, financial impact. In his research on censorship groups, Charles Lyons confirms that most films targeted by protesters have survived at the box office.[23] He cites, as examples, the protests of gays and lesbians that failed to affect the box office receipts for *Basic Instinct* (1992) and the Asian-American protests against *Year of the Dragon* (1985). Feminists, also, could not seriously damage the profits of DePalma's *Dressed to Kill* (1980). The lone exception to the rule seems to be religious films, particularly if they are perceived to be an attack upon a major religious group. Catholics and other Christian groups, for instance, vehemently protested Martin Scorsese's *The Last Temptation of Christ* (1988) because the clergy considered it "blasphemous."[24] The film suffered financially because three major theater chains decided against booking the movie, while the film's scheduled engagements were canceled in several cities. But when actor Mel Gibson, a devout Catholic, decided to buck the tradition fifteen years later, the results amazed the industry.[25] Gibson's movie, *The Passion of the Christ* (2004) recounts the last twelve hours of Jesus' life. Based on the four gospels of Matthew, Luke, Mark, and John, with dialogue in Aramaic and Latin, and featuring the considerable brutality of the crucifixion, it contained all the attributes of a personal project that was unlikely to succeed. Months before the film was scheduled to open, however, Gibson decided to have a series of private showings of the film to selected audiences. The strategy proved to be both a blessing and a curse. While Christian audiences were deeply moved by the film, several Jewish leaders expressed regret because it appeared that the film reexamined the question: Who was responsible for Jesus' death? Both the Anti-Defamation League and the American Jewish Committee criticized the film, expressing fear that it would encourage hatred, bigotry, and instances of anti-Semitism. The film did none of these things. Gibson went on national television to defend his film and deny the charges, insisting that his intention was not to assess blame but to record the suffering that Christ endured. Gibson invested $30 million of his own money in the project, which was produced by his film company. Unlike Scorsese's experience, people flocked to see the R-rated *The Passion of the Christ*. The film became a blockbuster hit, earning $355 million during its first five weeks, making it the eighth-highest-grossing movie ever.[26] Possibly the only generalization from this experience is that any film that is critical of Christianity is doomed to fail, while a religious film may or may not make money.

The fact that Hollywood is a capital-dependent industry that needs to borrow heavily from banks to finance its film projects requires that it be mindful of prevailing public tastes and sensitive to audience reaction during "sneak previews" as well as tickets sales. Hollywood also knows that the industry is capable of generating demand for certain films through emotional manipulation and creative advertising. Common sense dictates that Hollywood observes audience demands as expressed at the box office, but the industry has the ability to create the desires underlying the wish fulfillment. Writing in the late 1940s, anthropologist Hortense Powdermaker characterized Hollywood as the "dream factory,"[27] a place like Oz where dreams inevitably come true. Over the years, audiences have been conditioned to accept Hollywood's world as reality. Sadly, that cinematic fantasy world is becoming more populated with drug dealers, sadistic criminals, rapists, and sexually uninhibited young people.

The industry is cognizant of the changing American mores and morals since the sixties. The assumption is that Americans no longer find sex and violence offensive. Evidence can be found in the two sexual accusations against former President Clinton. At no time during the discovery and publication of these charges did polls indicate that a majority of Americans wanted the president to resign or be impeached by the Congress. Further evidence of changing social mores comes in the American Film Institute's (AFI) "100 Best American Movies" list, selected by 1500 voters. Half the list includes films that deal with such violent subjects as crime (*The Godfather* 1972), assassinations (*Taxi Driver* 1976), urban dysfunction (*Pulp Fiction* 1994), and the Vietnam War (*Platoon* 1986).[28]

While the explanations are not empirically verifiable, they suggest that the increase in the R-restricted category denotes a trend in the industry. Why has the industry moved in this direction? Is it really due to audience feedback, Hollywood's response to the more liberal social mores, or both?

From its infancy the industry has made the kind of emotional appeals that would attract customers into theaters. Silent films were not devoid of nudity. Violence and sexual suggestiveness were present in the films of the 20s and 30s. Westerns with shootouts, hangings, and other forms of mayhem were an industry staple into the 70s. War films usually do well at the box office too. Therefore, the emphasis on sex and violence is not a new development and is fairly typical, and yet these portrayals have been accompanied by public concern over their social and behavioral effects.

Film critic Peter Keough argues that whenever the country finds itself in the midst of an economic downturn, rapid social change, or political crisis, the public and the media scapegoat the entertainment industry rather than place blame on real villains such as arms manufacturers, industrial polluters, and the tobacco industry.[29] Keough insists that there is little hard evidence that film violence and explicit sexuality encourage or cause criminal behavior and moral decline. He argues, instead, that Hollywood is primarily a reactive business rather than an innovative industry. Hence its films reflect contemporary values already accepted in the larger society. He maintains that Hollywood serves to disguise the country's real culprits by suggesting in its films that America's real enemies are external; communism after World War II and terrorists after the Persian Gulf War.

Keough's defense of Hollywood, while not original, deserves analysis. Naturally, Hollywood should not be blamed for all of the country's social ills. The conventional social science view is to accept Keough as correct when he suggests that the causal connection between screen sex and violence and real-life crime and immorality are largely anecdotal rather than empirical. Nonetheless, he avoids entirely the issue of

Hollywood films as a contributory agent to social problems. Because no definitive causation theory exists does not necessarily rule out a correlation between film depictions and anti social and immoral behavior.

Some facts are inescapable. In R-rated movies scenes of film violence are as mandatory as sex scenes. It also appears that Hollywood has turned up the graphic and excessive nature of the violence since the 1990s: *GoodFellas, Reservoir Dogs, Natural Born Killers, Pulp Fiction, Braveheart, Gladiator, Gangs of New York*, and *Collateral Damage*, to cite just a few. Meanwhile, raunchy and vulgar films like *American Pie* are specifically earmarked for the teenage market. Worst still, are the explicit and mean-spirited presentations of screen nudity and sex (*Showgirls* 1995, *Monster's Ball* 2001), reducing audiences to voyeurs. And the tendency to interface sexual behavior with physical brutality (*Basic Instinct* 1992) is even more disconcerting. Therefore, what has changed in film content is not the presentation of sex and violence but an excessiveness and pervasive explicitness in the presentation. It seems that no detail is left to audience imagination. Violence and sexual behavior is no longer implied or presented off-screen; instead it confronts viewers directly. While adults may have the maturity to adequately deal with such material, children and impressionable youngsters, particularly those who come from homes without positive parental/guardian role models or from homes absent an established moral code to offset the temptations of a bad neighborhood environment, are more likely to become susceptible to imitating screen sex and violence. In this conditional sense, Hollywood films do influence antisocial behavior. Therefore, should the film industry not have a social obligation to avoid gratuitous screen sex and violence while it provides positive role models for children and youngsters?

Former MPAA president Jack Valenti insisted that the ratings are meant to assist parents who bear the primary responsibility for their children's film fare. Valenti's words can be tested to see if the current rating system satisfies the two criteria: first, parents should expect the ratings to have internal integrity and second, they are systematically enforced at the theater.

Internal Integrity

No film classification system could ever be flawless and guarantee universal satisfaction because a certain amount of subjectivity is inherent in the evaluation process. Even conceding that the CARA reviewers are intelligent and sincere people and the majority of parents are concerned with their children's welfare, differences of opinion are still likely to occur. The real issue is not quantity or explicitness but the context. At what point do scenes become excessive? In one sense, the serious portrayal of the holocaust on screen makes violence, as well as evil, banal. There is a qualitative difference, however, between gratuitous violence in a film without serious purpose and the bloody violence that erupts throughout *Michael Collins*, a film depicting the IRA's guerrilla warfare against the British presence in Ireland. Similarly, when does the showing of sexuality on screen succumb to pandering and exploitation? The explicit sexuality expressed in Louis Malle's *Damage* (1992) is quite different in intent from the vulgar display of sexuality in *Showgirls* or the moronic teenage sexuality displayed throughout *American Pie*. How do the CARA reviewers distinguish one characteristic from another? What factors are compelling in arriving at the assigned rating? Unfortunately, the industry provides viewers with minimal information because the deliberation process is secret and internal rating discussions are generally not made public, except for the occasional leak.

However, the increasing popularity of the R rating in Hollywood means that a majority of films being released are restricted to viewers seventeen and over unless accompanied by a parent or guardian. The problem extends beyond the rating *per se* to the criteria utilized for the category. CARA claims not to employ a litmus-paper test for the R category, that is, x number of shootings, knife stabbings, drug abuse scenes, explicit sexuality, and bad language automatically earn the restricted rating. Instead CARA literature states that an R-rated film may include "hard language, or tough violence, or nudity within sensual scenes, or drug abuse or other elements, or a combination of some of the above."[30] These guidelines are vague enough to allow CARA great latitude in application. The discretionary power turns the rating process into a game of negotiations, much like the old production code. Take the case of Stanley Kubrick's *Eyes Wide Shut* (1999). A film intended for adults, both in subject matter and treatment, originally received an NC-17 rating for the explicitness of its sexual orgy scene. After considerable haggling, hooded figures were digitally inserted in the scene to block out the more offensive sexual activity, which permitted the film to be released in the United States with an R rating. The original Kubrick version was retained, however, for European distribution.[31]

This is not to deny that negotiations are totally useless exercises. CARA has been successful in securing changes in selected R-rated films to elevate them to PG-13, thus making them available to wider audiences. CARA engages in these constant negotiating games because, on the one hand, a litmus test can be overly rigid and restrictive and, ultimately, harmful to the creative process. On the other hand, the current bartering system is sometimes demeaning to intelligent directors and embarrassing to CARA reviewers. The process would be unnecessary if rather than require deletions and other changes, CARA followed the British Board of Film Classification (BBFC) and placed films with adult content in an 18-and-over category. Adoption of the British 18 classification would enable Hollywood to eliminate both the R and NC-17 categories, substituting instead an age classification grouping that permits serious filmmakers to treat adult subject matter in a mature way. The preference for age eighteen as the benchmark for an adult film category can be justified on the ground that eighteen is almost universally recognized in the United States as the legal demarcation point for being treated as an adult. While all age distinctions are arbitrary, eighteen, rather than seventeen, is a more appropriate division since at age eighteen, most American youngsters will have graduated from high school, joined the workforce, entered the military, or begun their college careers. Also, the Twenty-Sixth Amendment granted voting power to eighteen-year-olds. And with a few exceptions, eighteen is the minimum age to marry without parental consent, make a valid will, serve on a jury, and purchase tobacco products. Under this proposed reorganization of the rating system, former NC-17 rated films like *Bad Lieutenant* (1992), *Henry and June* (1990), and *Showgirls* would qualify for the 18 rating while films like Louis Malle's *Damage* and Oliver Stone's *Natural Born Killers*, which required cuts to receive the R-rating, also would be assigned the 18 rating—but without subjecting the films to deletions. When the 18 category is supplemented by detailed content information provided by the industry and film critics, adults will be in a better position to make informed decisions about screen fare.

When CARA is unsure of how to classify a troublesome film, why not allow it to call in outside experts for assistance as the BBFC is permitted to do? Why is CARA such an insular body that shuns outsiders? When director David Cronenberg's disturbing film, *Crash* (1996), about people who receive sexual stimulation from auto crashes, came before CARA it originally received an NC-17 rating. After cutting approximately ten minutes from the film, an R version was approved. In England, where the film's anticipated distribution led to government opposition and public indignation, the BBFC assigned the film an 18 rating after consultation with a psychologist and feedback from disabled people who attended a special screening.[32]

What can be done to shield youngsters from seeing restricted, adult movie fare? Hollywood needs to adopt the practice of the British film classification system of applying the film rating to every patron who enters the theater. The logic of the British system is quite simple. Violent films along the lines of *Reservoir Dogs* and *Natural Born Killers* and films with explicit sexual content like *Showgirls* and *Basic Instinct* are not suitable for children, with or without adult accompaniment. It defies logic to have a rating system that permits youngsters to see an adult film because a parent or adult purchases the tickets. The content of an adult film does not magically change and become acceptable for viewing by youngsters simply because they are accompanied by a parent or guardian. Rather, the current Hollywood rating system encourages deception and circumvention. To discourage youngsters from viewing an adult (18-rated) film, theaters should require a valid photo-ID (such as a school ID card or driver's license) in cases where the age of the viewer is in doubt. Whatever initial delays this procedure brings to the box office eventually will be minimized as youngsters discover that they will need a photo ID to prove their age.

It is imperative that the 18 rating system apply to videos and DVDs as well. This requirement should include theatrical films released on video, films released directly to video, and versions of theatrical films that differ from the print initially shown in theaters. In a technical sense, CARA does rate videos. But there are loopholes that need to be plugged. For example, a theatrical film that has been reedited for video is considered to be a different film from the original. Such "director's cuts" or "unrated" versions often include material omitted from the initial theatrical release. This material, usually sexual or violent in nature, that CARA considered too strong for movie audiences, miraculously becomes acceptable on videotape for home viewing. Stone's R-rated theatrical film, *Natural Born Killers*, required the director to make 150 cuts that were restored when a "director's version" was released on video. Also, R-rated films such as *American Pie* and the lesbian thriller *Bound* (1996) were reissued on video with additional footage that had been cut from their theatrical version. These videos then become available for rental to teenagers. In addition, a small percentage of films are produced for video distribution only. These do not pass through CARA's rating system and show up on the video shelf without a classification label. These loopholes make a mockery of the entire rating process since they permit youngsters to view adult material on video that they were prohibited from seeing on the theater screen.

Box Office Enforcement

No film classification system is meaningful unless its ratings are consistently enforced at the theatre. Unfortunately, no systematic study pertaining to the level of enforcement of film ratings at the box office has been undertaken. Hollywood, citing as its source the National Association of Theater Owners (NATO), claims that 85 percent of the theater owners in the nation voluntarily subscribe to the rating system, which obligates the theaters to make certain that underage children are not admitted to restricted film fare.[33] NATO insists that if underage viewers are gaining entrance to R-rated and NC-17-rated films it is because parents and guardians are purchasing the tickets. No hard evidence exists to support that assertion. Most moviegoers, however, probably have viewed R-rated and NC-17-rated films with an audience that included underage youngsters, alone or in groups without adults. The enforcement problem is exacerbated at the suburban multiplex theaters with their dozen or more screens. One metro New York reporter observed teenagers buying tickets to R-rated violent films, *12 Monkeys* (1995) and *Sudden Death* (1995), at a suburban multiplex where a fourteen-year-old boy bought three tickets to an R-rated film for his younger siblings, age twelve, eleven, and eight.[34] *USA Today*[35] also conducted a field experiment a few years ago by asking a selected group of teens, from Virginia to California, to buy tickets to R-rated films at their local theaters. The newspaper reported that a majority of the theaters flunked this informal test as teenagers had little trouble securing admission to restricted films. How did the youngsters do it? After sifting through the various responses, the newspaper found the following three methods most utilized. One popular method that was especially successful in multiplexes was for a teen to purchase a ticket to a PG or PG-13 movie and then sneak into an R-rated one when the ushers are preoccupied with collecting tickets rather than guarding each entrance door. A second box office maneuver is for a seventeen-year-old to purchase multiple tickets, which are distributed to underage teens, as was the case cited above. These two strategies work well when the theaters are especially busy. A third technique involves a conspiracy of adults and youngsters as parents and guardians buy tickets for their children but not for themselves. The teens view the restricted films alone even though R-rated films require an accompanied parent or guardian. In fact, this method is sometimes inadvertently encouraged by theaters. For instance, a recent policy of the Keystone theatres, a Pennsylvania chain, requires parental permission before underage teens are allowed into the theater. However, parents may provide the required permission by showing up at the box office or by addressing a signed note to the theater box office.[36] The news that the midwestern chain, GKC Theatres, has introduced the R-card will only aggravate the enforcement problem. Under the chain's new policy, any youngster under seventeen will be allowed into an R-rated movie without their parents or guardians once the latter visit the box office, pay a two-dollar fee, and sign the photo ID card. In its defense, GKC Theatres justified the policy change as beneficial to those parents who are unwilling to see the R-rated films themselves. Now teenagers will be able to see films like *American Psycho* and *American Pie* while Mom, Dad and Grandma stay home and watch reruns of *Leave It to Beaver*. Even former MPAA president, Jack Valenti, was critical of the new initiative to lure teens into GKC Theatres with a blanket endorsement.[37]

Because youngsters are so cleaver and skillful in seeing the films of their choice regardless of their parents, theatre owners, or the MPAA, even a photo-ID requirement might fail to resolve the problem. Though a photo-ID system may address the more blatant attempts to gain admission to restricted film fare, it is not the final solution. A foolproof way to insure box office enforcement probably does not exist. Still a cooperative effort by parents and local theaters, together with the photo-ID requirement, may diminish the circumvention. That is why the introduction of the R-card is so disheartening. It will make a mockery of the rating system itself. That is not the kind of parent-theater cooperation that is needed to restore confidence in the integrity of the classification system.

CENSORSHIP VS. CLASSIFICATION

What options exist for a democratic society such as the United States to regulate screen sex and violence? Democratic theory provides governments with three choices. First, they may take a laissez-faire attitude toward popular entertainment, leaving the choice entirely up to market forces and public demand. Under a "hands-off" policy, films like *Natural Born Killers* and *Basic Instinct* would be free to contain any content and be shown to any audience. Government would abstain from playing any regulatory role. Although the Supreme Court's decision in *Burstyn v. Wilson* brought movies under the protection of the First Amendment, the justices have yet to endorse an absolute view of free speech. Obscene material, for example, is still outside of constitutional protection. Furthermore, many politicians and parents would consider such a laissez-faire policy irresponsible.

Government censorship, where the state either owns or controls the production and distribution of films or has the authority to exercise final approval prior to general distribution, is anathema to First Amendment theory and unacceptable to a free society. Such action is what Blackstone called "prior restraint." When the Chinese government banned Joan Chen's film *Xiu Xiu the Sent-down Girl* (1999) because of its critique of the policies of the Cultural Revolution, it was exercising the kind of censorship familiar to all authoritarian regimes.

Such control by an American government would run counter to Supreme Court decisions dating back to the twenties, where the judicial decisions consistently have ruled against government efforts at censorship, except for national security reasons and for the distribution of obscene material.[38] No Washington administration could impose such content restrictions even if it had the desire. One caveat is that not every censorship attempt qualifies as unconstitutional prior restraint. When director/producer Stanley Kubrick decided to withhold his 1971 film, *A Clockwork Orange*, from distribution in the United Kingdom, he was not exercising censorship in the legal sense. Similarly, when Adrian Lyne's R-rated version of *Lolita* (1998),[39] which featured a romance between a twelve-year-old girl and a middle-aged man, experienced trouble finding an American distributor, this also was not censorship in the First Amendment sense. Such actions involving a majority of theatre owners working in concert, however, may raise issues of restraint of trade.

Common sense rules out laissez-faire while democratic theory repudiates government censorship. Where feasible, internal or self-regulation is preferred over government control, and this is the route taken by the film industry with creation of the rating system. By internal policing, Hollywood has avoided government intervention. In its present form, however, the Hollywood-based age-classification system fails to either shield children from adult material or reassure parents that their children are viewing films appropriate for their respective age group.

A rather lengthy discussion on the Internet H-film Web site[40] implied that classification and censorship are interrelated terms that in practice often result in similar consequences. This theory claims that any film classification system seeks to control content through control over the audience (those who may view the film) as opposed to censorship, which instead regulates film images during production or afterward through control over distribution. In either case, the argument is that the film industry controls the kind of images viewed by audiences.

There is just enough truth in this assertion to make it compelling, yet disingenuous. In a film classification system such as Hollywood's rating system, the purpose is to align the film's content with the appropriate audience maturity level. Obviously, subjectivity will always be an issue in the application of the rating category. That is a factor in any system involving human judgment, whether calling balls and strikes in a baseball game or imposing film ratings. The heart of the argument, however, is not so much subjectivity but the fact that in application, the rating process produces changes in the film's content since, according to the recent economic study, a PG-13 is economically preferably to an R rating and an R rating to an NC-17 rating. Like any other business, the film industry seeks to maximize profits and minimize losses. Thus producers and directors are under economic pressure to agree to the suggested cuts and revisions. While this is no doubt an accurate assessment, studios and filmmakers still have the choice of maintaining the film intact and accepting the restricted rating or making the necessary changes to receive the less restrictive rating. If the film receives a more restrictive rating, it is likely, but not inevitable, that the box office would be affected. Those excluded from seeing a restricted film experience only a deferred viewing. Such a system is not censorship in the legal or constitutional sense, even though in application it results in a teenage audience that must wait until adulthood to see the film with its content unchanged. It is argued that this is a small price to pay for protecting impressionable youth from a bombardment of violent and sexual images.

All classification systems are arbitrary. Why deny teenagers access to alcoholic beverages until age twenty-one? Why not sell them cigarettes at any age? Why have them wait to get married or to exercise the vote? A classification system that selects films according to age suitability governs the composition of the audience, temporarily denying access to a certain age group. Therefore youngsters are not permanently banned from the film in question but must wait to view it at a later date. Censorship, on the other hand, denies access to adults as well as children. Stanley Kubrick's decision to withhold distribution of *A Clockwork Orange* meant that no one in the United Kingdom could see the film. When the government, rather than the individual, makes that decision, that action constitutes the exercise of prior restraint in the constitutional or legal sense. Censorship and classification are distinct activities, often imposed by different bodies and for dissimilar reasons. When scholars identify the film classification system as "censorship," they fail to acknowledge any distinction and only confuse the public. When the Chinese government banned *Xiu Xiu: The Sent-down Girl*, that was censorship. When President Reagan denied entry to three Canadian antinuclear films, that was censorship.[41] When the New York State Board of Regents edits out any references to sex, religion, race, or ethnicity from great works of literature on the Regents English exam, that is censorship. These are far more serious intrusions on free speech than telling a teenager that he/she cannot see *American Pie* until the age of seventeen or unless accompanied by a parent or guardian. The Hollywood rating system may require some producers to make choices in their film content in order for their films to be seen by a specific audience, but that is not censorship. It is time for all the participants in this debate—politicians, academics, and film critics—to define their terms and use the appropriate language.

In a free society it is preferable for institutions to regulate themselves. At least, that is a basic tenet of American political theory: government intervention should be the last resort. But what if an institution fails to fulfill its regulatory role? Public opinion, then, might support government action. That is why Hollywood has acted to police its films, first through the Production Code and later through the rating system. What happens when the policing is flawed and the system is not working? What alternative is there when Hollywood refuses to accept necessary reforms within the present classification system? What choice does the movie audience have against a system that is notoriously inbred and immune to external criticism and action?

Film critic Michael Medved has called for stricter guidelines and a return to the restrictions imposed by the 1930s code.[42] Medved's characterization of most Hollywood films as being against the nuclear family, opposed to the institution of marriage, and against traditional moral values, even if an accurate assessment, ignores the reality that not all movies under the code were wholesome and sanitized representations. The studios continued to make gangster and sexually suggestive films, although within the limits of code guidelines. Trying to make honest movies under the numerous code restrictions made filming serious subjects a course in jumping hurdles. Serious social problems like racism, sexism, child abuse, and drug or alcohol addiction could not be easily presented in an intelligent and realistic manner under the old code. And the code's guidelines did not apply to independents or films made outside of the studio system.

While Medved has cause to be concerned about the pervasive amount of screen sex and violence in current Hollywood films, his solution is faulty. Valenti was correct in 1968 to abolish the code and replace it with a classification system based upon audience suitability. Americans prefer self-regulation to government interference, and the rating system is a way to satisfy two desires simultaneously—the absence of content control (censorship) with the preference for viewer freedom of choice. The major flaw in the rating system lies not in the self-regulatory concept but in its implementation. Instead of abolishing the rating system or returning to the antiquated Production Code, Hollywood should adopt three reforms of the British classification system: an 18 classification for adult material to replace the current R and NC-17 categories, application of the film rating to each theater patron, and more effective age enforcement at the box office.

Apparently, the British accept the fact that science may never provide the kind of proof necessary to establish a causal link between film viewing and bad conduct, but common sense dictates that society need not have to wait until the linkage is demonstrated and the damage is done. Films and videos need to be regulated as to sexual and violent content and the classification system is the least intrusive remedy. When the BBFC is in doubt about a particular film, it exercises caution. For instance, the release of Stone's *Natural Born Killers* in the United Kingdom was delayed until an investigation was made into allegations that the film caused imitation killings in both France and the United States. When the allegations were not substantiated, the film was given an 18 rating and released for distribution. Also, when *Money Train* came before the BBFC, the Board asked the London Transport police to review the incendiary scene that caused such controversy in the United States. The film was certified for theatrical showing after the Transport police decided that a similar incident was unlikely to occur in the London underground.[43] Similar precautions were taken with the film *Crash* before its theatrical release.

Adoption of these changes, taken together with external film reviews available in daily newspapers, magazines, religious literature, and on the Internet, would assist parents in selecting appropriate films for their children's viewing. Adults also might profit from the British approach since the studios and filmmakers would enjoy greater creative freedom to make serious films in the adult classification without the threat of deletions.

HOLLYWOOD'S SOCIAL RESPONSIBILITY

If Hollywood were in the business of selling tobacco and alcohol to youngsters or dispensing prescription drugs instead of providing entertainment, the American public would expect some sort of regulation to protect children and the public interest. The use of tobacco, alcohol, and drugs has been demonstrated as harmful to individual health, and their abuse may pose a serious danger to public safety. Entertainment, specifically film, is not harmful *per se*, but is it harmless? Because social science has failed to prove a causal connection between exposure to fantasy violence, including sexual images, and the perpetuation of real violence does not absolve the film industry of all social responsibility. Since social science has difficulty in establishing causal connections for understanding human behavior, their failure to prove the sex and violence-antisocial behavior nexus, should not serve as an obstruction to reform.

The results of the Federal Trade Commission (FTC) Report exposed Hollywood as indifferent to the welfare of children when such consideration interfered with industry profits. The Commission's review of the entertainment industries revealed, not surprisingly, that Hollywood was in the practice of marketing violent fare to children. Specifically, the FTC report exposed the following wrongdoings: (1) previewing R-rated (for violence) films during the showing of G-rated movies; (2) using youngsters (nine to twelve years old) to test-market their R-rated films; (3) targeting R-rated films to youngsters under seventeen; and (4) at least half of the theatres reviewed admitted underage children to R-rated films that required an accompanied adult.[44] Despite these findings, Congress failed to take any legislative action, and after days of hearings, could solicit only a promise from some of the film studios to cease the above practices. Whether the failure to act was due to congressional First Amendment concerns, the strength of the Hollywood lobby, a lack of any visible interest on the part of parents, or a combination of these factors, the film industry escaped the bullet and departed Washington chastised, but undeterred.

The question of the effects of film images on social behavior is still under scrutiny. Powerful organizations such as the American Medical Association, American Psychology Association, and the National Institutes of Mental Health, among others, maintain that a limited and circumstantial linkage exists between violent images and behavior, especially on the young and impressionable. In the first longitudinal study[45] of the long-term effects of media violence on youngsters, University of Michigan researchers examined aggressive behavior of children exposed to media violence in 1977 and then reexamined them fifteen years later. While the researchers admitted that aggression is the product of complex variables, they nonetheless concluded that, other factors being equal, children who view a substantial amount of media violence are more likely to express aggressive behavior as adults, particularly when the children identify with an aggressor who is rewarded for his/her bad behavior. Even though most of the exposure was to television violence, the study implied extension to film violence as well.

Other research studies, here and abroad, refute these findings and argue that real violence, rather than fictional violence, is the culprit. The debate is similar to the one fought over pornography in the seventies and eighties and is unlikely to be resolved empirically. Moreover, attempts by plaintiffs to use the courts to win damages against particular films that allegedly caused harm to them or others have been unsuccessful.[46] Therefore, the real issue should be whether the film industry, like other businesses, has an obligation to act with greater circumspection. In fact, is this not what Hollywood did after September 11, 2001, when the studios delayed the distribution of films with terrorist themes such as *Collateral Damage* and *Bad Company* until the following year? If film lacks the power to persuade or influence, why postpone the scheduled openings? Could it be that the distribution of these films soon after 9/11 would demonstrate that art and reality had the potential to be disturbingly similar?

Rather than respond defensively to the issue, Hollywood has an opportunity to be constructive. Industry leaders admit that the purpose of the industry's rating system is to provide assistance to parents in selecting appropriate film fare for their children. The FTC report confirms that a majority of parents rely on the rating system, a fact that supports the industry's self-regulation process, but in a modified format. What the report exposed, however, are the weaknesses inherent in any film classification system, namely, that to be effective it requires a social conscience on the part of the industry and a serious commitment from parents. The FTC findings confirm, on the one hand, the popularity of the R rating, since it is assigned to two-thirds of all Hollywood films, while, on the other hand, more than half of movie theaters sampled admit youngsters without a parent or adult guardian. So explicit sex and excessive violence, along with bad language—the usual reasons for the R rating—have become the content staples of the industry.

The logical conclusion is obvious: the rating system is a profitable working arrangement for the industry that is neither helpful to parents nor protective of their children. Unless a significant change occurs in the industry, the gratuitous sex and violence will not disappear. That is why the industry needs to adopt the three changes inherent in the British system, namely: films presently placed in the R and NC-17 categories should be located in a new adult (18 and over) classification, film ratings should apply to each patron so that no parent can take a child to a film with adult content, and age identification should be strictly required at the box office as it is at the local liquor store or cigarette counter.

Parents, naturally, have the primary responsibility for their children's welfare. Unless parents play an active role in selecting suitable films for their children, particularly during the teen years, Hollywood will continue to produce profitable R-rated movies like *American Pie* and its sequels, that are specifically designed to attract youngsters.[47] Fortunately for parents today there are Internet sources to assist them in providing content information. Several Internet sites provide film reviews from a religious perspective. Chuck Colson, a born-again former Watergate participant, includes a list of recommended films with Christian themes on his Breakpoint.com Web site. Another Christian Web site is movieguide.org, which rates films on their "redemptive themes and inspiration." Catholic parents may refer to the film classification system used by the U.S. Catholic Conference, a five-category rating scale based on moral values. Their reviews are available online at CatholicDigest.org.

Parents also may consult www.moviemom.com, a Web site that reviews films specifically for children. Two nonsectarian Web sites, screenit.com and filmvalues.com also provide fairly comprehensive film guides useful to parents. For instance, screenit.com's review of *American Pie2*, runs nine pages, informing parents that the film contains a heavy dose of profanity, sex/nudity, and alcohol and drug use. This is probably more than parents want to read but at least there no longer is an excuse for parents to claim ignorance about the content of a particular film.

Together, parents and the film industry have an opportunity to transform self-regulation into an effective instrument to protect children from adult material and to prevent possible government intervention. The potential exists for a meaningful film rating system if parents exert their will and if Hollywood accepts its social responsibility.

HUAC AND THE BLACKLIST

The Red Scare Comes to Hollywood

"I could answer the question . . . but if I did I would hate myself in the morning."

RING LARDNER, JR.

"Joe couldn't find a Communist in Red Square—he didn't know Karl Marx from Groucho."

GEORGE REEDY ON McCARTHY

"I wouldn't know a communist if I saw one."

JACK WARNER

In a scene at the end of Irwin Winkler's 1991 film, *Guilty by Suspicion*, actor Robert DeNiro, playing a prominent film director falsely accused of being a communist, rises from his chair and shouts at the members of the congressional committee interrogating him: "Shame on you! Shame on you!" Television viewers old enough to remember the Army-McCarthy hearings might recall a similar scene where special counsel for the army, Joseph Welch, turns to the senator from Wisconsin and says: "Have you no sense of decency, sir, at long last? Have you left no sense of decency?"

Unfortunately, that final scene in *Suspicion* is the highlight of a rather lackluster film about life in post-World War II Hollywood where the real drama being played out was far more exciting and tumultuous than anything portrayed on screen. The industry was so embarrassed by its performance during the HUAC hearings that *Guilty by Suspicion* represents one of four major feature films that Hollywood has released about that dark period in film history when friends turned against friends, colleagues accused other colleagues, and the studios, succumbing to the political pressure of the day, instituted an industry blacklist in an effort to demonstrate their loyalty and patriotism. Of course, a few filmmakers masked their insinuations behind the facade of western melodrama such as *High Noon* (1952) and *Johnny Guitar* (1953). Although both these films had western narratives, insiders recognized them as metaphors for HUAC and the blacklist.[1]

Of the four films with explicit blacklist plots, the first film, *The Way We Were* (1973), and the most recent one, *The Majestic* (2001), are essentially love stories sugar-coated with nostalgia for the good old days of the 1950s. In *The Way We Were*, a WASPish Robert Redford falls in love with leftist radical Barbra Streisand. This two-hour film portrays their wavering romance and marriage as they relocate from New York to Hollywood where Redford works as a screenwriter while Streisand embarrasses him with her leftist politics. It is during the second hour that the film focuses on the HUAC hearings with Redford's character choosing not to get involved while Streisand supports the Hollywood Ten. Eventually the pair split and go their separate ways although it is clear to the audience that they still love each other. Arthur Laurents, who wrote the screenplay, later would claim that the film was altered to soften the politics and emphasize the love story.[2] *The Majestic* is an overlong dramatic vehicle for actor Jim Carrey who stars as a Hollywood writer blacklisted for communist activities during his college years. Depressed and drunk, Carrey is involved in an auto accident, loses his memory, settles in a small coastal town and is mistaken by the local theater owner for his lost son. The bulk of the film concerns renovation of the town's old movie theater and a budding romance. Eventually the FBI catches up with Carrey and he is subpoenaed to appear before HUAC. His memory restored, Carrey's character rejects his previous willingness to "name names" and even make up names in favor of a heroic stand that challenges the committee on First Amendment grounds, a position that was never accepted either by Congress or the courts. Carrey walks out of the committee a hero and returns to the small town where he is last seen selling tickets for the movie, *Invasion of the Body Snatchers*.

At least in *The Front* (1976) and *Guilty by Suspicion* HUAC and the blacklist were dealt with more directly. *The Front* is the first feature film that compelled Hollywood to confront its past. In the film, Woody Allen plays a cashier bookie who lends his name to blacklisted writers, a tactic used by several of the Hollywood Ten. Allen's character is apolitical but his willingness to serve as a "front" has more to do with paying off his gambling debts than to principle. When he is discovered and called to testify, Allen does a Hollywood turnabout, develops a political conscience, and refuses to name names. He defiantly walks out of the hearings, telling the committee members "you can go fuck yourselves." Possibly to protect itself, the film concerned blacklisting in the television industry rather than the movies, surprising since the screen credits listed half-a-dozen Hollywood artists who had suffered through the real blacklist. Still the film comes closest to showing the tragic effects of black-listing, which the film industry refused to acknowledge until recently.

Guilty by Suspicion touches on the effect the blacklist had on people in the indus-try. It could have expressed stronger sentiments against HUAC and the blacklist except for the fact that even after forty years Hollywood lacked the courage to face up to its past. In the original screenplay by blacklisted writer Abraham Polonsky, the DeNiro character, was supposed to be a former party member called before HUAC, a factual situation closer to the real events played out in 1947. When director Irwin Winkler changed the status of the DeNiro character from party mem-ber to non-communist, Polonsky had his name removed from the film credits.[3] Though Polonsky's stand may have been a victory for the integrity of the creative process, it also was a tacit admission that communists had worked in the film industry.

The truth of the matter is that the film industry succumbed to the hysteria of the Red Scare of the 1950s. The one significant resistance to the HUAC hearings was the failure of the Screen Directors Guild to impose a loyalty oath on all film-makers, a proposal that would have barred a director with communist membership or affiliation from making any more films in Hollywood.[4] The fact is the industry resorted to blacklisting as an industrial weapon, first against the trade unions and later against employees named during the HUAC investigations. To put the Hollywood blacklist in perspective, a brief summary of the post-World War II peri-od is in order.

COLD WAR AMERICA, 1945–55

In retrospect, the decade following the end of World War II might best be described as another watershed in American history. The United States emerged as the eco-nomic and political leader of the democratic West in a bipolarized world fraught with danger, where a wrong decision or misunderstood movement could trigger nuclear war. That fear of total destruction hung like Damocles' sword over the decade, leading schools to prepare children for a possible atomic attack and fright-ening some people into building bomb shelters in their backyards.

Culturally, the more interesting projects of the decade were being created for the new medium of television, while Hollywood retreated into producing pre-dictable dramas, inane comedies, and musicals as the studios sought to meet the challenge of TV with gimmicks (3-D movies) and new technology (cinemascope projection). A few "message" films about racism and bigotry were made at this time, but in the wake of the prison sentences handed out to the Hollywood Ten and the blacklisting of unfriendly witnesses, the studios played it safe. Hollywood, however, was not reluctant to produce a number of films that warned of the communist menace.

As the fifties approached, Americans had settled down in their suburban homes, content to enjoy their new consumer goods. But the break with the Soviet Union over numerous postwar issues provided the catalyst for the anticommunism campaign that erupted in the country. This campaign of fear was manipulated by a political opportunist named Joseph McCarthy, the senator from Wisconsin, whose wild assertions and unsubstantiated charges created an atmosphere of such terror that the term, "McCarthyism," came to define the decade.

MCCARTHYISM AND THE RED SCARE

The Red Scare

In truth, there were two "red scares" in American history. The first occurred after the First World War when Attorney General Palmer in the Wilson administration conducted a series of "roundup raids," led by a young FBI agent named J. Edgar Hoover. This was in response to the Bolshevik victory in Russia, attacks against prominent capitalists and government officials, and threats against the lives of public figures. The raids took on the character of "collective sweeps" common to totalitarian regimes, where government arrests political activists, suspected radicals, and "outsiders" with the wrong religion or ethnicity and places them into one generic category labeled "subversive" and "dangerous" to national security. In one 1919 twelve-city sweep against the Union of Russian Workers, the federal government made 300 arrests, resulting in the deportation of 199. The following year, raids in thirty-three cities led to 591 deportations and over 4,000 arrests; more than half of those arrested were subsequently released.[5] This fear of subversion from within led to the imposition of immigration quotas in the 1920s and helped to create the atmosphere of intolerance that led to the injustice inherent in the Sacco and Vanzetti trial. There was no middle ground in this internal war: you were either for America or against it, either a patriot or a traitor. The seeds of nativism and anti-radical hysteria were planted after World War I and waiting to resurface when the "right person at the right time" appeared. That person turned out to be the junior senator from Wisconsin.

McCarthyism

So much has been written about Joe McCarthy that his life story is easily accessible:[6] his early childhood in Appleton, Wisconsin, his rather humble beginnings, his decision to quit school and go to work, his subsequent return to education to complete law school, and finally, his determination to enter politics. What is remarkable about McCarthy's early career is its lack of any discernible characteristics; he loses some electoral races and wins others. His military service record is also undistinguished. His first significant electoral victory came in 1946 when he defeated the popular senator Robert Lafollette for the Republican nomination and went on to whip his Democratic opponent in the general election. After three years in the U.S. senate, McCarthy has a moderate voting record: in foreign affairs, he votes for NATO, the Marshall Plan, and aid to Greece and Turkey; in domestic matters he votes for high price supports for farmers and follows the advice of Republican Party leaders. His political career languishing, McCarthy seized the opportunity presented during the traditional Lincoln Day Birthday address and turned it into political capital when he discarded his prepared speech on housing in favor of one on communism, and the rest is history. McCarthy never had a list of State Department employees who were communists nor did he have any plan in mind. He was an astute politician, grabbing headlines by announcing daily charges of new communists discovered in the government, academia, and the military. His accusation that there were 205 communists in the State Department would be pared down to fifty-seven and eventually reduced to four names supplied by his staff. McCarthy had a knack for manipulating the media, providing newspapers and broadcasters with tomorrow's headlines. At the same time he was as much a creation of the media as any contemporary rock star, whose entourage of reporters printed accusations without checking or verifying them first. McCarthy was instant news, driving even President Eisenhower off the front page. The senator came to dominate the news during the five years of his ascendancy (1950–54) to such an extent that historians refer to this period as "McCarthyism," adding a new word to the American political vocabulary. That word became synonymous with "the practice of publicizing accusations of political disloyalty or subversion with insufficient regard to evidence."[7] In sum, McCarthy exploited the political situation and capitalized on weakness and vulnerability. Recently released documents[8] from the fifties revealed that McCarthy held secret examinations of witnesses as a sort of dress rehearsal for his subcommittee's public hearings. The results of these quasi-official hearings determined whether the witness would be subpoenaed to appear before the whole committee. As a consequence, some witnesses like writer Dashiell Hammett were recalled while others like composer Aaron Copland were excused, apparently on the basis of their resistance to McCarthy's bullying tactics or their perceived inability to provide dramatic theater for his media appearances.

Historian Albert Fried maintains that McCarthyism cannot be adequately understood by a simple explanation.[9] Instead Fried offers a more complex definition of McCarthyism and demonstrates that unlike previous red scares that were brief, the effects of McCarthyism lasted for decades. For example, as a result of the

FIGURE 7 McCarthy-Terrorist cartoon: 2003. Reprinted with permission, *Green Bay Press Gazette.*

decades-long impact of the HUAC hearings and the imposition of the industry blacklist, Hollywood refused until recently to acknowledged the wrong done to blacklisted writers and directors by restoring their screen credits to their work. The pseudonyms and "fronts" were removed from forty-seven films produced during the red scare era and replaced by the names of their creators, the blacklisted writers.[10] Second, Fried holds McCarthy responsible for creating anxiety in the hearts of liberal Democrats in the 1960s who feared a political backlash from public perception during the Cold War of any sign of weakness toward communism. This fear, according to Fried, supposedly drove the administrations of John Kennedy and Lyndon Johnson into the Bay of Pigs and Vietnam. Finally, Fried believes McCarthyism illustrates the abuse of power by government and its agents, encouraging errant behavior on the part of the FBI and the Justice Department.

McCarthyism was not nurtured in a vacuum. Its context is best understood as a mixture of fact and fiction stimulated by public fear and intolerance. While an active American Communist Party (CPUSA) did exist, the U.S. government only could speculate on the actual number of hardcore Stalinists dedicated to overthrowing the institutions of government by force and violence. It seems fruitless to guess that there were 100,000 or 10,000 members because joiners moved in and out of the party and others attended local meetings without becoming members. What is much easier to account for in the Cold War hysteria was Soviet imperialism in Eastern Europe, the fall of China, the outbreak of the Korean War, the disclosure of the Amerasis spy ring that left the Foreign Service vulnerable to accusations, the passing of atomic secrets to the Soviets by the Rosenbergs, and the subsequent Soviet explosion of a nuclear device. These political realities provided substance to the perception of a legitimate communist threat; opinion polls overwhelmingly showed that the public would allow the government to outlaw the Communist Party, force communists to register, and bar them from college and university teaching.[11] In other words, current events and public opinion lent comfort and support to McCarthy and his political allies. Biographer Ted Morgan[12] insists, however, that the most sordid aspect of McCarthyism was the failure and cowardice of his Senate colleagues, who knew him best, to stand up and expose him for what he was—a bully and a drunk. Instead, Washington encouraged him by its silence.

As a political phenomenon, McCarthyism may be interpreted in three ways. One is to see it as the articulation of working-class intolerance, a sort of lower-class reaction against intellectualism, as McCarthy regularly railed against academics and intellectuals. Another is to place it within a historical line of American paranoia that exhibits a deep distrust of elites and strangers, a suspicion ripe for exploitation by an adept demagogue dating back to the nativism and populism of the nineteenth century. Third, and more positively, his downfall after the Army-McCarthy hearings represents a national rejection of extremism. Simply put, McCarthy had gone too far in his accusations and had exceeded American limits of tolerance.[13] On the negative side, Americans also shared in the blame by their public support of his methods. Quite possibly Shakespeare summed it up best in *Julius Caesar* when he wrote: "The fault, dear Brutus, lies not in our stars but in ourselves."

HOLLYWOOD AND THE BLACKLIST

Against Labor

Hollywood has never admitted the practice of "blacklisting," an underhanded way of depriving a person of his/her livelihood without formal acknowledgment. Those blacklisted are frequently locked out of a whole industry or line of work as employers conspire against them. It is a form of punishment without trial and Hollywood has used it twice against its artists and employees. Years before HUAC came to Hollywood and McCarthyism became a national phenomenon; the film industry resorted to the blacklist in an attempt to discourage unionization.

Mike Nielsen and Gene Mailes, have documented the complete story of early blacklisting in the film industry.[14] The authors argue that Hollywood was not only anticommunist; it was also antiunion. The industry fought unionization in the courts and on the streets.[15] Labor organizing in the entertainment industry began in the 1890s when stagehands sought to protect themselves against exploitation by theater managers. The organizing process eventually would reach the motion picture industry, involving all craft workers (carpenters, electricians, and painters) employed in film production. These laborers worked long hours under poor conditions and without benefits. While the studios employed a hard core of regular workers, most of the laborers had to "shape up" everyday, similar to conditions on the waterfront. Apparently, the industry had a "sweetheart" arrangement with organized crime whereby mob bosses "fronted" for the company union, keeping wages and benefits low in return for payoffs from the studios. This is not a story likely to show up in a Hollywood film.

Not until 1926 did the International Alliance of Theatrical & Stage Employees (IA) and the studios sign the first labor agreement that provided for negotiations over wages, hours, working conditions, and grievances. Referred to as the Studio Basic Agreement, it became the cornerstone for labor relations within the film industry. In the thirties, discontent over labor conditions led the professional employees—the writers, actors, and directors—to create their own unions along the lines of the medieval guilds. Later these active leaders in the labor movement were the ones called to appear before HUAC, where they learned that their names were on the industry's blacklist.

As elsewhere, labor organizing in Hollywood did not come easily or peacefully. In fact, labor unrest and violence cover three decades of Hollywood history; this was a labor-management war every bit as intense as any military engagement, with reports of arbitrary firings, beatings by goon squads, mob murders, violent clashes on picket lines, and collusion of the studios with organized crime figures like Chicago gangster Frank Nitti. It is also a story of jurisdictional strikes and clashes within the labor movement for control of the film industry. Although several strikes occurred in the thirties, labor was committed to its "no strike" pledge during World War II, a pledge that the American Communist Party endorsed against the wishes of a few labor leaders. But it was during the postwar strikes from 1945 to 1947 that union-studio confrontations became quite nasty. One 1945 strike at Warner Brothers, in particular, was so vicious that it earned the label, "Bloody Friday." Some 1,000 strikers set up a mass picket line around the Warner Studios and were confronted by company security, non-strikers, and local police. The ensuing two-hour melee resulted in forty injuries as the picketers were dispersed with tear gas, clubs, and fire hoses. Screenwriter Dalton Trumbo, one of the Hollywood Ten, described the day as "fascism in action."[16] The following Monday, the picket line was broken by police and non-strikers using metal chains, clubs, and battery cables, resulting in more bloodshed. Additional injuries occurred when Warner Brothers had its security cops drop heavy bolts from a five-story sound stage down on unsuspecting pick-eters. To make sure that strikers did not return the next day, the studio hired a private "goon squad" to beat up those who were still walking the picket line. In total, almost 150 persons required hospitalization or suffered physical injuries during the course of the strike.

Even more insidious than the physical violence was the conspiracy by the major studios to "blackball" the participating strikers by placing the names of union activists on a sheet of unsigned paper, which circulated among the film studios and the independents. The Hollywood blacklist indicated that the persons named should be fired if they were working or not hired if they applied for work. For example, labor organizer Irv Hentschel, who formed the IA Progressives, lost his job because of his union activities. Under union rules, Hentschel, a machinist by trade, was listed as eligible to work, but he received no calls from the studios. He finally decided to call the studios directly and was told that the word around the industry was not to hire him.[17] Hentschel's name had landed on the "invisible" blacklist.

Another tactic used by the film studios and their mobster henchmen at this time was to label union organizers and activists as "communists." This strategy aimed to discredit union advocates and isolate studio dissenters as "un-American." When the union bosses who fronted for the mob and the film studios wanted to purge the IA of local troublemakers, they filed "conduct unbecoming a loyal member of the union" charges, which required a union trial. All the IA progressives were cited as "communists," even though only one of the five local leaders was a party member at the time.[18]

The Hollywood blacklist, then, was a product of the early labor wars in the industry; this strategy of labeling foes as "communists" or "un-American" was later used during the HUAC hearings to discredit both the post-World War II peace movement and the promotion of civil rights. Discrediting a foe or a movement by labeling was still in vogue in the 1980s as evidenced by President Reagan's characterization of the nuclear freeze proponents as "communists."[19] When HUAC came to town in 1947, the atmosphere in Hollywood was conducive to a public trial that would expose, and then exorcise, the evil forces that plagued the industry. The hearings provided an opportunity for the studios to silence activists, individuals to pay-back personal grudges, and politicians to exploit patriotism to advance their careers.

Against Communists, Radicals and Liberals

The HUAC investigation of the film industry occurred in three stages. Initially, HUAC met informally with studio heads and individual actors, many of whom were members of the conservative Motion Picture Alliance for the Preservation of American Ideals (the Alliance), an organization that worked with the committee to cleanse Hollywood of communists and other radicals. These were the so-called "friendly" witnesses, who either provided the committee with names of communists or reinforced the suspicion already held by the committee about particular people.[20] Often their testimony was based on rumor and gossip. For example, Walt Disney could name the League of Women Voters as a communist group without proof or fear of cross-examination. Film stars Adolphe Menjou and Gary Cooper cited persons who associated with actor-singer Paul Robeson or who had criticized the Constitution and the government in Washington. Based on this sort of testimony, HUAC created a list of seventy-nine "named communists" scheduled to be called before the committee. In October 1947, HUAC narrowed the list to nineteen Hollywood writers, directors, producers, and actors, issuing them subpoenas to appear before the committee. Of the nineteen subpoenaed, eleven appeared, (Bertolt Brecht was the last to appear, claimed that he was not a communist, and departed for Europe), leaving the ten "unfriendly" witnesses (the Hollywood Ten) to be cited for contempt. As punishment they were sent to prison for their refusal to answer the committee's questions. The final act in the drama occurred during the second round of hearings between 1951 and 1953, when HUAC subpoenaed the remaining eight names on the original list in addition to others identified during the hearings. It was during this stage that witnesses broke down (actor Larry Parks begged the committee not to force him to "name names"), others recanted (director Edward Dmytryk, one of the original Hollywood Ten admitted his communist past and named twenty-six of his colleagues as communists), while still others purged themselves of their radical pasts by reciting every conceivable name that came to memory. According to one source,[21] fifty-eight informers recited 902 names before the committee, an average of 29 names per witness. Some witnesses, like former communist turned FBI informer Harvey Matusow, provided hundreds of names to the committee but later recanted and admitted most were lies.[22] If you discount duplications, the informers identified roughly 200 Hollywood artists as "communists" associated with the film industry. Those who were blacklisted probably exceeded 200 since the ones with valid passports left the country to seek work elsewhere and the others who remained were "graylisted," that is, they found work in the industry scarce because they had supported the Hollywood Ten or worked for liberal causes. The "graylisted" were victims of "guilt by association," best illustrated on screen by the DeNiro character in *Guilty by Suspicion*. The exact number of film industry people blacklisted is unlikely to be ever publicized but estimates range as high as 250.[23] A few like Trumbo, Lawson, and Polonsky eventually would resume their film careers, while others were less fortunate and often forced to take odd jobs to survive. It is estimated that only 10 percent of those blacklisted returned to work in the film industry.[24] Possibly the saddest aspect of the HUAC hearings was that the committee already knew about the activities of many of those named.

What the committee wanted from witnesses was a public confession, similar to the Stalinist purges of the 1930s. This aspect of the Hollywood investigations left an impression that the purpose of the hearings was for public entertainment staged by members of the committee to advance their political careers.

The Hollywood Ten: Heroes or Villains?

The drama that unfolded during the hearings of the original ten "unfriendly witnesses" was not accidental or even spontaneous. HUAC singled out the most professionally successful Hollywood radicals to interrogate, and while the 1947 hearings were about communism, some of the politicians and friendly witnesses took the opportunity also to strike a blow against aggressive trade unionism and left-liberal political activism. Membership in popular front, radical, and peace organizations automatically placed an individual under HUAC's suspicion.[25] A majority of the Hollywood Ten, who were or had been members of CPUSA, adopted the strategy of attacking the committee's authority and its constitutionality under the First Amendment. Because of their CPUSA membership, if any one had answered "no" to the question: "Are you now or have you ever been a member of the Communist Party?" he would have been subject to perjury charges. By answering "yes" to that question, the witness was subjected to even more intensive questioning, increasing the chances of breaking down and "naming names." To the political left, the Hollywood Ten were heroes, standing up to demagogues and fascists. They drew support from their liberal colleagues, many of whom joined the "Committee for the First Amendment" and traveled to Washington for the hearings. They petitioned Congress to disband HUAC and they donated their time and names to fund-raising campaigns. However, most of the studio heads, the leadership of the various screen guilds, and the members of the Motion Picture Alliance believed the Ten were everything from dangerous to naive. Actor Ward Bond, a leader in the Alliance and a close friend of John Wayne, lobbied the Motion Picture Academy not to give an Oscar to actor Jose Ferrer, whom Bond considered to be a communist well *before* the actor was named on a subpoena to appear before the committee.[26]

On the other hand, the informers were either praised or despised. Some former party members, like director Edward Dmytryk, finally testified because they did not want to be punished for their past associations, especially since they no longer believed in the cause.[27] Others such as screenwriter Leo Townsend admitted their communist past and repented, seeking salvation through public confession. To Albert Maltz, one of the Hollywood Ten, there was no justification for "naming names"; he considered the informers to be rats and he hated their guts. He went so far as to pay for a two-page advertisement to correct the *Saturday Evening Post* story on Dmytryk's change of political heart. Trumbo, on the other hand, was more conciliatory, citing both "friendly" and "unfriendly" witnesses as victims of the postwar hysteria.[28]

THE UNFRIENDLY WITNESSES

The Original Eleven Witnesses

ALVAH BESSIE: novelist and screenwriter; author of *Bread in the Stone*; wrote screenplay for two Errol Flynn World War II movies, *Northern Pursuit*, and *Objective Burma* (with Lester Cole). Supported Spanish Republic and served in the International Brigade and later in the Second World War.

HERBERT BIBERMAN: director and producer; coproduced film *New Orleans*, and directed another film, *The Master Race*; married to blacklisted actress Gale Sondergaard. Directed *Salt of the Earth*, a film project of blacklisted writers, directors, and actors.

LESTER COLE: writer of forty screenplays, including *None Shall Escape* and *Blood on the Sun* and coauthor of *Objective Burma*; founder of Screen Writer's Guild (SWG).*

EDWARD DMYTRYK: noted director of such films as *Hitler's Children, Back to Bataan, Tender Comrade,* and *Crossfire*. Resumed his career after becoming an informer.*

RING LARDNER, JR.: writer, author of screenplays *Woman of the Year* and *Forever Amber*; coauthor with Albert Maltz of film *Cloak and Dagger*; served as officer of SWG; did not write under his own name until the 1965 script for *The Cincinnati Kid*.*

JOHN HOWARD LAWSON: critic and writer; author of numerous screenplays, including two Humphrey Bogart World War II films, *Action in the North Atlantic* and *Sahara*; served as president of SWG.*

ALBERT MALTZ: novelist, playwright, and screenwriter; wrote scripts for *Destination Tokyo* and *Pride of the Marines* and the award-winning documentary, *The House I Live In*. Was "ghost writer" on film scripts for *The Robe* and *Broken Arrow*, receiving no screen credits.

SAMUEL ORNITZ: novelist and author; wrote screenplays for *The Man Who Claimed His Head* and *Three Faces West*. After prison he turned his attention to research and writing.*

ADRIAN SCOTT: screenwriter and film producer of such films as *Crossfire* and *Murder My Sweet*; wrote script for film *Mr. Lucky*.*

DALTON TRUMBO: novelist and screenwriter; author of *Johnny Got His Gun*; wrote scripts for *Thirty Seconds Over Tokyo, A Guy Named Joe,* and *Our Vines Have*

Tender Grapes. Active in Hollywood trade union movement and Screen Writers Guild. Wrote thirty scripts under pseudonyms during the blacklist.*

BERTOLT BRECHT: novelist, poet, and playwright. After HUAC appearance, fled to Europe, thereby avoiding further interrogation and prosecution.

The Remaining Eight Witnesses

RICHARD COLLINS: screenwriter for *Song of Russia*; served on the executive board of the Screen Writers Guild; turned informer during second round of HUAC hearings, 1951–53.*

GORDON KAHN: author and correspondent for the *Atlantic Monthly*; managing editor of the *Screen Writer*; served on SWG executive board.*

HOWARD KOCH: scriptwriter for *Casablanca, Sergeant York*, and *Mission to Moscow*; served on SWG executive board.*

LEWIS MILESTONE: film director of *All Quiet on the Western Front, A Walk in the Sun, Arch of Triumph*, and *Of Mice and Men*.

IRVING PICHEL: actor and director; directed *The Moon Is Down, OSS*, and *A Medal for Benny*.

LARRY PARKS: actor on verge of stardom after playing the lead in *The Jolson Story*; became informer, which ruined his film career.

ROBERT ROSSEN: author and director; wrote screenplays for World War II films *Edge of Darkness* and *A Walk in the Sun*; directed *Body and Soul* and *Johnny O'Clock*; served as officer in SWG; also became an informer.*

WALDO SALT: screenwriter for films like *Shopworn Angel* and *Mr. Winkle Goes to War*.*

---

* Self-confessed or named as member of the Communist Party.

The Communist Threat in Hollywood

The search for communists, real and imagined, by HUAC and McCarthy's Senate committee took a wide swipe through the unions, education, the legal profession, the military, and even the clergy. Few occupations were spared during this national campaign allegedly designed to protect America's internal security from its enemies. But how strong was the CPUSA? The estimates of party membership ranged from J. Edgar Hoover's exaggerated half-million to several thousand at the other extreme. As mentioned earlier, the exact number is impossible to determine since people moved freely in and out of the party. For example, writer and director Cy Endfield, named in the 1951 HUAC hearings, attended communist meetings during the thirties and forties but actually never joined the party.[29] Were people like Endfield included? The best estimate of CPUSA membership at this time ranged anywhere from 10,000 to 100,000 members, most likely fluctuating between 30,000 and 50,000.[30] In addition to the transitory nature of party membership, left-liberals joined communists in a number of Popular Front causes against fascism during this period. An example is the case of Charlie Chaplin. The actor was accused of being a communist for his leftist speeches and political activities. Amidst charges of tax evasion and paternity suits, Chaplin fled to his native England in 1952, eventually establishing residency in Switzerland. He did not return to the United States until twenty years later when Hollywood honored him for his lifetime achievement in the cinema.[31] However, Chaplin's politics were inconsistent. He flirted with communism in the 1920s, deserted the cause in the thirties, only to return when he believed that the Soviets were the singular anti-Nazi power in Europe.[32] Should people like Chaplin have been counted in the membership figures? How many other Hollywood entertainment figures besides Chaplin pursued politically erratic paths but were counted as committed communists?

While the red scare dragnet snared many in its net, the logical question remains: why focus on the entertainment industry? What harm could communists do in Hollywood? There are two very plausible reasons why HUAC would find Hollywood an attractive venue. First, and of paramount importance, was the obvious publicity that the discovery of communists active in the film industry would provide to the committee and its members. The Hollywood hearings had the potential to be as dramatic as anything on the silver screen since the appearance of recognized stars lent an air of show business to the entire proceedings. As it turned out, the hearings had the effect of furthering the political career of a young California representative named Richard Nixon.[33] The second reason is that Hollywood, like the rest of the popular arts, is vulnerable to public scrutiny. The arts attract creative people, free spirits who often ignore the rules of social conventions. Artists are particularly drawn to new ideas and to critical analysis of the existing order. When the vulnerability of the arts is combined with whispered allegations by the American Legion[34] and printed accusations of publications like *Red Stars and Fellow Travelers in Hollywood*,[35] which listed some 200 Hollywood stars as "reds" and partners in a fifth column aimed at overthrowing the government, HUAC's focus on Hollywood is not surprising.

How strong was the Communist Party in Hollywood? Out of thousands of studio employees, one source estimate puts local party membership around 300 between 1936 and 1949.[36] That estimate is corroborated by another source[37] that breaks down party members according to their work in the film industry: 145 screenwriters, some 50 to 60 actors, 15 to 20 producers and directors, and some 60 to 90 backlot workers and office staff. That figure totals 315, using the maximum estimates.

Regardless of their number, how influential were they? Their greatest effectiveness seemed to be in the trade union movement and in the screenwriters' guild. HUAC focused in on the latter group since sixteen of the first nineteen witnesses were writers. This was likely due to the misguided assumption that the scripts written by these writers were tainted with communist propaganda or else contained material dangerous to the social order. In reality, however, the old studio system operated like the American system of checks and balances; all film scripts were subject to internal review by studio heads and producers. Screenwriters *never* had the last word. As Dorothy B. Jones confirmed in her study of film content, it was virtually impossible to incorporate Marxist ideology into films produced by the major studios because

> the very nature of the film-making process which divides creative responsibility among a number of different people and which keeps ultimate control of content in the hands of top studio executives; the habitual caution of moviemakers with respect to film content; and the self-regulating practices of the motion picture industry . . . prevented such propaganda from reaching the screen in all but possibly rare instances.[38]

If HUAC considered the films themselves to be "subversive" or "dangerous," why did the committee reject Dalton Trumbo's offer to examine eighteen of his film scripts, including several written for movies on the Second World War?[39] Furthermore, subjecting the films that involved the Hollywood Ten to content analysis reveals that the majority of films included topics that were strictly nonpolitical. For example, between 1929 and 1949, the Hollywood Ten participated in the making of 159 feature films in the following subject categories:

- 45 were a combination of biography and historical films, romances, love stories, and comedies;
- 28 were murder, mystery, and espionage films;
- 23 were war or military service films;
- 22 were social message films;
- 17 were westerns and action/adventure films;
- 15 were gangster, crime, and prison films.[40]

Combining the above film subjects with strict studio supervision leaves little doubt that the bulk of the films made by the Hollywood Ten were typical Hollywood entertainment fare, free from political ideology save for the war films.

History has brought the HUAC hearings into perspective. The committee could not have been interested in film content *per se* because if it had been, the studio heads would have been held accountable rather than the writers, directors, and actors. Films like *Song of Russia* and *Mission to Moscow*, for instance, were considered by HUAC's "friendly witnesses" to be pro-Red. Even if written or directed by hardcore Stalinists, they were made with the blessing of MGM and Warner Brothers. Louis Mayer told HUAC he made *Song of Russia* because "Russia was an ally. It seemed the patriotic thing to do."[41] Producer Jack Warner supposedly agreed to do *Mission to Moscow* at the request of the Roosevelt administration; the film presented such a kindly Soviet leader that American parents might be tempted to recruit "Uncle Joe" Stalin as godfather for their children.[42] Furthermore, both these films as well as the pro-Soviet movie scripted by Lillian Hellman, *The North Star*, had to be cleared through the Office of War Information. However, neither Mayer nor Jack Warner's loyalty was questioned at the time. Ironically, two of HUAC's friendliest witnesses, director Sam Wood (first president of the Motion Picture Alliance) and actor Gary Cooper, both involved in *For Whom the Bell Tolls*, the pro-Republican film of the Spanish Civil War that was based on the Hemingway novel, never had their loyalty or patriotism questioned despite the film's preference for the coalition government rather than the U.S.-supported forces of Generalissimo Franco. Clearly, film content was not what most concerned HUAC.

Even had the Hollywood Ten and the other unfriendly witnesses been committed Stalinists who attended every cell meeting and followed every communist command, the content of their films under the old studio system required approval at the executive level. It is now clear that the Ten and the other blacklisted were singled out because they posed a threat to the industry due to their union and off-screen political activities rather than for the content that appeared on the screen. Possibly Ronald Reagan, head of the Screen Actors' Guild at the time, hit the nail on the head when he characterized the risk of having communists and subversives in the film industry in these terms: "The danger is not what is on the screen. It is what these people do behind the scenes to gain power in organizations to further their beliefs."[43] Thus, the committee, with the collaboration of the film studios and the Motion Picture Alliance, appears to have intended the 1947 HUAC hearings in Hollywood and those held from 1951 to 1953 to put an end to what they considered to be radical unionism and leftist-liberal politics.

THE IMPACT OF THE RED SCARE AND THE BLACKLIST
Personal Harm

The Hollywood hearings had personal and professional repercussions, both on the informers and on those named. Which group had the heaviest burden to bear? In economic terms, all the unfriendly witnesses suffered personal loss and endured economic hardship through blacklisting. The informers, on the other hand, carried the mark of Judas around with them throughout the remainder of their careers. Trumbo was right when he characterized the informers and the blacklisted as victims because both were shunned by former friends and despised by their enemies. Blacklisted actors, directors, and producers were hardest hit because they were visible to their enemies; however some writers such as Trumbo, Michael Wilson, and Ned Young could still work under pseudonyms. Even though they were paid for their scripts, these blacklisted writers worked without recognition. Furthermore, blacklisting was open-ended; there was no deadline or date when redemption began and careers resumed. Actress Lee Grant spent sixteen years on the blacklist while actress Gale Sondergaard, Herbert Biberman's wife, went seven years without a paid acting engagement. Meanwhile, turning informer did not provide actor Larry Parks with salvation; he played a supporting role in only one major Hollywood film after his HUAC appearance. His actress wife, Betty Garrett, also found work in the industry hard to come by.[44] Blacklisted director Abraham Polonsky would not direct another film for twenty years, while screenwriter Samuel Ornitz deserted the film industry altogether for lack of work.[45] Others, like Albert Maltz, had screen projects pulled out from underneath them. Maltz was hired by Frank Sinatra, who held the film rights, to do the screenplay for *The Execution of Eddie Slovak* (1974), a story about an American deserter in World War II. Maltz claims that he did considerable research for the film script and even had a first draft ready for review when Sinatra fired him, presumably because of intense pressure from the Motion Picture Alliance and the Kennedy White House.[46]

Those writers who were unable to find work even with pseudonyms and those who were unsuccessful in locating "fronts" for submitting their scripts to the studios, resorted to any kind of work just to survive. Ned Young was forced to work as a bartender, salesman, and junkman; meanwhile others left the country to pursue their film work in England (Joseph Losey, Carl Foreman, Adrian Scott), France (Jules Dassin, John Howard Lawson), and Mexico (Maltz, Trumbo). Others formed the Blacklist Company to produce their own films, but the failure of their first feature, *Salt of the Earth*, led them to abandon the effort.

There were personal casualties as well. Ned Young's wife, blacklisted along with her husband, committed suicide after years of depression. There is some suggestion that at least a half-dozen Hollywood deaths, including actors John Garfield, J. Edward Bromberg, and Canada Lee, can be attributed directly to the hearings and the blacklist.[47] Garfield, for example, was rejected for military service because of heart trouble. Although he was not a communist, he worried that HUAC would ask him about his wife, who had been a party member. Garfield died from a heart attack at age thirty-nine and his family and friends blamed HUAC, citing the stress associated with his subpoena.

There were marriage breakups and divorces and the effect the blacklist had on the children of those on the list has been recognized only recently. In gatherings in Los Angeles and New York called for the purpose of filming a documentary on the subject,[48] the children of the blacklist, middle-aged at the time of the interviews, offered bittersweet recollections of their parents with occasional reproaches against their accusers. Julie Garfield described the studio heads as "racists" who went after her father because he was Jewish; Joshua Mostel claimed his father, Zero, was apolitical, if anything he likely was an anarchist; Martha Randolph told how her father was allowed to work in the theater but not on radio or in film; Liz Schwartz talked about her mother's suicide; others recalled being prohibited to play with or socialize with the children of informers; still others had memories of fleeing California in the middle of the night and hiding out in desert motels. Although their evidence is largely anecdotal, these personal stories reveal a second generation scarred by the blacklist. Thus the blacklist continues to touch the lives of its victims to this very day.[49]

The Defiant Ones

Several of the blacklisted sought to continue their professional careers by forming the independent Blacklist Company to produce their own films. Led by Herbert Biberman, Paul Jarrico, and Michael Wilson, the newly formed Independent Productions Corporation sought stories to transfer to the big screen. When the group learned of a labor strike in southwestern New Mexico that had lasted a year, writer Michael Wilson was sent to investigate. After discussions with union leaders; mine workers from the International Union of Mine, Mill, and Smelter Workers; and local citizens, Wilson drafted a fictional account from facts derived from the actual events. The completed film, entitled *Salt of the Earth*, starred five professionals, including Mexican actress Rosaura Revueltas and blacklisted American actor Will Geer, but the majority of the cast roles were filled with nonprofessionals. Shot on location and in black and white, the Wilson script integrated three plots into its story line. As briefly mentioned in an earlier chapter, the dominant narrative featured the labor-management dispute over wage discrimination, worker benefits, and mine safety conditions that precipitated the strike. This is the heart of the film that provides its dramatic center. But two subplots involving class and gender issues have since taken on more significance. The union leaders were white and middle class; the miners largely Mexican and lower class. The workers' families lived in abominable conditions without adequate sanitation and hot running water. When the striking miners were denied the right to picket under a Taft-Hartley restraining order, the women took their places on the line. Although subjected to verbal and physical abuse, the women prevailed and the workers won important concessions from the mine owners.

The story[50] behind the making of the film proved more dramatic than the events depicted on screen. *Salt of the Earth* encountered opposition at every stage during production, postproduction, and distribution. Mexican actress Rosaura Revueltas, who played the main female character, was arrested by Immigration authorities and deported. Filming was constantly interrupted by physical threats from local vigilante groups. When the shooting was finished and the film was ready for final editing, it was locked out of Hollywood's technical facilities commonly used in post-production. Film critics were generally negative about *Salt of the Earth*, with Pauline Kael labeling it "communist propaganda." Theater exhibitors dealt the final blow when they boycotted the film's original release in 1954. As a consequence, *Salt of the Earth* played briefly in only thirteen theaters in the entire country.

Denied commercial exhibition in the United States, the film was praised in Europe and became a cult favorite on American college campuses. In 2003, on the film's fiftieth anniversary, the College of Santa Fe paid tribute to its legacy by hosting a national conference that included several of the original participants along with noted scholars, artists, filmmakers, and labor organizers. During the conference it was announced that a remake was being planned because the film was as relevant today as in the 1950s.

Professional Consequences

Many of the participants in the HUAC proceedings—friendly witnesses, inform-ers, unfriendly witnesses—not only knew each other but worked together on film projects, belonged to the same guilds, and occasionally, joined the same Popular Front organizations. Their political and working association possibly explains the depth of the bitterness held by the unfriendly witnesses toward the informers.

The personal conflict between informer and unfriendly witness ultimately moved from the congressional hearing room to the big screen and is best epitomized in the dispute between film director Elia Kazan and playwright Arthur Miller. Witnesses before HUAC were limited to three choices: talk as the friendly witness-es did or remain silent, which was the tactic of the unfriendly witnesses. The third option, a compromised position whereby the witness speaks about him/herself but not about others, is best exemplified by the testimony of Lillian Hellman. Kazan, however, was a willing witness before HUAC, talking freely about the political activ-ities of himself and his colleagues. Miller, on the other hand, took the same posi-tion as Lillian Hellman, namely, that it was honorable to talk about yourself but not about others.[51]

Prior to the hearings, Kazan and Miller talked of collaborating on a film about longshoreman and their life on the docks. When Kazan named "names" before HUAC, Miller broke off their relationship. Kazan, meanwhile, went ahead with the

FIGURE 8. Salt of the Earth: 1953. Reprinted with permission of *Movie Stars News* and Jerry Ohlinger.

project, which became the critically acclaimed film, *On the Waterfront* (1954). Kazan persuaded Marlon Brando to play the main character, the washed-up fighter, Terry Malloy, who through the efforts of the local priest (Karl Malden) and the love of a good woman (Eva Marie Saint), turns state informer against the organized crime mob that controls the waterfront. In a dramatic ending, Terry receives a vicious beating from the mob but still leads the strikers back to work against the wishes of the crime boss (Lee J. Cobb). In *On the Waterfront*, the informer is transformed into a hero by cooperating with the authorities. Kazan used the film to justify his decision to name names.[52] Budd Schulberg,[53] who wrote the screenplay for the film, claims that the source for the story originated with the true-life story of Reverend John Corridon, a Catholic priest who persuaded a contingent of honest longshoremen to testify to the Waterfront Commission against the mob that controlled the union.

Miller, meanwhile, countered with *The Crucible*,[54] a play about the Salem witch trials, which was clearly intended to demonstrate the evils associated with paranoia and public hysteria. In his play, Miller argues that the informer is a villain whose action supports and encourages wrongdoing.

Because Miller's play took place in seventeenth-century New England, it could be viewed as a historical recreation. But in order to directly confront Kazan's informer as hero, Miller wrote *A View from the Bridge*, a play about the Brooklyn waterfront that subsequently became a motion picture. In the Miller version of *On the Waterfront*, Eddie Carbone, a longshoreman who lives with his wife and his sister's daughter Catherine, agrees to hide illegal immigrants (called "submarines"), from the immigration authorities. Eddie understands the law of the waterfront: act deaf, dumb, and blind. But when Eddie takes in these two illegals, all the pieces for a Greek tragedy are in place. When the younger illegal falls in love with Catherine, Eddie becomes jealous because he also harbors suppressed feelings of affection for his niece. These feelings lead Eddie to inform, to break the unwritten code of silence on the waterfront by reporting the location of the two submarines to immigration. It is this act of betrayal that the Miller play dramatizes; this treacherous deed results in Eddie's death since there is no honor in informing.

The Kazan-Miller clash was but one piece of personal drama played out as a result of the HUAC hearings and the subsequent blacklisting. Although neither Kazan nor Miller had their careers destroyed by the blacklist, each suffered from its effects. Miller felt betrayed by a friend and colleague; Kazan's career endured but not without retribution from his peers in the industry who denied him professional recognition.[55] As Dalton Trumbo might have observed, both Kazan and Miller were victims of the Hollywood blacklist.

The initial use of the blacklist in the twenties and thirties was to curb union organizing and threaten the jobs of Hollywood workers. Then in the fifties, the industry sought to impress the government with its patriotism by refusing to hire named "communists" and by insisting that anyone named by HUAC pass a loyalty clearance before being employed.

The studios also sought to illustrate their allegiance by making over forty anticommunist films between 1949 and 1953.[56] Films like *The Red Menace* (1949), *I Married a Communist* (1950), *I Was a Communist for the FBI* (1951), *My Son John* (1952), and *Big Jim McLain* (1952) were blatant pieces of patriotic propaganda that would hardly qualify for Academy Awards in any era. In *The Red Menace*, for example, an ex-serviceman joins a local communist party cell with the assistance of a seductive woman. If all Americans were as naive as the main character, the United States would have voted for the Communist Party in 1952 instead of Eisenhower. Similarly, the film *Big Jim McLain* has John Wayne smashing a communist cell in Hawaii, thereby preventing a takeover of the island. Actually, the film adhered to a formula plot that would have enabled the producers to substitute the Nazis, Japanese, or cattle rustlers for the communists without too many script changes. It so happened that the communists were the "bad guys" of the day and Hollywood capitalized on the current mood in the country.

Few films dared to criticize the anticommunist message directly. Instead a smattering challenged the communist paranoia and the effects of McCarthyism allegorically, expressing their condemnation of HUAC and the blacklist in plots that dealt with subjects ranging from space aliens to westerns. *The Thing* (1951), for example, a film about a frozen creature that comes to life and threatens an Arctic expedition, was interpreted as a metaphor for the spate of communist invasion movies; one scriptwriter insisted that the evil creature, *The Thing*, represented McCarthy(ism).[57] Another film released in 1951, *The Day the Earth Stood Still*, concerned a flying saucer that lands in Washington, D.C. The two aliens aboard have come to the nation's capital on a peace mission, to warn planet Earth against a global nuclear war. Of course, no one in government pays any attention to the peace message and, subsequently, events turn ugly as the alien leader is shot due to public fear and ignorance. Eventually the aliens return to their own planet. Certainly, the pro-peace message of *The Day the Earth Stood Still* was a daring theme in an age when atom bombs and nuclear weapons were part of military strategy and when release of the film coincided with McCarthy's announcement about communists in the State Department.[58] Meanwhile, another film, *Invasion of the Body Snatchers* (1956) dealt with giant seedpods that take over the bodies of people and turn them into cold, Godless creatures similar to the Soviets. Supposedly the pods represented the three dominant forces of the fifties: conformity, paranoia, and alienation. The film was designed to confront America for exhibiting similar characteristics during the Cold War.[59] A Nicholas Ray western, *Johnny Guitar* (1953), featured a guitar-playing drifter (actor Sterling Hayden, HUAC informer) in the middle of a town feud between two women, saloon-owner Joan Crawford, who befriends outlaws, and upright citizen and banker, Mercedes McCambridge. Was the film intended to be a western parody or a political allegory about McCarthyism? If you accept the latter interpretation, then the outlaws represent the communists, Hayden is the former communist, Crawford the fellow traveler, and McCambridge the McCarthy-clone who manipulates the townspeople into "naming names," converting their fear and ignorance into an ugly lynch mob.[60] When the mob turns on the Crawford character, the script gives the actress an opportunity to address the crowd and deliver a speech against the making of false accusations (friendly witnesses and informers) and against the making of guilty judgments on the basis of the company she keeps (guilt by association). Such films reveal that there were at least a few in the industry who tried to counter the propaganda of the studios' anticommunist films.

Film Content

Except for a handful of serious films that confronted American racism and prejudice, Hollywood played it safe in the fifties, concentrating on musicals, Doris Day-Rock Hudson romantic comedies, crime thrillers, and westerns. This rather bland film diet is not so surprising since some of the very best Hollywood writers were on the blacklist. Between 1938 and the 1947 HUAC hearings, the eight major Hollywood studios released over 3100 films, about 600, or one-fifth, were scripted by radicals or leftists. It is this group of writers who combined to win four Oscars and receive nineteen Academy Award nominations. No wonder the studios considered them a valuable commodity, paid them well (Dalton Trumbo received $3000 per week from MGM while Ring Lardner, Jr. received a salary of $2000 per week from Twentieth Century Fox), and agreed to let some of them write under pseudonyms or use "fronts" to submit their work.[61]

Why did these talented artists turn to the left? What attracted them to Marx and the Communist Party? Perhaps author Vivian Gornick summarized it best when she wrote:

It was characteristic of that world that during those hours at the kitchen table I didn't know we were poor. I didn't know that in those places beyond the streets of my Bronx neighborhood we were without power, position, material or social existence. I only knew that I felt the same electric thrill as when Rouben, my Yiddish teacher, pressed my upper arm between two bony fingers and, his eyes shining behind thick glasses, said to me: "Ideas, dolly, ideas. Without them, life is nothing. With them, life is everything." For the people among whom I grew this intensity of feeling was transmitted through Marxism as interpreted by the CPUSA. At the indisputable center of their world stood the Communist Party. It was the Party whose awesome structure harnessed that inchoate emotion which, with the force of a tidal wave drove millions of people around the globe toward Marxism. It was the Party whose moral authority gave shape and substance to the abstractions. It was the Party that brought to life a remarkably far-reaching sense of comradeship. For of this Party it could rightly be said, as Richard Wright in his bitterest moment did say, "There was no agency in the world so capable of making men feel the earth and the people upon it as the Communist Party."[62]

Hollywood released more than 2500 movies during the decade of the fifties; less than 1 percent were serious dramas that confronted the important social problems of the time. The witch hunt in Hollywood had succeeded in silencing dissent and stifling creativity. It was not until the mid sixties that Hollywood returned to the exploration of contemporary social issues.[63] Two decades would pass before the film industry recovered from the wounds inflicted by the Red Scare hysteria.

REEL POLITICIANS

Idealists, Saviors and Villains

CHAPTER SIX

"The sad duty of politics is to establish justice in a sinful world."

REINHOLD NIEBUHR

"It could probably be shown by facts and figures that there is no distinctly native American criminal class except Congress."

MARK TWAIN

"There's an honest graft, and I'm an example of how it works … Ain't it perfectly honest to charge a good price and make a profit on my investment and foresight? Of course, it is."

GEORGE WASHINGTON PLUNKITT OF TAMMANY HALL

"There are two great actors in the country today. You are the other one."

FDR TO ORSON WELLES

"Only two things can wreck a political career in this town [Washington]—being caught with a live boy or a dead girl."

FROM *TRUE COLORS*

Ehrlichman: "We don't mind being called crooks, but not stupid crooks."
Nixon: "That's right. We know we'll never convince them on our morality, but do they think we're that dumb?"

THE NEW NIXON TAPES

There is a marvelous scene at the end of Robert Redford's *The Candidate* (1972) where he is sitting in his hotel suite surrounded by staff and friends in celebration of his election to the United States Senate. In walks his father (Melvyn Douglas), the former governor of California and consummate wheeler-dealer. Douglas approaches Redford, who is seated on the bed looking rather glum, and with a quizzical grin that runs from ear to ear, says: "Congratulations, son. You're a politician now." If there is one scene in all the films on American politics that would discourage, if not seriously damage, the interest of young people to run for political office, this is it! The scene's cynicism offends two vital concepts in a democratic society; first, the notion that the electorate believes politicians hold office as a public trust and second, that politics is an honorable and commendable profession. Speaking facetiously, Congress ought to make it unlawful for any American youngster to view this scene on the ground that it could destroy whatever is left of the civic virtue. Does the scene represent reality or Hollywood's version of the U.S. Congress?

On second thought, Hollywood has not always been kind to the presidency either. Recent Hollywood presidents, such as Bill Pullman fighting alien invaders in *Independence Day* (1996) or Harrison Ford socking it to hijackers who have taken over his plane in *Air Force One* (1997) reinforce a macho image that defies credibility as well as historical accuracy. Americans expect their presidents to reside in Camelot, but also mingle with common folk, be compassionate but act tough against external enemies, be human but not too seriously flawed. The reel presidents—Pullman and Ford—however, are glamorous heroes, creative inventions rather than real people. Most American presidents have understood the difference between fact and fantasy, but occasionally a Nixon or a Reagan is inspired by the fictions on the screen: Nixon bombing Cambodia the day after viewing *Patton* (1970), Reagan watching *Rambo: First Blood, Part II* (1985), to reinforce his "evil empire" foreign policy against the old Soviet Union.[1]

Since Hollywood deals in illusions and fantasies, the industry should find politics an attractive partner in the entertainment business. Not true. Only a fraction of the more than 180,000 films turned out by Hollywood over the past century actually feature American politics as the primary subject and politicians as the central characters. Historically, the studios decided that serious films on politics would not fill theater seats. Whenever a studio disregarded the conventional wisdom and made a film depicting American politics, either the finished product was accorded a bland treatment or the plot took liberties with the facts and the historical record. Moreover, in films that attempt to present serious domestic or foreign policy issues, the script is likely to focus on the personal foibles of the political characters, dwell on their private lives rather than the actual workings of the legislative process, and ignore the means by which the president reaches a policy decision.[2] Seldom does the industry portray evil politicians as expressions of institutional wrongdoing or virtuous politicians as defenders of constitutional principles.[3]

However, it is not the case that the film industry has ignored American politics completely. Several silent films, e.g., *The Senator* (1915) dealt with politics, but Hollywood's interest in the subject waned, only to be revived again in the thirties and sixties. Hollywood preferred political biographies in the 1930s, including three on Lincoln. In the sixties, four feature films (*The Best Man, Dr. Strangelove, Fail Safe,* and *Seven Days in May*) released in 1964 centered on the presidency. Hollywood returned to the presidency in the 1990s with a vengeance, placing the Oval Office center stage in over two dozen major features. These screen presidents are a varied bunch: they are romantically involved (*The American President*), womanizers and sex abusers (*Executive Power, Absolute Power*), macho patriots (*Independence Day, Air Force One*), enigmatic political figures (*Nixon*), fatherly figures (*Dick*), wimpy impostors, (*Dave*), calculating politicians (*The Contender*), decisive leaders (*Thirteen Days*), and political hacks, (*My Fellow Americans*). Quite a mélange.

Despite these bursts of periodic interest, Hollywood has avoided the treatment of American politicians because ideological or partisan politics is bad box office. Whenever attempted, the politics is diluted. Essentially, what happens in Hollywood is that if politics is the central story line, it serves as a framework for more familiar plots, such as assassination thrillers or as an ambiance for love and romance.

AMERICAN POLITICS ON SCREEN

When Hollywood enters the world of politics, it often does so through the back door. Political activities in feature films frequently express individual behavior that is motivated by self-interest; bad politicians act out of greed and ambition while good politicians act in response to the deeds of bad politicians. Few act out of a deep commitment to democratic principles. Observe the intentions of the screen politicians below and draw your own conclusion.

Political Campaigns and Conventions

Political elections provide scriptwriters with a dramatized event around which to develop a narrative that can be melodramatic, exciting, and funny. Some of Hollywood's finest political films have depicted the electoral process. Hollywood became interested in political elections as screen fare as early as the 1930s with the release of several films on campaign politics, including *Judge Priest* (1934), a star vehicle for humorist Will Rogers. This early John Ford film has Rogers playing a small town judge in 1890s Kentucky, dispensing justice and wisdom equally from his courtroom seat and his front porch. Although up for reelection, Rogers's judge seldom leaves his home or works up a sweat campaigning. The film is best viewed for contrast with contemporary elections dominated by high technology and media promotion.

Hollywood took a hiatus from the political campaign film until the post-World War II era when three features, *The Dark Horse* (1946), *The Farmer's Daughter* (1947) and *State of the Union* (1948) hit theater screens. *The Dark Horse* is a serious political drama about a veteran of the Second World War who runs for city alderman only to discover that the local political machine is exploiting his war record for personal gain. In *The Farmer's Daughter*, a young Swedish woman (Loretta Young) goes to work as a maid for a wealthy family and falls in love with the son (Joseph Cotten), a congressman. Billed as a comedy in the advertisements, most of the screen action concerns the budding romance between the two stars. When a local congressman dies in office, Young decides to run for the vacant seat even though her lover's family supports her opponent. She is successful despite an attempted smear by the opposition. The script, however, avoids the details of a real election. The film's political campaign consumes about five minutes of screen time; a majority of the political events occur off-camera and the most impressive political speech is given by a supporting actor rather than the candidate herself.

Frank Capra's *State of the Union* features Spencer Tracy and Katherine Hepburn in one of their nine films together. The plot has Tracy playing Grant Matthews, a successful and idealistic industrialist, persuaded by an ambitious newspaper owner to run for the presidential nomination on the Republican ticket. Mary (Hepburn), his estranged wife, reluctantly agrees to accompany her husband on the campaign trail. Except for one or two unnecessary scenes in an airplane, the film sticks to the business of electioneering, which allows the major characters to make speeches expressing Capra's liberal philosophy and general belief in the wisdom and essential decency of the common man. When Grant discovers that the party bosses are using him, he withdraws from the race but not from politics. Reunited with his wife at film's end, he intends to go to the convention and influence the selection of the Republican candidate. The film is best remembered today for the one-liner, "Politics makes strange bedfellows."

During the days of the Red Scare, Hollywood was too preoccupied with the HUAC hearings and Cold War themes to be concerned with political elections. The industry returned to the subject in the sixties. On the surface, John Ford's *The Man Who Shot Liberty Valance* (1962) appears to be a traditional western with John Wayne playing rancher-gunman Tom Doniphon. But the story quickly shifts to the other major character, a tenderfoot Eastern lawyer named Ransom Stoddard (James Stewart), who, in contrast to Doniphon's penchant for violence, believes the West can be civilized by adherence to the rule of law rather than the gun. When Stoddard is beaten and threatened by the town bully and outlaw, Liberty Valance (Lee

Marvin), it is Doniphon who comes to his rescue in the climactic shootout. The town folks, however, believe it was Stoddard's gun that rid the community of Valance; an act that makes Stoddard the town hero and catapults him into politics, first as a representative to the territorial legislature and later as one of the state's U.S. senators. Ford intends Stoddard's political career to parallel the development of the West from a lawless frontier into statehood and civilization. While Stoddard goes east to civilized Washington, Doniphon remains in the West. Doniphon's death signals the passing of the Old West as well; its future development delivered into the hands of businessmen, railroaders, shopkeepers, and law-abiding citizens like Ransom Stoddard. The fact that Stoddard profited from a lie should not be overlooked; his political career was built on a fabrication he benefited from because he chose not to disclose the truth to the electorate. The local editor, who knows the truth about Stoddard, refuses to print the story, preferring to keep the legend alive. Released at a time when campaign managers, public relation specialists, and media experts had begun to market candidates as commodities to be sold to the public like commercial products, Ford's film is a reminder of the significant role that myth plays in American politics.

The first Hollywood entry into convention politics, *The Best Man* (1964), was based on the Gore Vidal play. The action revolves around the politics of a presidential nominating convention. The film studios, apparently, were so apprehensive about offending Democrats or Republicans that the convention depicted in *The Best Man* remains unidentified. The narrative has two candidates seeking the endorsement of the incumbent president, who is dying of cancer. William Russell (Henry Fonda), the principled secretary of state, is seeking the nomination against a rival candidate, the ambitious and unscrupulous U.S. senator, Dan Cantwell (Cliff Robertson). The president's endorsement will virtually guarantee the nomination. Which one will the president select? That question lies at the heart of the drama because each candidate has a flawed past—Russell's bout with depression raises questions of his competency under stress while Cantwell's homosexual affair fosters concerns about his electability. In the end, the president selects neither, throwing his support instead behind a third candidate who goes on to win the nomination. *The Best Man* is rich in backroom convention politics as it explores the characteristics that make for an "ideal" presidential candidate. It also proved prescient since during the 1972 campaign, Senator Tom Eagleton's vice presidential candidacy was derailed when the media revealed that he had suffered a nervous breakdown and received electroshock therapy.

Of the more recent films about political campaigning, Robert Redford's *The Candidate* (1972) is usually singled out for acclamation. Scripted by a former staffer for Eugene McCarthy's 1968 presidential race, the film concerns a liberal antipoverty lawyer, Bill McKay (Redford), son of the former governor of California. When the Democrats ask him to run against the incumbent Republican U.S. senator, McKay is reluctant to join the race. He finally consents after receiving assurance that he can discuss the real issues and run his own campaign, even if doing so will guarantee his defeat. Since he is expected to lose, McKay enters the race discussing the issues to bored audiences. When he outperforms his opponent in a televised debate and his election chances improve according to the polls, McKay relinquishes more and more of the control over his campaign to his managers, who exploit his good looks and charisma. On the campaign trail, McKay begins to spout ready-made slogans and clichés while he accepts the support of his father's old cronies. To illustrate that he has become a media-managed candidate, the film contains a scene at a women's luncheon where McKay's speech is reduced to the apology: "I'm sorry, ladies, that I ate all the shrimp." McKay smiles, the women laugh. Removed from his own ideals, McKay has succumbed to the manipulation of his campaign managers. He wins the election, and as the reinvented U.S. senator-elect in the fade-out scene, McKay asks his manager, "What do we do now?" Criticized by some as lacking substance,[4] The Candidate, on the contrary, warns the audience of the pitfalls of contemporary electioneering where superficiality is preferred over hard content, personal appeal is celebrated over intelligence and ethical principles, and thirty-second campaign sound bites are favored over detailed analysis of complex issues. Can an image-created candidate win a national election? After the two terms of Ronald Reagan, is there anyone today who would wager against a successful race by a Tom Cruise, a Kevin Costner, or a Tom Hanks? The successful election of prowrestler Jessie Ventura and movie star Arnold Schwarzenegger to governorships reminds us that politics is as much a celebrity game today as popular entertainment.

Actor Tim Robbins depicted a nineties version of a political campaign in his film *Bob Roberts* (1992). Whereas Redford's film was a commercial and critical success, *Bob Roberts* failed at the box office. Robbins, who wrote the script and served as director, plays the title character, a self-made, guitar-playing right-wing conservative millionaire from Pennsylvania, who runs for the U.S. Senate. Filmed in mock documentary style, *Bob Roberts* unfolds as a diary of a political campaign, from the initial announcement to Election Day victory. Roberts's campaign slogan is PRIDE, which he displays on his motorbus as he tours the state campaigning against drugs, sexual promiscuity, and wasteful social programs. On the surface, Roberts is a sincere charmer who preaches family values and national pride but off-camera is prone to dirty campaign tricks. When a local reporter threatens to expose him as a fraud, Roberts and his staff plot a fake assassination attempt on the candidate's life. The strategy works as the reporter is killed, but Roberts supposedly is seriously wounded and confined to a wheelchair. However, in the ironic conclusion, Roberts is seen tapping his feet under the blanket that covers his legs as he celebrates his election victory with a song. The film's failure at the box office may have been due to its portrayal of a gullible electorate; an assessment too harsh for American audiences to accept.

The latest entries in the political campaigning mold include Mike Nichols's *Primary Colors* (1998) and Warren Beatty's *Bulworth* (1998). *Primary Colors*, based on the book by a former Clinton staffer, makes no attempt to hide the fact that it is a recreation of the Clinton 1992 presidential campaign. The John Travolta character is a southern governor with a weakness for Krispy Kremes and women, not necessarily in that order. *Bulworth*, however, is quite different. In this film, Beatty plays a despondent U.S. senator whose life is transformed after he falls in love with a political activist. He changes campaign strategy in his reelection bid and adopts rap music to express his ideas on campaign financing and race relations. Knowing that he has sold out to corporate interests, Bulworth expresses his dismay in rapper style:

> One man, one vote/now izzat real?
> The name of the game is/let's make a deal
> Now the people got their problems/the haves and have-nots
> But the ones that make me listen/pay for 30-second spots . . .
> You've been taught in this country/there's speech that is free
> But free do not get you/no spots on tv
> If you want to have senators/not on the take
> Then give them free airtime/they won't have to fake.

The film has many of the attributes of *Bob Roberts*, particularly in using comedy to deliver its timely political message of the necessity for campaign finance reform. Beatty, a life-long liberal who worked with the Democratic Party and the McGovern, Bobby Kennedy, and Gary Hart campaigns, however, could not deliver a political message film that audiences wanted to see.

Probably the most realistic presentation of a political campaign remains *Tanner '88* (1988), the result of the collaboration of director Robert Altman and cartoonist Gary Trudeau. The film has never been shown in theaters but aired originally as a miniseries on cable television. *Tanner '88* runs six hours and depicts in documentary style the story of the 1988 presidential race from the New Hampshire primary to the convention in Atlanta as viewed through the eyes of one Democratic hopeful, Jack Tanner. Tanner is a divorced former congressman with a college-aged daughter and a lover whom he meets occasionally for trysts while on the campaign trail. Despite his academic credentials (he holds a Ph.D. in economics), Tanner is very much a manufactured candidate—the product of his campaign staff. Similar in style to Altman's earlier film, *Nashville* (1975), *Tanner '88* weaves a rich tapestry of American electioneering that includes attempted assassinations, dirty tricks, media-styled campaign slogans, and appearances by real presidential candidates Bob Dole, Gary Hart, Bruce Babbitt, and Pat Robertson. Whether the series impressed viewers as the real campaign or whether some voters decided to play a prank, the fact remains that the fictitious Jack Tanner actually received write-in votes in the November election. By interweaving Tanner together with the real candidates in the New Hampshire and Tennessee primaries, Altman was able to depict the grungy work of running a major campaign along with the gaffs and disasters. For instance, when Tanner is speaking to an outdoor rally in New Hampshire he is upstaged by a group of snowmobilers. Later, when he attends a quilting party with his daughter, the women are more interested in his daughter than in his prepared remarks. As the campaign moves toward the convention and Democratic candidates begin to drop out of the race, Tanner's remaining opponents are Michael Dukakis and Jesse Jackson. In an effort to influence convention delegates, Tanner announces his Cabinet choices, which include, among others, Ralph Nader, Gloria Steinheim, Barbara Jordan, and Robert Redford. But when Jackson releases his votes to Dukakis at the convention, Tanner's chances for the nomination are squashed. At film's end, Tanner turns down a Cabinet post in the Dukakis administration while he ponders a presidential race as an independent. Taking full advantage of the expanded running time, Altman produced a commercial film on political campaigns that is eclipsed only by documentaries like *The War Room* and *A Perfect Candidate*. The Sundance channel aired *Tanner '88* during the spring of 2004 when the Democratic primaries were being held, complete with updated material.

Political Machines

Hollywood movies about political machines usually depict two very different attitudes about politics. On the one hand, the films portray the machine as a monolithic force that controls votes and remains in power through corrupt deals made by self-serving politicians and justified on grounds of political necessity. On the other hand, the existing machine becomes the target of reform politicians who overthrow it only to succumb to the temptations provided by absolute power.

What exactly is a political machine? Most political scientists agree that any acceptable definition must include a political party organization, longevity, and the exchange of patronage and social services for Election Day votes. In the U.S. the machine was primarily associated with big cities and with the arrival of an immigrant population that required jobs, housing, and assistance with the English language. Ellis Island became the primary arrival point for immigrants from Europe, who were met at the Customs House by Tammany Hall bosses and helped with the assimilation process into their new environment. In exchange for this assistance, immigrants were asked to vote for Democratic candidates, an arrangement that kept Tammany Hall in control of New York City for virtually eighty years. George Washington Plunkitt, ward boss for the city's Fifteenth Assembly District, explained the secret of Tammany's power: understand human nature, familiarize yourself with the local neighborhood, and make government friendly and personal.[5]

Films that depict a cynical view of machine politics include Preston Sturges's *The Great McGinty* (1940) and *The Glass Key* (1942), based on the Dashiel Hammett novel. The Sturges film is a satirical look at big-city politics with a moral message that honesty in politics does not pay. On the other hand, *The Glass Key* depicts both reformers and machine bosses as double-crossing, unscrupulous politicians, reducing political reform to changing personnel but not policies. Although Frank Capra's *Meet John Doe* (1941) has a happy ending, the film's message is that the masses are easily swayed by sentimentality and democratic clichés, weaknesses that leave the people vulnerable to domination by political machines.

Can there be a decent political boss? Novelist Edwin O'Connor thought so in *The Last Hurrah* (1958), which John Ford transferred to the big screen. In this paean to Irish politics, Spencer Tracy plays Frank Skeffington, a Boston political boss who resembles the charismatic Beantown mayor Frank Curley. Skeffington is a wily old politician, ruthless yet charming, whose power base rests on personal favors and debts collected at election time. Skeffington is the consummate politician, even campaigning at the wake of Jocko, a not particularly admired constituent. Skeffington makes sure, however, that a crowd shows up at the wake to pay tribute to Jocko, who now has more friends in death than he ever had in life. In the film, personal politics are no match for a sophisticated television crusade by his opponent in the new era of media-based campaigns. Skeffington loses his bid for a fourth term, a victim of mediated politics. While *The Last Hurrah* is a nostalgic and romantic examination of machine politics, it does serve as an indictment of contemporary media-created politicians. After viewing *The Last Hurrah*, audiences may wonder whether the replacement of the political machine by reform candidates without character or concern for individual welfare actually has improved the public good.

Two decent politicians who are corrupted by machine politics turn up in *All the King's Men* (1949) and *City Hall* (1996). The former film was based on Robert Penn Warren's Pulitzer Prize winning novel and transferred to the screen with the message that unchecked power can destroy political reformers. Warren's novel is a thinly disguised biography of the political career of Louisiana governor Huey Long. In the film version, Broderick Crawford plays Willie Stark, a poor backwoods Southern lawyer who gains political power through a populist attack on state corruption. But once in office, Stark becomes as ruthless and corrupt as the political machine he ousted. Although Stark sets up a fascist government complete with thugs and goons and resorts to blackmail, beatings, and even murder, he remains popular with the masses because of his building projects, which create jobs, result in school improvements, and advance social programs. Stark's popularity reaches its peak after an unsuccessful impeachment attempt by the state legislature. Like the real Huey Long, Stark has his eye on the White House but an assassin's bullet cuts his political career short. After more than 200 years of American politics, Huey Long's regime in 1930s Louisiana came closest to homegrown fascism and a threat to democratic state government.[6]

In the other film, Al Pacino plays a beleaguered mayor in *City Hall* (1996), scripted by Ken Lipper, former deputy mayor in the Ed Koch administration, and filmed on location in New York City. *City Hall* relates the story of Mayor John Pappas (Pacino), a popular and liberal mayor, who has had to make deals with the political bosses, especially Frank Anselmo's (Danny Aiello) Kings County political leader, in order to rebuild the city, create jobs, and foster race relations. This richly detailed film portrays the political process as a series of compromises and tradeoffs; Pacino's Mayor plays this game until one unacceptable deal is struck that comes back to haunt him and the other politicians and judges involved. The film's location shots and finely detailed characters will prove recognizable to New Yorkers with memories of city politics in the 1980s, complete with revelations of political cover-ups, shady deals, and personal corruption. *City Hall* will help New Yorkers to recall the scandal-ridden Koch administration in the eighties that sent one political boss to prison and another to commit suicide.[7] Pacino's alter-ego and conscience is the deputy mayor, Kevin Calhoun (John Cusack), whose investigation uncovers murder and drug deals that ultimately destroy the political aspirations of his boss. At its center, *City Hall*, questions whether any elected official, however decent, can be an effective politician without support from the power brokers. This film comes closest to challenging the simplistic textbook explanation of machine politics as evil *per se* and reformers as "white knight" politicians in its depiction of the realities of governing our cities where policy choices are reduced to compromises among legitimate, but competing, interests.

Capital Crimes and Misdemeanors

A number of very good dramatic films exploit the Washington, D.C., location in narratives that both praise and damn the federal government. Foremost among this group is Frank Capra's film, *Mr. Smith Goes to Washington*. Jimmy Stewart's character, Jefferson Smith, boy ranger and ingenuous idealist, is appointed to the Senate because he is expected to serve as a patsy for his state's corrupt political machine, headed by Jim Taylor (Edward Arnold). Incidentally, Arnold made a film career out of playing corrupt politicians and unscrupulous characters. Capra's movies often revolve around decent, common men, exploited by the rich and the powerful, who, nonetheless, manage to triumph over their adversaries in the final reel. In order for Smith to win his battle against the political bosses, however, he must engage in a filibuster. While Capra utilizes this political tactic for a good cause in the film, historically the filibuster has been employed to defeat and delay liberal legislation such as civil rights.

Meanwhile, in *Advise and Consent* (1962), the film version of the Allen Drury novel, the appointment of a secretary of state provides the basis for the drama. In the American political system, the presidential appointment of a cabinet-level post, federal judgeship, or ambassadorship requires senatorial approval. When the film president (Franchot Tone) nominates the controversial Robert Leffingwell (Henry Fonda) to be secretary of state, the Senate divides over his selection. Foes of the president take the appointment as an opportunity to settle old scores. Dixiecrats (Southern Democrats) object to Leffingwell's liberalism while conservatives are concerned that he is soft on communism. To neutralize one of Leffingwell's Senate supporters (Don Murray), the opposition threatens to expose a homosexual incident in his past, which leads the young senator to commit suicide. At the end, the president dies and the vice president decides to name his own candidate. While the film reflects America's Cold War concern of Soviet expansion and the need for policy-making officials to be committed to the containment of communism as the cornerstone of foreign policy, it also exposes Capitol Hill as a ruthlessly competitive place.

The Seduction of Joe Tynan (1979), a film scripted by and starring Alan Alda, is another film with a plot grounded in the politics of the U.S. Senate. Alda plays the title character, a young, liberal senator and contented family man. The political issue at the forefront of this film is a presidential appointment to the U.S. Supreme Court, which requires Senate confirmation. Southern senators, led by senior senator Birney (Melvyn Douglas), favor a candidate that the NAACP characterizes as "racist" and unacceptable. Both sides lobby for Tynan's support. Should he side with the black lobby or should he do the expedient thing and promote his career by standing with the Southern coalition? Tynan's eventual decision to oppose the Southerners' candidate aborts the nomination and rewards him with the political plum of making the presidential nominating speech at the convention, a selection normally reserved for potential presidential candidates.[8] Although Tynan makes the right choice politically, he makes the wrong choice morally when he has an affair with a Southern lobbyist (Meryl Streep) that almost destroys his marriage. But true to Hollywood form, reconciliation, if not repentance, is implied at the end along with fulfillment of presidential ambitions.

Legally Blonde II (2003) aspires to duplicate the "Capresque" world of Jefferson Smith but the film proves to be a poor substitute. In this sequel, Elle Wells (Reese Witherspoon) has graduated from Harvard Law and is preparing for her upcoming wedding. She gets sidetracked into becoming an advocate for animal rights when she discovers that her pet Chihuahua's mother is being used to test cosmetics at a Boston research lab. Shocked by this revelation, Witherspoon goes to Washington to persuade Congress to enact animal rights legislation. She is successful but the film's simplistic approach to politics led one film scholar to observe: "The film's preposterous premise that silly costuming and naïve rhetorical masturbation will win the day is a disservice to those who seek real change."[9]

Political skullduggery is at the heart of a couple of films about Washington politics that deal with the abuse of political power. *True Colors* (1991) tracks the careers of two bright law school students, Peter Burton (John Cusack) and Tim Garrity (James Spader). Burton is an ambitious manipulator with a Nixon personality, who chooses politics as a career while his law school friend, Garrity, joins the Justice Department. Burton romances and marries the daughter of an influential senator (Richard Widmark) and becomes his father-in-law's aide as part of his ambitious political scheme. Using an assortment of dirty tricks, blackmail, and his father-in-law's money and influence, Burton decides to run for Congress. Meanwhile, Garrity is content to prosecute cases for the government. Their paths cross when Burton implicates Garrity in a shady deal with a land developer, which guarantees Burton the developer's financial support. To save his job and his reputation, Garrity turns informer, becoming Burton's campaign manager in a plan to secure incriminating evidence for a Justice Department prosecution. At film's end, Burton wins his congressional seat, loses his wife, and likely will go to prison for his illegal dealings with the land developer. Still the final scene implies that an unrepentant Burton is ready to resume his political career after serving his prison term, which is not an encouraging assessment of what Hollywood thinks of the American electorate.

More serious crimes are committed in *No Way Out* (1987) where Lt. Cmdr. Tom Farrell (Kevin Costner) is a Naval intelligence officer assigned to locate a suspected mole inside the Pentagon. The mole story is part of an elaborate cover-up to protect the secretary of defense (Gene Hackman), who accidentally has killed his mistress during a lover's quarrel. Farrell is the one person who knows the mole story is a fake because the secretary's mistress was his mistress, too. Worse yet, Farrell is the last person to see her alive. Thus, the film's Washington, D.C., locale serves to authenticate this suspenseful thriller in which Farrell must expose the real killer before the authorities turn on him. While much of the action in the film takes place inside the Pentagon, the audience receives virtually no information about this octagonal building or the workings of the defense department, except that the secretary is a cheat and a coward who is willing to allow someone else to be punished for a crime he committed.

A portrait of political in-fighting is at the heart of Rod Lurie's film, *The Contender* (2000), deliberately released one month before the presidential election. Democratic president Jackson Evans (Jeff Bridges), a good ol' boy who loves to eat, bowl and smoke tobacco, nominates the female senator from Ohio (Joan Allen) to fill the vacant vice presidency position. However, the villainous Chair of the House Judiciary Committee, Republican Shelly Runyon (Gary Oldman), opposes her nomination and sets out to destroy her candidacy through the release of photos that supposedly show Allen involved in a college sex orgy. Although the charges are false and the president urges her to fight back, Allen refuses to respond to them or to withdraw her candidacy. Runyon is depicted as such a mean-spirited, evil character that Joe McCarthy would have been proud of him. After the film's release, Oldman, who also was one of the producers, accused DreamWorks, Steven Spielberg's company, of deliberately changing the film's emphasis to support a Democratic agenda.[10] The true story of the backstage politicking is unlikely to be made public, but the incident demonstrates that at least some people in Hollywood take their politics seriously.

Macho Men

With few exceptions, the film industry has treated the American presidency with respect and dignity, if not reverence. Before the Second World War, the films of American presidents usually were historical biographies in which the future presidents were portrayed as statesmen. In the 1990s, Hollywood turned to representations of strong and decisive leaders, capable of handling Cold War machinations and crisis situations. The portrayal of Presidents Thomas Whitmore (Bill Pullman in *Independence Day*) and James Marshall (Harrison Ford in *Air Force One*) as action-adventure heroes appealed to the American public as both films grossed over $100 million. President Whitmore almost single-handedly takes on and defeats enemy aliens in outer space combat while president Marshall engages in hand-to-hand combat to save his wife and family. When Air Force One is taken over by Russian terrorists, President Marshall decides to stay on the plane rather than take the safety chute. As a combat veteran and Medal of Honor winner, who refuses to negotiate with terrorists, Marshall is the right person to handle this situation. Single-handedly, he kills all the terrorists and recaptures the plane. He is certainly no middle-aged, soft-bellied wimp of a president. During the struggle with the terrorist leader, Marshall overpowers him and shoves him out the open door yelling: "Get off my plane!" Audiences clapped and cheered, demonstrating that Americans prefer their presidents to be larger-than-life heroes as in the movies. No wonder Americans loved President Reagan; he too was perceived to be the dashing hero of his films.

Other recent activist fictional presidents include Stanley Anderson (*Armageddon* 1998) and Morgan Freeman (*Deep Impact* 1998) who try to save the United States and the world from an asteroid and Kevin Pollak (*Deterrence* 2000) who exercises firm leadership in a foreign policy crisis despite being trapped in a blizzard. Pollak's president, Walter Emerson, is campaigning in Colorado when he and his staff get caught in a snowstorm and take refuge in a local diner. When Emerson learns that Saddam's son has reinvaded Kuwait and overrun UN and American forces, he is faced with a major international crisis. Turning the diner into a mini war room, Emerson and his staff discuss their options, which are limited because the majority of American troops are stationed near North Korea. At this point, Emerson decides that his only recourse is to threaten the Iraqis with a nuclear attack unless their armies withdraw from Kuwaiti soil. On the surface, Emerson appears to be a resolute leader who refuses to negotiate with terrorists. As portrayed, his decision to bomb Baghdad brings the world to the brink of nuclear war. These strong fictional presidents may help to explain the rising popularity of macho men in American political life. Can it be that Hollywood has profiled the future occupants of the Oval Office where only the Venturas and Schwarzeneggers need apply?

Real Presidents vs Reel Presidents

Without doubt, the office of the presidency has changed since the early days of the Republic. The evolving transformation in the power, prestige, and expansion of the presidency reached its zenith after World War II. Whereas the early presidents had small staffs and few advisers, the contemporary Executive Branch has created a bureaucracy of its own. To understand this growth, President Wilson employed a full-time staff of 7 aides and Franklin Roosevelt only 5 more. Neither administration had staff layering where aides hired additional assistants. In FDR's second term, the White House employed 45 full-time staff. By 1988 with Bush the elder in the Oval Office, the staff had swelled to 605.[11] It would be hard to imagine today's White House described as "relatively small, personal, and homey,"[12] a place where FDR's houseguests would be invited for dinner only to remain indefinitely. Winston Churchill, for example, stayed at the White House for weeks at a time. The environment was so friendly that FDR knew the names of the White House press corps and could be seen, on occasion, joking with them. That was partly due to FDR's personal charm and his ability to control and manipulate the media. That talent helps to explain why FDR was often photographed and filmed sitting down behind a desk, his wheelchair hidden from view. The personal relationship that existed between a small, still manageable media and the president is one consideration in understanding why their private lives went unreported. Chastity and fidelity were certainly not the reason why the public was kept ignorant of their mistresses and their affairs while they occupied the Oval Office.

The film industry joined the political media as coconspirators in protecting the public image of the early presidents. In pre-WWII Hollywood, the studios made only two kinds of films involving presidents: biographical and fictional. For the first half-century, historical-biographical films dominated the studio output. From 1908 until the 1950s, more than half of the presidential films were biographies of some sort.[13] Although many film historians consider these factually inaccurate in detail, they treated the president and the office with respect. The fact that Hollywood produced over 130 films, including impersonations, of Abraham Lincoln, reflects on the industry's requirements under the old Production Code and on the loyalty of the early studio heads. Lincoln is a perfect example. Three major films about Lincoln's life before his ascendancy to the presidency were distributed in the 1930s and in each one Lincoln is depicted as humble, modest, even saintly. From this one-dimensional characterization it seems that Hollywood wanted Americans to believe that Lincoln lacked personal ambition, political skills, and character flaws.

Hollywood treated the real presidents with respect and deference but their fictional presidents in pre-WWII movies were men of action who took risks, sometimes stretching the boundaries of constitutionality. As one illustration, take the screen president Judd Hammond (Walter Houston) in *Gabriel Over the White House* (1933). He begins as an indifferent and corrupt politician who is transformed into a decent and caring leader after a visit from the angel Gabriel. At the beginning of the film, Hammond acts like real president Hoover, expressing political platitudes but doing nothing to meet the challenge of the Depression. When the angel Gabriel visits him after a serious automobile accident puts him at death's door, Hammond is miraculously converted into a political activist, taking steps for economic recovery, rooting out political corruption, and supporting the efforts for world peace.[14] Unfortunately, his methods border on the dictatorial—dismissing the legislature, creating military tribunals, organizing the unemployed into Brownshirt cadre. The public, meanwhile, saw in the screen Hammond a welcome relief from the real do-nothing Hoover.[15]

Hollywood continued to turn out screen biographies of presidents after World War II on an occasional basis. What might be described as "old-fashioned" screen biographies were made of Wilson, Franklin Roosevelt, and Harry Truman (for cable TV). *Wilson* (1944) followed the president from his early years into the White House. *Sunrise at Campobello* (1960) focused on FDR's battle with polio and ends with his nomination speech at the 1928 Democratic Convention. On the other hand, *Truman* (1995) is more interested in the decisions he faced during his time in office. The three were reverential towards their subjects. Usually the action unfolded chronologically and these screen biographies were intended to be mythic personal stories of human courage and sacrifice rather than controversial political tracts. What moviegoer will forget President Wilson's stirring speeches or FDR's efforts to battle polio? Uplifting yes, but biased presentations because *Wilson* (1944) ignored the president's prejudicial views on race and gender while Roosevelt's adultery was omitted from *Sunrise at Campobello* (1960).

However, the presidential biography of Harry Truman, made for cable distribution rather than commercial theaters, was more honest than most. The film
reverts to the format of the pre-World War II biography where the film's intent is
to elevate Truman's presidency above the 32 percent approval rating his administration received in 1952 at the end of its second term. Gary Sinise is a very credi-
ble Truman, in both appearance and mannerisms. Beginning with the 1948
campaign, the film unfolds in a series of flashbacks, commencing in 1917 with the
young Truman volunteering for the First World War and ending in his second term.
Between these two events, Truman enters politics with the support of the Pendergast
Kansas City machine and ascends to the presidency on the death of FDR. The second half concentrates on the difficult issues Truman faced in the White House:
namely, whether to use the atom bomb during World War II; how to desegregate
the military; if he should seize the steel mills during the Korean War; how to
thwart Soviet aggression; whether to recognize the new state of Israel; and whether
he should fire the popular General MacArthur during the Korean conflict over issues
of authority and command. These momentous political issues, as usual in commercial films, are treated superficially during the 135-minute running time. Still,
Truman represents a more balanced approach to political biography.

It is hard to imagine that contemporary Hollywood would make a traditional
screen biography of even a dead president, let alone a living one. Live presidents pose
almost insurmountable problems for filmmakers and studios. A perfect example of
inherent problems with living presidents occurred when CBS made a miniseries
about the Reagans. The former president, suffering from Alzheimer's and living in
isolation on his Malibu ranch, apparently was portrayed in unflattering terms and
the public outcry led the network to cancel the program from its schedule. Whether
the portrayal was criticized for being in poor taste or considered politically incorrect, it reinforced the view that filming the biographies of living presidents can cause
as much trouble as having sex in the White House.

The change in practice from respectful and accepting to disrespectful and antiestablishment occurred sometime in the sixties. This was consistent with that era's
rejection of political hypocrisy that held the presidency sacrosanct. This attitude
influenced the perspective of many young filmmakers. With a few notable exceptions, the film studios were willing to examine the cherished institutions of
American life, from the military to the Oval Office. Beginning with the fictional
president Muffley in Kubrick's *Dr. Strangelove* (1964), American films have been
inhabited with national leaders who are weak and ineffectual, deranged and drunk-
en paranoids, passive-aggressive personality types, womanizers and sex abusers, liars
and scoundrels—enough characters to give democratic government a bad name. The
filmic assault on the presidency escalated to such a degree in the nineties that two

political scientists described the representation as ones of "shysters, sycophants, and sexual deviants."[16]

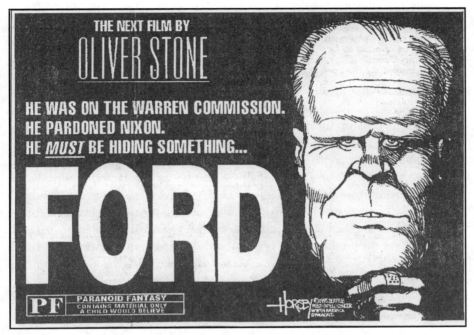

FIGURE 9. Ford cartoon: 1995. Reprinted with permission, *Seattle Post-Intelligencer*.

Two films about President Nixon would not have been made by pre-WWII Hollywood. Oliver Stone's *Nixon* (1995) reconstructs the presidency as a dark and secret place inhabited by an unstable leader. Stone's three-hour-plus film is a psychology study of a tortured and lonely man whose ego constantly requires social acceptance and public love. Although the Nixon family found fault with the portrayed image, George McGovern, Nixon's Democratic opponent in the 1972 presidential race, considered Stone's treatment to be balanced.[17] Stone himself thought Nixon a tragic figure, incapable of taming a system dominated by power elites, corporate greed, and political intrigue.[18] This theme is dramatically portrayed in the night scene at Lincoln Memorial where Nixon is confronted by student protesters. When Nixon tells the students that he wants to end the war, one protester replies: "The system won't let you stop it." Nixon repeats this observation as the Secret Service lead him away from the group. Stone tells Nixon's story in flashback, culminating in the Watergate break-in and his subsequent resignation. Despite his personal fall from grace, Nixon was still an important political player in the twentieth century, particularly in foreign affairs. Although he left office in disgrace, recent history has been kinder and remembers Nixon as the president who brought Vietnam to closure and who opened China to the West. If Stone's film is considered harsh, Robert Altman's view of Nixon in *Secret Honor* (1985) is absolutely devastating. Although not a screen biography *per se*, *Secret Honor* is a ninety-minute monologue filmed on a set designed to represent Nixon's private White House quarters, where actor Philip Baker Hall paces, raves, and curses his fate. Altman's Nixon is a sad, lonely figure who drinks too much and blames everyone else—Kennedy, Eisenhower, his mother—for his misfortune. This Nixon is a foul-mouthed whiner continually conjuring up enemies, real and imagined, and searching for scapegoats. The only prop missing from the film is a straightjacket.

Character issues are crucial to four other films about the presidency. In Clint Eastwood's *Absolute Power* (1997), the president (Gene Hackman) is portrayed as a boozy womanizer who enjoys rough sex. During a sexual encounter, the president's penchant for rough sexual foreplay goes too far and his mistress fights back. As she gets the upper hand and has the president on the ground, secret service men mistakenly believe the president's life is at risk and shoot her. As the story unfolds, the president's staff devises an elaborate cover-up scheme to hide the murder from the Washington police. This screen president lacks even one redeeming quality.

Dave, a 1993 comedy, is about another screen president whose extracurricular sexual activities drive the plot. Here the philandering president suffers a stroke and later dies during a sexual encounter with an aide. His wicked chief of staff decides to cover up the death by recruiting a presidential look-alike, Dave Kovic (Kevin Kline), to impersonate the dead president as part of a devious plot to deny the executive office to the liberal vice president.[19] Being a comedy, the plan naturally fails as the impostor Kovic becomes a more compassionate president than the one he replaced. *Dave* is a Hollywood fairy tale as Kovic returns to his real job at the end and wins the heart of the president's widow, too.

Another satire, Barry Levinson's *Wag the Dog* (1997) finds the occupant of the Oval Office in deep trouble as he is accused of molesting a Girl Scout (no less) during a White House tour. Although this deed drives the screenplay, the president does not appear on the screen. Instead his staff contrives an international crisis to distract the public. Finally, in *Primary Colors* presidential hopeful Governor Jack Stanton (John Travolta), a thinly veiled Clinton impersonation, is a womanizing junk-food addict who, liberal social policies notwithstanding, pitted against his campaign staffers when he decides to expose harmful material about his opponent's private life. The morality message delivered here seems to imply that the ends justify the means, that since Stanton would make the better president he is justified in blackmailing his opponent into quitting the race. These screen presidents have not only demystified the office; they have thrown dirt on it. Is Hollywood telling us that this is politics as usual?

Naturally, there are alternatives to these negative screen characterizations. The action heroes of *Independence Day* and *Air Force One* (actors Bill Pullman and Harrison Ford) are the presidents of our dreams. While it is true that a few of our national leaders were military men, they usually entered the White House a bit old for hand-to-hand combat. It is also true that a few of our presidents found romance in the White House similar to the fictional president Andrew Sheppard (Michael Douglas) in Rob Reiner's *The American President* (1995). Sheppard is a decent man, a widower trying to run the country and raise a daughter as well. When Sheppard falls in love with an environmental lobbyist (Annette Bening) his affair jeopardizes his reelection campaign. Furthermore, over the objections of his staff, Sheppard decides to support her environmental legislation. Whether any real politician would elevate love over politics is problematic, but at least it is romantic. Even Richard Nixon receives kind treatment in *Dick* (1999) as a gentle, fatherly figure to two teenage girls who become dog walkers for the White House. This spoof presents Nixon as a bumbling cookie-eating innocent, a deviation from his traditional image as the consummate scheming politician.

Political Assassinations

Conspiracies abound in the minds of Hollywood screenwriters because films about assassinations and attempted assassinations make highly dramatic movies, full of suspense and action sequences that draw well at the box office. History and cultural factors provide another reason why political assassinations interest the film studios. The United States is a country with a violent past, from the war for independence to slavery, the winning of the West, the systematic extermination of Native American tribes, the exploitation of women and children as cheap labor (many of them immigrants and illegals), the birth of organized crime during Prohibition, the development of urban street gangs in the post-World War II era, and the growth in violent crime by youthful offenders. These historical benchmarks provide the background for the crime rate in the United States today, including a high murder rate compared to other Western industrial nations.

Political figures have not escaped becoming victims of violence. Of the forty-three American presidents, ten have had attempts made on their lives. Four presidents actually died at the hands of assassins: Lincoln, Garfield, McKinley, and Kennedy. Six unsuccessful attempts were made: Presidents Jackson, Teddy Roosevelt, Franklin Roosevelt, Truman, Ford, and Reagan. Added to this list are the assassinations of such prominent political figures as Martin Luther King, Medgar Evers,

Bobby Kennedy, and Malcolm X, and the attack on former Governor George Wallace, which left him permanently paralyzed. It is a sobering statistic that almost one-fourth of American presidents have been the targets of assassins.

What do foreigners make of this? Do they believe violence is inherent in America's genetic makeup? Is it perhaps due to the racial and class economic differences that breed discontent and hate? Or might it be the increasingly gratuitous violence found in Hollywood films? Whatever the reason, officials and political figures in contemporary America perform their public duties at considerable personal risk.

Virtually all of Hollywood's assassination films have focused on the presidency, including John Frankenheimer's *The Manchurian Candidate* (1962), a film about a conspiracy to plant a communist functionary inside the White House. Although the final assassination attempt on the life of a U.S. senator is thwarted, the film's conspiracy theory preceded Oliver Stone by almost three decades. The film stars Laurence Harvey as Korean War POW, Raymond Shaw, who is brainwashed by the North Koreans and their communist allies into becoming a sleeper assassin. He returns to the States to be reunited with his mother, the politically ambitious wife of a right wing, McCarthyesque senator. Her intention is to promote her husband as vice president as a ruse to infiltrate communists into the White House. The plan is to have the president assassinated so her buffoonish husband would move into the Oval Office and she would be the power behind the throne. Her scheme is foiled by Harvey's former army commander, Lt. Bennett Marco (Frank Sinatra).

Forty years later, a modernized version of the film hit the theaters. The original *Manchurian Candidate* explored the new brainwashing technique of the fifties, with the villains part of a communist conspiracy. The film's paranoia resonated with the reality of the Cuban Missile Crisis. The 2004 version is not really a remake since the plot and some characters have changed. The villains here include an incestuous mother and her corporate power base, Manchurian Global (MC), a multinational equity fund. This time around, Marco (Denzel Washington) and Shaw (Liev Schreiber) are soldiers in the 1991 Persian Gulf War. Captured, they become unwitting henchmen for MC, since implanted with command chips, they are to serve as sleeper assassins. The scheme is to have Shaw enter national politics, aided by his mother (Meryl Streep), a powerful and influential U.S. Senator. Mother maneuvers her son onto the national ticket as vice president with the intention of assassinating the president, allowing Shaw to move into the Oval Office where Mother and MG can control him. With the assistance of an F.B.I. agent, Marco fortunately uncovers the conspiracy in time. The film contains timely references to terrorists, terror alerts, and intense security measures, but its paranoia of total control by a vague equity fund may no longer frighten audiences accustomed to the machinations of a Halliburton.

Frank Sinatra figured prominently in another assassination film, *Suddenly* (1954), where he plays the role of a presidential assassin. Sinatra portrays a disgruntled war veteran, John Baron, turned professional assassin, who arrives in the small town of Suddenly, California, to wait for the president to appear on his scheduled whistle-stop tour. To carry out the planned assassination, Baron and his gang take over a strategically located home, hold the family hostage and set up headquarters in a second floor room with a good vantage point from which to shoot the president. The motivation for the assassination attempt in this film is more personal than political: Baron believes that only by killing the president will he "become somebody." Because Baron's character slightly matched that of Lee Harvey Oswald, the film was temporarily withdrawn from television after 1963.[20]

A number of films have dealt directly with President Kennedy's assassination and its aftermath. In addition, several films used the assassination as a reference point from which to develop the subsequent narrative. For instance, the culmination of Robert Altman's metaphor on the seventies, *Nashville*, assembles all its characters together for the grand finale—an outdoor country-western songfest as a prelude to a political rally for fictitious presidential candidate, Hal Phillip Walker. Before Walker's motorcar reaches the Nashville Partheon Theater where the rally is being held, a disturbed young man shoots the lead singer, Barbara Jean,[21] frightening off the Walker cavalcade. As the shooter is subdued, the audience is persuaded to remain calm by the master of ceremonies, Haven Hamilton, who reminds the crowd "This isn't Dallas, this is Nashville." Although candidate Walker is never seen in the film, his name, nonetheless, ended up on several write-in ballots in 1976, just as the fictitious Jack Tanner, from the *Tanner '88* film, received votes in the 1988 presidential election.

Since the Kennedy assassination, five feature films have used this tragic event as the basis for screen material involving conspiracies of one kind or another. Robert Robins and Jerrold Post[22] maintain that the conspiracy theme is attractive to filmmakers because such plots appeal to the political paranoia by which the public seeks to explain tragedies that appear incomprehensible to them. An early entry into political paranoia, *Executive Action* (1973), is pure speculation, as screenwriter Dalton Trumbo reconstructs a conspiracy theory in which a group of millionaires, joined by military leaders, plot to kill Kennedy and use Oswald as the patsy. To give the appearance of being a documentary, the film is constructed around a daily log of events leading up to the assassination day and supported with newsreels from the Kennedy era that are interspersed with fictitious characters from the film. To further enhance its appearance of authenticity, the film's prologue contends that the evidence warrants its conspiracy conclusion. Actualy, the film is based on Mark Lane's book, *Rush to Judgment*, an attempt to prove a more plausible explanation than the "lone assassin" theory accepted by the Warren Commission Report. *Executive*

Action would have the audience believe that Kennedy was targeted for death because of three fears: that he would withdraw the United States from Vietnam, that he would eventually end nuclear testing, and that he would encourage the civil rights revolution. There is not, however, one shred of evidence to support these suspicions. Furthermore, the film advances a three-gunmen thesis rather than the Commission's "lone assassin" or the alternative, the two-gunmen theory. In this scenario, Oswald is guilty of murderous intentions, but innocent of the deed itself.

Two subsequent films, *The Parallax View* (1974) and *Winter Kills* (1979), have scenarios that parallel the Kennedy assassination. In *The Parallax View*, Joseph Frady (Warren Beatty) is a Seattle television reporter who stumbles into an old political assassination story. When Frady digs deeper into the mystery, he discovers parallels with the Kennedy assassination, such as the lone assassin being killed by the police and several eyewitnesses dying under mysterious circumstances. Sound familiar? Frady's investigation leads him to the monolithic Parallax Corporation, an organization that specializes in political assassinations. This discovery puts Frady's life in danger. In *Winter Kills*, Jeff Bridges is Nick Kegan, the younger brother of an assassinated president. Based on the Richard Condon novel, Kegan's investigation into his brother's death uncovers an implausible conspiracy. This time the assassination occurs in Philadelphia rather than Dallas. However, the convicted assassin is shot dead by a nightclub owner prior to trial. Why did the president have to be killed? The film script wants the audience to believe that the president had taken money from the mob but had failed to deliver favors as his part of the bargain. Kegan's family is obscenely rich and conspicuously dysfunctional—a womanizing bully of a father, an alcoholic mother, a weak older brother, and the dead president, who had a madame supply him with an endless array of women. If all this sounds too familiar, the similarities with the real Kennedys are meant to be intentional.

Like *Executive Action*, Oliver Stone's conspiracy version of the Kennedy assassination depicted in *JFK* deals directly with the subject and the personalities involved. Based on several books, including one by New Orleans District Attorney Jim Garrison (played by Kevin Costner), Stone's film, however, mixes fact with fiction, interfaces historical newsreel footage with filmed events, and includes a "deep throat" informer to weave a sweeping conspiracy tale that embraces the military, the Dallas police, the intelligence community, and multinational corporations.[23] Stone's film centers on Garrison's efforts to prosecute businessman Clay Shaw (Tommy Lee Jones) for complicity in Kennedy's assassination. The actual legal record indicates that the trial was a fraud, an attempt by Garrison to blame Kennedy's death on a small group of homosexuals, including Shaw, together with an unidentified military-industrial complex. Shaw's jury took just forty-five minutes to acquit him, while Stone took over three hours on screen to convict him. Stone's supposedly "documented evidence" neglected to include Shaw's trial record.[24] The film's distributor, Warner Brothers, contributed to the deception by promoting the film as if the contents were the truth rather than Stone's version of events.[25] Stone's film deceptively intertwines the two worlds of illusion—Washington and Hollywood—to propagandize an unsubstantiated theory.

Conspiracy theories appear to be the most recent fad in American popular culture, as evidenced by Stone's *JFK*, Mel Gibson's *Conspiracy Theory* (1997), and the popular television series, *The X-Files*. Why this fascination with conspiracy theories today? Political scientist Michael Barkun believes that there are two reasons for this attraction.[26] First, Barkun suggests that in the human need to make sense of the world, conspiracy theories greatly simplify reality, which appears inordinately complex. The end of the Cold War and the dissolution of the old Soviet Union, for instance, removed an identifiable enemy that could be blamed for world problems. Even Hollywood has been at a loss to locate new screen enemies for audiences to hate, vacillating between aliens and creatures from outer space and rogue terrorists who want to reinstate the hostility of the Cold War and terrorize the world. Second, Barkun speculates that the approach of the millennium is often associated with a literal or metaphysical Armageddon—a New World Order—ranging from religious fundamentalists preaching against the Antichrist to UFO enthusiasts who believe the government deliberately denies the truth about extraterrestrial life. Hollywood conspiracy films, therefore, provide us with convenient scapegoats to blame for the ills of the world rather than struggle with the complex problems that confront humanity in the twenty-first century.

Historian Robert Alan Goldberg[27] goes further than Barkun, blaming Hollywood for validating conspiracy theories in such major films as *JFK*, *The Manchurian Candidate*, and *Wag the Dog*. These films serve as catalysts for skeptics, the gullible uninformed, and antigovernment groups. Credibility for conspiracy theories are aided, sometimes unintentionally, by government denials and cover-ups, mainstream media's often unquestioned acceptance of the official government line, and by government attempts to discredit or silence its critics. Goldberg claims that political conspiracies represent but one of several contemporary plots evident in modern America.

REEL POLITICIANS: FROM SAINTS TO SINNERS?

What generalization can be derived from this overview of American politics and politicians as portrayed in Hollywood feature films? Some moviegoers who remember the early days of Hollywood might be tempted to answer that the film industry made a 180-degree turnabout in its attitude toward American politics. While there is a kernel of truth to that observation, particularly as applied to political biographies, it is seriously flawed because it wrongly suggests that historically Hollywood treated politicians with more respect and depicted political institutions in the past with greater deference than the present.

The truth is more complicated. American politicians have been depicted as less than honorable figures as early as the silent movies. For instance, *The Racket* (1928), portrayed politicians in cahoots with Prohibition bootleggers; the president was depicted as a crook in *Gabriel Over the White House*; and the Congress in Capra's *Mr. Smith Goes to Washington* was characterized as one huge trading market, where corrupt deals were struck for power and profit. It is much more accurate to state that the film industry always has been willing to take a critical look at its political leaders and institutions. In fact, Hollywood frequently depicted politicians (and lawyers too) as screen villains. What separates the present from the past is that pre-WWII Hollywood sought to balance the negative portrayals with more positive attributes of political heroes. Recall that in *Gabriel Over the White House* Judd Hammond's crooked president is redeemed and transformed into a man of the people after a visit from the angel Gabriel. Meanwhile, Jefferson Smith's idealistic freshman senator triumphs at the end of the film over the weak and flawed Senator Paine and the corrupt political machine. Capra was willing to criticize the political system and point a disapproving finger at some of the people in it, but he never attributed their flaws and failures to representative government.[28] And Loretta Young's resourceful farmer's daughter wins her novice congressional race despite the opposition's attempt to smear her reputation. In pre-WWII Hollywood, more often than not, decent screen politicians prevailed over crooked machines and corrupt politics.

However, there have been few Jefferson Smith "white knight" type heroes on the silver screen since the sixties. In recent decades, the fictional political characters are more than flawed human beings. They seem to lack any redeeming personal qualities. Instead, they are depicted as political opportunists interested more in personal advancement and rewards than the public good, willing to cheat on their spouses, and not above abusing their friends and colleagues—sometimes without having to pay the price of disgrace and rejection. As a scheming and ambitious political animal in *True Colors*, the John Cusack character shows little remorse for his criminal behavior. Instead of displaying shame and disgrace for his misdeeds, he defiantly intends to remain in politics. Less than a decade later, President Clinton lied about his affair with Monica Lewinsky and even when the lie was disclosed, he refused to admit it or to consider that he owed the American people a public apology. Clinton did not hesitate to announce to the American public that "I have not had sex with that woman" but he refused to go on television to apologize for the lie. Although Alan Alda's philandering Joe Tynan reconciles with his wife at the end of *The Seduction of Joe Tynan*, it is less a case of regenerated love as pragmatic politics because he needs her for his run for the presidency. Tim Robbins's Bob Roberts schemes and tricks his way into the U.S. Senate, raising questions as to what nefarious ventures he plans for the Congress. Even Robert Redford's Bill McKay is a victorious, but imperfect senator, unsure of himself since in winning the election, he lost his soul in the process. Warren Beatty's Senator Bulworth raises some serious questions about class and race in America, yet tempers them with tongue-in-cheek comedy.

Recently, Hollywood has been bold enough to feature politicians as despicable characters, like the womanizing governor in *Primary Colors* and the rapist president in *Absolute Power*. Whenever the political figure is portrayed in a totally positive light, however, the film character is apt to be cast in the unlikely role of action-hero presidents like Harrison Ford (*Air Force One*) and Bill Pullman (*Independence Day*). In an age when the average film budget exceeds $50–$60 million, the major studios are unlikely to take risks with multidimensional politicians and complex political issues. The president in *Deterrence* threatens the city of Baghdad with nuclear annihilation after five minutes of reflection when, in the real political world, President Kennedy and his staff spent days negotiating with the Soviets during the Cuban Missile Crisis. Oversimplification and resort to violent solutions are the buzzwords in the entertainment industry today, where human characteristics and people-oriented plots are replaced by special effects featuring the latest destructive weapons. The trend is possibly inevitable. In studying feature films on the Congress, one scholar has concluded that Hollywood's need for simplification is irrevocably at odds with the complexities of life on Capitol Hill where cooperation and compromise are often necessary for the passage of legislation or the enactment of a balanced budget.[29] This is impossible to portray in a 90–120-minute film.

Admittedly, the working life of a politician is routine and lacking in high drama, much like police work where most police officers never fire their weapons. Hollywood and the public may fantasize that the life of a politician is exciting, where important and dramatic decisions are made every day. More often than not, the days of politicians are filled with committee meetings, reading reports, talking on the phone, listening to speeches, responding to constituents, and interacting with lobbyists and colleagues. This is the stuff of ordinary life. Because Hollywood's purpose is to entertain rather than to educate, their films dare not focus on the intricacies of the political process. The studios prefer depiction of an imaginary political world, filled with unlikely characters engaged in behavior that is sheer fantasy, but potentially more profitable. Since these negative views often are reinforced by other social institutions and by the news media, the end result has been a complete debunking of American politics, defined on screen as a corrupting process fit only for villains.[30] No wonder many American students reject politics as a career choice. Possibly this contributes as well to the failure of young people to vote more so than any other age group.

The present mood depicted in Hollywood films is a misrepresentation of the majority of decent, honest, hard-working people, elected and appointed, in government. The current climate recalls the time when, as a young man in Missouri, Harry Truman told his disapproving mother that he intended to run for political office. Her response was terse: "Politics cheapens a man." Recent Hollywood films have given new life to her words.

PICTURING JUSTICE

CHAPTER SEVEN

The Law and Lawyers in Hollywood Films

"The first thing we do, let's kill all the lawyers."

SHAKESPEARE, *HENRY VI, PART II*

"If there were no bad people, there would be no good lawyers."

MARK TWAIN

"Freedom, Justice, Equality—Without lawyers, they're just words"

ABA SLOGAN

"God works wonders now and then—here lies a lawyer, an honest man"

ON AN ENGLISH TOMBSTONE

"I have three rules. I never believe what the prosecutor or the police say, I never believe what the media say and I never believe what my client says."

ALAN DERSHOWITZ

LAW AND POPULAR CULTURE

Lawyers, like politicians, make dramatic film subjects because their characters have the capacity for both good and evil. Furthermore, their actions affect the lives of others in significant ways. The good lawyer insures a client's personal freedom or economic security; the client who has a mediocre lawyer may end up in prison or the poorhouse. Moreover, lawyers, judges, and the police are perceived by the citizenry to be representatives of the country's values as expressed through its legal system. That system is supposed to dispense justice in every case; failure to provide a right decision adversely affects the system's credibility. Therefore, images that represent the legal culture can reinforce its authority or undermine its popular support.

According to law professor Stewart Macaulay,[1] representations of the legal culture are present in everyday life, from the schoolroom to the sports arena. Particularly of importance to Macaulay is the contribution of the entertainment arts because, as he correctly suggests, the visual media formulate an especially significant popular image of the law and the legal profession. Why is the media's influence so compelling? The legal culture consists of statutes, case law, and scholarly essays on jurisprudence—all of which shape and affect ordinary life. Yet as Macaulay observes, relatively few Americans read the legal literature; only a smaller number are involved in litigation or see the inside of a courtroom. He cites the study by the Hearst Corporation[2] where it was discovered that only 20 percent of the survey population had ever been a party in a civil suit, that only 16 percent had actually served on a jury, that 15 percent had been witnesses in a personal injury suit and that as few as 10 percent had been victims. Therefore, where do Americans learn about the law? Macaulay's response is that they learn the law from the experiences of ordinary life—work, school, sports, and entertainment. He reasons that more Americans learn about the legal system from the visual arts, especially film and television, than from any firsthand experience.[3]

Macaulay's thesis has been expanded by another law professor, John Denvir,[4] who advances the notion that films can serve as visual opportunities for filmmakers to challenge the conventional wisdom and established doctrine on particular legal issues such as abortion and capital punishment. According to Denvir, films like *The Godfather* can serve as legal texts, supplementing material found in the law reports. In the legal culture, law is but one of the images seeking popular acceptance. Hence, to investigate movies is to actually study one aspect of the legal culture.

Why study films about the law or fictitious plots involving courts, judges, and lawyers when newspapers and television provide extensive real coverage? There are three good reasons, according to professor Timothy Lenz.[5] First, Lenz makes the point that much of what appears in legal fiction is often related to real facts and the story lines are perused by specialists for accuracy about the law. Especially in crime stories, Lenz believes that fictionalized stories about the law center around the search by individuals or groups to achieve justice for themselves or their loved ones. Finally, Lenz believes films can provide models for an ideal justice system, reflecting the public's preference for a just society.

Lenz believes that some good can come from viewing "legal nonsense," fictitious stories about the law that are exaggerated for dramatic effect. He sites as an example the two versions of the film *Cape Fear*, involving a psychopathic character, as providing a lesson in the changing image of the law. In the original 1961 version, Max Cady, the psychopath, is released from prison intent on seeking revenge against the former prosecutor who sent him to prison. Cady, however, is a wily convict who understands enough about the legal rules to use the law in his favor. Cady threatens the prosecutor and his family, but always making sure that he is within the legal boundaries to prevent the police from arresting him. The film, then, touches on the due process rights of criminals, a perennial issue before the U.S. Supreme Court. This version of the film focuses on convicts who menace but do no physical harm. What action can a prosecutor, acting as an ordinary citizen, take against such people? At film's end, the prosecutor wounds Cady in a physical confrontation but does not kill him. Cady will stand trial again and likely return to prison.

Thirty years later, Martin Scorsese remade *Cape Fear* (1991). In this version Cady plots vengeance against his negligent public defender when released from prison. Apparently, his lawyer refused to introduce evidence that Cady's rape victim was promiscuous. As a result, Cady is convicted and sent to prison. But Lenz reminds us that rape shield laws prohibit the use of such evidence in a criminal trial. In the Scorsese version, Cady is killed in a violent struggle with his lawyer instead of then being arrested and processed through the criminal justice system. In the context of the 1990s, the film relayed the message that Cady had to die because the legal system no longer could be trusted to deliver justice. If you want justice, Scorsese's film says, do it yourself.[6]

These are the not the worst examples of legal nonsense. In *Runaway Jury* (2003), based on the John Grisham bestseller, a woman sues a gun manufacturer after her husband is killed in an office shooting. The gun manufacturer brings in a noted consultant to help select a jury favorable to the defense. In a convoluted plot development that hinges on an event thirty years before, a juror on the inside and a woman on the outside work to manipulate the jury verdict and deliver it to the highest bidder. The legal nonsense is considerable. The inside juror sneaks out of his motel despite being sequestered. He also receives outside phone calls into his motel room. Another juror is an alcoholic who is able to bring a whiskey bottle into the jury room without being detected. Finally, the jury consultant, who is the villain of the piece, hires thugs to trash the inside juror's home and set it on fire. These are major felonies that carry prison time. It is unlikely viewers will learn anything from this film except a completely ill-founded disdain for the jury system, an integral part of the American justice system.

THE REEL WORLD OF THE LAW

Lenz and Macaulay contend that movies reflect the legal culture, contradictions and all. On the one hand, there are the film texts that reinforce the legal principles, which lend support to the ruling authority and foster compliance with the established law. On the other hand, there are legal texts in film that challenge those in control and portray public officials and authority figures as dishonest and corrupt. However, as in the case of film texts on American politics, Hollywood movies often try to avoid direct attacks on the institutions of government, including the justice system, preferring instead to present the imperfections in a context that blames human weakness rather than a flawed legal system. Exceptions exist, of course, but do not negate the generalization. The following discussion examines Hollywood movies as legal texts in different circumstances.

Frontier Violence

Historians describe the frontier as the demarcation line that divides civilization from the wilderness. In the American past, the frontier's edge moved westward from Pittsburgh until it met the Pacific. Historian Frederick Jackson Turner believed that those pioneers who settled the West shaped the American character.[7]

Hollywood exploited the dramatic potential of the Turner thesis in its visual exploration of the migration westward. Thus, it should not come as a surprise that the first narrative to come out of Hollywood, *The Great Train Robbery* (1903), had a western action plot. Thereafter, westerns became a staple of the film industry well into the sixties. Hollywood's version of the western genre often reduced the plots to simplified morality tales in which the forces of evil are dispatched, usually violently, after the climactic barroom brawl or street shootout with the virtuous good guys. Frontier justice was normally achieved by brute strength and the quick draw rather than by persuasion or the appeal to reason.

Occasionally the western film served as a legal text.[8] Recall that James Stewart's lawyer character (Ransome Stoddard), in *The Man Who Shot Liberty Valance* eventually proved that in the new West, the law book would replace Tom Doniphon's (John Wayne's character) six-shooter. Remember that Wayne began his film career in the thirties by appearing in a series of short westerns for Republic Pictures. In one such film set in the 1870s, *King of the Pecos* (1936), Wayne plays John Clayborn, a young lawyer out to avenge his parents' murder at the hands of the local cattle baron, Alexander Stiles. Somehow the young Clayborn manages to escape unharmed from the shootout that killed his parents. Stiles's strategy is to claim most of the open range for himself, either through buying out deceived ranchers or killing those, like Clayborn's parents, who refuse to sell. Stiles, however, fails to file legal claim to the land, preferring instead to control the water rights. Unless ranchers sell their cattle to him at a low price, Stiles threatens to cut off their water supply. Ten years pass and the grown-up Clayborn returns to town as a lawyer and persuades the court to accept the waterholes as property held in the public domain.

When the legal system rules against him, Stiles resorts to violence. Although Clayborn is committed to using the law to settle disputes, he comes to realize that his law books are no match for Stiles's guns. Reluctantly, Clayborn straps on his gun belt and after a fierce battle, shoots Stiles and kills most of his gang in the climactic gunfight. Afterwards, Clayborn throws away his guns, an act symbolic of his new commitment to the practice of law.

King of the Pecos relied on the legal system and the use of force to achieve justice. Sometimes, however, frontier justice on the big screen meant vigilantism and mob rule.[9] In *The Ox-Box Incident* (1943), a pair of saddle tramps, Henry Fonda and Harry Morgan, reluctantly join a posse in search of cattle rustlers who have killed a local rancher. Disregarding the instructions of the sheriff, the posse, led by an ex-Confederate major, stumble onto three men, preside over a kangaroo trial, and then lynch them for the crime. Fonda and Morgan try to persuade the men to wait for the sheriff to arrive but they are overruled by the mob. On their way back to town, the posse meets the sheriff who informs them that the real culprits are in custody and that the rancher who was shot had not died. When the sheriff learns about the lynching, he promises to hold those involved accountable. Back in town, the major commits suicide while the rest of the posse gathers in the local saloon to drown their guilt. Fonda, however, reads aloud the letter one of the victims had written to his wife in which he refers to the law as the "conscience of humanity." In taking the lives of three innocent men, the posse had become judge and jury, losing its humanity and deteriorating into an uncivilized mob.

A variation on the mob vigilantism theme, but still within the western genre, is found in the film story of *The Life and Times of Judge Roy Bean* (1972). Paul Newman plays the title character, a drifter who declares himself "the law" in a small town west of the Pecos. There he dispenses his brand of justice, usually at the end of a rope. Based on a post-Civil War character, Bean comes into the frontier town of Vinegaroon, Texas, where there is neither law nor order. He proceeds to kill or drive out all the outlaws and, armed only with a copy of *The Revised Statutes of Texas*, proclaims himself "Judge of the territory." Converting the town brothel into a saloon/courthouse, he dispenses justice so harshly that he acquires a reputation as the "hanging judge." In this film, the law literally is what Bean says it is. When the statute book fails to conform to his predetermination, Bean rips the page out of the law book. When an outlaw is brought before Bean for killing a Chinese man, Bean's jurisdiction is challenged because "Chinks, Niggers, and Injuns" are excluded as "persons" in the statute books. Judge Bean will not hear of it; regardless of the statute book, all persons are considered equal before him. Since Bean and the law share the same body, the outlaw is sentenced to hang. Part history and part legend,[10] the film constructs an idol out of an outlaw who tried and sentenced his victims arbitrarily, sometimes on the basis of personal whim. Roy Bean had to be the worst kind of judge to represent the legal system. His story demonstrates, though, what happened when a vacuum existed in territories where official authority had yet to be established.

While hangings, lynchings, and shootouts fit the mythology of the old West, such violence in the twentieth century is more likely to arouse public wrath. Yet lynchings and mob brutality continued well into the 1930s, especially in selected regions of the country. While lynchings occurred throughout the United States, the act had become primarily a southern and racial phenomenon by the late nineteenth century. Studies indicate that almost 4,000 lynchings took place in the South between 1880 and 1930;[11] the vast majority of the victims were blacks lynched by white mobs. A correlation usually existed between economic conditions and the prevalence of lynching. When economic times were good, lynchings decreased; when prices paid to white farmers dropped, lynchings increased. Economically distressed whites found blacks to be convenient scapegoats on which to take out their aggression and frustration.

During the Depression era, Hollywood produced several social-message films, including two on mob rule. Both German director Fritz Lang's *Fury* (1936) and Warner Brothers' *They Won't Forget* (1937) confronted the issue of mob violence directly. *Fury* starred Spencer Tracy as an innocent young man, mistakenly arrested for a fugitive kidnapper. Tracy is arrested on the basis of circumstantial evidence together with being an outsider unknown to the townsfolk. While he languishes in the local jail, a large angry mob develops outside. The sheriff asks for state assistance but the governor is up for reelection and reluctant to intervene. The self-appointed vigilantes, unable to break into the jail to lynch Tracy, set it on fire instead. Tracy is presumed dead. Unknown to the mob, he has managed to escape. Meanwhile, the real kidnappers are captured and the local district attorney brings murder charges against twenty-two identified members of the lynch mob. Embittered by the events, Tracy refuses to reveal himself, content to allow his persecutors to be tried for a murder they did not commit. After the defendants are found guilty, Tracy has a change of heart and decides to intervene. He walks into the courtroom in the final scene while the trial judge is handing out the sentences. Although Tracy's reappearance saved the defendants from certain death, he tells the court that he has lost faith in the ability of the legal system to deliver justice. Lang's film failed at the box office, but it did help to establish his reputation in Hollywood.

Unlike *Fury*, *They Won't Forget* (1937) is a fictionalized account of the 1913 Leo Frank case. Set in a Southern town, *They Won't Forget* retells the story of a teenage secretarial student found murdered in her school building. The politically ambitious district attorney pounces on the case as a potential springboard into the U.S. Senate. He needs to make an arrest and secure a conviction if the crime is to advance his career. The D.A. narrows his suspects to a young teacher, a Northerner and outsider, who was in the school building on the day the student was murdered. The teacher is quickly arrested and convicted, largely on the basis of circumstantial evidence. The governor, however, commutes his sentence from death to life imprisonment. On his way to prison, the teacher is taken off the train by a vicious mob and lynched. As was true in the actual case, the accumulation of circumstantial evidence supported by anti-Yankee prejudice, yellow journalism, and political ambition led to Leo Frank's conviction and eventual death because it was assumed that "we can lynch a nigger anytime but when do we get the chance to hang a Yankee Jew?"[12] Georgia Governor John Slaton commuted Frank's sentence; a brave act that destroyed his political career. The real Leo Frank was taken from the prison farm a few months later and lynched.[13] His killers were not prosecuted even though several were identified. Films like *Fury* and *They Won't Forget* serve as reminders that prejudice and violence did not end at the frontier.

Urban Vigilantism: Dirty Harry Meets Paul Kersey

In 1968 criminologist Herbert Packer[14] theorized a dual model for the criminal justice system. One model, the due process model, resonated with liberals since it was predicated on the presumption of innocence, advocated rights for those accused and charged, and proscribed treatment and rehabilitation for those convicted. Its opposite, the crime control model, appealed to conservatives because it expressed confidence that, unfettered, law enforcement personnel could apprehend criminals and reduce street crime. The crime control model favored community security over individual rights, punishment over treatment. Like most social science models, Packer's represented "ideal types" rather then the prevailing legal reality. The escalating crime rate and U.S. Supreme Court decisions[15] creating protective rights for those accused of crime fueled disaffection for the courts and support for the crime control advocates. Public opinion polls between 1972 and 1983 consistently reported that Americans believed the courts were much too lenient with criminals. The prevalent impression was that the courts had handcuffed the police in dealing with crime and that judges were dispensing light sentences for those convicted. Like the fictional Howard Beale, the deranged newscaster in *Network* (1976), the public was "mad as hell and not going to take it any more" regarding crime.

Hollywood, always ready to capitalize on the prevailing public mood, responded by creating two film characters: Lt. Harry Callahan (Clint Eastward) in *Dirty Harry* (1971) and New York City businessman Paul Kersey (Charles Bronson) in *Death Wish* (1974), both reflected the popular sentiment that criminals had taken over the cities, thanks to an overly liberal Warren Court. While Callahan was a rogue cop operating under the color of law, Kersey represented the ordinary citizen driven by circumstances into becoming an urban vigilante. Being an equal opportunity employer, Hollywood produced five films in each series—the *Dirty Harry* films covering 1971 to 1988, the *Death Wish* films extending from 1974 through 1994. Both series testify to the Hollywood strategy that you continue production until the money dries up at the box office.

Vigilantism is part of the American tradition, according to Lenz.[16] He traces its roots to the concept of popular sovereignty in a culture where the people, not the government, represent the ultimate authority. Vigilantism occurs when individuals or a mob decide to dispense justice without consideration for due process or other legal requirements. If government is a social contract between the people and the ruling authority, then the latter have the responsibility to protect the people in return for their relinquishing certain rights to the government. Should the government fail in its responsibility, the people have the right to take the law into their own hands. At least, that is the justification theory behind vigilantism. More often than not, it was a charade to mask the real reasons of underlying hated, prejudice, and personal vengeance.

Lt. Callahan has no use for criminals or legal technicalities like due process of law, the exclusionary rule of evidence, or the Miranda warning read to those apprehended. In *Dirty Harry*, Callahan is after a serial killer named Scorpio who kidnaps victims and extorts money for their return. He is a thoroughly despicable character, a sociopath who has little regard for his victims. Callahan is a dedicated officer who has little regard for police rules or constitutional rights. He has no regard for the Fourth, Sixth, or Fourteenth Amendments. Moreover, he has a mean streak that approaches those on the opposite side of the law. He baits criminals, tempting them with lines like: "Do you feel lucky—well, do you, punk?" and "Go ahead, make my day" before he shoots them dead. The *Dirty Harry* character appealed to an America tired of criminals like Scorpio, street gangs, and urban punks—and best of all, he did his killing under the authority of law.

Paul Kersey is a decent family man, and according to the *Death Wish* films, a bleeding-heart liberal. He is transformed into an urban killing machine after his wife and daughter are brutally attacked. His wife dies from the assault; his daughter is so traumatized that she requires institutional care. The police inform him that the attackers are unlikely to be apprehended. On a business trip to Arizona, Kersey is given a handgun as a gift. Returning to New York, he begins to roam the streets at night, gun in pocket. One night he shoots a man who intends to rob him; later he shoots three thugs who threaten him. The New York City public likes this urban avenger so that when the police discover his identity, he is not arrested and instead asked to leave town. Shades of the old west. In *Death Wish II* (1982) Kersey resurfaces in Los Angeles where he pursues a gang of thugs who rape and murder his housekeeper. The rape scenes were considered so brutal that the British Film Board ordered the scene cut from the film. Kersey continues his manhunt until he has killed each member of the gang, the last one under treatment in a mental hospital. Once again, the film ends with Kersey escaping punishment so he can pursue his vigilantism in three more *Death Wish* films. The public spotlight shone on the *Death Wish* motif of unpunished urban vigilantism when life imitated art on the New York subway. There is a scene in the original *Death Wish* film where Kersey shoots three black youths who threaten him on a New York City subway car. In 1984, Bernard Goetz, a white man who had been a mugging victim previously, shot and seriously wounded four black youths who approached him on a subway car and asked him for five dollars. While Goetz was charged with several felonies, he argued that his actions were justified because he felt threatened that he would be robbed and mugged again. The black youths, through their lawyers, said that panhandling, not robbery was their intention. In a celebrated trial, the jury could not decide on the serious felonies. They did convict Goetz on the illegal weapons charge for which he received six months in jail. Had the crime been committed during a more liberal era when criminals were considered products of social dysfunction, the sentence might have been longer. Here a crime-weary jury could not find it in their hearts to punish a mild-mannered shooter who carried a gun for protection in the urban jungle.

Military Justice

Because the United States was designed as a federal system with powers shared by both the national and state governments, the country has fifty-one legal systems— one for the federal government and one for each of the fifty states. In addition, two types of courts distinguish the federal court system: constitutional and legislative. Constitutional courts are created under the language of Article III of the U.S. Constitution, which authorizes the Congress to establish courts inferior to the Supreme Court. Legislative courts, on the other hand, are created pursuant to a congressional legislative function. For example, under Article I Congress has the power to organize, arm, and discipline the militia. Discipline is held so vital for military success that even the U.S. Supreme Court has ruled that an orthodox Jew cannot wear his Yarmulke instead of regulation headgear.[17] The Congress, therefore, has the power to establish military tribunals to discipline soldiers.

One example of a legislative court is the U.S. Court of Military Appeals, which reviews the decisions of courts-martial. Its caseload consists primarily of military personnel discharged for bad conduct or sentenced to the stockade for violations of the Uniform Code of Military Justice. Offenses while in the military service, crimes committed on military bases, and other infractions that are "service connected" fall within the jurisdiction of the Uniform Code. Though military personnel do not forfeit their constitutional rights while in the service, the application of the code differs from legal practices in civilian life. For instance, while the Fourth Amendment protection against "unreasonable searches and seizures" applies to service personnel, routine inspections and shakedowns are not considered searches and are therefore permissible. Nor do military personnel accused of a crime have a right to post bail. Military courts substitute military personnel, appointed by commanding officers, for jurors in civilian trials. And while a unanimous verdict is required in civilian criminal trials, courts-martial permit a two-thirds vote to convict in noncapital cases. Only in cases where conviction requires the death penalty is a unanimous verdict required in military trials. The justification for these differences in the Uniform Code is that military necessity requires absolute discipline and adherence to the chain of command.

Hollywood has ignored military trials as screen material with several notable post-World War II exceptions. In *The Court Martial of Billy Mitchell* (1955), Gary Cooper plays the title role of the brigadier general who commanded the American Expeditionary Air Force during the First World War and later served as assistant chief of the Army Air Service. He differed with his superiors over the role of air power in future wars, including the military potential of strategic bombing, airborne forces, and polar air routes. His incessant and sharp criticism of military leaders led to his court-martial in 1925. The film recounts Mitchell's advocacy of a strong air force against military leaders in both the war and navy departments who were committed to naval power and the infantry. When one of Mitchell's friends dies in an air crash, he accuses the war and navy departments of incompetence and negligence. His accusations and insubordination lead to his court-martial under Article 134 of the Uniform Code, which prohibits conduct that discredits the armed forces or is prejudicial to order and discipline. Mitchell's legal strategy was to use the courtroom as a public forum, a place where he could expound his ideas, including the vulnerability of Pearl Harbor to air attack. Mitchell is found guilty because, as a maverick, he dared to question the entrenched establishment. What the trial demonstrates is that the military chain of command requires blind obedience to orders regardless of the consequences. As punishment, Mitchell was suspended for five years. He subsequently resigned from the army, but continued to lecture on the use of air power until his death. Unfortunately, his ideas were not accepted by the military until the advent of World War II.

Mutiny, rather than insubordination, is at the heart of the 1955 film, *The Caine Mutiny*. Article 184 of the Uniform Code defines mutiny as the refusal to obey orders from a proper authority in concert with others with the intention to override military authority. Mutiny, of course, is one of the most serious offenses under the Military Code and is punishable by death. The mutiny in the film occurs in World War II during a Pacific typhoon when a group of naval officers led by Lt.

Maryk (Van Johnson) and Ensign Keith (Robert Francis) seize control of the *Caine* from its commanding officer, Captain Queeg (Humphrey Bogart). Queeg, a strict disciplinarian, had assumed command of the *Caine*, a battered minesweeper, from a lackadaisical officer. He manages to get the ship back in shape but has become increasingly paranoid as a result of excessive combat. He becomes preoccupied with unimportant details like improper dress on board ship. His erratic behavior comes to a climax in his obsession with locating a box of missing strawberries. Queeg orders a thorough investigation for the strawberries, even though it is obvious to the other officers that they had been eaten and no longer available to be produced. When Queeg freezes during the typhoon and hesitates to take action, Maryk and Keith assume command. Both are subsequently charged with mutiny. Their military lawyer, Barney Greenwald (Jose Ferrer) reluctantly defends them at the court-martial by attacking Queeg in an attempt to destroy his credibility. Under intense questioning, Queeg breaks down on the stand, rolling the steel balls in his hands more violently as the cross-examination intensifies. Greenwald's strategy works as Queeg cracks under pressure and Maryk and Keith are cleared of all charges. Later at a post-victory celebration, Greenwald defends Queeg as a good officer who was worn down by the stress of command. In return for the cooperation of the U.S. Navy, film changes had to be made in the Herman Wouk novel to direct blame for the mutiny on the conduct of individuals rather than on the military establishment. Still, the film conveys both a sense of the importance of hierarchical decision making for military effectiveness and a perception of fairness within the military justice system.

Severe hazing (Code Red) that leads to murder on a military base forms the basis for the film, *A Few Good Men* (1992). Loosely based on an incident at the marine base in Guantanamo Bay in the 1980s, *A Few Good Men* recounts the story of Pvt. Santiago, an unhappy marine scheduled to snitch to the authorities on two fellow marines for shooting on the fenceline in Cuba. To frighten him into silence, the two marines initiate Code Red when they stuff a rag down Santiago's throat and tape his mouth shut. As a consequence, Santiago dies and the two marines are charged with his murder. Their base commander, Col. Nathan Jessep (Jack Nicholson), a gung-ho marine who refused to transfer Santiago, tries to minimize the incident as an accident. The U.S. Navy also would like to whitewash the incident; it therefore appoints a young and brash, but untested trial lawyer, Lt. Daniel Kaffe (Tom Cruise) to head the court-martial defense team. Initially Kaffe is willing to accept the prosecutor's plea bargain because he has never tried a case. He changes his mind after a meeting with Jessep and after the constant goading of his colleague, Lt. Cmdr. JoAnne Galloway (Demi Moore). Kaffe and Galloway believe their clients did not act on their own and to substantiate their suspicions, they subpoena Jessep. The strategy works as Jessep, under intense examination, admits the

Code Red order. During the heated court-martial exchange, Jessep defends the hazing order because Santiago was a whiner, a weakling, and not a true marine. He berates Kaffe as well, arguing that when the United States goes to war it calls upon men like himself—real marines—instead of the soft, bookish lawyers in white dress like Kaffe, to do the dirty work. When the country is in crisis, discipline and strength, not weakness and self-indulgence, are required of the military services. As he is being led out of the courtroom by the Military Police, Jessep screams that men like Kaffe undermine the strength of the country. From one viewpoint, Kaffe's first trial is a success; his clients are acquitted of the murder charge. Since they are dishonorably discharged from the corps, the sentence raises the question of whether it is fair to punish lower echelon military personnel for carrying out a crime under orders from a superior officer. Yet the Nuremberg War Crimes Trial after World War II,[18] established the principle that military personnel cannot rely on illegal orders, such as a Code Red, to absolve them of wrongdoing. However, for subordinates to disobey an order is a serious offense under military law. Within the context of the film, the two marines would have had to pass judgment on Jessep's order—which was not to kill Santiago but simply to toughen him up, frighten him into becoming a real marine. That is a no-win situation for military personnel who apply the Uniform Code to preserve discipline and obedience rather than the attainment of just ends.

TRIALS AND TRIBULATIONS: LAWYERS ON THE BIG SCREEN

In the American legal system it is the lawyer who is the pivotal character in the resolution of legal contests. Having an adversarial legal system places the lawyer center stage. Hollywood films about the law tend to portray the profession in three contexts: as larger-than-life heroes, as sleazy shysters available for hire, and as fallen idols seeking redemption through their clients.

Heroic Lawyers

A hero or heroine is usually characterized as a person who has committed an act of courage or bravery without regard for personal consequences. Heroes are admired and held in high esteem by the rest of society. Hollywood action-adventure films consistently feature characters that perform heroic deeds or overcome extreme obstacles to right a wrong. Such heroes usually cannot serve as role models because their escapades are often implausible and belong more to the realm of the imagination than to real life.

Courtroom movies, however, can utilize the trial as a paradigm for the confrontation between good and evil. Trial movies provide opportunities for lawyers to become heroic figures as their legal strategy saves the life of an innocent client or delivers just compensation to the plaintiff in a civil suit. For more than half a century the film industry has exploited the dramatic potential of the heroic lawyer in pursuit of truth and justice. What young person would not want to grow up to become Abe Lincoln (Henry Fonda), the advocate with a social conscience, in *Young Mr. Lincoln* (1939)? Not only does the Springfield lawyer prove the innocence of two brothers accused of murder, he saves them from a lynch mob and, in typical Perry Mason fashion, exposes the real killer in the final scene. Nor is attorney Lincoln reluctant to engage in courtroom tricks, including reliance on the *Farmers' Almanac* to identify the real killer.

Could there be a more heroic lawyer than Atticus Finch in *To Kill a Mockingbird*? Gregory Peck plays Finch in the 1962 film adaptation of the Harper Lee novel about a small-town Southern lawyer who defends a black man accused of raping a white woman. Finch, a widower and a respected lawyer, is struggling to raise his two children during the Depression years. When asked by the local judge to accept the rape case, he never hesitates although his client's case appears hopeless. Finch's acceptance is a lesson to audiences that even marginalized groups are entitled to the best defense possible under the American legal system. Like the young Lincoln, Finch also faces down a lynch mob. Still, despite an impassioned closing argument in which he asks the all-white jury to lay aside their racial prejudices, the jury convicts his client. Unfortunately, in 1930s Alabama, a black man accused of raping a white woman had no chance whatsoever. Blacks were sent to prison just for "leering" at white women. While it is unlikely that any lawyer could have saved Finch's client, his insistence on uncovering the truth despite the personal consequences represents the best tradition of defense lawyers.

Lincoln and Atticus Finch are noble characters, fighting for justice in the courtroom. They symbolize Hollywood's most ideal representation of lawyers on the big screen. They are flawless characters, a credit to the legal profession. Other screen lawyers who fit this mold include Humphrey Bogart in *Knock on Any Door* (1949) and Glenn Ford in *Trial* (1955), both represent minority defendants in trials permeated with prejudice and ethnic hostility.

In *Knock on Any Door*, attorney Andrew Morton (Bogart) defends a young hoodlum, Nick Romano (John Derek) accused of murdering a policeman during a robbery. Morton takes the case despite a warning that his acceptance jeopardizes his chance for a full partnership. He identifies with Romano because both were products of the urban slum; yet Morton became a respected attorney. He believes that Romano, the son of immigrant parents, can also be rehabilitated. However, Romano is too weak to stay out of trouble, flaunting an attitude of "Live fast, die young and have a good-looking corpse." Morton's defense strategy is to put society on trial, to have the jury believe that Romano is a decent kid who never had a chance to go straight. But when cross-examined on the stand, the D.A. provokes Romano into confessing to the crime. Morton, then, has no choice but to make an impassioned plea to the judge to save Romano's life, citing the arguments of the social determinists that environment is largely responsible for crime. If Romano is guilty, Morton argues, then so is society because it failed to provide him with a decent home and a good neighborhood. Despite his passionate defense, Romano is sentenced to death in the electric chair, thereby making his prophecy of dying young and having a good-looking corpse come true.

David Blake's (Glenn Ford) client, Angel Chavez, in *Trial,* is a Mexican-American high school student accused of murdering his WASP girlfriend. Blake is a law professor on the verge of getting fired because he lacks trial experience. To save his job, Blake accepts an offer to spend the summer as an assistant to local attorney, Barney Castle (Arthur Kennedy). Castle convinces Chavez's mother to let him handle the case. Instead of doing the trial work he assigns it to Blake on the pretense that he will be too busy raising the legal funds necessary for the defense. Unknown to Blake, Castle actively promotes the Chavez case, turning it into a cause celebre for the Communist Party. The party needs a martyr (Chavez), and an inexperienced trial lawyer like Blake is the perfect candidate to lose the case. Meanwhile, local bigots surround the courthouse, anxious to dispense with the trial altogether and lynch Chavez on the spot. In response the National Guard is called out and the local sheriff dissuades the crowd from doing violence. Back in the courtroom, Blake is learning the law on the job, his mistakes corrected by the patient trial judge. At least Blake has enough sense not to put Chavez on the stand. Castle, who has the support of Chavez's mother, overrules him on this matter. As expected, the vulnerable Chavez crumbles under cross-examination and the jury finds him guilty. Blake is devastated by the verdict. Nonetheless, because he believes that somewhere in the law, "where there is a wrong, there is a remedy," he decides to try one last legal tactic. During the sentencing hearing, Blake convinces the judge, with the consent of the prosecution, to send Chavez to reform school rather than the gas chamber. In order to save Chavez, however, Blake must confess to his incompetence and admit that Castle had duped him in an effort to aid the communist cause. The film concludes at this point with the implication that while Blake did the right thing, he should return to the classroom and avoid the courtroom at all cost. Because of its content, MGM, the film's distributor, released it after the Army-McCarthy hearings and McCarthy's censure by the U.S. Senate.

Al Pacino plays beleaguered Baltimore criminal defense attorney, Arthur Kirkland, in *And Justice For All* (1979). The opening scene finds Kirkland in jail for contempt after he takes a swing at his nemesis, Judge Fleming (John Forsythe). Kirkland represents the sensitive lawyer with a conscience. He is angry with Fleming for refusing to reopen the case of a wrongly convicted client. In addition to the jail time, Kirkland is under investigation by the judicial ethics committee to determine whether he continues to be fit to practice law. After his release from jail, Kirkland is asked by Fleming to defend him against a rape charge. Kirkland is put in a catch-22 situation since he despises the judge, yet if he refuses to take the case, he most likely will be disbarred. Laying aside his personal feelings, Kirkland accepts the case and provides an aggressive defense until he discovers that the judge is guilty. In the final scene, Kirkland confesses his client's guilt to the stunned courtroom, an act that leads to his disbarment.

While Kirkland is an improbable lawyer, *And Justice for All* is the rare Hollywood film that is willing to cast aspersions on the criminal justice system itself rather than on the individual participants. The film presents an unending parade of corrupt officials, scenes of judicial abuse of power, and questionable plea bargain deals. Although it tends toward exaggeration, the audience leaves the theater with a feeling that the urban legal system requires not justice but compromise and expediency in order to survive. Kirkland represents the idealistic and ethical lawyer trying to exist in an irrational system that overwhelms, and eventually, destroys him.

Michigan attorney Paul Biegler, Jimmy Stewart's character in *Anatomy of a Murder* (1959) would rather fish for trout and play jazz on the piano than practice law. Based on the best-selling novel that recounts an actual Michigan case, *Anatomy of a Murder* is an ironic depiction of the criminal law in practice. The major character, Paul Biegler is less the heroic lawyer than the duped attorney depicted in Harvard Law Professor Alan Dershowitz's story of the lawyer who cables his client that "Justice has prevailed," to which the client responds: "Appeal immediately."[19] Biegler agrees to handle the case of an Army officer, Lt. Manion (Ben Gazzara), charged with killing the man who allegedly raped his wife. When Biegler interviews Manion at the local jail, he tells his client that there is no such thing in the law as an unwritten rule that acquits a husband who protects his wife's honor. In desperate need of a viable defense, Biegler skirts the code of ethics when he lays out the various excuses for such a crime and, after repeated questioning, gets Manion to admit that he "must have been crazy" when he shot and killed his wife's attacker. The lead allows Biegler to develop the "irresistible impulse" strategy, a defense permitted under Michigan law. Legal scholars contend that Biegler's coaching is just one of several legal improprieties evident in the film.[20] Biegler's legal tactics prove successful, as Manion is acquitted. Afterward, Biegler goes to the trailer court to collect his fee, only to learn that the Manions had an irresistible impulse to skip town. Like the client in the Dershowitz story, Manion was guilty as sin.

Occasionally, Hollywood will take a real lawyer or a famous case to dramatize on the big screen. Actor Ron Silver portrayed Dershowitz in *Reversal of Fortune* (1990), the film version of the Claus von Bulow case. Dershowitz and his Harvard law students were successful in convincing the Rhode Island Supreme Court to reverse von Bulow's attempted murder conviction. In another film, noted criminal lawyer Clarence Darrow is represented on screen in two of his famous cases. In the so-called "Monkey Trial," Darrow was retained by the American Civil Liberties Union (ACLU) to defend teacher John T. Scopes on trial for teaching the theory of evolution against state law. The film version of the Scopes trial, *Inherit the Wind* (1960), had Spencer Tracy playing Darrow. As in the actual trial, Darrow made his adversary, William Jennings Bryant, appear foolish on the stand. What is often not known about the real trial (and omitted from the film) is that the Scopes trial represents a legal "test case." The ACLU sought to challenge the Tennessee anti-evolution statute and needed a teacher to volunteer to break the law. Scopes answered the ACLU advertisement. Moreover, unlike the rest of the fundamentalist Dayton, Tennessee, community, the town merchants actually believed that a national trial would be good for business.[21]

In the other film, *Compulsion* (1959), Orson Welles played Darrow in a fictionalized account of the famous Leopold-Loeb murder case of the 1920s. The film story concerns two brilliant law students who want to commit the "perfect crime" and plot to kidnap and kill a small boy. Arrested for the crime, their families hire Darrow to defend them. While his bravado courtroom performance failed to win an acquittal, Darrow's two-day closing argument that the boys were mentally disturbed and unable to comprehend the enormity of their crime saved them from the death penalty. Darrow's summation, in which he asked the court to be more compassionate and kinder than his clients, still serves as a convincing argument against capital punishment. These two cases secured Darrow's reputation as America's most outstanding criminal lawyer.

Grisham's Lawyers

The film studios are enamored with John Grisham's novels, making screen adaptations of his first seven books. There are two apparent reasons for Hollywood's interest. The Grisham books are popular best sellers because the author has developed a substantial readership and his novels are often distributed through several book clubs. When adapted for the big screen, Grisham's novels have done well at the box office. Another reason for Hollywood's interest is that Grisham's fiction contains at least one good lawyer, a hero or heroine, who fights for the underdog, the disfranchised, and the disposed. Even though the novels contain bad lawyers, they are usually on the losing side and their characters are balanced by honest, usually young lawyers intent on seeing that justice is done. An example is the Matthew McConaughey character in *A Time to Kill* (1996), Grisham's first novel. McConaughey's liberal lawyer, Jake Brigance, has the formidable task of defending Carl Lee Hailey, the black Mississippi farmer accused of killing the two rednecks who raped and beat his ten-year-old daughter. That Brigance does it success-fully in a southern town renders his victory even more heroic.

In Grisham's *The Firm* (1993), Tom Cruise's young lawyer, fresh out of law school, is seduced by the money and gifts showered on him by "the Firm" and obliv-ious to the company's association with organized crime. Then two law associates are murdered and Cruise, working with the F.B.I., must help expose the company's shady dealings. In *The Pelican Brief* (1993) Julia Roberts plays a law student who stumbles onto a plot that gets two Supreme Court justices killed. It seems a friend of the president is trying to manipulate the outcome of a trial before the Supreme Court and Roberts is drawn into this unlikely plot through her law professor, with whom she is having an affair. Roberts solves the mystery and satisfactorily resolves the case by the final reel with the help of an investigative reporter (Denzel Washington). Reggie Love (Susan Sarandon) is another heroine in a Grisham novel, *The Client* (1994), who tries to help a young boy being pursued by the Mafia and harassed by the local prosecutor. Although obviously out of her league, Reggie manages to protect the boy from both dangers. Like Roberts, the Reggie Love char-acter is a larger-than-life heroine.

Another young lawyer (Matt Damon), clearly overmatched, takes on corporate America in *The Rainmaker* (1997) and in true Hollywood fashion, wins his case with the aid of an assistant who never passed the state bar exam. As they used to say in Brooklyn, "if you believe that, I have a bridge to sell you." Damon's case involves a woman suing a large insurance company that refused to pay her son's medical bills. Now the boy is terminally ill and Damon and his assistant are locked in a struggle with a high-powered law firm that represents the interest of the insurance compa-ny. It is the familiar Hollywood scenario of David versus Goliath and the film's happy ending could only happen in the movies. What separates these heroic Grisham lawyers from the young Abe Lincoln and the idealistic Atticus Finch is their total lack of believability. Grisham's lawyers are usually overmatched upstarts, with limited resources and staff, who achieve the impossible for their clients against powerful interests that employ expensive law firms with huge staffs to insure suc-cess. The fact that Grisham's lawyers always are victorious is what appeals to both Hollywood and a willing American public that believes in miracles.

Shyster Lawyers

Unlike the serious heroic lawyers of the Grisham-based films, the movies where lawyers are portrayed as disreputable characters are either silly comedies or crime and gangster movies. There are exceptions to that generalization. As early as the 1930s, Hollywood films characterized lawyers as "ambulance chasers," unscrupulous leeches who thrived on the misfortune of others. One film, *The Nuisance* (1933) featured a lawyer who works legal scams with the aid of a drunken doctor and a professional accident victim.[22]

More common were Hollywood comedies where the laughs were at the expense of an incompetent or unscrupulous lawyer. A case in point is the Joe Pesci character, Vincent Gambini, in the 1992 film *My Cousin Vinny*. Vinny is a recent graduate from an unidentified law school who travels to the Deep South to defend his nephew against a wrongful murder charge. Armed with his fiancé, Mona Lisa Vito, and his cowboy boots, Vinny is the kind of relative most people would like to disown. He is brash, vulgar, dresses in black leather and chains, and has failed the bar exam six times. Nonetheless, he still manages to get his cousin acquitted in a silly, but harmless, film.

Funny, but not quite as harmless, is Willie Gingrich (Walter Matthau), the lawyer character Billy Wilder created for his film, *The Fortune Cookie* (1966). If you would not want Vinny Gambini as a cousin, you certainly would not want Willie Gingrich as a brother-in-law. Willie is an ambulance-chasing personal injury lawyer who richly deserves his nickname: "Whiplash Willie." When his brother-in-law, Harry Hinkle (Jack Lemmon), a CBS sportscaster, is run over by a Cleveland Browns football player and ends up in the hospital, Willie sees an opportunity for a megabuck insurance settlement. Harry, of course, is not seriously injured but Willie convinces him to accept the splints, neck braces, and wheelchair charade, at least until the insurance settlement. The insurance scam almost works until Harry's conscience upsets the fraudulent scheme. In Willie Gingrich, Wilder created one of the funniest lawyers in film history but also one of the sleaziest. Willie is an unprincipled opportunist whose philosophy is summed up in the phase, "life is a racket." Matthau's performance won him an Oscar because, in the opinion of one reviewer, it came close to the truth.[23]

While the origin for "shyster"[24] remains unclear, the word found its way into Hollywood gangster movies in the 1930s. The lawyers in these crime films worked for the mob and valued money and power over the legal code of ethics. Illustrations of the shyster lawyer can be found in two 1930s films, *The Mouthpiece* and *Lawyer Man*. As their titles suggest, these are portraits of charming rogues who either work for the underworld or for crooked politicians.[25] The attorney in *The Mouthpiece* (1932) is an assistant D.A. who turns to drink when he discovers that the defendant he convicted, and later executed, was actually innocent of the crime. Unable to overcome his guilt, he becomes an attorney for hire, even to the criminal class. He receives his just deserts when mobsters shoot him down at film's end. The fortunes of unscrupulous lawyers like *The Mouthpiece* were usually tied to the mobsters they defended.[26]

The importance of the lawyer to the criminal and to organized crime is best exemplified by *The Godfather* trilogy (1972, 1974, and 1990). The collaboration of writer Mario Puzo and director Francis Ford Coppola, *The Godfather* films are the saga of the "Corleones"—Vito and Michael—two generations of Mafia chieftains. A key figure in this intergenerational story of a Mafia family is the role of the "consigliore," the Corleones' adopted son and legal adviser. Played by actor Robert Duvall in Parts I & II and by actor George Hamilton in Part III, the consigliore acted similarly to the legal department in the modern corporation. As the Corleones' illegal business empire grows, the greater the need for the Don—"the Godfather"— to rely upon him for advice and counsel. It would be inconceivable that the consigliore later could deny knowledge of the organization's illegal activities. To make that point clear, the Puzo novel included a line, cut from the film version, where Don Corleone says: "A lawyer with his briefcase can steal more than a hundred men with guns."[27] To the Mafia leadership, lawyers were "hired guns"; yet they also were important players within the organizational structure. In every sense of the word, they were lawyers for the mob.

Fallen Idols

A common theme in the entertainment arts is the concept of redemption; narratives built around a major character who falls from a position of prestige and high status downward to the lower depths, usually due to alcohol, drugs, or bad women (restricted to women since men dominated positions of power in the film industry). Hollywood has applied this traditional plot idea in its films to all sorts of occupations, including the legal profession.

As early as the thirties, the studios began to grind out films in which prominent lawyers succumb to the pleasures of the flesh. Occasionally, Hollywood produced a film where the lawyer's descent was not due to a "femme fatale" or to substance abuse but to a failure to live up to personal ideals. Two films, both involving Jewish lawyers, concern characters that have lost their souls to greed and the temptations of a lifestyle that only money can buy. Elmer Rice's stage play, *Counsellor At Law* was adapted for the screen in 1933 and starred John Barrymore as George Simon, a successful Jewish lawyer with an office in the Empire State Building. Simon has progressed from humble boyhood in the lower East Side ghetto to become a highly respected and successful attorney. From all outward appearances, Simon has a flourishing practice. Yet he has a troubled soul. His socialite wife and her two children from a previous marriage look down on him because of his humble background, while his mother reprimands him for rejecting his heritage. For example, his mother embarrasses Simon into defending the son of a Jewish woman from the old neighborhood, a communist arrested for making speeches in Union Square. The young man is completely out of place in Simon's plush offices, and during their consultation, he refuses to listen to Simon's advice that he refrain from making more speeches. The disparity between Simon's wealth and the young man's Marxist ideals are so obvious to Simon that all the attorney can do is shrug his shoulders. Simon's descent begins when a rival lawyer threatens to expose some wrongdoing in Simon's past, knowledge of a false alibi provided to a former client. To add even more misery to his possible disbarment, Simon discovers that his wife has been unfaithful. In a moment of utter despair, he considers jumping out his office window. He is prevented from jumping by a loyal secretary who adores him. With new inspiration and true love, Simon decides to fight the disbarment charge rather than commit suicide.

John Garfield is another beleaguered Jewish lawyer, Joe Morse, who has climbed his way out of the New York slums and into a plush Wall Street office in *Force of Evil* (1948). Joe's decision to make lots of money by working for Tucker, a racketeer and mobster, has made him a successful lawyer, albeit one without scruples. In contrast, Joe's older brother, Leo (Thomas Gomez), sacrificed to put him through college and law school, a familiar scenario among lower-class immigrant families. Without an education, Leo tries his hand at several businesses that fail. Eventually, he goes to work in the illegal numbers policy racket as an independent operator. When Joe's boss, Tucker, has a scheme to control the numbers racket, Joe tries to warn Leo, but his brother refuses his help. In a plot too complicated to detail here, Tucker's men kidnap Leo and his bookkeeper. In the process, the bookkeeper is killed and Leo dies from a heart attack brought on by the shock. Joe learns of Leo's death and takes revenge on Tucker in a dramatic shootout. At film's end, Joe decides to turn himself in to the special prosecutor who has been appointed to investigate the numbers racket. Looking at Leo's body on the banks of the Hudson River, Joe's voice-over expresses his remorse and his hope for redemption:

> I found my brother's body at the bottom there, like an old dirty rag nobody wants. He was dead and I felt that I had killed him. I turned back to give myself up to Hall. Because if a man's life can be lived so long and come out this way, like rubbish, it's something that is horrible and has to be ended one way or another. And I decided to help.[28]

Force of Evil is one of those multifaceted films that operate on several levels. At its most obvious level of understanding, it is a gangster story. On a second level, it is a retelling of the story of Cain and Abel. At a third level, it is also a story of personal redemption. Finally, at its highest level of understanding, it can be construed as a critique of the capitalist system. The story of Joe Morse's rise from ghetto to Wall Street raises the moral question of whether it is possible to become financially successful within the capitalist system without becoming corrupted by it.[28] This is not an inappropriate interpretation of the film since it was the collaboration of Abraham Polonsky, who directed and did the screenplay, and actor John Garfield's short-lived independent company, Enterprise Productions. Both men came under the scrutiny of HUAC during the Hollywood hearings. Polonsky would be black-listed as one member of the Hollywood Ten while Garfield was subpoenaed but refused to appear and died shortly thereafter.

Counsellor-At-Law and *Force of Evil* were not typical Hollywood redemption films. More common within the industry were films where the major character's fall from grace is due to a personal flaw or addiction. For instance, alcoholism is the cause of the descent in films like *The People Against O'Hara* (1951) and *The Verdict* (1982).

Spencer Tracy plays a noted criminal attorney forced to retire because of alcoholism in *The People Against O'Hara*. He agrees to defend young O'Hara on a murder charge because the family is poor and can only afford to pay a fee of $325 for legal services (a situation rectified by the creation of the public defender system in the 1960s). Unfortunately, due to inebriation, carelessness, and old age, Tracy loses the case. He still believes O'Hara is innocent, however, and launches his own investigation that leads him to the real killer. Although he secures sufficient evidence to free O'Hara, he is killed in the process, thus providing redemption through death.

Alcoholism proves the downfall, also, of Frank Gavin (Paul Newman) in *The Verdict*. Gavin is a shabby, alcoholic attorney who begins his day with a shot and a beer chaser. Understandable, since he has not had a decent case in years and is reduced to ambulance chasing and hustling up business at wakes. His career is at rock bottom and he is one step from disbarment when he is given a medical malpractice suit by default. Since the suit is against a Catholic hospital, few lawyers in Boston are willing to take a case where the Catholic Church is the defendant. Gavin rejects an out-of-court settlement by the Boston Archdiocese after he visits the comatose victim in the hospital and decides to go to trial and seek a greater justice and a larger settlement. He sobers up and his pre-alcoholic legal skills return. Meanwhile, the Diocese has hired a high-priced law firm to defend its case. Gavin once again proves his competence as an attorney but he must contend with considerable opposition: the defense team has put a corporate spy (Charlotte Rampling) onto him, many of his witnesses are discredited, and the rulings of a prejudicial judge eliminate most of his evidence. A surprise witness, a hospital nurse, saves his case when her testimony establishes the negligence Gavin requires for a victorious verdict. At film's end, Gavin is sober, has won his big case to restore his reputation, and his clients have received substantial personal injury damages. While it is true that almost half the lawyers who are disbarred or disciplined are alcoholics or drug addicts, the legal community was most unhappy with the film for its erroneous presentation of tort law, trial lawyering, and judicial behavior. The film's legal lapses led two law professors to complain, "If justice is blind, justice got lucky in *The Verdict*."[29]

The substance that brings down Eddie Dodd in *True Believer* (1989) is drugs, not alcohol. Eddie (James Woods) is the former civil rights activist turned drug addict and ambulance chaser. A fighter for liberal causes in the sixties, Eddie's law practice has been neglected by his addiction and his clients are mostly drug deal-ers and dope pushers. He has become so disillusioned by the legal system that he accepts the injustice of it: "everybody's guilty of something," therefore justice is an irrelevant commodity. Goaded by his young protégé, Eddie is pressured to take one last "lost cause"—the kind of hopeless cause Jefferson Smith reminds Senator Paine of in *Mr. Smith Goes to Washington*. Eddie agrees to defend Kim, an Asian-American inmate accused of murdering another prisoner. Supported by his protégé, who reminds Eddie of himself in his early years, and the legitimacy of his client's self-defense claim, Eddie's investigation reveals that his client is innocent of the crime that sent him to prison in the first place. In the final scene, his family meets Kim as he leaves prison while Eddie looks on, his confidence renewed and his faith in the justice system restored.

A new twist on the redemption plot is found in *The Devil's Advocate* (1997). Keanu Reeves goes to work for a prestigious New York law firm headed by a slick lawyer (Al Pacino) who serves as a metaphor for Satan. Pacino recruits Reeves after the young lawyer has successfully defended a child molester he knew to be guilty of the crime. In fact, Reeves has a perfect record as prosecutor and defense coun-sel. It is his desire to win regardless of whether justice is done that makes him the perfect candidate for Pacino's firm. Thus, blind ambition and the lure of financial success seduces Reeves into the New York firm where he learns what it means to work for the devil. During the fiery climax, Reeves asks Pacino why he selected lawyers to do his bidding. Pacino's answer is similar to the reason Macaulay gave: the law touches everyone at some point in life.

Another overly ambitious personal injury lawyer (John Travolta) takes on the case of eight families in Woburn, Massachusetts, whose household members con-tract leukemia and die. Based on the Jonathan Harr best-selling book, *A Civil Action* (1998), the film identifies two large corporate giants, W. R. Grace and Beatrice Foods, as the industrial polluters who poison the town's water supply. Playing real life Boston lawyer, Jan Schlichtmann, Travolta appears to be the "white knight" for these families. His personal greed, legal mistakes, and oversized ego, unfortunately, result in the bankruptcy of his law firm and no compensation to his clients. In real-life, Schlichtmann has undergone a transformation of sorts, as he spe-cializes in legal suits against business America in an effort to recover damages due to corporate negligence or indifference.

Women Trial Lawyers

With the exception of the 1930s, women trial lawyers were not major characters in Hollywood films until the decade of the eighties. Contrary to popular belief, Hollywood churned out a dozen or more films in the thirties that featured women lawyers.[30] This is somewhat surprising since at the time women comprised 24 percent of the workforce but only 3 percent of the national bar.[31] Nonetheless, the film industry turned to depicting female lawyers for screen plots in the thirties and forties. Some of these movies were "B" films like *Scarlet Pages* (1930) where actress Elsie Ferguson defends a murderess who turns out to be her illegitimate daughter. Others, however, featured established female stars like Fay Wray (*Ann Carver's Profession*, 1933), Jean Arthur (*The Defense Rests*, 1934) and Claire Trevor (*Career Woman*, 1936). The trend continued until World War II movies put a halt to films centered on women lawyers. But what distinguishes these films from the ones that will reappear in the 1980s is the pre-feminist message that women lawyers cannot have successful professional careers and happy personal lives. For instance, Fay Wray's character in *Ann Carver's Profession* wins an important murder case but afterward relinquishes her career to save her marriage.

Plots involving women lawyers largely disappeared from the screen over the next four decades, due largely to the industry's interest in war movies, westerns, and musicals. The one notable exception is Katharine Hepburn's character, Amanda Bonner, in the 1950 film, *Adam's Rib*, where she costarred with Spencer Tracy. *Adam's Rib* is a romantic comedy where Hepburn and Tracy play a husband-and-wife attorney team, except Tracy (Adam Bonner) is an assistant D.A. When Amanda takes the case of a ditzy blonde (Judy Holliday) charged with the attempted murder of her unfaithful spouse, she does not know that Adam has been assigned to prosecute. The comedy comes from the complications caused by spouses representing different sides of the law. What provides the film with substance is the fact that Amanda sees in the case an opportunity to criticize the socially acceptable double standard and preach the cause of legal equality. Adam insists that the facts, which are not in dispute, logically lead to an inevitable guilty verdict. For her defense Amanda maintains that if her client were a man, her actions would be excused under the "unwritten law" that married men have a right to protect their home and their honor. In her summation, Amanda tells the jury that equality is on trial, rather than her client, who had just as much right to defend her family and home as her husband. The argument proves persuasive and Amanda wins the case. Although the trial has caused domestic problems, Adam and Amanda are reconciled at the end. It is not hyperbole to suggest that Amanda Bonner is an early feminist who would have made an excellent screen attorney for the twenty-first century.[32]

The film industry woke from its slumber in the 1980s to resume making movies featuring women trial lawyers. Whether this was in response to the feminist movement, a desire to be politically correct, or an attempt to lure women into movie theaters, the answer is best left to Hollywood insiders. What is obvious to even the most casual Hollywood follower is the fact that the industry could hardly continue to ignore the significant gains by women in law school acceptances, private sector practice, and judicial prominence. One notable statistical trend involved applications to law school. Women applicants went from 3 percent of the total law school enrollment in the late 1940s to 34 percent in the 1980s. The greatest surge occurred in the seventies where the number of women law students tripled. By the mid nineties, women comprised 44 percent of the law school population.[33] Meanwhile, the number of women practicing law moved from pre-World War II single digits to roughly one-quarter of the almost 900,000 practicing lawyers in the United States, with 70 percent in private practice rather than government employ as district attorneys or public defenders.[34] Additionally, women hold virtually every professional legal role, including U.S. Supreme Court Justice.

Beginning in the mid eighties, Hollywood recognized the change in the legal demographics by releasing more than half-a-dozen feature films with major actresses portraying women lawyers as central characters. Glenn Close, Barbara Hershey, and Jessica Lange played defense lawyers in *Jagged Edge* (1985), *Defenseless* (1991) and *Music Box* (1989), Debra Winger and Kelly McGillis were district attorneys in *Legal Eagles* (1986) and *The Accused* (1988), Cher portrayed a public defender in *Suspect* (1987), and Mary Elizabeth Mastrantonio a corporate lawyer in *Class Action* (1991).

Men have long dominated the film industry. Inequalities in leadership roles, star status, and picture salaries characterized the industry well into the eighties when the situation began to change. Women now hold executive posts, and a few female stars, like Julia Roberts, can command salaries comparable to their male costars. In the spirit of equal opportunity, Hollywood is to be commended for producing films that provide starring roles that previously had been reserved almost exclusively for male actors. Even so, the female-lawyer characters in the films cited above raise serious questions regarding screen depictions. The acceptance of women in professional roles is offset by the manner in which these screen women conduct their professional and personal lives. On a personal level, women lawyers in films are portrayed as either unmarried or divorced, lonely, and frequently without children. Their private lives are often out of synch, giving the appearance of an unfulfilled life. When children are present, the relationship with their mother is often estranged. Glenn Close's defense lawyer in *Jagged Edge*, for example, has a son who resents her working.[35]

As members of the legal profession, women trial lawyers are depicted in stereotypical terms as incompetent and unethical attorneys who often exercise poor judgment. For instance, Glenn Close (*Jagged Edge*) sleeps with her client (Jeff Bridges) during his murder trial while Barbara Hershey (*Defenseless*) has an on-going affair with her married client. Both women breach professional ethics and contradict the conventional wisdom that a lawyer should never become involved with a client in order to retain objectivity. Jessica Lange violates a corollary of that principle in *Music Box* when she decides (unwisely) to represent her father against charges that he had been a war criminal. Meanwhile, Mary Elizabeth Mastrantonio (*Class Action*) is carrying on an office affair with her law supervisor, which clouds her judgment in a civil suit where her father represents the plaintiff. Actress Cher (*Suspect*) allows a juror (Dennis Quaid) to provide her with clues in a murder case. Consorting with a juror, for whatever reason, is grounds for disbarment. In *Defenseless*, Hershey defends a client in a murder case without informing her or the police that she is a material witness to the crime. Kelly McGillis's district attorney does a disservice to a crime victim (Jodie Foster) in *The Accused* when she plea-bargains away the gang rape charge in favor of going after the witnesses to the crime who encouraged and supported the rape. Worse yet, in *Class Action*, Mastrantonio conspires with her father in a civil case to destroy her own client.[36]

The examples of outright negative screen portrayals of women lawyers are too numerous to document here. A few examples will suffice. Take the film adaptation of Scott Turow's novel, *Presumed Innocent* (1990), where D.A. Harrison Ford is having an affair with one of the female assistants in his office. Apparently this woman has slept her way up the career ladder since previously she had been the mistress of the chief district attorney. Christine Lahti's character in *And Justice For All* is having an affair with attorney Al Pacino while she sits on the ethics panel that will decide whether he should be disbarred. Charlotte Rampling's ambitious lawyer, seeking to restart her career after a failed marriage, allows herself to be exploited by the legal team representing the Boston Archdiocese in *The Verdict*. She agrees to seduce the opposition lawyer, Frank Gavin (Paul Newman) and spy on him, feeding the collected information back to her boss. Rebecca DeMornay's criminal defense lawyer in *Guilty as Sin* (1993) plants evidence to implicate her own client (Don Johnson) once she realizes that he is guilty of the murder of his wife. Mary Elizabeth Mastrantonio commits several serious blunders in *Class Action*. For openers, she is sleeping with her immediate supervisor, a partner in a prestigious law firm who is in a position to control her career ladder. She also is guilty of a conflict of interest since she defends a client that is being sued by her father's client. Finally, she knowingly permits her bedmate boss to perjure himself on the stand while she remains mute. Not only do these actions violate the ethical rules of the profession, they are all grounds for disbarment. These are certainly not the kind of lawyers to recommend to your friends.

Feminists might disapprove of the above analysis by citing Steven Soderbergh's hugely popular film, *Erin Brockovich* (2000), which won an academy award for actress Julia Roberts. The film is based on a real person, a single mother who goes after a large corporation, Pacific Gas & Electric (PG&E), after she discovers that the utility is poisoning the water supply of a small California town. Brockovich, while not a lawyer, is a file clerk in a North Hollywood law office. Shunned by the other office workers, Brockovich spends her lunch hour perusing the files. One day she learns of a pro bono case involving a Hinkley, California, woman who is suing PG&E because of health problems related to the company's toxic waste dump. On her own initiative, Brockovich visits the town, interviews the woman, and is convinced that the utility is culpable. She convinces 634 town residents to initiate a class action suit and persuades the law firm to take on the case. Doing most of the legwork herself in gathering the evidence, Brockovich and the townspeople are rewarded when an arbitration panel awards a $333 million settlement. Brockovich is given a $2 million bonus and a new job; the law firm receives $133 million for its services, while the residents receive the remainder. It is the typical Hollywood fairy tale of how one ordinary individual (think *Rocky)* overcomes the odds, brings a large corporation to its knees, and secures justice for the underdog. Brockovich became a media celebrity after Hollywood brought her story to the big screen. She currently is a motivational speaker on the lecture circuit, inspiring women to achieve great things. However, the film ended while the real story continued. An Internet[37] report claims the film misrepresented the facts. While the story cannot be substantiated because, unlike trials, arbitration proceedings are secret, a number of complaints were registered concerning the awards. First, there were complaints that the award money was held for six months without interest added to the distribution. Other complaints involved unequal distribution of award monies without regard to medical histories. For example, the average award divided among the plaintiffs came to roughly $300,000 each but some residents received only $50,000 to $60,000, including one man who was awarded $80,000 despite surgery to remove seventeen tumors from his throat. Since no reasons were provided for the individual awards and the amounts were secret, several residents filed lawsuits against the firm that won them their awards. Possibly someday the full Erin Brockovich story will become part of the public record. Meantime, as the newspaper editor in John Ford's *The Man Who Shot Liberty Valence* remarks when questioned about the truth behind the shooting, "When the truth becomes legend, print the legend." Hollywood loves to film legends.

DOING JUSTICE, HOLLYWOOD STYLE

Statistics reveal that there are more practicing lawyers in the United States than in any other country in the world. There is one lawyer for every 300 Americans. Hollywood has released about 180,000 feature films. Using the same proportion as lawyers to population, the industry would have had to make at least 600 law-centered films. Though lawyers[38] differ as to what constitutes a bona fide law film, still the number of law-related films produced remains conspicuously low.

One observation to be drawn from the evidence presented here is that Hollywood is just as ambivalent about lawyers as it is toward politicians. On the one hand, Hollywood tends to underrepresent lawyers and politicians as screen material. On the other hand, when the industry portrays law and lawyers in films, it either gets the legal facts wrong or it portrays lawyers as one-dimensional characters, usually as unlikely/unsavory people. To this point, Hollywood has an aversion to presenting a balanced, objective view of the profession. Screen lawyers are more likely to be ready for sainthood (*Young Mr. Lincoln*, *To Kill a Mockingbird*) or candidates for prison (*True Believer*) and the unemployment line (*The Verdict*). Even if we grant dramatic license to the filmmaker, lawyers as a distinct class are no more likely to be one-dimensional characters than politicians, teachers, or doctors. Additionally, screen lawyers behave as if they flunked law school, repeating the kind of mistakes that are usually corrected during moot court. The public reputation of lawyers (politicians too) as an honorable profession declined considerably after the Watergate scandal and their portrayal in recent Hollywood films has done little, if anything, to alter that perception. Film lawyers not only make stupid mistakes and behave badly, but worse yet, they commit serious offenses that in real life would most certainly lead to disbarment.

What does Hollywood have against lawyers? The answer is "nothing" because the studios hire many and work closely with them. How, then, to explain their screen portrayals? One explanation[39] is that the entertainment media has turned lawyering into a performance art. In a culture dominated by the visual media, the screen courtroom no longer is a venue for sifting through the facts to discover the truth. Rather it is an opportunity for lawyers to sway jurors with emotional appeals, bombastic rhetoric, and courtroom tricks. The public, so the argument goes, has come to expect lawyers to behave badly. Law professor Michael Asimow[40] agrees and sees the portrayal transition in Hollywood between the more positive image of lawyers in 1930s and 1940s films with the more negative, unpleasant representations today as occurring in the decade of the seventies. The shift reflects a change in public attitudes, according to Asimow, that is reinforced by the largely negative stereotypes portrayed in Hollywood films. In a content analysis of 284 Hollywood films in which lawyers are significant characters, Asimow found around two-thirds contained at least one bad lawyer. Were the earlier positive portrayals due to the requirements of the old Production Code? Asimow does not think so but the code did require respect for the law, authority figures, and practicing professionals.

Asimow is not the only lawyer concerned with the profession's public image. The negative screen portrayals have distressed the American Bar Association (ABA) as well. In a committee report[41] delivered at the 2002 ABA conference, it was noted that a survey of public confidence in nine institutions and their practioners ranked lawyers eighth. Doctors were first, while only the news media kept lawyers out of last place. In a Harris Poll[42] conducted about the same time, people were asked a question about who could be trusted to tell the truth. Doctors, teachers, and college professors were held to be most trustworthy, while lawyers were at the bottom of the list along with members of Congress and trade union leaders. Two-thirds of the respondents, in fact, would not trust lawyers to tell the truth. Admittedly, part of the public negativity is understandable because unlike doctors and teachers, lawyers interact with people when they are in crisis and most vulnerable—sorting through a messy divorce, trying to reach agreement in a nasty custody battle, handling the probate and estate taxes when a loved one has died. These are traumatic experiences for people, and it is at these times that individuals rely upon lawyers. Still the excessive negativity is hard to accept. After all, doctors do lose patients and teachers do fail students. It is conceivable that the public's love-hate relationship with the law and its practitioners has always existed but the dominance of the negative relationship after the 1970s is due to factors beyond the control of the profession. Remember that of the forty individuals charged in the Watergate scandal, thirty pleaded guilty or were found guilty and nineteen went to prison. Many involved in the crime and cover-up had studied and practiced law, including the president of the United States. The legal profession and their political counterparts have not recovered from that debacle.

Hollywood has been especially unkind to women lawyers in this regard. Their depictions convey the impression that modern women who opt for legal careers are likely to end up unhappy and alone and sometimes indebted to a male colleague. Mary Elizabeth Mastrantonio's lawyer in *Class Action*, for example, defends an automaker in a personal injury suit whose car self-destructs on impact due to a faulty design. Her father (Gene Hackman), a famous liberal attorney, represents the plaintiff. The script discriminates against Mastrantonio's character because she works for a law firm that hides damaging evidence, steals documents, and generally lies to cover up its illegal activities. At the end, Mastrantonio has a change of heart and works with her father (against her client, the automaker) to achieve a settlement for the plaintiff. At a victory party in a local hangout, father and daughter dance and reconcile; daughter will join dad's law firm and work for the good guys. This sappy ending reinforced the film's message that "father still knows best."[43] Moreover, film depictions of women lawyers have had an influence on the real world expectations, particularly regarding appropriate dress, demeanor, and lifestyle. According to one source, these screen portrayals have led to the "androgynous female attorney" who wears pants suits and adopts other male characteristics in order to avoid appearing too feminine.[44]

Rather than view these characterizations as a conspiracy of the male power structure within the film industry,[45] a more plausible scenario has to do with box office receipts than political ideology. The discussion in this chapter indicates that male lawyers on screen are often just as flawed as their female counterparts. Spencer Tracy and Paul Newman portrayed alcoholic lawyers while James Woods's attorney was a drug addict. In addition, no female screen lawyer yet has even come close to Walter Matthau's unscrupulous sleazy lawyer, "Whiplash Willie" in Billy Wilder's *The Fortune Cookie*.

What is of greater concern for the legal profession than gender representation is the question of how justice is achieved in Hollywood films. Aristotle considers two kinds of justice in his *Nicomachean Ethics*: distributive and corrective. Distributive justice concerns how honor, prestige, and material goods are distributed throughout society. Hollywood virtually never constructs a film plot around the unequal share of the goods and rewards of society. *Force of Evil* is the rare exception that challenges the economics and the morality of the capitalist system. However, it was not a conventional film for its time since an independent company owned by a Marxist writer-director and a leftist-liberal actor produced it.

Aristotle's second kind of justice is corrective, where the law is used as an instrument to provide remedies for those wrongly victimized. Hence, Aristotle's concept of corrective justice requires both an injury and a wrongdoing. The party that has committed the wrong should be identified and punished for it and the law is much more interested in the wrongful injury than in the character of the parties involved. Hollywood films usually achieve justice through unlawful procedures, a timely accident, or last-minute evidentiary discovery. This unrealistic depiction serves to remind us once again that Hollywood is in the business of marketing products that sell at the box office. In so doing, the film industry has done a disservice to the moral principles underlying the American legal system and to the men and women who serve as its practitioners.

HOLLYWOOD GOES TO WAR

From the Great War to the Good War

CHAPTER
EIGHT

"In war, truth is the first casualty."

AESCHYLUS

"War is hell."

GENERAL WILLIAM SHERMAN, CIVIL WAR

"I want you to remember that no bastard ever won a war by dying for his country. He won it by making the other poor dumb bastard die for his country."
GENERAL GEORGE S. PATTON TO HIS TROOPS.

"World War II? Isn't that the one they fought in black-and-white?"
A STUDENT IN HISTORIAN STEPHEN AMBROSE'S CLASS

"It seems as if all my life I have been waiting for men to return from war: In the 40s my uncle. In the 50s my college friends. Some did not return. In the 60s I waited for my husband to return from two tours in Vietnam."

HOMEFRONT WOMAN

The film industry has a special interest in the combat/warfare film genre since the typical war movie is a variation on the standard action-adventure film that traditionally does well at the box office. It may surprise the reader to learn that 5000 war-related film titles were released during Hollywood's first century.[1] The persistent popularity of war movies is evident by their peacetime production; some like Steven Spielberg's *Saving Private Ryan* (1998) do remarkably well at the box office, while others, like Terrence Malick's *The*

Thin Red Line (1998) do poorly. On the other hand, Michael Bay's WWII block-buster film *Pearl Harbor* (2001) cost $135–140 million to complete and grossed under $200 million in the United States; certainly a financial disappointment. However, its overseas gross of more than $250 million turned it into a moneymaker.[2]

The appeal of the war movie to the film industry is understandable since the genre allows the studios to fulfill the audience's heroic fantasies while it celebrates national patriotism. The war movie permits the industry to rally round the flag while exploring the dualities of the human condition: individual decency and courage versus brutality of the enemy, individual loyalty and duty versus self-interest and survival, and self-sacrifice versus the collective good. The genre also is vulnerable to jingoistic preaching and government enticement since often it is necessary to secure the assistance of the Pentagon or a government agency like the Department of Defense (DOD) to shoot a war film. John Wayne, for instance, could not have made his pro-Vietnam film, *The Green Berets*, without government support, both financial and material.[3] However, when the war film is produced at the direction of the state or under its control, it can easily serve as an instrument for government propaganda. It is highly unlikely that any government, democratic or totalitarian, would support films that question or raise doubts about the wisdom or necessity of the war it is conducting. A nation's power to wage war, Supreme Court Chief Justice Hughes wrote in the Minnesota Moratorium case,[4] is the power to wage it successfully.

Historian Arthur Schlesinger, Jr., writing at the close of the twentieth century, remarked that of all our wars, only three were necessary: the Revolutionary War, the Civil War, and World War II because they were "driven by decent purposes and produced beneficial results."[5] Hollywood, in its turn, has sanctified both the American Revolution and World War II but has fudged on the Civil War for fear of alienating either the North or the South. The Revolution has been mythologized; for evidence think no further than Mel Gibson's *The Patriot*, where the American militia were glorified while the British Colonel Tavington was demonized and portrayed as an inhuman beast. In fact, the historical British officer was Lt. Colonel Banastre Tarleton, considered by biographers to have been an aggressive and ruthless commander but definitely not a butcher. Unlike the film version, the real Tarleton returned to England after the war and served in Parliament. Furthermore, even the most severe film critic would be hard put to find a negative movie about World War II that was produced in Hollywood. Even before Tom Brokaw dubbed them the "greatest generation," these WWII veterans had been glorified by the film industry. Therefore, when John Huston's WWII documentary, *Let There Be Light*, was previewed for the military the War Department refused to show it to the troops because its stark realism would have a demoralizing effect.[6] In Hollywood terms, these were good wars fought for noble causes and with considerable popular support. At least, that would be the version shown to the American people even if it was less than the truth.

Photographing combat scenes dates back to the Civil War and the work of Matthew Brady. By the late nineteenth century, the French film pioneers, the Lumiere brothers, were taking pictures of training maneuvers. Other filmmakers, however, were not as adventurous, preferring to stay at home and recreate the Boxer Rebellion or the Russo-Japanese War in their backyards. Still others, seeking more realism, urged the military to do battle in daylight to facilitate the shooting. One such incident occurred during the Mexican Revolution when a film company paid Pancho Villa to engage in battle only if the filming conditions were right. Sometimes audiences were at a loss to decipher whether the film they were watching on the Boer War was shot in South Africa or New Jersey.[7] More recently, Vietnam-era films were either staged or shot on locations that could duplicate for Hanoi or Saigon. Stanley Kubrick filmed the second half of his *Full Metal Jacket* inside an abandoned London factory while Oliver Stone and Francis Ford Coppola went to the Philippines for their Vietnam films *Platoon* and *Apocalypse Now*, respectively. Real combat may be hell but making a war movie often posed no more threat to the participants than suffering from the vagaries of the local weather.

WORLD WAR I: THE GREAT WAR

Historians consider the First World War as the first modern war in which the number of deaths and casualties exceeded those from disease. It is estimated that more than 9 million died during the war's four years. American deaths totaled more than 114,000 for the nineteen months of its participation. The British, for example, lost 29,000 in one day at the Battle of the Somme.[8] World War I also was the first war to use modern weapons of death such as tanks, airplanes, and poison gas. The superlative "great" refers to the number of nations involved and populations affected by the war rather than to any displays of modernity.

One area where modernity played an important factor was in portraying the war on film. The technology and economics of the motion picture business had advanced sufficiently by the time war broke out in Europe in 1914 such that many of the countries involved—particularly Germany, France, and Britain—already had established film industries. Hollywood, however, was still preoccupied with the growing pains associated with the development of a new industry. Prior to 1917, when the United States entered the European war, the film industry imitated the "official" government neutrality policy by making films that would appease both isolationists and interventionists. Films like J. Stuart Blackton's *Battle Cry of Peace* (1915) and Thomas Ince's *Civilization* (1916) cancelled each other out, preaching warmongering and pacifism, respectively. Hollywood produced films that characterized the

Germans as "Huns" and brutes, alternating these with antiwar movies, which cautioned Americans against becoming cannon fodder in a predominantly European conflict.

The situation changed dramatically after President Wilson's 1916 election to a second term. Wilson appointed George Creel to head the Committee on Public Information (CPI) with authority to oversee all propaganda activities, including a special department "to sell the war to America" once the United States officially joined the Allied side. The Creel Committee was responsible for the distribution of official Army and Navy war footage and for the production of such films as *Pershing's Crusaders*, about the Army Expeditionary Forces, *America's Answer*, which dealt with mobilization efforts, and *Under Four Flags*, which promoted the role of the Allies in the war—all released in 1918. Since U.S. involvement in the war was relatively brief (around nineteen months) little documentary footage was shot of trench warfare involving American troops.[9] Hollywood neglected the European war until after 1917 when twenty-three feature films about the war were released, amounting to almost one-quarter of Hollywood's total film production for that year. With the arrival of the armistice in November 1918, however, Hollywood was left with a plethora of war movies that American audiences largely ignored.[10]

When the mood of the country turned toward isolationism under the presidencies of Harding and Coolidge, the film industry rejected narratives that portrayed war in idealistic images in favor of stories that depicted the futility of war and the virtues of pacifism. Consequently, for two decades Hollywood made films about the war that were skeptical, or at least, contradictory. Unlike previous patriotic World War I films, *The Big Parade* (1925), *What Price Glory?* (1926), and *Wings* (1928) presented ambivalent images of suffering as noble events while they questioned the validity of American anti-German propaganda. Disillusionment with the war is the theme of *The Big Parade*, where silent screen star John Gilbert played a wounded veteran returning to an indifferent, and even callous, homefront. Then in *All Quiet on the Western Front* (1930), the classic antiwar film of trench combat presented from the German point of view, a young recruit is killed by a sniper's bullet as he reaches over the parapet for a butterfly in the closing days of the war. This scene epitomized the futility of war for almost all the participants. Nor can a moviegoer find a stronger antiwar sentiment expressed than the one in *The Eagle and the Hawk* (1933) where a burnt-out pilot (Fredric March) regrets the shooting down of German planes during air combat. In a scene filled with sarcasm and self-loathing, he raises his glass in a toast, saying: "I give you war," before he goes off and shoots himself.[11]

When war swept across Europe and Asia in the 1930s, Hollywood reacted cautiously. The industry continued to sell mostly entertainment to American audiences, while the interventionist-isolationist scenario from the First World War replayed itself to another generation. But as fascism gained a stronghold in Europe, and Japan waged an imperialist war in Asia, several film studios sought to reverse the demythologization of World War I as meaningless slaughter and wasted idealism in a series of films that warned the county against the threat of fascism and that justified war as a necessary means to protect democracy. Between 1939 and 1941, the studios turned out fourteen anti-Nazi films, six military preparedness movies, and two World War I films that glorified wartime heroics.[12]

Warner Brothers' *Confessions of a Nazi Spy* (1939) brought the threat of fascism close to home as it depicted the FBI crackdown on a Nazi spy ring in America. The film's message was clear: America was not immune against Nazi subversion. The film, however, drew the ire of Father Charles Coughlin and was picketed by the priest's followers who saw it as a Jewish plot to lure America into the European war. The following year, Alfred Hitchcock's *Foreign Correspondent* (1940) reiterated the warning to an indifferent America when the film's hero, an American correspondent based in London, broadcasts a message in terms reminiscent of Edward R. Murrow: "The lights have gone out in Europe! Hang on to your lights, America—they're the only lights still on in the world!" Meanwhile, MGM's *The Mortal Storm* (1940) portrayed the evils of Nazism in personal terms as a university professor is sent to a concentration camp for his anti-Nazi opposition and his daughter is killed trying to escape to Switzerland. In that same year, Charlie Chaplin used satire and comedy to poke fun at Hitler and Mussolini in *The Great Dictator*, but turned quite serious in the final scene where Hynkel, Chaplin's alter ego, asks the army to overthrow the dictators and restore power to the people. Even Bogart's character in *Casablanca*, the disillusioned owner of "Rick's Cafe," comes to realize that the threat of fascism takes precedence over his love for Ingrid Bergman. By giving his visa papers to Bergman and her husband, a leader of the Resistance, Bogart facilitates their escape from North Africa to continue the fight against fascism.

Still it would be misleading to conclude that all the studios were turning out pro-interventionist films. Although many of the studios were headed by Jewish émigrés, the major film companies did not overemphasize the war in Europe. Between 1937–41, slightly more than half of the films produced by the nine major Hollywood studios had any connection to the wars raging in Europe and the Far East. Fearful that Germany, Italy, and Spain would boycott their films, the Hollywood studios encouraged nonpolitical screen plots and an attitude of neutrality toward the warring sides.[13]

Only Warner Brothers, the producers of *Casablanca*, continued its enthusiasm for war by portraying combat death as a form of personal redemption. In both *The Fighting 69th* (1940) and *Sergeant York* (1941), the major characters are transformed by their war experiences. Both films sought to revive positive memories of the "Great War" despite statistics that proved the First World War as the costliest war in human history up to that time. *The Fighting 69th* confined itself to recounting the adventures of a tough New York kid (James Cagney) assigned to an Irish regiment that acquitted itself nobly in battle. The story centers around the Cagney character as he goes from cowardice under fire to heroic death. The New York regiment suffered heavy casualties, but the film neglected the pain and suffering in favor of the value of wartime camaraderie. The actual war, however, was not quite as romantic since it was fought with the new technologies of its time: machine guns, air bombing, armored tanks, flame-throwers, and poison gas, resulting in enormous casualties on both sides. In the first five months of the war, for instance, the French suffered casualties that exceeded all the British losses in World War II. One campaign, the Battle of the Somme, was fought over a four-month period for six miles of French soil at the cost of over 300,000 lives.[14] In yet another engagement, the 1916 Battle of Verdun, a staggering 700,000 French and German soldiers were killed.[15] For its nineteen-month participation in the war, American casualties, dead and wounded, exceeded 320,000.[16]

On the other hand, the major character in *Sergeant York* is a poor Tennessee country boy who is transformed from Christian pacifist to combat hero while serving in the trenches. The film biography of Alvin York allowed Warner Brothers to glorify war and make it morally respectable when fought for honorable ends. In the film, York becomes a one-man army after he concludes that killing Germans would help to end the war and bring about peace. In this sense, *Sergeant York* represents an attempt to erase the memory of those antiwar films of the twenties and early thirties.

The Japanese attack on Pearl Harbor altered the course of world events and transformed Hollywood along with the rest of the country. President Roosevelt followed the lead of his predecessor, President Wilson, by creating an Office of War Information (OWI) as a successor to the Creel Committee. In 1942, the administration established a Bureau of Motion Pictures within the OWI to provide leadership and guidance on how the industry could best contribute to the war effort. Between Hitler's invasion of Poland in 1939 and the Japanese surrender in September 1945, Hollywood released a significant number of motion pictures that touched on the war, either directly through films of military training and combat or through stories that dealt with the hardships of life at home.

WORLD WAR II: THE GOOD WAR

If the First World War was dubbed the "Great War" because of the number of nations involved and the tremendous human cost in waging it, these losses pale in comparison to the millions[17] of lives lost in World War II. It was considered by Americans to be a "good war" in the sense that it unified the nation to wage a successful battle against an ideology that sought world domination while it stimulated a depressed economy at home, providing jobs and opportunities for women and minorities that could not be denied in the future. And these objectives were achieved without physical damage to the country. Yet describing World War II as the "good war" is an oxymoron to the rest of the world when the actual damage of the war is realized: more than 45 million dead, including 20 million Russians, whole cities like London and Dresden virtually leveled by systematic bombing, six million Jews and another five million gentiles, Jehovah's Witnesses, gypsies, and homosexuals victims of the European holocaust, the cities of Hiroshima and Nagasaki demolished by atomic bombs, and much of Europe and Asia left in ruins that would take decades to rebuild.[18]

The war proved advantageous for some Americans who traded in the black market or for corporations that enjoyed surplus profits from the war machine. Corporations and businesses that were converted to war production or engaged in the manufacture of war-related goods enjoyed soaring profits. The shift from civilian goods to war production created jobs in defense plants and war factories that were filled by women and minorities complemented by 4-F (nondraftable) men.

The film industry also profited from the war financially but not without paying a price. Some of its most established male stars—Edward Albert, Douglas Fairbanks, Jr., Henry Fonda, Clark Gable, Robert Montgomery, Tyrone Power, James Stewart, and Robert Taylor—entered the military, with most seeing combat duty.[19] On the other hand, declaring oneself a conscientious objector (CO) like actor Lew Ayres ruined his film career.[20] Several movie stars lost their lives during the war years. British actor Leslie Howard, one of the leads in *Gone With the Wind*, had his plane shot down by the Germans over Portugal, while actress Carole Lombard died in a plane crash on her return home from a war bond drive. Many entertainers toured with the United Service Organization (USO) or worked in local service canteens. Other Hollywood stars were active in raising money for the war or in supporting rationing efforts. Gene Kelly, for example, came to Williamsport, a small town in northcentral Pennsylvania, to make a war bond film that featured local servicemen.

The film industry also profited as film attendance increased during the war. Going to the local movie theater became a weekly activity. Movie attendance skyrocketed, resulting in the doubling of box office receipts.[21] Defense plant workers, often working overtime shifts, looked forward to the weekly three hours of relaxation at the movies. Parents and spouses sought respite from the boredom and anxiety of waiting for their loved ones to return home. School-aged youngsters eagerly

FIGURE 10. Actor Gene Kelly and local citizens of Williamsport, Pennsylvania: 1945. Reprinted with permission of Charlotte Gordon.

awaited the Saturday matinee where their heroes outwitted and defeated the enemy on a weekly basis. For these youngsters, the lessons of war were learned from films and newsreels.

Hollywood responded to the public demand for entertainment by grinding out almost 400 films a year to meet the needs of all age groups. While the film industry continued to churn out musicals, comedies, and westerns, it is estimated that one-fifth to one-quarter of the 1,500 films released between 1942 and 1945 were movies with war-related themes.[22] These are broadly classified into combat films, including military training and prebattle preparation, and homefront movies about the domestic impact of the war. The government contributed to the mix with its own documentaries and propaganda films. All shared a common purpose, namely, to depict the world as divided into good and evil forces, slave and free states, and that the fighting of the war would regenerate the country and lead to national harmony and unity.

Combat Films

World War II movies fall into four categories: the pure combat film, the hybrid training-battle action film, the resistance of our Allies film, and the homefront film when men were away in the service and women entered the workforce. Jeanine Basinger,[23] in her seminal work on movies of the Second World War, insists that Hollywood produced few combat films, particularly before 1943. According to Basinger, the industry produced many more films where combat was secondary to the military training or preparation for battle. These hybrid films—part training, part combat—were less expensive to shoot and often did not require government assistance. The formula was successful because it could be recycled, substituting one branch of the service for another. For example, *Crash Dive* (1943) depicts naval training before the crew goes into combat, while *Sands of Iwo Jima* (1949) depicts a similar scenario for the marines. The latter half of *Iwo Jima* depicts the fierceness of the actual battle where 29,000 soldiers died during one month of fighting, including 7,000 GIs. What Americans tend to remember today is the story of the raising of the flag on Mt. Suribachi, brilliantly retold in James Bradley's book, *Flags of Our Fathers*.[24] Bradley's father was one of the six marines from EASY company that raised the replacement flag. Three of the men were killed. The remaining ones, including Bradley's father, played small roles in the film version. However, what Hollywood failed to show in the film was the personal cost, not only of those who died but also of the three survivors. Maybe that is why Hollywood made less than two dozen films where the action centers around combat fought on the ground, in the air, or on the sea and where the armed forces face death and destruction in reaching, or holding, a military objective. Basinger considers these films "special" because many included actual newsreel footage that added to the realism of the action scenes and because most required the support of the military and the Department of Defense to be made.

Wake Island (1942) was the first World War II combat film distributed to movie theaters. The film deposits the audience on a small Pacific island where a marine detachment's job is to protect the island because it serves as a refueling base for flights from the West Coast to Asia. After the attack on Pearl Harbor, the Japanese fleet bombarded the island, softening it up for a land invasion. Although outnumbered, the marines refuse to surrender, holding the enemy at bay for sixteen days. No American soldier is alive at film's end. Although U.S. forces suffered a military defeat at *Wake Island*, Hollywood, with the assistance of the OWI, could still turn the film into a positive propaganda piece by having the commanding officer send this final message to headquarters: "The enemy has landed; the issue is still in doubt." The Defense Department thought so highly of the film that it became an integral part of military training, providing a rationale for the value of the human sacrifice against what the film described as "the forces of destruction."

The pace picked up considerably in 1943 as thirteen combat films were released to theaters. Several, like *Bataan* and *Action in the North Atlantic*, depicted American defeats or unsuccessful forays against the enemy similar to *Wake Island*. Such films disappeared once the war turned in favor of the Allies; in the Pacific the U.S. victory in the Battle of Midway proved decisive, while in Europe, the surrender of Italy not only took the Italians out of the war but also paved the way for the Normandy invasion. The American defeat suffered at Wake Island was reversed in *Guadalcanal Diary*, which glorified the marines' victory over the Japanese in several battles in the Solomon Islands. The film was based on an eyewitness account, yet it contained stock characters that appeared in most war movies: the stereotypical group of tough sergeants, sensitive chaplains, and the typical melting-pot GI platoon featuring rural Southerners, ethnic and racial minorities, and the always-present wise guy from Brooklyn. Fifty years later, Terrence Malick's *The Thin Red Line* revisits Guadalcanal for a new generation of moviegoers. In depicting the fierce battle between American and Japanese forces for control of this strategic island, Malick's film preaches that war transforms its participants into less than human characters. It remains problematic whether *The Thin Red Line* could have been made while the United States was engaged in the Second World War.

Combat movies after *Guadalcanal Diary* featured established male stars like John Wayne in predictable plots that depicted successful combat missions against the enemy. Wayne was kept busy during the war years because he did not qualify for military duty and leading men were in demand. Wayne played a PT commander fighting the Japanese in John Ford's *They Were Expendable* (1945) and also portrayed an American officer working with the Filipino resistance movement in *Back to Bataan* (1945). Wayne did not star in the first *Bataan* film (1943) but headed the cast of the sequel. By recreating MacArthur's return to the islands, the film sought to reverse the demoralizing effect of the infamous Bataan death march in which thousands of starving American and Filipino troops, captured by the Japanese in the early days of the war, died as a result of the forced march through the jungle. Made with the full cooperation of the U.S. government, *Back to Bataan* describes the almost three-year guerrilla war waged by the Filipino resistance against the Japanese invaders. Wayne again is cast as a heroic figure, leading his undermanned and poorly armed Filipino fighters against the superior Japanese forces. Though the two *Bataan* films depict the Japanese in particularly brutal terms, including scenes that detail the hanging of a school principal for refusing to take down the American flag; the beating of a young boy to extract information; and the shooting, stabbing, and inhumane treatment of the death marchers, it did not compare to the real experience. There is one scene where Wayne tries to explain the war to a young Filipino boy by saying, "You're the guy we're fighting this for." It is a line that Wayne would reuse thirty years later at the end of his pro-Vietnam film, *Green Berets*. Meanwhile, another Hollywood star (Errol Flynn) portrayed a leader of an American paratroop battalion dropped behind enemy lines on a mission to disable a Japanese radio station in *Objective Burma* (1945). After completing their mission Flynn and his men are cut off by Japanese forces and must fight their way back to Allied lines. The remainder of the film describes their escape from enemy forces.

On the European front, movies like *The Story of GI Joe* (1945), about war correspondent Ernie Pyle, and *A Walk in the Sun* (1946), about an infantry platoon in Italy that achieves its mission despite the loss of its officers, extolled the virtues of the foot soldier. Pyle is the centerpiece of *The Story of GI Joe*, a modest war film that concentrates on the ordeal of the infantry soldiers—the soldiers that would be characterized as the "grunts" of the Vietnam War. Although the real Pyle was in his forties, he insisted on walking along with the Army infantry unit during the Italian campaign. It was said that forty million Americans back home read his column. Pyle served as technical advisor on the film, and then returned to the front where he was killed by a sniper. He never did see the completed film. *A Walk in the Sun* also views war on a small scale as the film follows the adventures of one platoon in achieving its modest objective—the capture of a strategic farmhouse held by the Germans, not without significant casualties. War is hell for the infantrymen in these two films.

Hybrid World War II films usually began in boot camp as the military trains and prepares its troops for battle. This preparedness sequence may take up to half of the film's running time as it did in *Crash Dive*, where actors Tyrone Power and Dana Andrews play sub commanders who complete a successful raid against a Japanese installation. But as was common in these hybrid war films, the two men spend most of their time competing for the love of a woman back home. Meanwhile, in *Gung Ho!* (1943) Randolph Scott is placed in charge of a specially created marine battalion, Carlson's Raiders, that destroys the Japanese installation at Makin Island, signaling the beginning of the American offensive in the Pacific.

Another favorite wartime movie subject had to do with the resistance of our Allies against the Axis powers. These films portrayed ordinary people as heroes, engaged in extraordinary and courageous feats against an invading enemy. The Russians were portrayed heroically in two 1943 films, *The North Star* and *Days of Glory*. Both films extolled the virtues of the Russian people and the love expressed for their homeland. *The North Star* was the work of a talented group: writer Lillian Hellman, composers Aaron Copland and Ira Gershwin, and director Lewis Milestone. The film focused on a battle of wits between the German commander and the village leader. *Days of Glory*, on the other hand, was a B-movie with a cast of unknowns. Dedicated to the bravery of the Russian people, especially the peasants, the film stars Gregory Peck (in his film debut) as the leader of a small group of guerrillas, all of whom are dead by film's end. *Days of Glory* is an obvious effort to drum up American support for its Russian allies, but Hollywood could not resist the temptation to romanticize the war. While the Russians suffered tremendous losses, the film failed to do justice to their cause. Although there are enough "comrade" greetings in the film to fill Red Square, Hollywood dealt in cliché characterizations (Germans as brutes, Russians as happy, peace-loving people who sing, dance, and quote Pushkin) and fantasy images of the war on the Russian front. Ironically, some of the people involved in these sympathetic screen portrayals would later come under the scrutiny of HUAC, even though these pro-Russian films had received the approval of the OWI.

Meanwhile, the exploits of the Norwegians during World War II also were depicted in two 1943 films: *The Commandos Strike at Dawn* and *Edge of Darkness*. The question of Norwegian resistance, however, is equivocal. When war broke out in Europe, Norway proclaimed its neutrality and continued to trade iron ore to the Germans. It was in 1940 after Churchill ordered the Norwegian waters to be mined to prevent the Germans from reaching their iron ore supply that the Nazis responded by invading Norway. After the Norwegian government capitulated to the Germans, a growing guerrilla movement developed among the population; it is the resistance of ordinary people that is celebrated in these films. Made before Pearl Harbor, *The Commandos Strike at Dawn* was filmed with the cooperation of the Canadian and British governments and starred a contingent of American and British actors. On the other hand, *Edge of Darkness* was strictly Hollywood as Errol Flynn (an Australian by birth) played a local fisherman who leads the Norwegian underground against the Nazis. Meant as a tribute to the Norwegian resistance, the film was cast with stock actors from the Warner Brothers studio and it looked like it was filmed on the backlot. Still, the film contains two scenes of German brutality, involving the beating and public humiliation of the town's intellectual and the rape of a resistance woman, which, under Production Code guidelines, had to be implied rather than depicted. Both crimes were revenged in typical Hollywood fashion.

While men saw combat duty, women joined the armed services as nurses and as noncombatant replacements for the men at the front. Almost 400,000 women, including nurses, saw military service during the war; some lost their lives in the performance of that duty. The Army Air Force, for example, commissioned over 1,800 women as pilots in the newly formed WASP (Women Airforce Service Pilots) unit to fly ferry planes, to tow gunnery targets, and to serve as test pilots and flight instructors in an effort to release men for combat duty overseas. The government did not officially recognize this secret unit as military personnel, even though thirty-eight women died in plane crashes in the course of flying sixty million miles until Congress disbanded the unit in December 1944.[25]

FIGURE 11. Jackie Cochran instructing WASPs during World War II: 1943. Reprinted with permission, The Women's Collection, Texas Woman's University.

Regrettably, Hollywood chose to ignore these women and others like them. When women appeared in World War II films they usually were cast in the roles of USO entertainers, homefront workers, and sometimes as spies. Mainly, however, Hollywood minimized their contribution by portraying them as romantic interests or as volunteers and workers in field hospitals. There were several notable exceptions to this generalization: A 1943 film, *Ladies Courageous*, starred Loretta Young and told the story of the first group of women pilots that later became the WASPs.[26] Both *So Proudly We Hail* (1943) and *Cry Havoc* (1944) depicted nurses under combat conditions. An estimated 50,000 nurses served in the military during the Second World War, receiving military as well as medical training. Nurses served in all military branches and in all the war zones; some became prisoners of war when Corregidor fell, others were killed when the enemy shelled field hospitals.[27] Both Paramount's *So Proudly We Hail* and MGM's *Cry Havoc* paid tribute to Red Cross nurses. In *So Proudly We Hail* an all-star cast of actresses is trapped in the early days of the Pacific war. The film depicts their daily hardships, including several encounters with the enemy. In one such confrontation, a nurse sacrifices herself by becoming a human bomb, permitting the other nurses to escape from the advancing Japanese. The story line requires virtually nonstop combat conditions, though Paramount, bowing to projected market demand, permitted a few romantic interludes. The film concludes with the fall of Bataan; despite that defeat the film remains more optimistic than is warranted by the actual status of the war at the time. Like the patriotism of the marines in *Wake Island*, the nurses in *So Proudly We Hail* represent an American confidence that democracy will prevail over the forces of evil.

MGM's *Cry Havoc*, another token entry by a major Hollywood film studio regarding the role of women during World War II, also relates the plight of nurses caught behind enemy lines during the American retreat from Bataan,[28] including one casualty when a nurse is machine-gunned to death while swimming. It remains a mystery why two film studios virtually made the identical movie on a similar subject and released them during the same year. Whether by accident or design, these films influenced the federal government to act to recognize the heroism of the women who served. Washington finally erected a Women's Memorial at the entrance to Arlington National Cemetery to commemorate the contribution of women to the country's military service, beginning with the American Revolution and continuing through the Persian Gulf War.[29]

Hollywood did not do right by women or minorities[30] during World War II but the film studios certainly knew how to churn out hate propaganda against the enemy. No one expected Hollywood to present heroic images of the enemy, but the studios took every opportunity to inject propaganda into their screenplays. The war, of course, was being fought at home as well as at the front. The research of film scholars,[31] applying content analysis to World War II movies, reveals a strong film bias against the Japanese relative to the Germans and the Italians. The Japanese bias led to racist images on the screen. This was less true of war films involving the Germans because the war with Germany was being waged ideologically in wartime movies, that is, it was being waged against the German government—the Nazis—and not necessarily against the German people. As a matter of fact, even before *Schindler's List*, there were a few films where Germans befriend Allied soldiers or protect civilians from potential harm. Such an event occurs in *Desperate Journey* (1942) where some "good" Germans aid Errol Flynn and his squadron. Again, in *The Moon Is Down* (1943), a film about the Nazi occupation of Norway, one of the German officers is portrayed rather sympathetically. He is tired of the war and is homesick. His softness leads to his death, but not before his character has the opportunity to voice the sentiments of a sane Germany. This is definitely not the case for the Japanese, who fared so badly in these war movies as to suggest a more racist depiction rather than an ideological treatment. Take the 1942 B-movie, *Little Tokyo, U.S.A.*, for instance. In this story of domestic espionage in Southern California, the film implied that any person of Japanese ancestry was a spy or sabo-

teur. All the Japanese characters were portrayed as treacherous and not to be trusted. The movie was considered so prejudicial that even the War Relocation Authority,
the government agency that administered the internment camps, complained to the
OWI about the film.[32] The following year, RKO Pictures released *Behind the Rising
Sun* (1943), a piece of anti-Japanese propaganda that concerned the efforts of a
Japanese father to persuade his Americanized son to join the Sino-Japanese war. In
approximately ninety minutes of running time, the film contains scenes of Japanese
raping women, bayoneting children, and torturing prisoners by placing needles
under their fingernails, burning them with cigarettes and hanging them by their
wrists until dead.[33] While it is true that these were primarily low-budget B-films
rushed into release after Pearl Harbor and could be excused on that account, the
depictions of Japanese soldiers in feature films like *Wake Island* and *Guadalcanal
Diary* also were overtly racist. Derogatory terms like "Nips," "monkeys," and "apes"
were used to refer to the Japanese. Nor did Japanese soldiers fight by the rules in
Hollywood films. In contrast, American GIs harbored little hatred toward their enemies and even tended to their wounds. On the screen, the Japanese had no redeeming qualities.[34] These negative depictions of the Japanese can be considered part of
a continuous line of racial stereotypes of Asians historically traceable to the
Philippine insurgency following the Spanish-American War and reinforced during
the war in Vietnam.

Whatever misgivings film scholars and historians have regarding Hollywood
war movies, there is no denying the staying power of the genre. The box office success of World War II films challenged the conventional wisdom in the film industry that the public would not go to war movies. To test the market, Hollywood
released nine combat films in 1949 alone, including *Sands of Iwo Jima*, which
grossed $25 million, a considerable figure at the time. The financial success of these
war films a few years after the end of hostilities encouraged the industry to generate more movies in the same genre over the next four decades. Combat films
included *The Longest Day* (1962), *Battle of the Bulge* (1965), and *Patton* (1970); prison
camps were featured in *Stalag 17* (1953), *The Bridge on the River Kwai* (1957), and
The Great Escape (1963). In fact, between 1948 and 1970, Hollywood released at
least one World War II combat film every year.[35] Even into the nineties, the studios continued to find the Second World War good box office with several major
films critical and financial successes, including Steven Spielberg's *Schindler's List*
(1993) and *Saving Private Ryan* (1998).[36]

Homefront

Action/combat films remained in the Hollywood repertory for a good forty years
after World War II. A few Hollywood films had plots that revolved around life at

home during the war, showing the housing shortage, scarcity of consumer goods, and food rationing. Hollywood produced just two major feature films about the homefront during the war, *Tender Comrade* (1943) and *Since You Went Away* (1944). In *Tender Comrade*, five women (girlfriends, wives, and mothers) live together while their men are in the service.[37] Ginger Rogers stars as a woman who decides to share a house with three other women who work with her in the same defense plant after her husband is drafted. The fifth member of the group is a German woman who, because she is not a citizen and cannot work in the defense plant, serves as cook and housemaid for the others. The women in *Tender Comrade* are depicted as independent characters and not mere extensions of their menfolk. The film was considered a "woman's" picture because the audience learns details about the war off-camera. *Tender Comrade* was written by Dalton Trumbo and directed by Edward Dmytryk, later to be identified as members of the Hollywood Ten. Their involvement with the film, coupled with the word "tender" in its title and its communal living arrangements ("Share and share alike"), led HUAC to label it "un-American" after the war.

In *Since You Went Away* (1944), Claudette Colbert's husband is called to military duty, leaving her to care for their two children. The film focuses on the plight of a middle-class family struggling to survive the war years. Money becomes a primary concern as the family is forced to take in a boarder. Similar to *Tender Comrade*, *Since You Went Away* features major female characters, (even Colbert's children are girls in the film), with the studio's intention to appeal to women in the audience who could relate to the situation on the screen. Much like the World War II combat film, these homefront movies glorified individual sacrifice for the good of the country. Colbert's character is compelled to enter the workforce as a welder (a/k/a Rosie the Riveter) in a defense plant.

However, the most honored film about the homefront turned out to be *The Best Years of Our Lives* (1946), based on a story published in 1944 about problems that veterans faced in adjusting to civilian life. Production was delayed for two years and the film was not released until the war had ended. Using three different characters—Al Stephenson (Fredric March), a middle-aged banker turned army sergeant, Fred Derry (Dana Andrews), an Air Force hero and former drugstore clerk, and Homer Parrish (non-actor Harold Russell in his first film role), as a Navy vet who lost both hands in combat—as composites to represent war veterans, the film focused on issues that faced the discharged soldiers' return to civilian life, namely, employment, marriage, family, and social acceptance.[38] The film was a box office hit and proved to be an artistic success as it won seven Oscars, including best picture.

Contrary to popular belief, Hollywood films about the civilian population during World War II did not imitate government propaganda slogans promoting duty, obligation and patriotic responsibility. Instead the homefront movies emphasized democratic values while they encouraged civilians to protect their home and family.[39] These wholesome themes contributed to the mythology that World War II was a "good war" fought by the "greatest generation" as described by Tom Brokaw.[40] That generation, Brokaw reminds us, survived the Great Depression and went on to defeat the Axis Powers in the Second World War. The popularity of that war spurred interest in building new monuments to the men and women for fought "the good war." A new WWII memorial has recently been dedicated on the Washington Mall between the Washington Monument and the Lincoln Memorial. Meanwhile, funds were being solicited to expand the National D-Day Museum in New Orleans to include the Pacific and other war areas.

While credit is due to the generation who, although ordinary people, managed to perform extraordinary feats of courage and self-sacrifice, still Brokaw failed to mention that these same decent people lived in (and possibly contributed to) a racist and sexist society, generally supported McCarthyism, HUAC, and the anti-communist hysteria in the 1950s as well as the Vietnam War in the sixties. Possibly Hollywood has contributed to the hype, but as James Bradley noted in his book, *Flags of Our Fathers*, the Iwo Jima veterans never talked about themselves or the war. Maybe, unlike Hollywood, these veterans understood that media labels do not always reflect the whole truth.

Documentaries

Possibly Hollywood could be excused for glamorizing the war film, exploiting the setting to depict acts of heroism and self-sacrifice and to show individual deeds of glory as the means to build character and test manhood. But the federal government cannot be absolved from treating the film medium as another weapon of war. The OWI, through its Bureau of Motion Pictures, had primary responsibility for over-sight of Hollywood films produced during the war years. The OWI also commissioned war movies of its own, some intended for the armed forces, others for general release. The U.S. government distributed 164 films between 1941 and 1945, with thirteen pre-Pearl Harbor films acting as promotionals for the USO and the Red Cross.[41] Commencing in 1942, however, the emphasis shifted to films that would directly aid the war effort through recruitment in the Coast Guard and through special pleadings to women to consider working in defense plants. For instance, government-made movies appealed to feelings of patriotism in soliciting war bonds sales, conserving resources, and planting victory gardens. On the other hand, some government films served as warnings against profiting from the war (black marketeering) and the dangers of loose lips and careless talk.

The government sought to offset the more romantic and fantasized images of the Hollywood war film by shooting its own combat footage. These films were commercially distributed through five newsreel companies, including MGM's News of the Day, Paramount News, RKO-Pathe News, Twentieth Century Fox's Movietone News, and Universal Newsreel, and were shown as part of the weekly movie program in at least two-thirds of the nation's theaters.[42] These government-produced films, known as official reports, supposedly cost the government $50 million a year to produce and distribute. Many of these are still available in the National Archives. The government was fortunate to have the services of such prominent Hollywood directors as John Ford, Frank Capra, George Stevens, William Wyler, and John Huston at its disposal, either as civilians under contract or as military personnel assigned to a combat unit. Some of the more important documentaries made by these men included *The Memphis Belle* (1943) in which Wyler depicted the last mission of a B-52 bomber, part of the Eighth U.S. Air Force Command, from ground crew preparation to its return from a bombing mission over Germany. John Huston was commissioned by the War Department to make two films; one, *Report from the Aleutians* (1943) about a bombing raid and the second, *The Battle of San Pietro* (1944) about the Italian campaign. To capture the sense of combat, Huston accompanied a front-line unit and shot footage while the battle raged. Because it shattered the warrior myth, the army disliked the film and gave it a "secret" classification, insuring that it would be kept out of public circulation. Huston's documentary was not distributed to the public until almost one-third of its footage was cut from the original.[43] Another Hollywood director, John Ford, recreated the attack on Pearl Harbor in *December 7th: The Movie* (1943).[44] Previously, Lt. Commander Ford, on duty in the Pacific, shot film during the fierce naval and air war being waged at the time. Ford filmed as the battle raged and then edited and released the result as *The Battle of Midway* (1942). The Navy was so impressed with the film that it was used to stimulate war bond sales.[45] Films like *The Battle of Midway* and commercial newsreels containing actual footage depicted the war in terms that even Hollywood, with all its money, talent, and technical resources, failed to replicate. Although edited in some cases, these documentaries portrayed the Second World War in more realistic terms than the traditional Hollywood version, at least until the first half-hour of *Saving Private Ryan*.[46] In order to get the gritty feel of Omaha Beach on D-Day, Spielberg stripped the coating off the lenses on his Panasonic cameras, adjusted the shutter openings, and then attached blood packs to handheld cameras to stimulate their vibrations.[47] Audiences agreed that he had succeeded in capturing the atmosphere of battle on film.

KOREA: THE FORGOTTEN WAR

There are many reasons why the Korean conflict (1950–53) (Congress did not declare war) has been dubbed "the forgotten war." One explanation is that the war was fought under the auspices of the United Nations (UN), even though the United States contributed a majority of the troops and supplies. In effect, the UN sanctioned the sending of troops as part of America's right to meet its treaty obligations since the North Koreans were the aggressors. Eventually other UN members contributed troops to what was referred to as an "international police action." Moreover, it was a war fought for limited objectives. From the UN viewpoint, the war was not about gaining territory or furthering political or military objectives. The sole purpose of the UN action was to drive the North Koreans back over the 38th parallel and restore the territorial status quo. Meanwhile, the fighting between North and South waged for three years and included Chinese and U.S. intervention. A year after the initial clash between North and South Korean troops, cease-fire talks were initiated, while sporadic fighting continued for two more years until an armistice was signed in 1953. Unlike Vietnam, however, Korea was not a television war. Instead, the networks continued to rely on government reports for their news rather than journalists in the field, a facsimile of the way news was collected during World War II. Therefore, the Korean War was not filmed as it happened.

FIGURE 12. Local Korean War parade, Williamsport, Pennsylvania: 1997. Reprinted with permission, *Williamsport Sun-Gazette.*

FIGURE 13. Marilyn Monroe in Korea: 1954. Personal Collection.

Nor did the war affect the collective conscience of the nation as its predeces-sor did. A memorial to its veterans was not constructed in Washington until 1995, more than forty years after the armistice and thirteen years after the erection of the Vietnam Wall, despite the more than 54,000 deaths suffered in the Korean conflict. Finally, Hollywood did not seem terribly interested in the war; it failed to stir the emotions of the stars or serve as a resource for screen plots. Possibly because the war in Korea was one of attrition and stalemate rather than liberation and military victory, the film studios believed they could not duplicate the patriotism and idealism of the World War II movies.

A reliable indication of how Hollywood neglected Korea is found in the production statistics covering the years between 1950 and 1970 when the industry released four times as many World War II movies as films on the Korean War. The two most popular war movies during this period were films about the Second World War: *From Here to Eternity* (1953) and *The Bridge on the River Kwai*(1957). Also, no film on the Korean War has won an Oscar in any of the major categories in contrast to the number of awards presented to World War II and Vietnam War films.

When Hollywood treated the subject, it usually did so in low-budget B-movies without production values and minus strong marketing campaigns. Basinger reports that many of the Korean War films were replays of World War II combat films in terms of narrative development, characterizations, and symbolic events.[48] For example, the Korean War films continued to utilize the composite combat group, including ethnic diversity, as the basis for plot development. The film's hero was still the tough officer or sergeant and the central action was a "single mission" to knock out an enemy objective or to make a last stand against overwhelming enemy forces. To make the films more plausible, Hollywood updated its military hardware to match the requirements of the new conflict, hence, the carbine replaced the M1 rifle, the helicopter and jet plane replaced the B-52 bomber and fighter planes, and the Mobile Army Surgical Hospitals (MASH) replaced base hospitals.

In addition to the updated military hardware, Hollywood differentiates Korean War films from those of World War II in another significant way. In the WWII prisoner of war films, the American captives were defiant and heroic and usually plotted to escape from their camps. With a few exceptions, such as in the film *Stalag 17* (1953), WWII POWs were always patriotic and loyal to their country. Not so in Korean War films where the POWs were often portrayed as "brainwashed victims" or traitors. At least in a half-dozen films, the POWs cooperated and even collaborated with their captors. It is true that after the war, fourteen POWs were officially tried as collaborators, with eleven convicted. Yet this is a small number compared to the more than 7,000 POWs interned during the war, half of whom did not survive their captivity.[49]

Hollywood exploited this fact in a series of POW-type films. The most prominent film of this type, *The Manchurian Candidate*, is not a Korean combat film but rather a study of communist brainwashing. The plot concerns a noncommissioned officer, captured in Korea, who is programmed to carry out political assassinations. At the end, he deliberately avoids his intended target (a presidential candidate) and shoots his mother and McCarthy-type stepfather (VP candidate) instead. Released two days before the Cuban Missile Crisis, the film became a cult classic with viewers intrigued by conspiracy theories and Hollywood mythology. Not overly popular with audiences during its initial run, the film was shelved after the Kennedy assassination. The legend grew that its withdrawal from distribution was in respect to the fallen president but recent events indicate it may have had more to do with a contract dispute. Before he died, Frank Sinatra, whose film company held the rights, gave his daughter permission to remake the film. The 2004 version substitutes the Persian Gulf War for Korea, and a multinational corporation, Manchurian Global, is the villain.

Another Korean POW film, *Prisoner of War* (1954), starred Ronald Reagan as an Army Intelligence officer who allows himself to be captured by the North Koreans. He avoids the torture and brainwashing administered to the other prisoners by pretending to cooperate with the communists. In this way, he is able to collect evidence on the mistreatment of American POWs. Brainwashing was a major concern during the Korean War and it proved a sticking point during the two years of peace talks because the North Koreans insisted on a return of all their prisoners, while the United States. and its UN allies wanted POWs to have freedom of choice.

Several films on the combat aspects of the Korean War deserve consideration. Two, *The Steel Helmet* and *Fixed Bayonets*, were made by the decorated World War II combat veteran, Samuel Fuller, and released in 1951 during the early stages of the war; a third, *Pork Chop Hill* (1959), was released on the eve of the growing American presence in Vietnam. Like most of Fuller's war movies, *Steel Helmet* and *Fixed Bayonets* were lean, tough films, shot in black and white with their focus on the foot soldier, reminiscent of World War II combat movies. In *Fixed Bayonets*, Fuller's drama centers on a platoon of forty-eight men left behind during a Korean winter to fight a rear guard action against the enemy in order to save the 15,000 members of the battalion. Made with the cooperation of the War Department, *Fixed Bayonets* has a formula familiar to World War II audiences that remembered *Bataan* and *Wake Island*. It included acts of courage and self-sacrifice and the major character, a noncommissioned officer who must lead his platoon back to its regiment, displays the kind of courage under fire that symbolize the coming of manhood in World War II movies.

The Steel Helmet was Fuller's first war film; a *tour de force* since Fuller wrote the screenplay and served as producer and director. The film was completed in ten days and dedicated to the U.S. infantry. Like many of Fuller's films, it has a straightforward plot but its strength lies in its characterizations. The simple story concerns a tough, experienced sergeant and his platoon, who are ordered to capture and hold a Buddhist Temple to serve as an observation post for directing artillery fire. Most of the action takes place within the temple. The film ends with a fierce battle between the handful of American troops and hundreds of communist forces. Aside from the fighting, this B-movie touches on racial issues, a subject considered taboo by the traditional film studios at that time. The racial issue is raised when the platoon discovers a North Korean major hiding inside the temple. The major wants to know why the black medic and the Japanese-American (Nisei) soldier are fighting with white men against the oppressed peoples of color. The North Korean reminds the black medic that his platoon members are unlikely to eat with him in civilian life. Addressing the soldier, the major cannot understand why the Nisei would be fighting in Korea when his family had been interned in a relocation camp during the Second World War.[50] Although Fuller's characters provide unsatisfactory answers, raising the racial question in a film that was released three years before the desegregation decision in *Brown v. Board of Education*[51] is an expression of his personal sympathies toward the world's "underdogs," whether minorities mistreated by their homeland or infantry soldiers resigned to doing the dirty work of war.

Pork Chop Hill had the sound and smell of combat; not surprising since it was directed by Lewis Milestone of *All Quiet on the Western Front* fame, based on essays written by a veteran, S.L.A. Marshall, and made with the cooperation of the U.S. Army. Lt. Clemons's (Gregory Peck) outfit is ordered to retake Chinese-held Pork Chop Hill and hold the position until reinforcements arrive. His men suffer tremendous casualties before reaching the top of a hill that has no military value. Outnumbered by overwhelming Chinese forces, Clemons asks headquarters for reinforcements or permission to withdraw. He is ordered to hold the hill at all costs. Later on he learns that his platoon was used as a bargaining chip at the negotiating table at Panmunjon. As one U.S. general at the peace talks puts it: "Are we as willing as the Chinese to spend lives for nothing?" The answer is a qualified "yes" as reinforcements finally arrive, but only after 80 percent of Peck's unit has been sacrificed as political pawns. Although there were rumors that the film had been edited, what remains clearly illustrates the complexity of combining military and political ends. *Pork Chop Hill* serves to bridge the gap between the heroics of the World War II combat films and the later disillusionment of American involvement in Vietnam.

Hollywood made few films about the impact of the Korean War at home. One exception was *I Want You* (1951), starring Dana Andrews, who had appeared in *The Best Years of Our Lives* and a number of other World War II movies. Andrews plays an ex-GI, married with a family and living in small town America. His father had served in the First World War while he had seen action in the Second. Andrews has a younger brother and when the Korean War begins, the key plot issue involves the draft and military service. Should Andrews write a letter to the local draft board asking for a deferment for his brother who works in the family architectural firm?

Examining his conscience, Andrews decides against asking for special privileges for his brother, which leads to his induction into the army. The draft issue during the Korean conflict was not as dramatic or divisive as in the sixties with Vietnam; yet college-age males received automatic deferments until graduation. This special treatment of college students would reach a climax during the Vietnam era when males who sought refuge from the draft either bought time in college or skipped to Canada. In *I Want You*, complaints to draft boards about why a particular young man was not in the service came from the parents of those drafted into military duty while whispers and gossip around town questioned the fairness of the selective service system. The issue is conveniently resolved in the film as Andrews's brother is assigned to Germany rather than Korea; he therefore avoids combat duty. But when Andrews is asked by his former commanding officer to rejoin his old World War II outfit to help build airfields in Korea, Andrews chooses to reenter the military rather than seek an exemption. Their mother has the best line in the film when she declares to her family, "It seems all my life I've been saying goodbye to my sons."

Most Americans born after WW II learned about the Korean War from *M*A*S*H*, the popular television series in the seventies that was based on the Robert Altman film. The television show about a mobile medical unit in Korea became one of the most successful shows on the air, running for eleven seasons and many years of reruns. Considered irreverent towards the military and strongly antiwar in its sentiments, the TV show provided an opportunity to comment and express antiwar views during the Vietnam War. Its relationship to battlefield conditions in Korea, however, existed mostly in the imagination of sitcom writers. While the MASH units provided conditions for battlefield surgeries, a whole generation of Americans viewed the Korean conflict through the antics of fictional characters like Hawkeye, Radar, Trapper John, and "Hotlips" Houlihan. Only occasionally did the series tackle a serious subject such as deaths caused by friendly fire that were covered up by the military.

In his book, *Just and Unjust Wars*, Michael Walzer categorizes Korea as a "just war" for three reasons.[52] First, U.S. involvement rested on assisting South Korea against a full-scale invasion by 60,000 North Korean troops. Second, the United Nations authorized the American participation. Third, the military objective underneath the intervention was to restore the *status quo ante bellum* and reestablish the 38th parallel as the demarcation line between North and South as defined by treaty. But the very nature of a "just war" precludes a nation from bragging over the war's events. In fighting "just wars" nations do not punish their enemies or celebrate military victories; two necessary dramatic effects in any combat war movie. After years of decisive World War II films in which the enemy was clearly defined and in which commitment to total victory was absolute, it was understandable that the ambiguity of the Korean "police action" discouraged the making of salutary films about the war. The Korean War was not so much forgotten as ignored by Hollywood and the American people.

One aspect of the conflict that was deliberately forgotten by the military until 1999 were atrocities committed during the war. News stories[53] revealed two such incidents early in the war. The first involved the massacre of South Korean civilians, mostly refugees, at No Gun Ri. Apparently inexperienced American troops fired upon hundreds of these refugees in July 1950, mistakenly believing them to be North Korean infiltrators. The second incident did not directly involve American troops. Instead, U.S. Army officers stood by while the South Korean military executed more than 2,000 political prisoners during the early days of the war. Of course, the North Koreans did likewise when they occupied territory in the south, but they were not our allies.

If Americans were frustrated by the political stalemate in Korea that ended the fighting, their discontent was barely visible. On the horizon, however, loomed another conflict in Southeast Asia that would prove as divisive at home as the Civil War.

PICTURING
VIETNAM
ON FILM

CHAPTER NINE

Lessons Learned and Forgotten

"I love the smell of napalm in the morning."

COL. KILGORE, *APOCALYPSE NOW*

"The Oriental doesn't put the same high price on life as does the westerner."

GENERAL WILLIAM WESTMORELAND

"We are here to help the Vietnamese, because inside every gook, there is an American trying to get out."

MARINE COLONEL, *FULL METAL JACKET*

"Filmic images of death and carnage are pornography for the military man"

ANTHONY SWOFFORD, FORMER MARINE SNIPER

U nlike the Korean conflict, Vietnam was very much a television war, with the fighting and dying vividly displayed on the evening news. Bringing the war into the home was best expressed in a scene from the film *Summertree* (1971) where actor Michael Douglas drops out of college and is shipped to Vietnam. The poignant moment occurs in the final scene when his parents, watching the late night television news in their bedroom, click off the set just as their son's body bag is being loaded onto a helicopter. This dramatic scene depicts the pervasiveness of the war, from the soldiers at the front to civilians in the comfort of their home. To avoid its presence would have required a life of isolation, a monk's existence without access to the daily newspaper or television set. In urban centers and on university campuses, the war often preempted academic studies, as picketers waved their placards, demonstrators' chanted antiwar slogans, protesters blocked the entrances into campus buildings, and police clashed with students. In short, the spirit of the war permeated the country; its presence was felt even when its effects were not always visible.

The Vietnam War era was a time of affliction for Americans, generating pain and suffering at home and abroad. The war cost the United States an estimated $165 billion. The number of American dead exceeded 58,000, with another 300,000 wounded. A considerable number of veterans returned home either physically disabled or mentally impaired. The number of suicides among Vietnam vets is proportionally higher than among other segments of the population. Often neglected in the human tragedy are the casualties suffered by the Vietnamese people; over one million South Vietnamese troops, North Vietnamese Army regulars, and Vietcong (VC) guerrillas were killed, together with an additional one million civilian casualties. The bombing and napalm destroyed more than 5.2 million acres of Vietnamese land.[1] These are tremendous losses for what correspondent Bernard Fall once characterized as "a small war."[2] Fall had placed Vietnam within the era characterized as of a period of modest revolutionary wars. Once the casualties from these forty-eight minor wars are computed, Fall acknowledged that they would equal losses suffered in either of the two world wars.

The setback in Vietnam was difficult for Americans to accept since the national character is preconditioned to military victories rather than defeats. The Korean conflict, conducted under UN authority, was accepted by the country, albeit reluctantly, as a bona fide stalemate. At least after the Panmunjon negotiations, Korea remained a divided country, with the communists in control of the northern half. But in Vietnam, the entire country was lost to the communists once the United States withdrew its armed forces as part of the Paris Accords; the fall of Saigon in 1975 marked the official end of South Vietnam. Moreover the conclusion of this divisive war left thousands of loyal South Vietnamese to the mercy of the enemy. Critics of Vietnam policy considered this decision by the United States a shameful act of betrayal.

Furthermore, outside of the internal strife that accompanied the civil war in Vietnam, the increasing Americanization of the conflict divided generations, families, races, and socioeconomic classes. Fathers who served in the "Good War" clashed with their sons over the merits of the war just as actor Michael Douglas did with his father in *Summertree*. Laborers and the working-class generally supported the war, while intellectuals, academics, and college students opposed it. Civil rights leaders argued that young black men were being sent to Vietnam to fight against another minority, while the smart, rich white boys retreated to the security of a college or university campus and proceeded to protest the war from within their safe haven. Police entered college campuses to quell student demonstrations. Students, in turn, boycotted classes, harassed pro-war professors, and locked administrators in their offices. Antiwar students literally shut down colleges and universities. At Villanova, for example, a rally by Tom Hayden and the Students for a Democratic Society (SDS) led the university to suspend operations for five days. It seemed in the sixties that America was a fractured society, one part at war against a foreign foe, another segment at odds against the government in particular, and authority in general.

Vietnam was not a war that could be ignored. Taking a neutral position was virtually impossible, politically or philosophically; one was either for the war or against it. Also, unlike World War II soldiers, the Vietnam veterans did not receive a warm homecoming; there were no parades or marching bands to greet them. Instead Vietnam veterans returned to America in silence, either ignored or scorned by their country. There were no heroes in this war.

The national feeling of ambivalence toward Vietnam was reflected in the films of the era. While the war movie genre continued to do well at the box office, the film studios doubted that there was much commercial value in Vietnam during the early stages of the conflict. Eventually, Vietnam films would surpass the number of films the industry had released on the Korean conflict, although the studios proceeded cautiously. One early B-movie entry, *To the Shores of Hell* (1965), proved a commercial failure. It recounted the story of an American marine who attempts to rescue his brother from the Vietcong. Perhaps its failure was predictable given its low-budget production and largely unknown cast.

The film's poor reception, however, did not deter John Wayne, who with the assistance of the U.S. military, produced, directed, and starred in *The Green Berets* (1968). It turned out to be the only American film to unequivocally support U.S. involvement in the war. The major film studios were reluctant to fund such a project, but Wayne was willing to risk his money and his considerable reputation. Supposedly, Wayne wrote to President Johnson that it was "extremely important that not only the people of the United States but those all over the world should know why it is necessary for us to be there [Vietnam]" and that furthermore, the "most effective way to accomplish this is through the motion picture medium." Wayne told LBJ that the film "would inspire a patriotic attitude on the part of fellow Americans."[3] Jack Valenti, LBJ's aide, was receptive to Wayne's plea for government support and persuaded the president to grant the actor the military assistance required to complete the project. The aid included arms and equipment as well as advisors and permission to shoot the film at Fort Benning, Georgia. *The Green Berets* turned out to be a commercial for the Special Forces and an apologia for the Johnson administration's war policy. The film's rhetoric flaunted a Cold War mentality, since its message was that Vietnam was one small part of the worldwide communist conspiracy; therefore the American presence was necessary. Similar to many of the World War II combat movies, *The Green Berets* is a hybrid part training, part battle film. Using a skeptical journalist (David Janssen) as a convenient plot device, Wayne took every script opportunity to articulate the government's position that Vietnam was not a civil war since the North received aid from the Chinese and the Russians. America is in Vietnam, Wayne's film insisted, because the United States had to protect the Vietnamese people from communist domination. For the film's finale, Wayne would repeat almost verbatim the line he used in *Back to Bataan* almost three decades before, but this time to a Vietnamese orphan, explaining that America was fighting the war for children like him. A similar use of force for humanitarian reasons was echoed thirty years later by President Clinton to justify a bombing campaign in Kosovo. *The Green Berets* turned a profit despite poor reviews, antiwar protests, and an ill-timed theatrical release during the year of the Tet offensive and the MyLai massacre. Its box office success was testimony to Wayne's star power, but the film was recognized as an attempt by Wayne to structure the film as if it were a formulaic western or World War II movie. Hence, *The Green Berets* proved to be nothing more than the standard action yarn about good guys (cowboys, U.S. cavalry, U.S. military) versus bad guys (Indians, North Vietnamese Army, Vietcong).[4] Its poor reception by critics ensured that it would garner no awards nor have any imitators.

Both *To the Shores of Hell* and *The Green Berets* were aberrations as Hollywood ignored the Vietnam War movie in the turbulent sixties. When the film industry decided to utilize the war as screen material, it did so with a vengeance. In the late seventies, the studios renewed their interest in the topic after the Tet offensive and the fall of Saigon. By 1975, the literature on the war was extensive and scholars from several fields, among them history, politics, and film studies, wrote scripts and directed visual images of the Vietnam War from their respective disciplines. Their scholarship, although overlapping in analysis is best understood as two contrasting perspectives on Hollywood's version of the war, with each outlook reflecting the methodology of their particular discipline merged with their respective personal attitude.

THE WAVE THEORY

Several scholars[5] have advanced a "wave theory" analysis of Vietnam films characterized by saturation marketing where Hollywood releases a batch of war films within a concentrated time span. According to this theory, the film industry dealt with the war in clusters, releasing films about the war in two distinct waves; the first group released to theaters occurred in the years 1978 and 1979, the second appeared between 1985 and 1989.

The first wave of Vietnam war movies includes two combat (in country) films, *Go Tell the Spartans* (1978) and *Apocalypse Now* (1979), one hybrid training-combat film, *The Boys in Company C* (1977), one hybrid combat-returning veteran film, *The Deer Hunter* (1978) and one film, *Coming Home* (1978), that concerns the reassimilation of the returning veteran.

Contrary to World War II movies, the Vietnam combat films differ considerably from their predecessors in two respects: they refused to reconstruct a false image of American unity and military competence in Vietnam, and they avoided the unequivocal acts of courage by individual soldiers. It is difficult to find heroic acts in Vietnam-era films. In fact these "grunts" commit acts of cowardice and participate in unspeakable crimes. Revelations of torture and abuse of detainees at the Abu Ghraib prison in Baghdad during the military action to oust Saddam Hussein raise the fundamental question of whether war itself changes the nature of its participants. This issue reverberates throughout many Vietnam-era films.

In *Go Tell the Spartans*, a film that represents the early years of the war when the American military served primarily as advisers to the South Vietnamese government, the major characters explicitly criticize the strategy of the high command in fighting the war. When a veteran U.S. major (Burt Lancaster) is ordered to move his troops to defend an isolated outpost, he reluctantly obeys because the new position is vulnerable to attack and holds no strategic importance. True to his prediction, Lancaster's troops, composed of raw recruits and South Vietnamese militia, are overrun and killed by the Vietcong. Only one soldier, an idealistic volunteer, survives to relate the tragedy to headquarters. As a consequence his idealism is destroyed along with his fallen comrades. To add insult to injury, the Vietcong strip the bodies, leaving the naked soldiers as a symbol that the Americans will be unable to accomplish what the French had failed to achieve in over a century of administrative rule.

The other combat film, *Apocalypse Now*, could belong in a category of its own because it contains both positive (pro-war) and negative (antiwar) images of fighting an insurgency war where the enemy is dressed as soldier, farmer, or civilian. Drawing from Joseph Conrad's early-twentieth-century novella, *Heart of Darkness*,[6] the film relates the CIA-directed mission of Captain Willard (Martin Sheen) to locate the renegade ex-Special Forces Colonel Kurtz (Marlon Brando) and terminate him "with extreme prejudice." The renegade Kurtz has taken his army of Montagnards into Cambodia and established a camp from which his forces engage in indiscriminate killing. Willard's journey up river into Cambodia, where he locates Kurtz, is meant to represent America's intervention in Vietnam, and the film's commercial and artistic failure proved to be a perfect metaphor for the war itself. At some point in time, Kurtz realized that the war could not be fought by conventional means, nor could it be won by civilized methods. The imposition of brutality, however, led to even greater horror until the excesses of war changed the humanity of those who waged it. Whether meant as a metaphor for the end of civilization or a depiction of America's descent into hell, Coppola's *Apocalypse Now* would never be mistaken for a World War II film where the forces of good and evil are explicitly delineated.

On the other hand, *The Boys in Company C*, is the type of hybrid combat film that was familiar to World War II audiences. It traces the fortunes of five recruits from marine boot camp to combat in Vietnam. The contrast between the competence and efficiency of their drill sergeant (portrayed by a real marine DI) and the incompetence of their field commanders is not coincidental. Field officers put the troops at risk when, in order to deliver booze and other supplies for the commanding general's birthday, they lead their convoy into an ambush. Constant bickering among the company's officers over strategy needlessly cost the lives of their men. As further evidence of military corruption, the American forces are ordered to "lose" a soccer match with the South Vietnamese, an action the team rejects, even though it would guarantee that their remaining days in Vietnam be spent in the relative safety of base headquarters rather than on jungle patrol. Hence, the soccer match becomes a metaphor for the senselessness of the war itself.

Both Michael Cimino's *The Deer Hunter* and Hal Ashby's *Coming Home* confront the physical and psychological problems that faced the Vietnam veteran on his return home. Cimino's film focuses on three working-class men, Michael (Robert DeNiro), Nick (Christopher Walken), and Steven (John Savage), living in a small Pennsylvania steel town that believes in God and country. The three enlist and are sent to Vietnam where the Vietcong capture them. During their imprisonment, they are subject to the torture of playing Russian roulette for the enjoyment of their captors. Eventually, the three friends engineer a daring escape from the prison camp but their experience in Vietnam has permanently altered their lives. Steven is wounded in the escape and returns home a paraplegic who prefers to remain in the VA hospital rather than go home to his wife. Nick remains in Vietnam, becoming a drug addict with such low self-esteem that he gambles and loses his life playing Russian roulette. Michael is the sole survivor, who returns home physically whole but psychologically damaged. This bleak portrait of the harm done to those who served in Vietnam is offset by the final scene at Nick's wake where, despite their personal suffering, the mourners still are able to sing God Bless America. In contrast, at the heart of the film *Coming Home* are the veterans who regret their Vietnam experience and are transformed into antiwar activists. Different though these films may be from each other, what they share in common is an ambiguity toward the war and America's involvement in it.

The films of the second wave (1985–89) are more explicitly critical of the war and symbolize greater cynicism about American involvement. Films such as Oliver Stone's *Platoon* (1986), Stanley Kubrick's *Full Metal Jacket* (1987), John Irvin's *Hamburger Hill* (1987) and Brian DePalma's *Casualties of War* (1989) express dismay, if not disgust, at American militarism. The soldiers in these films would not qualify for good conduct medals. Instead they are presented as cowards, murderers, and rapists. These films are revisionist exercises that indict the United States for its wrongful intervention in the war. One hybrid training-combat film, Stone's *Born on the Fourth of July* (1989), follows real-life Vietnam veteran, Ron Kovic, from gung-ho marine to antiwar activist. Kovic returns home, physically and emotionally scarred. He is consumed with guilt for atrocities over which he had little control. When his platoon invades a village and riddles it with gunfire, the company inadvertently kills women and children. Kovic and several of his buddies try to assist the wounded but are ordered to withdraw as an artillery strike is planned against the village.

These Vietnam combat films were flawed in two significant respects. First, the Vietnam War movies focused on the grunts, the infantry soldiers, who fought the ground war in villages and jungle terrain. These films led audiences to believe that the foot soldier was the heroic figure in Vietnam when most of the damage, in lives and property, resulted from air and artillery strikes rather than the limited firepower of combat soldiers. Second, the films presented an American perspective on the war. The Vietnamese are either portrayed as Vietcong or spectators to the conflict.[7] The second-wave films, therefore, are symbolic of the Americanization of the war.

Films that also would fit within the timeframe of the second wave include the first two Rambo (Sylvester Stallone) films *First Blood* (1982) and *Rambo: First Blood 2* (1985) and the Braddock (Chuck Norris) trilogy *Missing in Action* (1984), *Missing in Action 2: The Beginning* (1985) and *Braddock: Missing in Action III* (1988) as well. These films present a view of the war that places the blame for the failure squarely on politicians and civilian bureaucrats at home.[8] When ex-green beret John Rambo is asked by his former commanding officer, Colonel Trautman, in *Rambo: First Blood, Part 2* to return to Vietnam to rescue American POWs, Rambo replies: "Do we get to win this time?"[9] The question is rhetorical but the film answers it anyway. The Sylvester Stallone character had an immediate impact on the public, as visitors to the Vietnam Memorial Wall search for the name "Arthur John Rambo" to make rubbings to take home as souvenirs.[10]

The Phase Analysis

Social historian William Palmer[11] considers the Vietnam movies as progressive stages in the filmic representation of the war as a visual text, evolving from an epic phase (1976–79) to two overlapping phases in the 1980s—the comic book and the symbolic nihilist. Palmer's theory is that the Vietnam films are best understood as a series of evolving texts related to political and social developments. In the epic phase (1976–79) such films as *The Deer Hunter, Apocalypse Now,* and *Coming Home* renewed America's interest in the war as each film, in its own way, acted as consciousness-raising stimuli on film audiences. Palmer views these films as "the publicists of a Vietnam War consciousness that was abroad in the country yet dormant for various reasons (bitterness, shame, depression, decompression, inarticulateness)."[12] He considers these films to be traditional narratives that are related to previous literary texts (like Stephen Crane's *Red Badge of Courage*) and World War II movies like *Sergeant York* and *Sands of Iwo Jima*.

The first stage of the second phase of the Vietnam War films, the comic book period, occurred, not surprisingly, during the renascent nationalism of the Reagan administration. Films like the Rambo series and the Braddock trilogy supported the president's belief that America did not lose the war in Vietnam. Moreover, the Reagan administration implied that similar "small wars" could be refought and rewon in places like Grenada, the Middle East, and Central America. Palmer notes the similarities between the popular comic book figure at the time, Sergeant Rock, and the Rambo film character. As Rambo's picture appeared on magazines and in newspapers throughout the country, he became the icon for the restoration of American military power in the world. Stallone even was invited to dine with the Reagans at the White House and was treated as if he were a Congressional Medal of Honor recipient.[13]

The other part of the second phase, identified as the symbolic nihilist stage between 1987 and 1988, includes films like *Platoon, Full Metal Jacket,* and *Hamburger Hill*: visual attempts to capture the disorder, chaos, and futility of the war. Within a sixteen-month timeframe, Hollywood released six major features on the war, all except one set in Vietnam. Two films, *Platoon* and *Hamburger Hill*, were inspired by Vietnam veterans who saw combat in the war and who centered the action around foot soldiers—the grunts—who come to view the war as senseless. If Vietnam is commonly identified with the swish, swish, swish of the helicopter and the sound of artillery fire and aerial bombing, its "dirty war" was fought on the ground. In *Hamburger Hill*, for example, the 101st Airborne unit's objective is to take a hill away from the enemy. After a fierce ten-day firefight in which the outfit suffered 70 percent casualties, the Americans secured the hill, but then casually abandoned it as the fighting moved forward. Much like the hill in the Korean War film, *Pork Chop Hill*, the territory fought over in *Hamburger Hill* was of psychological rather than strategic importance.

The second half of Kubrick's *Full Metal Jacket* takes place in Vietnam during the 1968 Tet offensive where a squad of marines is picked off one by one by a

Vietcong sniper. The marines have been so thoroughly indoctrinated with the "born to kill" mentality that they become as brutal as the enemy. At film's end only one marine has survived and he has been dehumanized by the war. Similarly, the Everyman character in Stone's *Platoon*, Chris Taylor (Charlie Sheen) arrives in Vietnam a naive recruit and leaves three months later, alive but with a damaged soul. The film is as much a rite of passage story as a war movie, in which Taylor loses his innocence but becomes a man. During his short tour of duty, Taylor experiences the anguish of trying to survive in a war where the enemy lacks an identifiable face. In the process he becomes transformed into a murderer when he revenges the death of Sergeant Elias by shooting his killer, Sergeant Barnes. After the burning of a local village and the gang rape of a young Vietnamese girl, Taylor writes home "I don't know right from wrong anymore." If Taylor represents Everyman, then America lost its soul in Vietnam.

The Political Expediency Factor

These interpretations of Vietnam War films are valid explanations for how the war was presented to the American public. There is a third perspective that also is worth consideration. Historically, the film industry has been politically bifurcated; selected executives and movie stars are liberals while the traditional studios continue to be run by conservatives who view movies predominately as a business. Hollywood neglected the Vietnam War movie because there was no consensus in the country on the war. That would also explain why the major studios avoided treating Vietnam as source material until it was relatively safe to tackle the subject once American troops left Saigon. It would also explain why no other studio would duplicate Wayne's chauvinistic *Green Berets*. Those few films made about Vietnam before the 1970s were low-budget action pictures, not million-dollar projects. After the fall of Saigon, however, the film industry was willing to take a minimal risk and treat the war and its aftermath on film.

Examinations of those late-seventies' films reveal the traditional Hollywood practice of hedging its bets. What is *The Deer Hunter* save an affirmation of the attitude, "my country right or wrong!" Although the lives of the three major characters have been irrevocably altered by Vietnam (Nick is brought home dead, Steven is disabled, and Michael has lost his appetite for hunting and the kill), they and their townsfolk can still pay homage to flag and country in the final scene.

Apocalypse Now, on the other hand, is more ambiguous since it lends support for both pro and antiwar interpretations.[14] The battle at Charlie's Point, for instance, where gung-ho Colonel Kilgore (Robert Duvall) destroys a Vietnamese village, demonstrates the superiority of American firepower. But Kilgore's helicopter assault, intended to provide a place for soldiers to surf, while the loudspeakers blast Wagner's

"Ride of the Valkyries," also reveals the madness, the total insanity of the war long before Willard locates Kurtz. Even the returning veteran film, *Coming Home*, is most believable as a love story between a marine officer's wife (Jane Fonda) and a wounded veteran turned antiwar activist (Jon Voight) than as an antiwar polemic. The film conveniently neglected several important issues associated with the Vietnam veteran, namely, the government's denial of the effect of Agent Orange on troops and civilians alike, the difficulty of dealing with the veterans' administration bureaucracy, and the problem of post-traumatic stress disorder (PTSD) and the survivor guilt syndrome. One issue that Hollywood did exploit for screen material was the returning veteran as a "walking time bomb"—sick, angry and even psychotic.[15] The Travis Bickle (Robert DeNiro) character in *Taxi Driver* (1976) is an unstable veteran whose outburst of violence against urban immorality escalates into murder and assassination attempts. A year later *Rolling Thunder* (1977) reached the screen with a plot that had a Vietnam POW return home to an unloving wife and unfriendly son. When thieves rob his prized coin collection, disfigure him, and kill his family, the Vietnam veteran extracts his own brand of revenge. Revenge is the motive, also, in a number of B-movies about returning Vietnam veterans. For example, in *Angels from Hell* (1968), a Vietnam veteran returns home to organize his own motorcycle gang and tangles with both rival bikers and the police, while in *Chrome and Hot Leather* (1971), an ex-green beret seeks to extract his own brand of justice from bikers who are responsible for his fiancée's death. Contrary to the World War II veterans in *The Best Years of Our Lives*, these Vietnam vets are often portrayed as a menace to the community and a danger to society. The only comforting news about these B-films is that most Americans never saw them.

With President Reagan's election in 1980, the film studios acknowledged a change in government attitude and in the national mood and sought to take advantage of the transformation. What has been described as the comic book phase in representations of the war, also were political tracts and propaganda pieces that tried to blame misguided bureaucrats and impotent politicians, rather than the American military, for what happened in Vietnam. The "winning the war" syndrome films focused on the exploits of the individual superheroes—Rambo and Braddock—who single-handedly rescue MIAs and POWs and do considerable damage to the life and property of the enemy. Similarly, in *Uncommon Valor* (1983) the heroics are supplied by a commando team of experts and specialists put together by a former Vietnam officer (Gene Hackman) and supported with funds from the private sector. Their objective is to return to Vietnam/Laos to find POWs, including Hackman's son, despite objections from the CIA and Congress. Hackman tells his group of six that there are 2500 soldiers still missing and that the U.S. government either refuses or is unable to bring them home. Thus, this rogue band of misfits (most of the six recruits cannot adjust to civilian life), with the help of local guides, penetrate into Laos, locate the prison camp, and rescue a handful of prisoners. But Hackman's son is not among the group, having died in the camp. The mission, though, costs the lives of two guides and two Vietnam vets, hardly a cost-effective undertaking. Yet the film preaches that the United States remains a commanding military power to be reckoned with despite the fact that the film is about private armies rather than sanctioned military forces. The film's rather alarming lesson is that private armies can accomplish successful missions by force rather than wait for diplomatic negotiations. It is a lesson not lost on paramilitary groups scattered across the United States today.

Admittedly, the period from 1985 to 1989 also saw the release of films like *Platoon* and *Hamburger Hill* that came from independent filmmakers. These films, as well as *Casualties of War* (1989) also can be legitimately viewed as personal statements since Stone, *Hamburger Hill*'s Jim Carabatsos, and *Casualties of War*'s David Rabe, were Vietnam veterans whose scripts were memory plays. These films, together with *Full Metal Jacket*, share important similarities with the war-is-hell combat movies of the Second World War. The difference, of course, is that the World War II soldier was always cast as the hero.

The Vietnam War films can be viewed as reflecting the political expediency factor in Hollywood that requires that a film never alienate its audience, especially by challenging the dominant political ideology. While these interpretations may claim some modicum of validity, there is one criticism of the Vietnam war film that all share, namely, Hollywood focused on the American presence rather than on the Vietnamese people who endured and suffered through the war. Regardless of political ideology, there is no denying that the war was fought in their country—on their land, in their villages and rice paddies. What is largely missing from Hollywood's versions of the war are the Vietnamese. Not one Hollywood Vietnam film raised the fundamental question of who was morally responsible for all the human suffering and property damage.[16] Even independent filmmakers like Stone avoided the issue of American involvement in the war, preferring instead to dramatize the plight of the ordinary soldier. Of course, to focus on responsibility would require a classroom rather than a movie theater.

POST-VIETNAM INTERVENTIONS

Since the evacuation of Saigon in 1975, the United States has committed its troops to some dozen military operations around the world, with mixed results.[17] Several were military failures: the aborted Iranian hostage rescue, the intervention in Lebanon and the disastrous firefight on the streets of Mogadishu. But there were some military victories and operational successes scored in Grenada, Panama, the

Persian Gulf, and the ouster of the Taliban in Afghanistan. The jury is still out on the preemptive strike to oust Saddam Hussein and establish a democracy in Iraq. Limited troops were utilized in the skirmishes and military operations in Lebanon, Grenada, Panama, and Somalia. In the subsequent Persian Gulf and Iraqi wars, the interventions were full-scale, major military actions.

The American government used military force after Vietnam for three reasons: to evacuate or rescue its citizens from foreign countries under siege or caught in the midst of civil wars (Iran, Grenada, Panama), to act as peacekeepers on behalf of the United Nations and friendly nations or to provide humanitarian relief from mass killings and starvation (Lebanon, Somalia, the Balkans), and to liberate occupied lands at the request of friendly nations or as part of a coalition force (Persian Gulf, Iraq). The political reasons for intervention, however, do not lend themselves to neat compartmentalization. In politics, the motivation for military intervention is usually never singular. The invasion of Grenada, for example, was designed not only to protect the 1000 American medical students but also to topple the Marxist government. Similarly, the purpose in Panama was to depose Noriega before the Canal was turned over to Panama, although the administration stressed the security threat to the 34,000 Americans residing in the country at the time. The fact that the Panamanian dictator had ties to the Columbian drug cartel sealed the case for intervention.

For whatever reasons, Hollywood ignored these post-Vietnam military interventions as suitable screen fare. Only a handful of films were produced that concerned such interventions. Perhaps the studios thought audiences had been saturated with war films, even though the industry continued to churn out WWII movies. In some cases, perhaps, the superiority of American military would diminish the dramatic interest for viewers. Another consideration is that after Vietnam the major studios wished to avoid those military interventions that proved unsuccessful.

The disastrous 1982 U.S. involvement in Lebanon, where an 18-month peacekeeping mission ended in failure with 266 military dead and 151 wounded, was ignored completely by the film industry. The same could be said for the botched Iranian hostage rescue during the Carter administration. However, the Grenada intervention, although a minor military operation, turned out quite well for the Reagan administration. In October 1983, the Reagan White House responded to a request from the Organization of Eastern Caribbean States to invade the tiny island of Grenada to insure the safety of American students attending the local medical college. Within three days, the combined strength of 15,000 U.S. Marines and Army Rangers, joined by a token force from six Caribbean nations, overwhelmed the local militia and their "Cuban advisers," evacuated American citizens, and deposed the Marxist government. It was a quick victory with nineteen American soldiers killed in action. Politically, the Grenada invasion was to President Reagan what the Falkland Islands war was to Mrs. Thatcher—an opportunity to reassert military superiority at the expense of an unworthy foe.

With the exception of one major film, Hollywood overlooked the Grenada military success. Actor Clint Eastwood, an admirer of Sam Fuller's work, directed a hybrid-type WWII movie about the Grenada invasion, entitled *Heartbreak Ridge* (1986).[18] Eastwood hired Jim Carabatsos, the Vietnam veteran and writer of *Hamburger Hill*, to write the screenplay, while Eastwood starred as the tough, but antiestablishment, drill sergeant who saw action in Korea and Vietnam and who has problems adjusting to the new civilian volunteer army. Following the hybrid-WWII formula, Eastwood devoted two-thirds of the film to the preparation of his green recruits. As a consequence, *Heartbreak Ridge*, like many of its predecessors, failed to meet the criteria for a combat film and did poorly at the box office.

A second intervention—really a limited "police action"—occurred in December 1989 when the first President Bush sent 4,000 American troops into Panama to drive General Manuel Noriega from power. The brief military action led to Noriega's capture and deportation to the United States to stand trial, where he was convicted and sent to prison. The four-day invasion cost 23 American lives with an additional 300 wounded. The United States action was criticized in Latin America and other parts of the world. Hollywood preferred to turn the other cheek and ignore the entire episode altogether.

The film industry, however, expressed some interest in stories where American military forces assumed the role of peacekeepers. Operating under a United Nations resolution to provide humanitarian relief to Somalia's starving population by ensuring the safety and distribution of food shipments, U.S. forces moved from peacekeeping to military action against the local warlord, Muhammad Aideed. In retaliation, Somali forces attacked and killed Westerners as open warfare raged on the streets of Mogadishu, the capital city. While U.S. ground forces were in the process of rounding up prisoners, a rocket-propelled grenade brought down a Black Hawk helicopter. During a fierce firefight, eighteen Americans were killed along with several hundred Somalis. U.S. forces subsequently withdrew from Somalia without capturing Aideed and the lasting image of dead American pilots being dragged through the streets of Mogadishu raised serious questions as to the wisdom of interventionist policies. Two years later, when the Clinton administration took office, the situation in Somalia had deteriorated to the extent that America's role as a superpower was tarnished because of the inability to bring a local warlord to justice. Did this incident provide encouragement to local thugs and international terrorists? The question was never answered in the film reenactment directed by Ridley Scott and produced by Jerry Bruckheimer, although *Black Hawk Down* (2001) wants audiences to leave theaters impressed with American troops "kicking ass." True, 100 Army Rangers and Delta Forces killed hundreds of Somalis but the

U.S. neither won the battle nor accomplish its humanitarian mission. The film poses none of the serious interventionist questions, demonstrating once again that Hollywood is primarily in the business of selling tickets and avoiding political issues.

Another peacekeeping mission that drew some interest from Hollywood concerned the decade-long struggle in the Balkans, first in Bosnia and later in Kosovo. Neither the first President Bush nor President Clinton wanted to intervene in the war that developed among Serbs, Croats, and Muslims until the brutality and savagery of the horrors were reported in the daily press and appeared on the nightly newscasts. The Bush administration's failure to adopt a hard-line policy encouraged Yugoslavian President Slobodan Milosevic to use force to keep the various ethnic groups from seceding. A few days after Slovenia and Croatia declared their independence in 1991, three bloody wars began that would claim more than 100,000 lives and compel millions more to flee.

Three films were made about the Bosnian War. Each one reflected on different aspects of the conflict. The first was an English-American coproduction, *Welcome to Sarajevo* (1997) that focused on journalists covering the beginning of the war in Sarajevo. The film's intention was to show the horrors of a city under siege, intermingling the lives of the fictional reporters with actual news footage. The second film, *Savior* (1998), was an Oliver Stone production and starred American actor Dennis Quaid as a mercenary in the Foreign Legion sent to Bosnia to fight with Serbian forces against Muslims. Although the film adequately represents the brutality and senselessness of the war, the narrative seems more concerned with Quaid's redemption. Quaid had joined the Legion after his wife and son were killed by Islamic terrorists and in his grief and anger, he becomes an inhuman killing machine until one day he meets a Serbian woman and her baby. The third film, *Behind Enemy Lines* (2001), portrays the ethnic conflict through the eyes of an American pilot shot down over Bosnia and pursued by Serbian troops while his commanding officer tries to rescue him. The pilot, part of an American peacekeeping operation, is assigned to photograph Serbian ground movements when his plane is downed. Before he is rescued, the audience has an opportunity to speculate on the horrors that could result once the peacekeepers leave. While each film involves Americans in some active role, in actuality the U.S. government was a spectator to the conflict until President Clinton committed airpower to NATO in an effort to protect UN peacekeepers on the ground. In 1999 the United States participated in air strikes again in Kosovo against Serb forces until Milosevic agreed to the peace accords that ended the fighting. Although the Balkan wars contained enough dramatic material for several films, Hollywood adopted a "not interested" policy, similar to the U.S. government.

The United States, however, has fought two brief but full-scale wars in the Middle East since the end of the Vietnam hostilities. Both involved the presidencies of George H. W. and George W. Bush, father and son. The first war began rather suddenly in August 1990 when the Iraqi forces of Saddam Hussein invaded Kuwait. President Bush, Sr. acted quickly to organize American military forces to protect Saudi Arabia as part of Operation Desert Shield. By the end of January 1991, the defensive objective of the initial operation was replaced by the offensive firepower of Desert Storm with the intention of toppling Hussein and initiating a "New World Order" in the area. The Persian Gulf War, the president assured the nation, would not be another Vietnam. That promise was kept, as the war was over within months after U.S. military firepower reduced Iraq's infrastructure to the "preindustrial age." Hussein, however, was permitted to remain in power and the new world order was more slogan than reality. President Bush was delighted with the victory, exclaiming, "By God, we've kicked the Vietnam syndrome once and for all."[19] In the flush of military victory, the president could be forgiven for engaging in a bit of hyperbole but the war did serve to ease, if not erase, the burden of the defeat in Vietnam.

As was true for Vietnam, the Persian Gulf War lent itself to television as CNN filed nightly reports directly from the front. It was also a war that proved attractive to the video market and made celebrities out of Generals Schwarzkopf and Powell. At least a dozen videos were produced on various aspects of the war. Additionally, several documentaries were released about the war, having such titles as *Desert Storm: Eagles Over the Gulf* (1991) and *Sandstorm in the Gulf: Digging Out* (1991). One documentary video, *Desert Storm: Cockpit Videos of Bomb Runs* (1992) places the viewer in the pilot's seat on bombing missions. The video comes with a warning that it would never appear on national television because of the offensive language. TV journalists also secured a piece of the action as Dan Rather narrated the war from beginning to end in the three-volume set, *Desert Triumph*, while Diane Sawyer and Barbara Walters conducted interviews and provided commentary in a four-volume series, entitled *Persian Gulf: The Images of a Conflict*.

Once again, Hollywood refused to join in the national hoopla by flooding the theater screens with films about the war. Except for a couple of quickie B-films released in 1991, *The Finest Hour* and *The Heroes of Desert Storm*, the major studios largely ignored the war. By the mid nineties, Hollywood had released only one feature film, *Courage Under Fire* (1996) that concerned the conduct of the war. In this film, Denzel Washington stars as an officer assigned the task of investigating the merits of awarding the Congressional Medal of Honor to helicopter pilot Meg Ryan, the first woman in U.S. history to be so designated. Ryan is in charge of a flight rescue mission when her helicopter is shot down over Kuwait. The crew manages to hold off the Iraqis until another chopper arrives and most return to base safely, except for Ryan whose body is left behind. After interviewing the crew survivors and receiving conflicting versions of what happened in the field under fire, the question for Washington is to uncover the truth, that is, was Ryan a hero or a coward? Although the film contains occasional combat scenes, the action could have taken place in any war. In this sense, *Courage Under Fire* is more a mystery about the discovery of truth than a conventional combat film. As one reviewer[20] observed, film is the worst possible medium to discuss truth honestly since it is edited, cut, and reshot so as to construct a logical story that an audience will accept. War, on the other hand, is neither sensible nor logical.

In 1999, independent director David O. Russell, working from his own screenplay, made the second major Gulf War film, *Three Kings*, a quixotic, baffling movie that puzzled both critics and audiences. Though it starred the popular actor from television's *ER*, George Clooney, the film disappointed at the box office. One reason for the film's poor showing can be attributed to its ambiguous dramatic focus. It was unclear as to whether it was supposed to be a satiric action-adventure feature or whether it was intended as a critique of America's foreign policy indifference to the suffering of the Iraqi people. The plot centers around four U.S. soldiers who find a map at the end of the Gulf War that purportedly locates the place where Hussein has hid gold bullion stolen from Kuwait. The soldiers then design a plan to find the gold and steal it for themselves. During their quest, they encounter Iraqi resistance forces that are waging war against Hussein's elite guards. The resisters mistakenly believe that the soldiers have come to help them depose Hussein. Regrettably, Clooney and his pals are only interested in the gold bullion until, in typical Hollywood fashion, the American soldiers decide to help the resisters reach the safety of the Iranian border. At the film's climax, the gold is turned over to the American military in exchange for allowing the Iraqis to enter Iran. Despite several funny scenes, the film is filled with violence, torture, gas attacks, and other atrocities. Possibly, this mixture of comedy and suffering turned off American audiences. Certainly, the Iraqis living under Hussein's reign of terror would not find the film amusing.

American losses in the Persian Gulf War were 148 dead, including 15 women, and 467 wounded. The Iraqis paid a much heavier price. Their losses are estimates: Iraqi soldiers killed range from 75,000 to 100,000 and civilian casualties due to Allied bombing range from 35,000 to 40,000. In addition, the civilian population suffered considerably from imposed sanctions. Under UN Security Council Resolution 661, comprehensive international sanctions were imposed on Iraq and all its foreign assets were frozen. Although it had considerable oil reserves, Iraq could not feed itself and had to import about 70 percent of its food and medicine. Supposedly, the imposed sanctions served as both punishment and as an incentive for the Iraqi people to overthrow Hussein. Unfortunately, after thirteen years of sanctions, Hussein, his family, and henchmen remained firmly entrenched while the sanction policy resulted in the deaths of roughly 500,000 children due to starvation, medical shortages, and inadequate medical supplies.[21]

Saddam Hussein remained in power until March 2003 when Coalition Forces led by the United States and Great Britain deposed him. This second Iraqi war lasted three weeks and was initiated because Hussein refused to turn over nuclear and biological weapons to the UN. Consequently, the governments of Tony Blair (UK) and George W. Bush invaded Iraq in a preemptive strike against a potential enemy. From a war identified as necessary to protect America's security, the Bush administration, with the cooperation of the media, quietly shifted the war's focus from its initial concerns to freeing the Iraqi people from their tyrannical leader. This second Iraqi war was very much a television war. Unlike the Gulf War, when reporters were limited in their movements, the 2003 version embedded reporters with specific regiments. The result was twenty-four-hour coverage with every battle detailed and with constant commentary by what seemed to be every general who ever wore a uniform. The 2003 version was so extensive that the viewing and listening public may have wanted to shout: "War is not a spectator sport." Nonetheless the American public seemed to embrace this extensive media coverage as vicarious "recreational violence."[22] Because the wars were brief and militarily successful, Americans could accept, and even ambiguously support war as being a necessary good in a world filled with evil leaders. Wars that came into American homes could repulse and fascinate at the same time.

While the Iraqi fighting lasted three weeks, the guerrilla warfare against coalition forces and foreign governments continued on into the following year. No major nuclear or biological weapons were discovered, though Hussein was eventually captured after nine months in hiding. As the sporadic fighting and deadly ambushes continued, American losses escalated despite the president's official pronouncement that the three-week-old war was over. Eighteen months later, American losses had surpassed 1,000 while the wounded numbered into the thousands. As attacks against coalition forces continued and intensified, political pundits tried to compare the Iraqi situation with Vietnam, maintaining that the Bush administration had underestimated the resiliency of the enemy, misinterpreted the character of the Iraqis, and miscalculated the political difficulties of uniting the country. While all of these factors were applicable, the president's defenders sought to distinguish the two conflicts: the Iraqi operation involved limited military targets and objectives, tried to avoid civilian targets to minimize civilian casualties, and sought to overthrow a brutal despot.

Possibly because of the uncertainty of Iraq's political future or because of the extensive television coverage, Hollywood took a "wait and see" attitude toward utilizing the war for dramatic plot material. Hollywood, however, discovered a new screen enemy—terrorists, especially of Middle Eastern heritage, to populate their films.

POST 9/11: JUST WARS, REEL WARS

President Bush's preemptive strike against Iraq raised serious questions with just war theory,[23] which permits intervention but on a limited, justifiable basis. Under just war theory, intervention is justifiable on three grounds: self-defense, to prevent geno-cide or flagrant human rights violations, and for humanitarian reasons. A preemp-tive strike to ward off a potential attack does not fit into those reasons. Since September 11, 2001, the Bush administration sought to link that terrorist attack to an organized, if not always identifiable, enemy—Al Qaeda, supported by allies in Afghanistan and Iraq. The United States and the rest of the world is, in effect, in a war against terrorism. The attack on the Twin Towers transformed the nature of war itself. Hence, counterterrorism is justified on the grounds of self-preservation, that is, strike first before the enemy strikes you. According to this reasoning, the pre-emptive strike against Saddam, with his alleged weapons of mass destruction, was justifiable. The Bush administration used similar reasoning in Afghanistan. The administration demanded that the Taliban regime turn over Al Qaeda members and locations or, at least, the whereabouts of Osama bin Laden. When the Taliban refused to comply, President Bush ordered the bombing to begin prior to a military assault. The problem with this scenario is that almost any aggressor can justify mil-itary action under its rubric.

This might explain why Hollywood is reluctant to deal with such material in its films. Hardly ever has the industry used the medium to deliver ideological mes-sages, except in war movies. While these are popular with audiences, Hollywood, nonetheless, treats the genre with political sensitivity. When Europe was at war in 1914, the film studios observed the official American policy of neutrality. One pre-paredness or interventionist film was offset by another preaching peace and paci-fism. Once the United States entered the war, Hollywood condemned the enemy just as strongly as the government. In the period between the two world wars, the film industry was careful not to offend foreign governments. When Germany and Italy prohibited the importation of American films, Hollywood decided to be more adventurous and treat the subject of fascism on the screen. During the Second World War, the industry wholeheartedly devoted its resources to the war effort. However, when the wars are indecisive like Korea or unpopular like Vietnam, the pragmatism of the industry tests the audience market before plunging into film production. The studios avoided Vietnam until the remaining American troops were home. When Hollywood eventually plotted stories around the war, it omitted any consideration of the validity of the American involvement in Vietnam. According to Michael Walzer,[24] the answer to that fundamental question was pivotal to whether Vietnam was a just or unjust war. No Hollywood film on Vietnam, whether produced by the studios or by independents such as Stone, ever questioned directly the legality or morality of the American presence. The war may have been divisive and unpopular at home but political expediency dictated that Hollywood stick to tradition and play it safe.

The first sign of a revisionist attitude in Hollywood toward Vietnam occurs in *We Were Soldiers* (2002), based on the true story of Lt. Colonel Harold Moore (played by Mel Gibson). In recreating the three-day battle at la Drang Valley in the central highlands, the film pays tribute to the bravery of both the American forces and the North Vietnamese. This bloody battle claimed 50 percent of the Americans and 90 percent of the Vietnamese. In fact, it is a Vietnamese major who praises the American victory but cautions that the end result will be the same as it was for the French, Chinese, and all other invaders. The Vietnamese major knew his history; the invaders did not.

While these Vietnam combat films were praised for their gritty realism, they remain representations and creative inventions of that war rather than the war itself.[25] These films come close to letting the audience "experience Vietnam," yet they remain works of fiction. Films about the grunts (the dog soldiers) did not spare the realism of fighting a guerrilla war in the jungle, where the foot soldiers were subject to leeches, snakes, and heavy rains while slogging through mud and rice paddies to search for an enemy without an identifiable face. No audience would ever understand the disappointment, which intensified into anger and hatred, when the endurance of these conditions failed to secure loyalty and gratitude. Imagine the shock in the scene from *Go Tell the Spartans* when an idealistic soldier discovers the Vietnamese family he befriended has betrayed him. Or take the disk jockey character Robin Williams portrays in *Good Morning, Vietnam* (1987) who comes to realize that the brother of the Vietnamese woman he loves is a Vietcong terrorist.

Despite their attempts at authenticity, these Hollywood film wars remain fantasies, unsuccessful imitations of the realities of actual combat where air strikes are errant and artillery fire often goes astray, killing friend and foe alike. Helicopters, which appear on cue in the movies, do not always appear on time to pick up the wounded. Armies and troops are not always where they are supposed to be and, especially in a place like Vietnam, battles with the enemy were often characterized by confusion, disorder, and chaos. Except for *Saving Private Ryan*, what other war film has had the courage to depict a sense of fear before battle so strong that soldiers vomit and soil their pants? As one veteran in a VA hospital put it in the documentary, *Dear America: Letters Home from Vietnam* (1988), "Heroes are for the late show."

Maybe Hollywood will never get it right because no one save the soldier can understand the true nature of combat. As former marine sniper Anthony Swofford writes:

> The warrior becomes the hero, and the society celebrates the death and destruction of war, two things the warrior never celebrates. The warrior celebrates the fact of having survived, not of killing Japs or Krauts or gooks or Russkies or ragheads. That large and complex emotional mess called national victory holds no sway for the warrior. It is necessary to remind civilians of this fact, to make them hear the voice of the warrior.[26]

When World War II veteran Samuel Fuller was asked about the honesty in his combat films, *The Steel Helmet* (Korean) and *The Big Red One* (1980, Second World War), he supposedly replied that the only way to get at the truth in a war film was to put a machine gun behind the camera and gun down the audience.[27] No doubt Fuller's reply was not intended to be taken literally but it reminded moviegoers that viewing "war in the dark" is a far different experience from being there.

CHAPTER
TEN

HOLLYWOOD CONFRONTS THE NUCLEAR HOLOCAUST

"The seventeenth century was the century of mathematics, the eighteenth that of the physical sciences and the nineteenth that of biology. Our twentieth century is the century of fear."

ALBERT CAMUS

"I survived Three Mile Island."

1979 T-SHIRT

An exchange of dialogue between a California couple awakened from a sound sleep:
Wife: "What's that?"
Husband: "Oh, go back to sleep. It's only an atomic bomb test."
Wife: "All right. I was afraid one of the kids had fallen out of bed."

1952 ISSUE OF THE *READER'S DIGEST*

C amus, Nobel Prize winner, French philosopher and WWII resistance fighter, was referring, of course, to the new weapon of mass destruction—the atom bomb. August 6, 1945, is often cited as the beginning of the nuclear age, when "Little Boy," the code name for the uranium bomb, was dropped on Hiroshima. Three days later, "Fat Man," the plutonium bomb, leveled Nagasaki and persuaded the Japanese to surrender, thus bringing the Second World War to an end. The atomic era actually began years before when President Roosevelt gave approval to the Manhattan Project, the name assigned to the secret development of the atom bomb. The project united a number of European émigrés and American scientists to produce the bomb. It was a cold December day in 1942 at the University of Chicago where Enrico Fermi and his team of scientists achieved the first sustained nuclear reaction, which altered the course of human history. The initial atomic pile contained 385 tons of graphite and 50 tons of uranium and caused a chain reaction for only a few minutes. But the demonstration showed enough promise to warrant the movement of the Manhattan Project to Los Alamos, New Mexico, to be placed under the leadership of General Leslie Groves, who recruited J. Robert Oppenheimer to head the scientific team. Under Groves's command, the U.S. Army appropriated over 54,000 acres, relocated the residents, and built an entire self-contained community and military compound on the land. Eventually 7,000 people would come to live and work at the Los Alamos base.

Work on the bomb was anything but serene. A difference of opinion developed between physicist Edward Teller, who advocated building a hydrogen bomb, and Oppenheimer, who thought that an atomic bomb had to be built first. Although security was supposed to be tight, declassified documents and personal recollections by Russian scientists after the collapse of the Soviet Union revealed that there were spies at Los Alamos. Those identified such as Klaus Fuchs and David Greenglass had passed secrets on to the Soviets. New research,[1] however, suggests a more elaborate spy ring. What later became clear to all involved was that there existed more ideological sympathy for the Soviets among those working at Los Alamos than anyone suspected at the time. While the atomic lab was situated at Los Alamos, the actual testing ground, code name "Trinity," was set sixty miles south at the White Sands Missile Range near Alamogordo. There, on July 16, 1945, a successful nuclear bomb was detonated in the New Mexico desert as a prelude to Hiroshima.

As Paul Boyer[2] observes in his book, *By the Bomb's Early Light*, once news of the bomb became public, people knew that life would never be the same. H.V. Kaltenborn, the noted radio commentator, expressed this sentiment for mankind when he said: "We have created a Frankenstein!"[3] The bomb's devastation far exceeded the scientific estimates. Oppenheimer, for example, thought the death toll would be under 20,000. The actual figures proved to be much higher; 80,000 people were killed immediately at Hiroshima with another 60,000 deaths caused by radiation and other illnesses attributed to the fallout. At Nagasaki, 35,000 died immediately and another 35,000 died from the effects of the blast.[4]

While these statistics are tragic, still the fatalities from the atomic bombs rank ninth among the worst accidents and disasters in human history, far below the seventy-five million deaths attributed to the bubonic plague (Black Death) in fourteenth-century Eurasia, the thirty-five million Chinese slaughtered during the Mongol genocide in the same century, and the twenty-one million deaths attributed to the 1918 worldwide influenza epidemic. Another consideration, often forgotten, is that the two bombs persuaded the Japanese government to surrender, thereby saving millions of Allied and Japanese lives that would have been lost due to an invasion of the islands.[5]

Statistics alone do not define the aftermath of the atomic blasts. Boyer cites the dropping of the atom bombs as a benchmark for the twentieth century, setting off what came to be identified in the popular culture as the "nuclear age"; an era strangely marked by both public apprehension and a post-WWII consumer euphoria. Once the Soviets acquired the bomb, fear of a nuclear war between the two superpowers led to a renewed interest in civilian defense. Americans built over 100,000 bomb shelters during the fifties. Some families located these shelters in their backyards, stuffing them with canned goods, candles, blankets, and other amenities thought necessary to survive life after a nuclear attack. For those who could not afford a private bomb shelter, their old Fords and Chevys would do nicely. Buried in huge holes in the ground and stocked with provisions, these old cars were thought to be an adequate substitute. The civilian population was not the only naive participant in these survival strategies; the U.S. government's postal service printed emergency change of address cards to insure that the daily mail would continue to be delivered after a nuclear attack despite weather conditions, mad dogs, and radioactivity. The federal government apparently considered the delivery of the Sears catalog a high priority item while the country struggled with death, disease, contamination, and possible anarchy. Years later, Americans learned that the Eisenhower administration had made serious preparations in case of an atomic attack.[6] The federal government had built a mountainside bunker, an alternative to the aboveground Pentagon, sixty-five miles from the nation's capitol and six miles from Camp David. Insiders referred to the presidential bunker simply as Site R.

City governments also did their part in the preparedness drive; New York City installed over 700 sirens within the city limits and tested these every month until the mid sixties. Meanwhile, the nation's public schools included bomb drills as part of the normal curriculum. One popular civilian defense film shown to schoolchildren featured a cartoon character named Burt the Turtle, who instructed the youngsters that in case of a nuclear explosion they should "duck and cover."[7] Such misleading instructions severely underestimated the physical and psychological damage from an atomic attack. However, filmmakers Frank and Eleanor Perry were much more realistic than the government or the local school district. Their 1963 film, *Ladybug, Ladybug*, was based on an actual incident that documented the reaction of rural schoolchildren to a civil defense warning, signifying an impending nuclear attack. Although the warning turns out to be a false alarm, several children suffered harm under the stress of the expected attack. Unfortunately, *Ladybug, Ladybug* remains an ignored and forgotten film despite its accurate scenario.

Public concern also took the form of cooperative efforts by citizen groups to protest extensive government nuclear testing as part of the Cold War competition with the Soviet Union. American testing in the Pacific atoll during the fifties scattered radioactive dust over 7000 square miles, causing death and illness within an eighty-mile radius. Closer to home, reports of radioactive rain falling on Chicago, together with the discovery of deadly strontium 90 in the milk supply, extended public fear of nuclear war to anxiety over the effects of fallout from nuclear testing.[8]

Serious concerns over nuclear war and the effects of nuclear testing on humans and the environment also had its lighter side as demonstrated by the story of the California couple reported in a 1952 issue of the *Readers Digest,* reflected at the beginning of the chapter. The commercial sector also took advantage of the situation to profit from the new technology. Boyer reports the following: jewelry manufacturers marketing atomic earrings and pins, producers of breakfast foods stuffing atomic rings and other nuclear-related prizes in their cereal boxes, and the shameless commercialization even extended to a French designer who named his brief two-piece swimwear a "bikini" after the Pacific bomb tests because it would grab the attention of men.[9] Television as well sought to cash in on the latest interest with the development of new science fiction shows like *The Twilight Zone* and *The Outer Limits.*

Naturally, the film industry was not to be denied. The plot of the 1945 film, *The House on 92nd Street*, concerned Nazi spies but was revised by the studio prior to distribution to include a foreword that explained to the audience that what the Nazi agents were really after was the formula for the atomic bomb.[10] Fears that the atom bomb would be used against the United States in another world war,[11] were offset by surveys taken between 1954 and 1963 that revealed public ignorance about the bomb, indifference to the larger problem of nuclear weapons, and public apathy related to the dangers of radioactive fallout.[12] Even if the American people had equivocal feelings about the nuclear age, Hollywood perceived the subject as a potentially rich source for film plots.

FILMS OF THE NUCLEAR AGE

Hollywood was quick to cash in on the nuclear technology. Besides updating *The House on 92nd Street*, the film studios moved promptly to incorporate the bomb into forthcoming screen projects. Within eighteen months after "Little Boy" was dropped on Hiroshima, MGM studios released *The Beginning or the End?*, a docudrama on the making and deployment of the first atom bomb.[13] The 1947 film was an artistic disaster and a box office failure. The entire project was plagued from the beginning by internal and external squabbles within the scientific community, the military establishment, and the MGM studio. As a consequence, the film was revised several times, and the final version reflected the various compromises—a mixture of fact and fiction with entertainment values predominating over historical accuracy.

What began as an enlightened cooperative venture between the film industry and the liberal wing of the scientific community turned out to be a disappointing experience. It proved a bitter lesson for MGM and it may have encouraged other studios to avoid the subject altogether, particularly if the actual participants were still alive.

These reservations notwithstanding, Hollywood tackled the subject again in 1952 with another A-bomb film, *Above and Beyond*. The film focused on Colonel Paul Tibbets, the pilot of the Enola Gay, the plane that dropped the bomb on Hiroshima.[14] *Above and Beyond* became a personal story about Tibbets, his family, and the events leading up to the August 6 bombing. Hollywood did not produce another film on the subject until the 1980s when it released *Manhattan Project* and *Fat Man and Little Boy*. Neither film made much of an impact, even though the latter's political message doubted the wisdom of using the bomb. Actor Paul Newman accepted the role of General Groves since he was a committed antinuclear activist who had served as a delegate to the 1978 United Nations Special Session on Disarmament. His concern about the role was justified as the film directed most of the blame for the bomb on the military rather than the scientific community. While the film accurately depicts the team of scientists working to develop the bomb, it was Groves who manipulated Oppenheimer to remain on the project and bring it to a successful conclusion. The film strangely neglects to mention that both Klaus Fuchs and David Greenglass (Julius Rosenberg's brother-in-law) were Los Alamos employees who passed details of the bomb to the Soviets. Further, when Oppenheimer lost his security clearance during the Red Scare hysteria of the 1950s because of his past communist associations, General Groves's loyalty was never questioned, even though he was responsible for security at the Los Alamos facility. *Fat Man and Little Boy* conveniently places the blame for the bomb on the military even though, in fact, it was the scientists who urged Roosevelt to support the project lest the Germans develop the weapon before the United States. The urgency felt by the scientists, some of whom were émigrés from fascism, made the Manhattan Project a moral as well as a scientific challenge.[15] Still, the fact that these films were commercial failures reinforces the conventional wisdom that the public goes to the movies to be entertained, not informed. It also could have signaled that the American public had lost interest in the topic. Certainly by the mid eighties, liberals in the film industry, whose political activities either influence or reflect what is fashionable in the general culture, had deserted the nuclear disarmament/nuclear freeze campaign in favor of Aids research and environmental causes.[16]

Rather than avoid the subject, the film industry saw in nuclear technology the source of numerous dramatic plots. The post-World War II film formula transformed the Nazis and Japanese into the new Cold War enemies—the Soviets and communist agents—and the scripts converted weapon blueprints and war plans into spies and atomic secrets. One filmography[17] on nuclear movies listed some 874 films released in thirty-six countries, (with almost two-thirds produced in the United States). Their themes involved nuclear war, nuclear accident, or the after-effects of an atomic blast, including the battle against radioactive fallout. Not surprisingly, most of these films were distributed after the end of World War II, with more than one-third released in the 1980s. Included in the filmography are a dozen Godzilla movies and various clones of the "atomic monster" variety in films that dealt with annihilation and world destruction. At least a dozen of the James Bond films employed scenarios of nuclear technology, conflict over possession of nuclear weapons, and efforts to secure the materials to manufacture nuclear armaments.[18]

The new technology also proved a script bonanza for the weekly serials, which continued to be a staple of the Saturday afternoon matinee well into the 1950s. At least a dozen serials, some with the exotic titles of *Zombies of the Stratosphere* and *Radar Men from the Moon*, included the atom bomb or nuclear weaponry in their narratives. Naturally, a popular Saturday serial favorite like Superman did not ignore the potential scripts that could be culled from the new scientific discoveries. For instance, in 1950, Columbia Pictures produced fifteen episodes of the serial, *Atom Man versus Superman*, in which our hero saves Metropolis from an arsenal of atomic weapons and other gadgets of the space age such as thermal guns, flying saucers, and stratospheric vehicles. Previously, Universal-International had released a serial entitled, *Lost City of the Jungle* (1946), in which, for thirteen weeks, the hero, federal agent Rod Stanton, battled against a villain who had discovered a metal in the lost city with the capability to defend against atomic bombs and who planned to sell the discovery to the highest bidder. Some of the serial villains speak with a German accent, an obvious reference to Nazi war criminals not prosecuted at Nuremberg and other war crimes trials, while the crude "special effects" would not fool any contemporary youngster with access to a computer. Still, nuclear technology provided Hollywood writers with an opportunity to replay the old formulas by merely substituting the A-bomb for previous weapons of destruction.

When the Saturday matinee serials vanished from theater screens, displaced by television cartoons, feature films about the atomic age remained into the eighties. Rather than lose interest in the subject, Hollywood continued to mine it as if the industry had struck gold. Admittedly, films of the nuclear age could qualify as a separate "genre" and be organized into various categories since the breadth of the topic provides for overlap and identification with other more established genres. For example, should the genre include those dozen James Bond movies as well as films along the order of *The Fourth Protocol* (1987) and *The Package* (1989)? Or are these films really Cold War action thrillers where the new technology serves as a plot gimmick to advance the narrative?

Regardless, the hundreds of movies that comprise the genre can be topically subdivided into four distinct groups: (1) science fiction/horror films where nuclear power has released an assortment of beasts on the civilized world; (2) nuclear war/attack films where warring governments unleash disaster on the world; (3) nuclear accident or disaster films where human or mechanical error has caused a threat to life and the environment; and (4) nuclear survival films where the world has been destroyed and those unharmed after the blast or those who have survived the radioactive fallout struggle to remain alive.

Nuclear Age Science Fiction Films

The fifties have been characterized as a decade of paranoia and mass hysteria brought on by the creation of the atom bomb and the subsequent arms race competition between East and West that typified the Cold War. The science fiction films of this era reflected the national mood at the time since Hollywood had made few such films before 1950.[19] Most of these science fiction films are best characterized as low-budget B-flicks; "monster" movies where atomic testing or radioactivity produces mutations like giant grasshoppers, huge ants or overgrown spiders or awakens long buried beasts that proceed to create havoc and destruction on the human population.[20] What these films share in common is a warning of what is possible when science and technology transcend the boundaries of humanity in manufacturing weapons of mass destruction. One of the earliest of this type was the 1951 film, *The Thing*, featuring actor James Arness, who played a carrot-like creature defrosted as a result of nuclear testing. In order to survive, the creature needs blood. During the course of the film *The Thing* creates carnage and mayhem on an Arctic military base as it searches for human victims. When it is finally destroyed by fire in the final reel, a survivor says to the audience: "Tell the world. Watch the skies—everywhere—watch the skies!"

Hollywood, however, did not follow its own advice. While it is true that a few films like *Invasion of the Body Snatchers* involved creatures from outer space or aliens from another planet, more often than not the evil forces came from below the earth or from under the sea in films with titles like *Them!*, *Tarantula*, *The Deadly Mantis*, and *It Came from Beneath the Sea*. In *Them!* (1954), the creatures are twelve-foot mutant ants, a byproduct from the radioactivity deposited by the nuclear tests at Alamogordo. In *It Came from Beneath the Sea* (1955), the monster is a radioactive octopus that is transformed into a carnivorous giant intent on devouring San Francisco. Meanwhile, in *The Beast from 20,000 Fathoms* (1953), atomic testing in the Arctic dislodges a 100-million-year-old dinosaur that proceeds to eat its way southward until destroyed by a combined force of police and military personnel at

Coney Island Park in the Big Apple. Still, in another film, *The Terror from the Year 5000* (1958), scientists experimenting in their private laboratory somewhere in central Florida create a mutant creature, a highly radioactive woman who looks like a deformed cat dressed in a sequin gown and who speaks with a foreign accent. She proceeds to kill a few people before she is forced into a large oven-type apparatus that resembles an old washing machine and is melted down.

Although it is unlikely that adults took these films seriously, Hollywood, nonetheless, added a disclaimer that warned that experimentation with the new technology was dangerous. Rather than threatening, a few science fiction films of this period such as *The Day the Earth Stood Still* (1951) and *It Came from Outer Space* (1953) feature aliens that are kind and loving creatures in contrast to the harmful pods that take over human bodies in Don Siegel's 1956 film, *Invasion of the Body Snatchers*. Klaatu (Michael Rennie), the alien leader in *The Day the Earth Stood Still* has a powerful weapon of destruction (aka: atom bomb) but comes to earth to further interplanetary peace rather than war. He is met, however, by government mistrust, public fear, and accusations of being a communist agent.[21] Shot by the police, Klaatu warns Earth that unless it ceases its nuclear arms race, his planet will destroy the world. Such serious science fiction films, unfortunately, were atypical of the period.

Nuclear War Films

A few films delivered apocalyptic visions of a nuclear holocaust brought on by scheming politicians, deranged military commanders, and public officials who misjudge their ability to control modern technology. What these films express is a view of the bomb as a catastrophic force with the capability to destroy the entire world. In this sense, these films present the same kind of negative "end of civilization" scenario of the bomb found in the earlier science fiction films. An initial entry in this category was Stanley Kramer's 1959 film, *On the Beach*, based on the Nevil Shute novel. The film opens with the war a *fait accompli*, resulting in the destruction of much of the world except for Australia, where the survivors await the inevitable sickness and death brought on by radioactive dust ("Black Rain") carried by the winds to the South Pacific. Kramer's film featured an all-star cast and was a major production unlike the low budget B-science fiction films. With the exception of one scene where the scientists and military blame each other for what has happened, the film presents a sanitized version of extinction. While Kramer's film may have been intended as a warning to the nuclear powers that the next war would be the last for mankind, it never does assign responsibility for the bomb or its deployment, nor does it visualize the end of civilization in a horrific manner. Essentially, *On the Beach* is an old-fashioned romance, a love story involving married Gregory Peck, the

American submarine commander, and Ava Gardner, the single woman he meets and falls in love with. *On the Beach* is no nuclear horror show because it lacks even one scene of death or destruction. While Kramer's ending message is for mankind to reform before it is too late, the punch line of the final scene as the characters wait for the nuclear fallout to reach them loses its impact because of the romanticized perspective that dominates the film. Here is a film about the nuclear holocaust without pain or suffering. In light of the film's romanticism, why the Pentagon refused to provide Kramer with assistance on the film remains a mystery.[22]

To demonstrate just how romantic Kramer's film is, it should be contrasted with Peter Watkins short 1967 film, *The War Game*, made for the British Broadcasting Corporation (BBC). In the film's fictional narrative, the war begins when the United States threatens to use atomic weapons against the Chinese, who have invaded South Vietnam. The Soviet Union enters the picture when it warns the United States to desist or it will take over West Berlin. When NATO forces are overwhelmed by superior Russian military might, the West resorts to tactical nuclear weapons. The Soviets respond with missiles of their own, but several that were designed for military installations in Britain fall short of their targets and hit the civilian population of Kent. Given the military alliances of NATO and the Warsaw Pact during the Cold War, Watkins's launching of the war presented a plausible scenario. *The War Game* depicts the effects of a nuclear attack on the city of Kent in southeast England. Integrating newsreel footage and simulated events, the film visualizes the immediate effects suffered by the population after the bomb explodes. *The War Game* fills the screen with images of unending horrors—mass hysteria, panic, firestorms, suffocation due to a lack of oxygen, and even mercy killing of the sick and wounded. It proved to be too graphic for the BBC to televise. Although the film won an Academy Award as Best Feature Documentary and was eventually released to theaters, it had yet to be shown on British television in the 1980s.[23] *The War Game* proved too realistic for its own good.

Sidney Lumet's 1964 film *Fail Safe* concerns a limited nuclear war between the United States and the Soviets caused by a mechanical malfunction. The film could easily fit into the category of a nuclear accident except that its focus is on the decision-making process by which political leaders control the damage inflicted by the nuclear technology when the bomb's deployment is unintended. The plot has the U.S. president, played by Henry Fonda, offering the Soviet premier an opportunity to bomb New York City as a way to avoid World War III after an American plane breaks through the "fail-safe" security system and mistakenly drops a nuclear bomb on Moscow—a kind of tit for tat arrangement. Lumet's film is a well-crafted exercise in presidential decision-making. Purposely confining the action of the film to three interior sets, Lumet wants the audience to concentrate on the president's dilemma, that is, risk total nuclear war or offer the Soviets an opportunity to drop a bomb (unannounced) on a major American city. This may have been the only film during the Cold War where the audience was encouraged to cheer when the U.S. military shot down its own planes.

Like *Fail Safe*, Stanley Kubrick's *Dr. Strangelove or: How I Learned to Stop Worrying and Love the Bomb*, is also about the inadequacies of mechanical safeguards, military control, and communication devices to prevent unauthorized preemptive nuclear strikes against a political enemy. Contrary to the serious drama presented in *Fail Safe*, Kubrick's 1964 film is a satirical comedy populated with exaggerated characters like the lunatic officer (General Jack D. Ripper) who is convinced the communists are destroying his "precious bodily fluids" through fluoridation of the country's water supply and orders an unauthorized nuclear strike against the Soviets; a right-wing Cold War "nuke 'em dead" chief of staff (General Buck Turgidson) who acts more like an ape than a human being; a presidential advisor (Dr. Strangelove) whose bionic arm cannot stop giving the Nazi salute; and a cowboy Air Force pilot (Major Kong) who straddles a nuclear bomb like a bronco as it descends on the Soviet Union while the lyrics on the sound track sing: "We'll meet again, don't know where, don't know when."

Kubrick took a serious suspense story, *Red Alert*, and turned it into a black comedy about the nuclear apocalypse. He was denied assistance from the U.S. Air Force and shot the film in England, where he would enjoy greater artistic freedom. The result is a believable, yet devastatingly funny, film fantasy on how the world could end. There are many hilarious scenes in the film, but one in particular stands out. It takes place in the American war room as the world teeters on the brink of atomic annihilation and the U.S. president tries to reach his Soviet counterpart on the red phone:

> Hello, Dmitri? Listen, can't hear too well. Do you suppose you could turn the music down just a little? Oh, that's much better. Yes, fine. I can hear you now, Dmitri, clear and plain and coming through fine. I'm coming through fine too, eh? Good, then. Well, then, as you say, we're both coming through fine. Good. Well, it's good that you're fine and I'm fine. I agree with you. It's great to be fine. Now then, Dmitri, you know how we've always talked about the possibility of something going wrong with the bomb? The *bomb*, Dmitri. The *hydrogen bomb*. Well, now what happened, is, um, one of our base commanders, he had a sort of . . . well, he went a little funny in the head. You know, just a little *funny*, and he went and did a silly thing. Well, I'll tell you what he did: He ordered his planes to attack your country. Well, let me finish, Dmitri. Let me finish, Dmitri. Well, listen, how do you think I feel about it? Can you imagine how I feel about it, Dmitri? Why do you think I'm calling you? Just to say hello? Of course, I like to speak to you. Of course, I like to say hello. Not now but anytime, Dmitri. I'm just calling up to tell you something terrible has happened. It's a friendly call, of course, it's a friendly call. Listen, if it wasn't friendly, you probably wouldn't have even got it.

FIGURE 14. *Dr. Strangelove*. 1964. Reprinted with permission, Columbia Pictures.

The film's scenario may strike viewers today as dated after the end of the Cold War and the dissolution of the old Soviet Union. But how far-fetched was the film in the sixties? Political scientist Richard Ostrom[24] maintains that what audiences considered hilarious were the very ideas and equipment that were most realistic. For example, looney General Ripper's paranoia over fluoridation as part of a Soviet plot to destroy the United States could be found in the literature of the right-wing John Birch Society that flourished in the country for more than two decades. The Russians apparently explored the development of a Doomsday Machine that could destroy everything on earth, even though it was a highly improbable piece of technology. Additionally, a number of real scientists could have been the inspiration for the reel Dr. Strangelove. Candidates included, Edward Teller, Werner Von Braun and Herman Kahn. The consensus among film scholars is that Strangelove was a composite character.

More recently, Hollywood's film enemies are likely to be aliens (*Independence Day*, *Mars Attacks*)—creatures from another planet—who threaten the country's security. Still, the assumption that the world is safe from nuclear annihilation is incorrect because the nuclear threat is greater today due to the proliferation of nuclear weapons and the addition of Third World powers to the nuclear arms race. The knowledge that India, Pakistan, and Israel have the bomb, that North Korea has the capability and has threatened to begin testing, and that Iran is in the process of developing nuclear weapons increases, rather than diminishes, the prospects of a nuclear holocaust. If anything, Kubrick's film is more relevant today than when it was originally released forty years ago.

At least five nuclear war scenarios are plausible,[25] with one or two more likely than the rest. One possibility is that terrorists will touch off a nuclear war, while a second potential cause is mechanical failure due to shoddy or improper equipment. Human error could lead to the catastrophe in a third scenario. A fourth likelihood would revolve around a misunderstanding or miscommunication among nuclear club members such as the confrontation between the United States and the Soviets during the 1963 Cuban Missile Crisis. Finally, computer error could lead to a false alert that subsequently could trigger a real nuclear reaction. Hollywood explored this scenario in *War Games* (1983). Based on the premise that machines are not infallible, the film's scenario envisions a foul-up in the attack-alert warning system, which mistakenly indicates that the country is under attack, thereby precipitating the retaliatory strike. The film would have the audience believe that a young computer hacker (Matthew Broderick) could bring the country to the brink of thermonuclear war through accidental access into the command room of NORAD, the North American Radar Air Defense. Although the premise may have seemed implausible in the eighties, the subsequent revelation that a British teenager was able to break into U.S. government files from his home computer makes *War Games* less entertaining and more frightening. At film's end, the computer is asked to imagine the outcome of a nuclear war and determine a "game winner." The computer flashes out the words: "There is no winner."

The plot of *War Games* and similar films is predicated on the possibility of nuclear war. But is nuclear war possible today or just a screenwriter's fantasy? If you dare to think the unthinkable, remember that during the Cold War the U.S. government prepared for just such an eventuality in its secret Outpost Mission project which trained and prepared an elite corps of helicopter pilots to rescue the president from the White House in the event of a nuclear attack. Other so-called "doomsday" operations included saving important historical documents such as the Declaration of Independence and priceless works of art from the National Gallery in Washington. The Outpost Mission operation consumed twenty years of government preparation for the unthinkable—a nuclear strike against the United States.[26]

Nuclear Accidents

Ironically, Hollywood has made only two serious films about nuclear accidents although a significant number of incidents and mishaps have actually occurred.[27] With the release of *The China Syndrome* and *Silkwood*, an ecological dimension was added to the nuclear war-doomsday threat. *The China Syndrome* (1979) explored the issue of death at the hands of an invisible force—radiation. This perceptive film details an attempted cover-up of a nuclear accident at a California power plant. Plant manager (Jack Lemmon) realizes that the radiation leak could trigger a core meltdown—the "China Syndrome" of the film title—and tries to prevent the facility from reopening. He manages to take over the control room and the nuclear power company calls in the authorities to take care of Lemmon, described as an emotionally disturbed employee. Lemmon's plea falls on deaf ears; instead the S.W.A.T. team breaks into the control room and shoots him. What Lemmon was trying to do was to prevent the possibility of a core meltdown where many more people would be killed from the radiation leak than from any bomb blast. The film could not have been timelier since it was released to theaters two weeks before the leak at the Three Mile Island nuclear plant near Harrisburg, Pennsylvania. In this case, life imitated art.

The film was more prescient than first suspected. The situation in *The China Syndrome* was virtually duplicated in real life seven years later at the Chernobyl nuclear plant in the Ukraine. The explosion at Chernobyl was due to a combination of faulty design and human error, which resulted in an estimated 6000 deaths, numerous cases of thyroid cancer, birth deformities, and the contamination of some 16,000 square miles of fertile land. It should also be noted that the explosion affected almost nine million people in the Ukraine, Byelorussia, and the Russian Federation. Chernobyl remains the worst nuclear accident in global history.[28]

At the other end of the nuclear holocaust spectrum, a comparatively minor incident is at the heart of Mike Nichols's 1983 film, *Silkwood*, based on a true story.

FIGURE 15. Three Mile Island: 2004. Reprinted with permission, *Williamsport Sun-Gazette.*

Nichols's film is a reenactment of the real case of Karen Silkwood, a blue-collar worker in a plutonium plant, who died under mysterious circumstances while on her way to deliver documentary evidence to a *New York Times* reporter. Supposedly, the documents, which were never found, would verify the unsafe conditions at the Kerr-McGee factory where plutonium rods for nuclear weapons were being manufactured. Karen never made the interview, as her car went off the road. Nichols's film is multidimensional because at one level it is a mystery story that concerns itself with the strange death of Karen Silkwood. Did the corporate leaders at Kerr-McGee have Karen eliminated because she blew the whistle on the dangerous working conditions at their plant? Or was it merely a coincidence that a driving accident led to her death? *Silkwood* serves as a reminder that nuclear age weapons are unlike conventional weapons and require greater care. It also demonstrates the importance of insuring that the people who work with nuclear materials receive the highest level of protection and concern for their personal safety. One Chernobyl incident is enough.

Nuclear Survival Films

The last category of nuclear age films includes those that primarily concern them-selves with survival after an atomic explosion, blast, or attack. These films focus on individuals or families that must adjust to an entirely different, and often hostile, environment and overcome new challenges in order to stay alive. In some ways, the origin of such films are traceable to stories featuring the settlement of the frontier or the taming of the wilderness, except that in western films individuals had a chance against a human enemy or a wild beast. In the nuclear films, death from the bomb explosion or the radiation exposure is inescapable.

The nuclear survival film and its derivations proved to be a popular subject with the film studios, quite possibly because of their similarity to science fiction movies. Thus, while the topic itself is morbid and hardly a source for entertainment, the plot variations are endless. Still, three such films—*Five, Panic in Year Zero!* and *The World, the Flesh, and the Devil*—had optimistic endings. Two films, the made-for-television *The Day After* and the film *Testament,* were both more pessimistic and pro-vided little comfort to viewers. Meanwhile, Roger Corman's B-film, *The Last Woman on Earth* promised more intrigue and excitement in its title than it deliv-ered on the screen.

The plots of *Five* and *The World, the Flesh, and the Devil (WFD)* are similar. Arch Obler's 1951 film, *Five,* the first survivor film of the nuclear age, and the 1959 *WFD* both take place in limited worlds—contained environments—where the sur-vivors, groups of five and three persons, respectively, each contain one woman. This fact is crucial to plot development because each film finds hope through the repro-ductive organs of the surviving female. Both flirt with the issue of sexuality and race but are too timid to pursue that subject with any conviction. Also, the two films pre-sent fairly romanticized versions of a post-holocaust world without horror, pain, or human suffering.

The location for Roger Corman's film *The Last Woman on Earth* (1961) is Puerto Rico, and while the viewer is shown dead bodies lying in streets, cars, and jungle terrain, they are posed so peacefully as to suggest an afternoon siesta rather than nuclear death. Here the plot revolves around a married couple and the hus-band's lawyer (male) who survive the nuclear holocaust when deep-sea diving. Once it is established that they are the sole survivors on the island, the film sinks to a formulaic romantic love triangle and is unintentionally funny. For example, in a scene after the trio has learned of their rather desperate situation, they return to their hotel rooms and very carefully pack all their nice suits and dresses in suitcas-es as if preparing for a holiday rather than certain death.

Panic in Year Zero! (1962) is another variation on the nuclear survival film. Actor-director Ray Milland focuses on the struggle for survival of a single family fleeing Los Angeles after a nuclear attack. There are plenty of other survivors, and it is these people who pose more of a threat to this family than any nuclear bomb or radioactive matter. Theirs is a conventional middle-class family that adopts Herbert Spencer's principle of survival of the fittest. In order to protect his family, the father (Milland) takes guns and ammunition from a hardware store and gasoline from a service station. When three young thugs assault the father, the son comes to his rescue by wounding one of the hoodlums. Later, when his daughter is raped by this trio, the father and son track them down and kill two of them in cold blood. The film is filled with mixed messages. On the one hand, it supports individualism over cooperation in a crisis and promotes the idea that the ends justify the means. On the other hand, the film occasionally stops to allow the family members (primarily the mother) to engage in moralistic speeches whenever the family performs an act of kindness. At the end, when the unnamed warring powers have agreed to a truce and the family is headed home, Milland comes to realize that he has changed and that a future incident may force him to resort to similar behavior in order to survive. It becomes clear that this film is less about the horror of nuclear war than fear of human behavior under stress. An earthquake or tornado might have produced similar results.

Two 1983 films, *The Day After* and *Testament*, treat the subject of nuclear attack quite differently. Both personalize the experience, focusing on the impact of the attack on one family (*Testament*) and on several major characters (*The Day After*). The ABC network turned *The Day After* into a media event as it promoted the film's showing as an educational opportunity when it encouraged teachers, students, and their schools; churches and their congregations; and families to share the film experience together.[29] Before the film's showing, the network announced that while the film was based on scientific fact, it still was a work of fiction. After the screening, the network presented a discussion panel of experts to review the film. The story of ordinary people caught up in an unexpected nuclear attack contained many of the expected images: dead bodies, radiation sickness, virulent epidemics, scarce supply of uncontaminated food and water, and outbreaks of violence and lawlessness. Still, the film seems to want to shock its audience through special effects and gruesome makeup more than enlighten it. There was something artificial about the firing squad and the looters, so that at the film's end all that remained for the viewer was a feeling that nuclear war is terrible.

Testament, on the other hand, was a small, ninety-minute film about the effect of a nuclear attack on one California middle-class family. The opening scene finds the father away on business, leaving the mother and children to face the nuclear holocaust alone. After the initial blast, the film moves quickly to show the community covered by radioactive dust as a result of World War III. The remainder describes how the family and the community cope with the aftermath of such a catastrophe. There are no special effects or expensive makeup requirements in *Testament*. The emphasis is on the personal drama. For instance, in the final scene, when the mother, her son, and his friend await certain death, it is clear that the end of the family is a metaphor for the end of civilization. As T. S. Elliot wrote, that end is likely to come "not with a bang but with a whimper."

While the flashier *The Day After* drew a viewing audience of 100 million, *Testament* virtually disappeared from sight. The film had a strange history. Originally produced for Paramount Pictures and first screened at the New York Film Festival, the film starred Jane Alexander as the mother, a role that brought her an Academy Award nomination. Nonetheless the film had a limited theatrical release and eventually was shown on PBS as part of its American Playhouse television series. Unlike *The Day After*, the rather unemotional, but more realistic, ending of life as depicted in *Testament* failed to capture the public's imagination, and the film went virtually unnoticed.

A derivation of the nuclear survival genre can be found in films like *A Boy and His Dog* (1975) and the *Mad Max* trilogy starring Mel Gibson, which take place in a postapocalyptic world—an arid wasteland—inhabited by a population whose major preoccupation is with survival. While the dramatic situations in these films are byproducts of nuclear war, their narratives concern a more distant time, lending themselves closer to futuristic thrillers like *The Terminator* than to a film like *Testament* where the characters confront the immediate aftermath of nuclear destruction. The three *Terminator* films made Arnold Schwarzenegger, a Hollywood star, a millionaire, and a national celebrity. Machines and robots rather than human beings dominated these ultraviolent films. Film audiences might have preferred the "end of the world" scenario to the sterile future presented in the *Terminator* movies.

Disaster scenarios work well visually, especially on the big screen, in case the reader was among the handful that failed to see *Twister*, *Dante's Peak*, or *Independence Day*. In one sense, films with nuclear themes are disaster movies of a particular type. While tornados and volcanic eruptions are natural phenomena and alien invaders are hypothetical scenarios, nuclear war is manmade and, therefore, avoidable. Are there fundamental lessons to be learned from exposure to nuclear films? Unfortunately, social scientists have yet to provide a definitive answer. But limited experiments conducted on school-age children provide a clue. Using the same student population, studies conducted in North Carolina among high school students and college freshmen in 1982 and again in 1984 after the televising of *The Day After* reveal that young people are more affected by visual images than descriptive material on the printed page.[30] While the sample population in these surveys underwent an attitude change regarding nuclear weapons due to a better understanding of their destructive capabilities, there was no corresponding change in political knowledge after seeing *The Day After*, reading Jonathan Schell's *The Fate of the*

Earth, and being made aware of the Reagan administration's deployment of cruise and Pershing II missiles in Europe. The students, therefore, continued to divorce the horrors of a nuclear holocaust from the glamour of the administration's "star wars" project.

THE SECOND NUCLEAR AGE

The atomic era began in 1942 on a squash court at the University of Chicago, where the first nuclear reaction took place. Six decades later, it appears that the energy released by the atom has brought mankind more destruction than life improvement. It no longer matters who is responsible because all the participants in the development of the bomb should be held accountable: the scientists laid the foundation by splitting the atom, the military seized the opportunity to use that advantage by developing weapons of mass destruction, and the politicians made the decisions as to when, how, and under what circumstances these weapons should be utilized. Later, scientists like Oppenheimer regretted what they had done. Teller also had misgivings about the hydrogen bomb. By then it was too late. Had the Second World War continued longer, the Germans might have developed the bomb and used it against the Allies. Would the Japanese not have done so too had they had the capability? No matter. Scientific progress cannot be contained, only delayed. The real problem with atomic energy lies not in its discovery, but in its utilization. As Einstein remarked after the dropping of the A-bombs on Hiroshima and Nagasaki, "The release of atom power has changed everything except our way of thinking."[31]

Einstein proved to be prescient. Revisionist historians now claim that Truman used the A-bomb primarily as a future bargaining chip in negotiations with the Soviet Union rather than as a calculated means to save lives (American and Japanese) by bringing World War II to an end. Regardless, the president had the support of the American people. A Roper poll taken in the fall of 1945 revealed that three-fourths of Americans approved of the president's decision. In fact, more than one-fifth thought more atomic bombs should have been dropped. Only 5 percent expressed disapproval.[32]

Eisenhower, Truman's successor in the White House, also saw the bomb as a political rather than a purely military weapon, a means to regain the Cold War initiative from the Soviets. Reportedly, Eisenhower moved atomic warheads to Okinawa to impress the Chinese and later, during the Formosa Straits confrontation, ordered the military to be in a state of nuclear readiness. At one point in his administration, Eisenhower reportedly said: "I see no reason why they [nuclear weapons] shouldn't be used just exactly as you would use a bullet or anything else."[32] As Einstein's research predicted, Eisenhower the president failed to distinguish conventional armaments from nuclear weapons.

Fortunately, some international cooperation has occurred since the 1963 Partial Test Ban Treaty banned atmospheric nuclear testing. The five major nuclear powers (United States, Soviet Union, China, France, and the United Kingdom) have sought to prohibit aboveground testing and to limit underground tests. The 1968 Non-Proliferation Treaty, however, failed to accomplish its objective of restricting the spread of nuclear weapons as testing in India and Pakistan demonstrate. Since 1945, more than 2000 atmospheric and underground nuclear tests have been conducted worldwide.[34] An effort to ban all nuclear explosions was supported in the United Nations General Assembly by 158 members, but the United States along with India, Pakistan, China, Israel, and North Korea refused to sign the Comprehensive Test Ban Treaty. The treaty provides for worldwide monitoring as well as on-site inspections to ensure compliance. The failure of the U.S. Senate to ratify the test ban treaty was a blow to the prospects of world peace. To offset its rejection, the American government pointed to previous agreements, like the Start Treaties, with the old Soviet Union to reduce their nuclear stockpiles by two-thirds. Despite these reductions, each country still had over 3000 strategic nuclear weapons—land-based, air and submarine-launched nuclear warheads at their disposal in 2003—enough firepower to cause a nuclear Armageddon.

The first nuclear age, which began with Hiroshima and led to a stalemate between the two superpowers—the United States and the Soviet Union—had the effect of keeping nuclear weapons in check. Eventually, changing political and economic events brought these weapons under some semblance of control. Scientists mark 1998, when India and Pakistan detonated nuclear weapons, as the dawn of the second nuclear age.[35] Since then, North Korea claims to have developed such weapons and the present government in Iran makes no secret of its desire to join the nuclear club. The expansion of these weapons to insecure, relatively poorer, and with the exception of India, undemocratic nations exponentially multiply the risk of nuclear holocaust. In fact, several of these countries have reduced their conventional military forces to offset the costs involved in nuclear arms development. Consequently, when threatened such nations decide that their only choice is to resort to nuclear weapons as their sole option or contemplate using them earlier than anticipated. This is a frightening prospect for world security.

Furthermore, the second Bush administration is considering development of smaller nuclear bombs that would have the capability of entering the suspected 1400 underground ballistic missile sites and command posts scattered throughout the world. The administration strategy rests on the presumption that these smaller nukes would minimize collateral damage. The president sought to take advantage of the

1993 lifting of the congressional ban against research on nukes with explosive power of under five kilotons of TNT. Should the Congress approve of funding for these mininukes, it is conceivable that the United States will add nuclear bazookas to its arsenal.[36] The caveat, of course, is that these mininukes and smaller nuclear bombs might encourage rather than discourage their deployment in the case of any future war or military action. In this regard, the second nuclear age poses a greater risk to mankind than the atomic era that began with Hiroshima.

On the nonmilitary front, atomic energy has been utilized in the United States as a source of electric power since 1951. By the millennium, there were 103 operating nuclear power plants from Maine to California generating slightly more than one-fifth of the nation's energy. However, two problems have plagued the nuclear power industry. One is safety and the other is cost. Most Americans recall the partial meltdown incident at the Three Mile Island plant and a good deal of the world is unlikely to forget the Chernobyl disaster. Subsequently, Japan has experienced several frightening nuclear accidents. One sent high levels of radiation into the atmosphere, causing a few deaths, dozens of cases of radiation burns, and inconveniencing hundreds of thousands of people who were ordered to remain indoors. Of greater concern was the fact that this was the third such nuclear accident in Japan since 1997.[37]

Besides Three Mile Island, the United States has had other so-called "near misses" that raise grave concerns about plant safety. These "disasters-in-waiting" include complaints about shoddy workmanship, safety lapses, faulty equipment, and drug and alcohol usage by plant workers. The most serious incident so far occurred at the New England Haddam Neck plant where a seal failure in 1984 almost caused a complete meltdown.[38]

After the 9/11 terrorist attack, the federal government sought to insure the safety of populations living in the vicinity of a nuclear power plant after a post-9/11 F.B.I. report that stated that almost half of the operating plants had insufficient protective measures to guard against a possible terrorist attack. In some plants, the security surveillance equipment failed to function properly. In other plants, security clearance was given to employees with arrest records. In the nuclear power plant in Taft, Louisiana, it took three "mock attack" tests before the plant met government security standards.[39] The Nuclear Regulatory Commission (NRC) also insisted that every nuclear plant have an adequate evacuation plan in the event of a terrorist attack. What constitutes an "adequate" plan became the center of a dispute over the evacuation process for the Indian Point plant on the Hudson River in upstate New York. Indian Point lies ten miles north of Manhattan and any evacuation plan would affect hundreds of thousands of people. This would be a challenging feat for even the most brilliant minds but when politics intervened, recriminations replaced reason. The local Westchester County officials whose constituency lies within the radius of the Indian Point plant declared the facility's evacuation plan unsafe and asked that the plant be closed. Meanwhile, the Federal Emergency Management Agency (FEMA) declared the evacuation plan adequate after an on-site investigation. The squabble continued for several months and led Governor Pataki of New York (Republican) to disagree with President Bush's decision on the acceptability of the emergency evacuation plan, even though he supports keeping the plant open.[40] It put the governor in the awkward position of supporting the plant's operation while admitting that the existing evacuation plan was unlikely to protect the almost 300,000 people who live in the vicinity of Indian Point.

The other problem involves costs. Compared to hydroelectric power, coal, and gas, nuclear power produces electricity at modest costs. However, the construction costs of nuclear power plants are higher than the other electricity producers. This has led to plant closings or sale to private energy companies. A number of planned nuclear power plants, such as the one at Shoreham, Long Island, remain unfinished and others like the Connecticut Yankee plant in New England have been forced to close. As the nuclear power plants age, the United States will have to make some tough decisions concerning future power sources.

One thing is certain. Nuclear technology, whether designed to produce domestic energy or weapons of war, is a permanent fixture of modern life. The challenge facing political decision makers is daunting: how to harness nuclear energy to improve the quality of life rather than destroy it. Maybe the United Nations should screen the end of *On the Beach* and make it required viewing so that its members can focus on the film's final scene where the radioactive dust has extinguished all life and a draped banner reads: "There is still time, brother."

DOES POLITICAL FILM HAVE A FUTURE IN HOLLYWOOD?

CHAPTER ELEVEN

The brief simple answer to the chapter title's question is: yes, no, and maybe. This tentative and frustrating response best represents the current reality in Hollywood. The truth depends on factors and circumstances that have yet to be developed or that are still in the planning stages. Hollywood is undergoing a transition period marked by technical, financial, and administrative changes that render the future less predictable.

Technological advances, such as digital cameras, are altering the way movies are made. MPAA president Jack Valenti, who guided the film industry for almost forty years, has retired. His replacement, Dan Glickman, is another Washington insider, a former secretary of agriculture in the Clinton administration. Early reports indicate that he knows nothing about the film business but has strong ties to politicians in both parties.[1] In addition to leadership changes, youngsters coming out of film schools, replacing the old guard and familiar names, are having their films shown in festivals and other venues. In short, there are so many variables at work that it would be pure speculation to resolve the future of political film. The only sensible recourse is to analyze the changes in an effort to ascertain the possible directions that the film industry, and political films in particular, are likely to take.

THE BUSINESS OF FILMMAKING

The film industry is so unique that other business models are not applicable. Naturally, most businesses share certain core elements: a structure with an organizational chart, a product or service to be produced and marketed, an objective to earn a profit at year's end. There the similarities end.

Hollywood was founded by mostly foreign émigrés in a geographical location that was favorable to the industry. Filmmaking's early history[2] is best described as monopolistic, with five major studios producing and distributing movies to theaters under their ownership or control. The émigrés, who came to America to pursue their dreams, developed an industry that manufactured and marketed utopian visions to others. The émigrés lacked formal education and knew little about making movies. However, they understood what was necessary to become a successful business and they ran their studios like military units. They sat at the head of the chain of command. Producers presented their ideas and screen projects to the studio production chiefs, who served as gatekeepers to production. Directors and actors were considered hired hands. They might be consulted on casting and editing decisions but their choices were subject to final approval by the studios. Actors often were under contract to a studio, but could be "loaned out" to make a movie for a competitor. Banks became the moneylenders, financing film production at the current rate of interest. Studios had to "sell" the screen project to bankers to secure the necessary financing. This was no easy task because of the sums of money required and the high risk involved. The completed films were subject to the Hollywood censors in the Hays Office and subsequent Production Code before they were released into theaters.

In contrast to the days of the old studio moguls like the Warner Brothers, Louis Mayer, and Samuel Goldwyn, the vast majority of films in contemporary Hollywood[3] are produced and marketed by multinational corporations who operate a variety of other businesses as well. Under current conditions movies are not exclusive properties but merely represent one product line in a conglomerate of other economic interests. The CEOs of these conglomerates are Harvard-trained MBAs who may not even like the movies. Accountants and lawyers staff their offices. By the millennium, filmmaking in Hollywood was under the control of five multinational corporations: Twentieth Century Fox, Viacom (Paramount), Vivendi (Universal), Sony (Columbia), and AOL/Time Warner (Warner Bros.). Supplementing these major studios are Walt Disney, DreamWorks (Spielberg & Co.), and a growing number of independents (indies). Studios no longer own theaters and instead negotiate with theater chains like United Artists to release and distribute their films. Industry censors have been replaced by a less restrictive ratings system, which acts as an advisory guide for parents.

Whereas previously producers exercised considerable control over production, today the directors have taken their place. Established stars and prominent directors reign supreme in Hollywood and together they negotiate with the studio CEOs to get film projects made. In return, the studios use financial perks and personal favors to entice them. Picture fees for major stars like Tom Hanks and Julia Roberts reach as high as $15–20 million against 5–10 percent of the film's gross. Such high-profile stars earn even more because their contracts often contain a sliding scale where the percentage of the film's gross increases in accordance with the box office receipts. Being nominated or receiving an Academy Award adds a bonus to the star's financial package. Other perks might include a weekly nonaccountable expense allowance, availability of a jet aircraft complete with pilot, a full-size Mercedes-Benz, a first-class trailer, two personal assistants, a dialogue coach, bodyguards, a personal chef, and free hotel rooms for visiting friends.

It is not surprising, therefore, that the average cost of a major studio production reached $55 million by 2000, with another $27 million spent on distribution and marketing. The $82 million total cost means that not all films that gross $100 million are considered profitable investments within the industry because of residual additional costs.[4] What other businesses would make that claim? In addition, the revenue potential for a film has shifted from domestic to foreign. It is not enough today for a film to perform well at the domestic box office; it also must attract an international audience if it is to show a decent profit. It is now estimated that only 30 percent of box office receipts come from domestic distribution.[5] If 70 percent of a film's receipts come from foreign revenues, then studios must consider how their films will appeal to overseas customers.

Rising production costs have sent the studios scrambling to cut expenses. One major step taken in film production today is to shoot locations outside the United States. Canada, Mexico, Australia, and Eastern Europe are favorite production sites. For example, the American Civil War drama, *Cold Mountain* (2003), was filmed in Romania, while the martial arts feature, *The Matrix* (1999), was shot in Australia. Canadian cities like Vancouver and Toronto are frequently used to represent American cities like New York and Chicago. Local tax incentives and the strength of the American dollar in these Canadian locations result in lower production costs.

Another expense-saving measure is production cost sharing. In the new Hollywood, millionaire actors like Mel Gibson and Tom Hanks view films as investment opportunities. A number of Hollywood stars have financed or co-financed film projects that interest them. Others like Gibson set up their own production companies. Gibson's company, ICON, produced his film, *The Passion of the Christ*. Hanks, meanwhile, joined with several other investors to produce the surprise hit, *My Big Fat Greek Wedding* (2002). *Seabiscuit* (2003), the popular film about the famed underdog racehorse, cost $87 million that was shared by three Hollywood backers.[6] Cost-sharing partnerships have become a popular financial option for both major productions and for selected films with limited appeal. Another factor that grew out of the bull market of the nineties is the creation of a millionaire class of investors. People like Bob Yari, a real estate developer, and Steve Jobs, the founder of Apple Computer, are willing to invest their capital in film projects. Jobs, in fact, hit pure gold when his animated film *Finding Nemo* (2003) became the highest grossing movie of the year.[7]

Movie making is an expensive undertaking and a high-risk venture. Producers constantly are engaged in an audience guessing game. Increasingly, studios produce movies for specific markets and targeted audiences. When producers guess wrong, the results can be disastrous. This may explain why studios tend to "follow the money" and produce remakes, sequels, and mainstream films featuring established and popular stars. While the media readily reports on successful film projects that earn millions and break box office records, most failed films and unfulfilled projects go unnoticed.

Unfortunately, filmmaking is such an unpredictable business that depends on so many variables that it comes close to legalized gambling. Film production is at the mercy of weather conditions, labor delays and strikes, accidents on the set, script rewrites, and temperamental actors. Once completed, a film is subject to the uncertainties of distribution: release date (summer and Christmas are preferred), number of theaters involved in the film's opening weekend, reviews that the film receives from the critics, and external factors such as war and domestic crises. Most uncertain is the immeasurable variability of audience taste. Films that were expected to be hits due to casting, director's reputation, or a screenplay based on a best seller can backfire, resulting in considerable losses. Several examples can be cited. A film starring the popular actor Eddie Murphy appeared to be a certain success on paper yet *Adventures of Pluto Nash* (2002), a $100 million production, grossed a paltry $4 million during its first two weeks when interest normally is at its peak. The pairing of Oscar-winning actor Anthony Hopkins with popular comedian Chris Rock seemed to producers to be a natural hit. Yet their film, *Bad Company* (2002), delayed by 9/11, lost a reported $50 million. Even a film based on a popular children's book, *Stuart Little 2* (2002) failed to recoup its $120 million dollar cost. On the other hand, there are the unexpected surprises. Few in the industry expected a $5 million film without established stars like *My Big Fat Greek Wedding* to exceed $200 million at the box office.[8] With all these uncertainties, filmmaking in Hollywood has come to be dominated by projects that are most likely to appeal to teenagers who represent the audience group that buys the most tickets.

As if excessive costs and unpredictability were not enough negatives, geniuses and scalawags people the film industry. Hollywood films are not so much made as arranged through negotiations. And some of these film deals put Donald Trump to shame. If outsiders want to know how films get made in Hollywood, Peter Biskind's *Down and Dirty Pictures*[9] is a must read. Illustrative is the Gus Van Sant film *Good Will Hunting* (1997). The screenplay, written by two Boston actor-friends Matt Damon and Ben Affleck, concerns a mathematical genius who works as a janitor at MIT. Naturally, Damon and Affleck wanted to star in the film but their project drew little interest, particularly since the studios wanted Brad Pitt and Leonardo DiCaprio for the leads. Damon and Affleck's agent was able to sell the script to Castle Rock for $600,000. That was in 1994 but filming had yet to begin a year later. It was clear to Damon and Affleck that Castle Rock did not want them in the film and so the studio gave them thirty days to sell the project to another producer. Eventually the boys got a friend to bring it to producer Harvey Weinstein at Miramax. Weinstein bought the script for $1 million in 1995, agreeing to star the two boys in the film if they agreed to do a couple of other films for Weinstein at bargain prices. The boys agreed and the deal was done. Still there were glitches. The boys wanted Van Sant as director on the project and Weinstein objected. As a result, the project sat for another year. Finally Weinstein signed Van Sant to do it on the condition that an established star plays a supporting role in the film. Van Sant got Robin Williams to play the therapist and the project was ready for production. At this point Weinstein insisted on his own producer for the film and more arguments ensued. By April 1997, filming on *Good Will Hunting* began in Toronto, and by December, it had been released after previews indicated audiences liked the film. *Good Will Hunting* cost $20 million and had a total gross of $364 million, excluding profits from cable and video. It won two Academy Awards, one for original script and the other for Williams as best supporting actor. Damon and Affleck split the $1 million salary Weinstein gave them for the film. According to Biskind, the story behind the making of *Good Will Hunting* is business as usual in Hollywood.

The Rise of the Indies

The history of the independent film movement (the "indies") has no real beginning because movies have been produced outside of mainstream Hollywood since the film industry began. Furthermore, there is no one definition of the indies that is completely acceptable. A consensus does exist as to the characteristics usually present: first, the films are produced outside the traditional studio system; second, the films are generally made on modest budgets and are financed by the filmmakers themselves or by funds secured from nonconventional sources; third, the films are usually distributed, if at all, outside of the normal theater chains; and lastly, the films are made by young directors at the beginning of their careers or by established "auteurs" who are in a position to freelance.

The essence of the independent film is greater than its origin or distribution. Its most defining characteristics include ideas and imagery counter to commercial cinema in films that express the personal statement of their creators or reflect their idiosyncratic visions.[10] These young filmmakers find outlets for their work in film festivals like the one in Salt Lake City in 1978. The U.S. Film Festival's purpose is to serve as a showcase for the work of young filmmakers whose films are largely ignored by the national theater chains. At the same time another story[11] was unfolding in the West where actor Robert Redford, somewhat discontent with mainstream Hollywood, bought property in Utah on which he established a film workshop, the Sundance Institute, named after the character he played in *Butch Cassidy and the Sundance Kid* (1969). When the U.S. Film Festival experienced financial deficits, Redford took over the management of the festival in 1985 and moved it to Park City, Utah, where it was revived as the Sundance Film Festival.

It would not be inappropriate to single out Steven Soderbergh's work, *sex, lies, and videotape* (1989) as the breakout film for the independent movement. Before the success of Soderbergh's film, indies struggled for national distribution and consequently, their box office receipts were as modest as their production budgets. But Harvey Weinstein at Miramax bought *sex, lies, and videotape* at Sundance and marketed it to the multiplexes. A film that cost a little over $1 million eventually brought in $55 million at the box office. Soderbergh's film had become a commercial and critical success and a defining moment for the independent movement.[12] While Redford and Weinstein deserve credit for providing encouragement and business acumen to the indies movement, a video and cable market that was starved for new material aided their efforts. Even if an indie film failed to do much business on the big screen, additional revenue was now available from these other outlets.

Indies blossomed in the bull market of the 1990s. Films made for what in Hollywood is considered "pocket change" brought in millions in gross receipts. Producers like Weinstein were willing to buy films at festivals for one or two million and try to market them to a wider audience. Several 1990s films even broke the $100 million mark usually reserved for expensive major Hollywood productions. Films like *Good Will Hunting, Pulp Fiction* (1994), and *The Blair Witch Project* (1999) astounded people in the film industry. Not that every indie made money. Nonetheless the idea of a relatively inexpensive film grossing ten or twelve times its cost was seductive to the gambling nature inherent in the film business. The indies developed a reputation for being "good value for the money."

By early in the millennium, the indies had established a solid and growing niche in the film market. Whereas in the eighties possibly fifty independent productions were made, that number had increased to well over one hundred at the beginning of the new century. Not all, however, were bought for commercial distribution. Moreover, the ones that succeeded caught the attention of the major studios when twenty-five of them grossed at least $1 million.[13] Still it is a fact that in 1996 independents earned so little that they were not even listed in the box office receipts statistics for that year. But by 2000, independents had captured a 6 percent share of the domestic box office gross, a significant inroad.[14]

By this time, indies had redefined themselves in that they represent almost one quarter of the films produced in Hollywood. These independent films are released through subsidiaries of the major studios. For example, Miramax is the subsidiary of Walt Disney, New Line Cinema of Time-Warner, Samuel Goldwyn of MGM, October of Universal, and Fox-Searchlight of Twentieth Century Fox. The directors of the independent movement have become the next generation of Hollywood filmmakers: Steven Soderbergh (*Traffic*, 2003), Kevin Smith (*Dogma*, 1999), David O. Russell (*Three Kings*, 1999), Todd Haynes (*Far From Heaven*, 2003), Alexander Payne (*About Schmidt*, 2003), and Quentin Tarantino (*Kill Bill I* and *II*, 2003–04), among others. And to the surprise (and chagrin) of the Hollywood establishment, independents provided stiff competition at the Academy Awards[15] since distributors like Miramax[16] brought quality overseas films like *The English Patient* (1996), *Shakespeare in Love* (1999), and *The Quiet American* (2003) into the more traditional theater chains.

WHAT FUTURE FOR POLITICAL FILM IN HOLLYWOOD?

How does the business of filmmaking and the growth of the independent movement relate to the future of political film? The answer is contained in the reality that Hollywood is first and foremost in the entertainment business, where risks are high. While successes can be enormously profitable, failures can bankrupt studios and destroy reputations. One example suffices. Michael Cimino was at the peak of his career, having won an Oscar for directing *The Deer Hunter*. His next film project was a western, *Heaven's Gate* (1981) with a budget projected at under $10 million. The uncut version ran almost four hours, cost over $40 million, and was panned by virtually every film critic. It largely was responsible for the demise of United Artists and it ended Cimino's career.[17] Hence, the conventional wisdom in the industry is to play it safe, offend no one, and take no chances. As a consequence, the film industry is conservative, reactive, and audience driven.

On the other hand, the independent movement allows for more personal visions, opportunities to pursue controversial subjects, and provides freedom from studio interference. These attributes make it the ideal venue to treat adult material and deal with issues that challenge and even offend audiences. As mentioned previously, the term "adult" refers to intelligent stories populated with real characters found in such films as *The Door in the Floor* (2004), *In the Bedroom* (2001), and *You*

Can Count on Me (1999), to cite just a few. While these films lack political content, their sensitive treatment of human relationships and family tragedies provide a template for political filmmaking because of their modest budgets and critical acclaim.

There are three major obstacles still to overcome. One involves the cooptation of young independent filmmakers by the major studios. Success is like a virus in the film industry. If a filmmaker's indie is successful at the box office, the studios will trust him/her with a more expensive film project. When this scenario occurs, the tendency is for the studios to want greater control over the project. The exercise of that control could involve supervision over the budget, casting, and film content. The opportunity to move from a $1 million film budget to a $50 million budget is a great temptation to young filmmakers. The trick is to become successful without losing your independence.

Another obstacle is the reputation in Hollywood that political films seldom perform well at the box office. That obstacle can be mitigated in two ways. The first is to utilize the indies as a low-cost mechanism to revive the old "message" films of the thirties and forties. Thanks to digital cameras, many of these films can be made for under $1–$2 million and still contain quality production and commercial value. Filmmaker Rebecca Miller, for example, made *Personal Velocity* (2002), a film about three different women in crisis situations, for $150,000 using two Sony digital cameras.[18]

An alternative route to follow is the example of the film *The Contender*, about a woman nominee for vice president. DreamWorks, a major studio, produced this explicitly political film, for roughly $10 million because its participants—director and actors—were willing to work for lower than usual salaries and perks. Here is an ideal political movie: quality production values, recognized cast, modest (indies) budget—and it still made money. Both avenues afford Hollywood an opportunity to be more creative and challenging and not suffer for it.

A third impediment is more pervasive and offers a greater challenge to conquer because it lies within film industry values and those shared by the American character. Emanuel Levy,[19] professor of film and sociology, describes four jointly held values by Hollywood and the American majority. First, Americans dislike political movies because they distrust politicians and are wary about the exercise of power and authority. Certainly, a reader is able to trace an understandable line of political distrust from Vietnam through Watergate and into Iraq. Recognizing this distrust, Hollywood is reluctant to confront America's political institutions and instead substitutes criticism against impersonal bureaucracies. Next, Hollywood exploits the pervasive cult of individualism in the American character so that it's heroes and heroines are portrayed as individuals fighting alone (and often successfully) against overwhelming odds. Hollywood films glorify individuals such as Boy Ranger Jefferson Smith taking on the U.S. Senate, lawyer Frank Gavin arguing a malpractice suit against the Catholic Church, and plant manager Jack Godell shutting down a damaged nuclear power plant against the wishes of its CEOs. To reinforce the concept that it is individuals who can accomplish great feats, popular movie stars Jimmy Stewart, Paul Newman, and Jack Lemmon play these characters. Third, most of the action that occurs in Hollywood films is by characters operating as individuals rather than in groups or as part of larger communities. Whether the film characters are exposing political corruption, protecting the environment, or safeguarding the community, it is usually the work of one person rather than a political party or interest group. Collective action smacks too much of socialism for conservative Hollywood and mainstream America. Finally, the film industry avoids political ideology of any kind. It appeals to centrist, or even indifferent, America because it does not want to offend potential customers. Michael Moore's documentary *Fahrenheit 9/11*, considered by its distributor, Walt Disney, to be too critical of President George W. Bush, refused to release the film. Hollywood is not conservative because its CEOs are Republicans but because the studios want to make money or certainly not lose any. That often translates into supporting the status quo: capitalism, established institutions, and at least the remnants of the nuclear family.

These three obstacles interfere with the potentially promising future for political film. There is no simple solution to the first barrier since in Hollywood, as in other industries, success is measured in terms of status and money. How do you tell a Soderbergh or a Tarantino to turn down a major film project if they cannot have the final cut? The second obstacle can be diminished within the industry itself and by the vigilance of the independent movement to remain true to its origins as an alternative to mainstream Hollywood. There is a small market in American popular culture for filmmakers who challenge entrenched institutions and the underlying values of a consumer society. If this thought appears too utopian, remember that in the early days of film history, the American Federation of Labor and other labor organizations financed and produced some of their own films. Similar models exist in Hollywood's past: the Abraham Polonsky/John Garfield film *Force of Evil* was independently produced and still earned a profit. Imagine if environmental groups and public interest organizations joined with labor unions and consumer groups in financing and producing movies that had some commercial appeal? Admittedly such endeavors could lead to biased productions and propaganda tracts, but would they be worse than many of the films that populate movie screens today?

These new film ventures require mass distribution to substantially increase the independents 6 percent share of the marketplace. Just as labor struggled to find theaters for its films in the early part of the twentieth century, political films of the future may have to think outside of the Hollywood box and rely more on universities, public libraries, and film clubs for their venues. Today indies also have alternative outlets for their films, namely cable networks and the video and DVD market. Currently, some of the most original and interesting programming is being done by HBO and Showtime.

HBO did a miniseries, *Band of Brothers* (2001), based on the book by historian Stephen Ambrose that told the story of Easy Company, a paratrooper division in WWII France. The quality of the series, which involved Tom Hanks as director and coproducer, equaled the treatment of similar war material in the movies. From a different perspective, cable provides filmmakers with another option to the normal theatrical release. When an updated version of *Lolita* (1998) was considered too offensive for the big screen, it was picked up by cable and later released to theaters and video. In brief, independent filmmakers need to consider all these opportunities for their work.

There is another encouraging sign for the alternative cinema represented by the indies. The past two decades has witnessed a surge of interest in film festivals throughout the United States. The most popular festival is Sundance where the number of film entrees has escalated annually. In 1998, 110 works were selected by the judges to be screened. Five years later, over 800 films were selected, more than half made with digital cameras. This encouraging news is offset by the reality that only a small fraction of the films screened are bought for American distribution.[20] But it seems logical that the market for indies will expand as a greater number of their films are shown in an increasing number of annual film festivals held in the United States. There are at least eight film festivals in New York City alone, exhibiting each year the films of relative unknown filmmakers. It was at one of these festivals in the eighties that Michael Moore's *Roger and Me* was showcased. Unfortunately, Robert Redford's attempt to unite inner-city universities with a string of Sundance cinemas has yet to materialize. That venture would provide an outlet for documentaries and other independent projects attractive to college students. Hopefully, that effort will be revived in the future.

Political scientist Benjamin Barber,[21] reflecting on the tragic events of September 11, reminds us of the crucial role played by the media, particularly film and video, in an interconnected world. Contrasting the two worldly forces, which he identifies as Jihad and McWorld, Barber documents the replacement of print by filmic images transmitted around the globe. He is concerned about the uniformity of these Western images as filtered through the eyes of Eastern cultures. Since Hollywood has come to dominate the world market, it is American images and sound that the world sees and hears. Needless to state that in such a world, the film industry has a special responsibility to diversify its communicative messages and avoid cultural expansionism. If there ever was a need for an alternative film movement, now is the time. The best hope for peace and understanding in the world today lies in an expanded and truly independent film movement dominated by politically conscious filmmakers who are willing to take the risks avoided by mainstream

Hollywood. That spirit will only materialize if American audiences become more supportive and more selective filmgoers. If Americans really want to see fewer films that appeal to teenage hormones or macho masculinity, then they will have to prove it to Hollywood at the box office. In a democracy, the people have the power to exercise the final cut.

NOTES

ONE: IT'S SHOWTIME: THE HOLLYWOOD-WASHINGTON CONNECTION

1. Hortense Powdermaker, *Hollywood the Dream Factory: An Anthropologist Looks at the Movie-makers* (Boston: Little, Brown & Company, 1950).

2. Information on Schwarzenegger's background, early life, and movie career can be found on his Web site, joinarnold.com, with links to other sites, and in the *New York Times,* August 8, 2003, 1.

3. To understand the disaffection Californians had for their governor, see Michael Lewis, "The Personal is the Antipolitical," *New York Times Magazine,* September 28, 2003, sec. 6, 40–47ff.

4. In "Will California Elect a Superhero? Candidate Arnold Schwarzenegger Taps Film Myths," http://www.h-net.org/~filmhis/controversial_films/will_california.htm, Professor John Shelton Lawrence compares the recall election and Schwarzenegger's candidacy with Frank Capra's script for his 1930s film, *Mr. Smith Goes to Washington.*

5. http://MoveOn.org, October 3, 2003.

6. The recall election became the butt of jokes and cartoons, especially for monologues on *The Tonight Show* and *The Late Show with David Letterman.* See http://www.politicalhumor. about.com/cs/california for a comprehensive sample.

7. Quoted in Paul Krugman's column, the *New York Times,* May 30, 2003, A29.

8. For a more complete list of entertainers turned politicians before Schwarzenegger, see the *New York Times,* August 8, 2003, A14.

9. In her *New York Times* column, August 15, 1999, 15, Maureen Dowd asked: "Will You, Warren?" The *Times* carried his possible candidacy as a front-page story on September 9, 1999, 1, and a follow-up story on an inside page on October 1, 1999, A21.

10. See Neal Gabler, *Life: The Movie: How Entertainment Conquered Reality* (New York: Alfred A. Knopf, 1998).

11. ———, *An Empire of Their Own: How the Jews Invented Hollywood* (New York: Crown, 1988), 245, 311.

12. Leslie Wayne, "A Hollywood Production: Political Money," *New York Times*, Sept. 12, 1996, 1.

13. *International Herald Tribune*, August 11, 2000, 1, and August 14, 2000, 2. *Mother Jones*, March/April 2001, 82–83, reported that during the 1999–2000 election cycle, five individuals associated with the film industry were among the top 100 contributors to political campaigns. And all five gave to Democrats.

14. *Williamsport Sun-Gazette*, March 23, 2004, B8.

15. Reported in the *New York Times*, December 1, 1998, A24.

16. Reported in the *Williamsport Sun-Gazette*, December 8, 2000, A2.

17. R. W. Apple Jr., "On Washington," *New York Times Magazine*, Nov. 15, 1998, sec. 6, 42.

18. Ronald Brownstein develops this theme in Part II of his book, *The Power and the Glitter* (New York: Pantheon, 1990).

19. Neal Gabler in *An Empire of Their Own: How the Jews Invented Hollywood* tells their story.

20. Details of the campaign can be found in Greg Mitchell, *The Campaign of the Century* (New York: Random House, 1992) and in Immanul Ness and James Ciment, *The Encyclopedia of Third Parties in America*, Vol. 1 (New York: M.E. Sharpe, 2000), 249–250.

21. Paul Buhle and Dave Wagner, *Radical Hollywood* (New York: The New Press, 2002), Introduction. The film list would include such classics as: *Casablanca, Lawrence of Arabia, Mr. Smith Goes to Washington,* and *The Wizard of Oz*. For the view that Hollywood is under the control of left-liberals today, see James Hirsen, *Tales From the Left Coast* (New York: Crown Forum, 2003).

22. Gabler, *An Empire of Their Own*, 291.

23. See Frances Stoner Saunders, *The Cultural Cold War* (New York: The New Press, 1999).

24. John Daly, "*The Right Stuff* and the Wrong Stuff: The Curious History of an Epic Historical Film," (paper presented at the Far West Popular Culture meeting, Las Vegas, February, 2004).

25. Story in the *Williamsport Sun-Gazette*, December 1, 2000, A9.

26. Harvey B. Feigenbaum, "The Culture of Production and the Production of Culture" (paper presented at the annual meeting of the American Political Science Association, Chicago, August 31–September 3, 1995), 24.

27. *Variety*, June 22–28, 1998, 8.

28. The economic domination of Hollywood movies is demonstrated in David Puttnam, with Neil Watson, *Movies and Money* (New York: Knopf, 1997).

29. These facts and stories can be found in Gail Kinn and Jim Piazza, *The Complete Unofficial History of the Academy Awards* (New York: Black Dog & Leventhal Publishers, 2002).

30. http://www.cnn.com, December 10, 2002.

31. The Hollywood antiwar movement was featured prominently on the Internet. See http://www.islamonline.net, February 24, 2003; http://news.bbc.co.uk, January 19, 2003; and http://www.globalpolicy.org, March 10, 2003.

32. Richard Maltby and Dan Craven, *Hollywood Cinema* (Cambridge, MA: Blackwell Publishers, 1995) support the view that political movies are high box office risks, citing at least six pre-WWII political films, including *Abe Lincoln in Illinois*, that either lost money or were financial disappointments.

33. Quoted in Maltby and Craven, 363.

34. Gary Crowdus, ed., *The Political Companion to American Film* (Chicago: Lake View Press, 1994), x.

35. See reports and reviews of the film in the *New York Times*, Dec. 17, 1995, sec. 2, 1, and Dec. 20 1996, sec. C, 11.

36. See Charles Maland, "Politics and Auteurs: From Chaplin to Wajda," in James Combs, ed., *Movies and Politics* (New York: Garland Publishing, 1993), 239–269.

37. Walter Benjamin, "The work of Art in the Age of Mechanical Reproduction," in *Illuminations*, edited with an introduction by Hannah Arendt (New York: Schocken Books, 1968).

38. The quote by Cassavetes is in Michael Genovese, *Politics and the Cinema* (Lexington, MA: Ginn Press, 1986), 67. Certainly, Neal Gabler agreed with that assessment in his book, *An Empire of Their Own*, detailing how the Jewish immigrants who founded Hollywood portrayed an idealized version of their new homeland in their films.

39. Dan Nimmo, "Political Propaganda in the Movies: A Typology," in *Movies and Politics*, 271–294.

40. Ibid., 283–284.

41. Quoted in John E. O'Connor and Martin A. Jackson, eds., *American History/American Film*, with a Foreword by Arthur Schlesinger, Jr. (New York: Frederick Unger, 1979), xv. The film was the first motion picture shown at the White House.

42. See Mark C. Carnes, ed., *Past Imperfect* (New York: Henry Holt, 1995). Carnes takes the position that Hollywood filmmakers generally have distorted the historical facts.

43. See Ernest R. May, "Thirteen Days in 145 Minutes," *National Forum,* 81, No. 2 (Spring 2001), 34–37, and Michael Nelson, "Thirteen Days Doesn't Add Up," the *Chronicle of Higher Education*, February 2, 2001, sec. 2, B15–B16.

44. These three films are cited by Ernest Giglio, "Using Film to Teach Political Concepts," *European Political Science*, 1, No. 2 (Spring 2002), 53–58 as examples that require corrections and analysis before use in the classroom.

45. This is the viewpoint expressed by Richard B. Stinnett in his book, *Day of Deceit: The Truth About FDR & Pearl Harbor* (New York: Free Press, 1999).

46. Michael Haas, *Political Film Review*, Newsletter #195, April 15, 2004.

47. Stephen Vaughn, *Ronald Reagan in Hollywood* (New York: Cambridge University Press, 1994).

48. See Ernest Giglio, "The Decade of 'The Miracle' 1952–1962: A Study in the Censorship of the American Motion Picture" (Ph.D. diss., Syracuse University, 1964) and I. C. Jarvie et al. (eds.), *Children and the Movies: Media Influences and the Payne Fund Controversy* (New York: Cambridge University Press, 1996).

49. See comments in the *New York Times*, June 2, 1995, 24, and June 4, 1995, 20.

50. After the initial outcry had quieted, it was discovered that a number of fire-bombings had occurred in the New York subway system in the 1980s. Because of these incidents, the city's Transit Authority, while cooperating with Columbia Pictures, refused permission to film that scene in the subway. Actually, a Burt Reynolds police drama, *Fuzz*, released in the seventies, contained a scene where a man is doused with flammable liquor and set on fire. Public criticism was raised after a copycat crime occurred shortly after the film's theatrical release. But the furor declined as the crime became accepted as an isolated incident.

51. William R. Elliott and William J. Schenck-Hamlin, "Film, Politics and the Press: The Influence of '*All the President's Men*,'" *Journalism Quarterly* 56, no. 3 (1979): 546–553.

52. Thomas S. Bateman, Tomoaki Sakano, and Mokoto Fujita, "Roger, Me, and My Attitude: Film Propaganda and Cynicism toward Corporate Leadership," *Journal of Applied Psychology* 77, No. 5, (1992): 768–771.

TWO: IN SEARCH OF THE POLITICAL FILM: FROM RIEFENSTAHL TO THE THREE STOOGES

1. The literature on *Casablanca* is too large to cite here but a few noteworthy sources include: Aljean Harmetz, *Round Up the Usual Suspects* (New York: Hyperion, 1992), Howard Koch,

Casablanca: Script and Legend (New York: Overlook Express, 1992) and Randy Roberts and Robert E. May, "You Must Remember This: The Case of Hal Wallis's *Casablanca* in Roberts and May, *Learning to Think Critically: Film, Myth, and American History* (New York: HarperCollins, 1993).

2. Clifford Geertz, *The Interpretation of Cultures* (New York: Basic Books, 1973), 196.

3. See, e.g., Terry Christensen, *Reel Politics* (New York: Blackwell, 1987); Gary Crowdus, ed., *The Political Companion to American Film* (Chicago: Lake View Press, 1994) and Mark Litwak, *Reel Power* (London: Sedgwick & Jackson, 1987) as scholars, critics, and writers who fit into this group.

4. Peter Rainer, "Politicization of Films: A Mirror of Our Time," *Los Angeles Herald*, Dec. 16, 1984, 1, 14, analyzes the films of the eighties.

5. Herbert J. Gans, "Hollywood Entertainment: Commerce or Ideology?" *Social Science Quarterly* 74, no. 1 (1993): 150–153.

6. John Simon, *Movies Into Film* (New York: Dell Publishing Co., 1970), 66.

7. Ibid.

8. Georgakas and Rubenstein in *The Cineaste Interviews* do include a few American filmmakers such as John Sayles and Paul Schrader among their political directors as well as screenwriters like Budd Schulberg and John Howard Lawson. But Europeans and non-Americans dominate their exclusive list of political filmmakers.

9. See, Terry Christensen, *Reel Politics* (New York: Blackwell Publishers, 1987), Michael Genovese, *Politics and the Cinema* (Lexington, MA: Ginn Press, 1986), Don Georgakas and Lenny Rubenstein, eds., *The Cineaste Interviews* (Chicago: Lake View Press, 1983), Michael Ryan and Douglas Kellner, *Camera Politica: The Politics and Ideology of Contemporary Hollywood Film* (Bloomington: Indiana University Press, 1988), and Sidney Wise, "Politicians: A Film Perspective," *News for Teachers of Political Science*, 32 (winter 1982): 1.

10. Genovese, *Politics and the Cinema*, 2–3.

11. Political Film Society, "Political Film Review," http://PFS.cjb.net, April 1, 2001.

12. Peter J. Haas, "A Typology of Political Film," Working Paper #11, *Political Film Society* series, March 2000.

13. Cass Sunstein, "Free Speech Now," *University of Chicago Law Review* 59 (1992): 304.

14. On this point, see Nimmo, "Political Propaganda in the Movies: A Typology," in *Movies and Politics*, 277. For the view that the film was about Hollywood, see Crowdus, *A Political Companion to American Film*, 153–154 and Christensen, *Reel Power*, 93.

15. Christine Noll Brinckmann, "The Politics of *Force of Evil*: An Analysis of Abraham Polonsky's Preblacklisted Film," *Prospects* 6 (1981): 369.

16. Peter Biskind, *Seeing Is Believing: How Hollywood Taught Us to Stop Worrying and Love the Fifties* (New York: Pantheon Books, 1983), 5.

17. Crowdus, *A Political Companion to American Film*, 235–236, maintains that Kramer's social-message pictures were commercial successes because he provided simpleminded solutions to complex problems. For example, in *Guess Who's Coming to Dinner?* the film suggests that racism can be resolved at the personal level of two families having a friendly discussion over a cup of coffee. Furthermore, Crowdus questions Kramer's political liberalism since off-screen he deserted friends during the time of McCarthyism and the blacklist.

18. See Charles Chaplin, *My Autobiography* (New York: Simon and Schuster, 1964) and David Robinson, *Chaplin: His Life and Art* (New York: McGraw-Hill, 1985).

19. Don B. Morlan, "A Pie in the Face: The *Three Stooges* Anti-Aristocracy Theme in Depression-Era American Film" (paper presented at the annual meeting of the Popular Culture Association, Chicago, April 1994), "Slapstick Contributions to World War II Propaganda: The *Three Stooges*

and *Abbott & Costello*," *Studies in Popular Culture* 17 (Oct. 1994): 29–43, and "Pre-World War II Propaganda: Film as Controversy" (paper presented at the annual meeting of the American Political Science Association, Chicago, September 1995).

20. Leonard Maltin, *The Great Movie Shorts* (New York: Crown Publishers, 1972) identifies the Stooges as "low comedians" who recycled one basic plot formula in all their films, namely, where would they be most out of place? All story lines developed from that one premise. Maltin admits that the Stooges made one political film, *Three Dark Horses*, a satire about a crooked presidential campaign. But the public embraced the shorts and ignored the film.

21. *Jacobellis v. Ohio*, 378 U.S. 184 (1964), concurring at 197, Justice Stewart wrote: "I don't know what obscenity is, but I know it when I see it."

THREE: NONFICTION FILM: INVESTIGATING THE REAL

1. Bill Nichols, *Blurred Boundaries* (Bloomington: Indiana University Press, 1994), 47–48.

2. See Jill Godmilow, "How Real Is the Reality in Documentary Film?" *History and Theory* 36, no. 4 (December 1997), 80–81.

3. Richard M. Barsam, "From Nonfiction Film: A Critical History," in Gerald Mast and Marshall Cohen, eds. *Film Theory and Criticism*, 3rd ed. (New York: Oxford University Press, 1985), 583–585.

4. Guido Convents, "Documentaries and Propaganda Before 1914," *Framework*, no. 35 (1988): 107–108.

5. Reported in Tom W. Hoffer and Richard Alan Nelson, "Docudrama on American Television," *Journal of the University Film Association* 30, no. 2 (Spring 1978): 22, ft. #3.

6. The Library of Congress, "The Motion Picture Camera Goes to War." Online. Internet. February 19, 1998.

7. See Steven J. Ross, "Struggles for the Screen: Workers, Radicals, and the Political Uses of Silent Film," *American Historical Review* 96, no. 2 (April 1991): 333–367.

8. Richard M. Barsam, *Non-Fiction Film*, rev. ed. (Bloomington: Indiana University Press, 1992), 32–38.

9. Brian Winston, *Claiming the Real: The Documentary Film Revisited* (London: British Film Institute, 1995), 69–70.

10. Ross, "Struggles for the Screen," 349–361.

11. See Barsam, *Non-Fiction Film*, chapter 10, for a discussion of American films made during World War II.

12. Kopple's recent documentary, *Wild Man Blues* (1998), is about Woody Allen's jazz band.

13. See Barry Keith Grant, *Voyages of Discovery: The Cinema of Frederick Wiseman* (Urbana: University of Illinois Press, 1992) where the author describes Wiseman's films as "voyages of discovery" in which both the filmmaker and the viewer rediscover themselves; and Thomas W. Benson and Carolyn Anderson, *Reality Fictions: The Films of Frederick Wiseman* 2d ed.(Carbondale: Southern Illinois University Press, 2002).

14. For the complete story, see Benson and Anderson, *Reality Fictions,* chapter 2.

15. *Commonwealth v. Wiseman*, Superior Court, Civil Action No. 87538, 1 August 1991, Memorandum of Decision, Re: Motion for Reconsideration.

16. Grant, *Voyages of Discovery*, 27–34.

17. Ibid., 9.

18. Benson and Anderson, *Reality Fictions*, 306.

19. Ibid., 2.
20. See Raymond Fielding, *The March of Time, 1945–51* (New York: Oxford University Press, 1978), chapter 8, 187–201. Fielding claims that the newsreel took footage originally filmed in Germany and reshot most of it around Hoboken, New Jersey, using anti-Nazi German-Americans.
21. According to Matthew Bernstein, "Documentaphobia and Mixed Modes," in Barry Keith Grant and Jeannette Sloniowski, eds, *Documenting the Documentary* (Detroit: Wayne State University Press, 1998), 397, Moore admitted to the fact in an interview.
22. See the reviews and commentary by Richard Corliss in *Time*, February 12, 1990, 58, Pauline Kael in *The New Yorker*, January 8, 1990, 90–92 and John Simon in *National Review*, June 11, 1990, 54. Michael Moore's second endeavor, *Canadian Bacon*, a feature film with Hollywood actors, did not fare well at the box office or with critics.
23. Richard Bernstein, "'*Roger and Me*': Documentary? Satire? Or Both?" *New York Times*, February 1, 1990, C20.
24. See Miles Orwell, "Documentary and the Power of Interrogation: *American Dream* and *Roger & me*," *Film Quarterly*, 48 (winter 1994/95): 10–18.
25. Reported in Winston, *Claiming the Real*, 239.
26. See Alan Rosenthal, ed., *Why Docudrama?* (Carbondale: Southern Illinois University Press, 1999), Part One, 1–11.
27. Good background material is found in Tom W. Hoffer and Richard Alan Nelson, "Docudrama on American Television," 21–27 as well as Rosenthal, *Why Docudrama?*
28. Hoffer and Nelson, "Docudrama on American Television," 21.
29. Quoted in David Culbert, "Our Awkward Ally: Mission to Moscow," in O'Connor and Jackson, eds, *American History/American Film*, 145, ft. # 62.
30. For a history of the term, see Garth S. Jowett, "Propaganda and Communication: The Re-emergence of a Research Tradition," *Journal of Communication* 37, no. 1, (winter 1987), 113–114.
31. Barsam, *Non-Fiction Film*, 200–205. For a detailed account of the German film industry under Goebbels, see David Welch, *Propaganda and the German Cinema, 1933–1945* (New York: Oxford University Press, 1983).
32. Ibid., 123–125.
33. See Winston, *Claiming the Real*, 74–78 and 108–109, David Hackett, film review of "The Wonderful, Horrible Life of Leni Riefenstahl," *American Historical Review* 100, no. 4, (Oct. 1995), 1227–1228, and Frank P. Tomasulo, "The Mass Psychology of Fascist Cinema," in Grant and Sloniowski, eds., *Documenting the Documentary*, 99–118. Tomasulo argues that Riefenstahl's film created a spectacle rather than documented one because of the presence of sixteen cameramen, 135 technicians, and several high-ranking Nazi Officers—all for the purpose of constructing a mythic representation of Hitler and the nation as one entity, with Hitler in the role of the strong father-figure destined to lead a confused Germany in restoring its rightful place as a world power.
34. For more background on her association with Hitler and the Nazi leadership, see Dana Arieli-Horowitz, "The Devil's Advocate? Leni Riefenstahl in Nazi Germany," (paper presented at the European Conference on Political Research, Canterbury, England, September 2001).
35. Reported in Anna Maria Sigmund, *Women of the Third Reich* (Ontario, Canada: NDE Publishing, 2000), 101.
36. Ibid., 108.
37. Don B. Morlan, "Pre-WWII Propaganda: Film as Controversy," (paper presented at the annual meeting of the American Political Science Association, Chicago, Sept. 1995).

38. John Canemaker, "World War II Animated Propaganda Cartoons," in Crowdus, *A Political Companion to American Film*, 496–500. The cartoon won an Oscar for Best Animated Short.

39. See Melvin Small, "Buffoons and BraveHearts: Hollywood Portrays the Russians, 1939–1944," *California Historical Society* 52, (winter 1973), 326–337.

40. See Culbert in O'Connor and Jackson, *American History/American Film*, 121–145. Culbert insists that Stalin, acting as the Soviet censor, only permitted some two dozen American films, including *Mission to Moscow*, to be shown in the Soviet Union between 1939 and 1945. The film remains a source of embarrassment to Warner Brothers, its distributor, since the studio denied the author of the present text permission to use a photo still from the film.

41. For an eyewitness, but subjective account of the filming, consult blacklisted director Herbert Biberman's book, *Salt of the Earth* (Boston: Beacon Press, 1965).

42. See James E. Combs and Sara T. Combs, *Film Propaganda and American Politics* (New York: Garland Publishing Co., 1994), 3–13.

43. Nichols, *Blurred Boundaries*, 122–126.

44. Dan Nimmo, "Political Propaganda in the Movies: A Typology," in Combs ed., *Movies and Politics*, 271–294.

45. See Leon F. Litwack, "The Birth of a Nation," in Carnes, *Past Imperfect: History According to the Movies*, 136–141. While it is true that similar stereotypes appeared in Margaret Mitchell's 1936 novel, *Gone With the Wind*, much of the racially offensive material was omitted from the movie version.

FOUR: KISS, KISS, BANG, BANG: OR HOW I CAME TO LOVE SEX AND VIOLENCE ON THE BIG SCREEN

1. For a discussion of early film censorship, see Ernest Giglio, "The Decade of 'The Miracle' 1952–1962: A Study in the Censorship of the American Motion Picture" (Ph.D. diss., Syracuse University, 1964).

2. 343 U.S. 495 (1952). For an insight into Burstyn's historic role, see Laura Wittern Keller, "Freedom of the Screen: Joseph Burstyn and The Miracle," *New York Archives* 1, no. 4 (spring 2002): 23–25.

3. See Charles Lyons, *The New Censors: Movies and the Culture Wars* (Philadelphia: Temple University Press, 1997).

4. See Thomas Doherty, *Pre-Code Hollywood: Sex, Immorality, and Insurrection in American Cinema* (New York: Columbia University Press, 1999) and Mark Vieira, *Sin in Soft Focus: Pre-Code Hollywood* (New York: Harry N. Abrams, 1999).

5. *Congressional Record*, 67th Cong., 2d Sess., 1922, LXII, Part 9, 9657.

6. There has been renewed scholarly interest in the code, possibly due to its placement online at http://www.artsreformation.com/a001/hays-code.html.

7. Lyons, *The New Censors*, p. 14.

8. See Marybeth Hamilton, *When I'm Bad, I'm Better: Mae West, Sex, and American Entertainment* (Berkeley: University of California Press, 1997), 191.

9. Gregory D. Black, *Hollywood Censored: Morality Codes, Catholics, and the Movies* (Cambridge, UK: Cambridge University Press, 1994).

10. Ibid., see chapter 6, 149–197, for details on the activities of the Legion during the 1930s.

11. Richard Brisbin, Jr., "From State and Local Censorship to Ratings: Substantive Rationality, Political Entrepreneurship, and Sex in the Movies," *Political Film Society*, Working Paper Series #9, 5.

12. Vieira, in *Sin in Soft Focus*, refers to Breen as the "Hitler of Hollywood."

13. Michael Asimow, "Divorce in the Movies: From the Hays Code to *Kramer v. Kramer*," *Legal Studies Forum* 24, 2 (2000): 221–267.

14. For a detailed account of the battle between Selznick and the Breen Office, see Leonard J. Leff and Jerold L. Simmons, *The Dame in the Kimono: Hollywood, Censorship, and the Production Code from the 1920s to the 1960s* (New York: Grove Weidenfeld, 1990).

15. *U.S. v. Paramount Pictures*, 334 U.S. 131 (1947).

16. Jon Lewis, *Hollywood v. Hard Core: How the Struggle over Censorship Saved the Modern Film Industry* (New York: New York University Press, 2000) advances the theory that the rating system was in response to two occurrences; the first being a box office slump that plagued the industry in 1968–1973 and the financial success of soft-porn independent films like *Last Tango in Paris* (1973) and hard-core porno films like *Behind the Green Door* (1972) and *Deep Throat* (1972). Hollywood was saved from financial ruin, Lewis contends, because the studios rallied behind the rating system in order to control the production and distribution of mainstream films. Taken together with Supreme Court decisions that restricted porno films, the industry was able to reposition sexually explicit fare to the film fringes.

17. For a profile on Valenti and his achievements as MPAA president, see Connie Bruck, "The Personal Touch," *The New Yorker*, August 13, 2001, 42–59.

18. For the story behind the establishment of the rating system, see Jack Valenti, *The Voluntary Movie Rating System* (Washington, DC: Motion Picture Association of America, 1996).

19. Ibid., 3.

20. Stories of the film cuts were reported in the *New York Times*, January 30, 1992, C15 and March 15, 1992, H17 and the *Westchester Dispatch*, February 16, 1992, F1. The R-rated version contained scenes of sexual bondage, one rough sex scene that bordered on rape, and several brutal killings. Rumor had it that the cuts involved a shot of Michael Douglas's penis in a turgid state and an oral sex scene. Supposedly these scenes were included in the film version released in Europe. In the United States, however, an NC-17 version appeared on laser disc, while an unrated director's cut was made available on video in addition to the edited R-rated version.

21. CARA, Motion Picture Association of America, September 25, 1996 provided the statistical data. Updated, the MPAA reported in 2001 that, of the more than 17,000 films rated since 1968, 57% were R-rated and another 2% NC-17 rated.

22. Arthur DeVany and W. David Wells, "Does Hollywood Make Too Many R-rated Movies? Risk, Stochastic Dominance, and the Illusion of Expectation," *Journal of Business*, 75: No. 3 (July 2002), 425–452.

23. Lyons, *The New Censors*, 183–192.

24. See ibid., chapter 5, for a case study on the religious opposition to the film.

25. The story was followed and reported in the secular and religious press beginning as early as August 2003. The film was released on Ash Wednesday, February 25, 2004. Gibson appeared on Primetime with Diane Sawyer the previous week.

26. The *New York Times*, April 12, 2004, B1.

27. Hortense Powdermaker, *Hollywood the Dream Factory* (Boston: Little, Brown, 1950).

28. Frank Rich, "From Here to Zapruder," *New York Times*, July 4, 1998, A25. Echoing Powdermaker, Rich argues that Hollywood movies tend to substitute reel solutions to genuine social and eco-

nomic problems rather than confront these in the real ghettos of South Bronx (New York) and Watts (Los Angeles).

29. Peter Keough, ed., *Flesh and Blood* (San Francisco: Mercury House, 1995), Introduction.

30. Valenti, *The Voluntary Movie Rating System*, 9.

31. See Lewis, *Hollywood v. Hard Core*, 3.

32. The *Sunday Times*, February 9, 1997, 4.

33. Valenti, *The Voluntary Movie Rating System*, 11.

34. Trip Gabriel, "The Rating Game at the Cineplex," *New York Times*, Feb. 18, 1996, sec. 2, 1.

35. Trey Graham, "Despite ID Policy, R–rating Rarely Bars Teens from Screens," *USA Today*, June 16, 1999, 4D.

36. *Williamsport Sun-Gazette*, July 1, 1999, 1. The policy was in response to the Columbine and Georgia school shootings.

37. http://www.csmonitor.com/2004, story by Amanda Paulson, June 15, 2004; http://www.washingtonpost.com, story by Rebecca Kahlenberg, June 29, 2004, C10; and http://edition.cnn.com, June 7, 2004.

38. Before the 1952 *Burstyn* decision, consult: *Gitlow v. New York*, 268 U.S. 652 (1925); *Whitney v. California*, 274 U.S. 357 (1927); *Near v. Minnesota*, 283 U.S. 697 (1931); *Thornhill v. Alabama*, 310 U.S. 88 (1940); and *West Virginia State Board v. Barnette*, 319 U.S. 624 (1943).
After 1952, consult: *Roth v. U.S.*, 354 U.S. 476 (1957); *New York Times Co. v. Sullivan*, 376 U.S. 255 (1964); *Brandenburg v. Ohio*, 395 U.S. 444 (1969); *New York Times v. U.S.*, 403 U.S. 713 (1971).

39. For the story, see Caryn James, "A Movie America Can't See," *New York Times*, March 15, 1998, sec. 2, 1, 213. It should be noted that this second version of Vladimir Nabokov's novel was shown in several European cities before Lyne sold his film to cable television. Afterward, the film had a limited run in select theaters.

40. H-FILM@H-NET.MSU.EDU, May 24–29, 1998.

41. The president had the films confiscated by customs because they were not properly labeled as "political propaganda." The U.S. Supreme Court upheld the administration's action. After the films were labeled, they were distributed.

42. Michael Medved, *Hollywood v. America* (New York: HarperCollins, 1992).

43. British Board of Film Classification, *Annual Report for 1995–96* (London: BBFC, July 1996), 5–7.

44. Federal Trade Commission, Report on Marketing Violent Entertainment to Children (September 2000), especially pp. 4–21. President Clinton requested the report after the Columbine High School shootings.

45. See L. Rowell Huesmann, Jessica Moise-Titus, Cheryl-Lynn Podolski and Leonard D. Eron, "Longitudinal Relations Between Children's Exposure to TV Violence and Their Aggressive and Violent Behavior in Young Adulthood: 1977–1992," *Developmental Psychology*, vol. 39, No. 2, 2003, 201–221.

46. Because of free speech provision of the First Amendment, courts have been reluctant to award plaintiffs damages for "harm done" by literary texts and the entertainment media. Most recently, in a case involving Oliver Stone's film, *Natural Born Killers*, the victim of a holdup shooting sued Stone and Time Warner after her assailant told police she and her boyfriend saw the film and wanted to be like "Mickey and Mallory," the killers in the movie. *Byers v. Edmondson*, L.A. Court of Appeal, First Circuit, No. 2001 CA 1184, June 5, 2002.

47. *American Pie* had a budget of $11 million, *American Pie 2* a budget of $30 million and *American Wedding* (2003) a budget of $55 million. All had worldwide grosses of over $200 million. For some inexplicable reason, there is no plan to make a fourth.

FIVE: HUAC AND THE BLACKLIST: THE RED SCARE COMES TO HOLLYWOOD

1. See the work of Dan Nimmo, "Political Propaganda in the Movies: A Typology," in James Combs, ed., *Movies and Politics* (New York: Garland Publishing, 1993), Gary Crowdus, ed., *The Political Companion to American Film* (Chicago, Lake View Press, 1994), and Terry Christensen, *Reel Politics* (New York: Blackwell Publishers, 1987).

2. See his interview in the *New York Times*, March 14, 1999, sec. 2, 7.

3. Victor Navasky, "Has *Guilty by Suspicion* Missed the Point?" *New York Times*, March 31, 1991, H9.

4. See Greg Mitchell, *Tricky Dick and the Pink Lady: Richard Nixon vs. Helen Gahagan Douglas-Sexual Politics and the Red Scare* (New York: Random House, 1950).

5. Richard Fried, *Nightmare in Red* (New York: Oxford University Press, 1990), 42.

6. See, e.g., David M. Oshinsky, *A Conspiracy So Immense* (New York: Free Press, 1983); Richard Rovere, *Senator Joe McCarthy* (New York: Harcourt, Brace, 1959); Thomas C. Reeves, *The Life and Times of Senator Joe McCarthy* (New York: Stein and Day, 1982); and Albert Fried, *McCarthyism: The Great American Red Scare* (New York: Oxford University Press, 1997).

7. *American Heritage* 3d ed. (New York: Houghton Mifflin, 1992), 1114. But according to Richard Rovere, *Senator Joe McCarthy*, 7, cartoonist Herbert Block in the *Washington Post* first used the term.

8. S.Prt. 107–84, Executive Sessions of the Senate Permanent Subcommittee on Investigations of the Committee on Government Operations, vol. I–V, 83rd Congress, First Session, 1953–54.

9. Albert Fried, *McCarthyism: The Great American Red Scare*, introduction, 1–9.

10. See stories by Bernard Weinraub in the *New York Times*, Oct. 1, 1997, B3 and Oct. 5, 1997, sec. 4, 5.

11. Fried, *Nightmare in Red*, 88.

12. Ted Morgan, *Reds: McCarthyism in Twentieth-Century America* (New York: Random House, 2003).

13. John Patrick Diggins, *The Proud Decades* (New York: Norton, 1989), 175–176.

14. Mike Nielsen and Gene Mailes, *Hollywood's Other Blacklist* (London: British Film Institute, 1995).

15. Nielsen and Mailes's book has the advantage of being part scholarship and part oral history. Other valuable sources include: Richard and Louis Perry, *A History of the Los Angeles Labor Movement* (Berkeley: University of California Press, 1963); Hugh Lovell and Tasile Carter, *Collective Bargaining in the Motion Picture Industry* (Berkeley: University of California Press, 1955); Murray Ross, *Stars and Strikes* (New York: Columbia University Press, 1941); and U.S. House of Representatives, Committee on Education and Labor, *Jurisdictional Disputes in the Motion Picture Industry* (Washington: Government Printing Office, 1948).

16. Quoted in Nielsen and Mailes, *Hollywood's Other Blacklist*, 130.

17. The episode is described in Nielsen and Mailes, 155.

18. These episodes are recounted in Nielsen and Mailes, chapters 5 and 8.

19. See Robbie Lieberman, "Communism, Peace Activism, and Civil Liberties: From the Waldorf Conference to the Peekskill Riot," *Journal of Popular Culture* 18, no. 3 (fall 1995): 59–65.

20. See U.S. Congress, House Committee on Un-American Activities, *Hearings Regarding the Communist Infiltration of the Motion Picture Industry*, 80th Congress, 1st. sess., 1947.

21. Larry Ceplair and Steven Englund, *The Inquisition in Hollywood* (Garden City, NY: Anchor Press/Doubleday, 1980), 371–373. Of the fifty-eight informers, the authors identify thirty-one

or slightly more than half, as important Hollywood artists. The "naming of names" varied from one informer to another. For example, writer Martin Berkeley gave up 155 names to the committee while at the other extreme; writer Gertrude Purcell identified only one colleague as a communist. See Appendix 7, 447–448.

22. Reported in Walter Bernstein, *Inside Out: A Memoir of the Blacklist* (Cambridge, MA: Da Capo Press, 2000), pp. 153–154.

23. The high estimate of 250 Hollywood workers who lost jobs and were placed on the blacklist comes from the American Movie Classics 1995 documentary, *Blacklist: Hollywood on Trial* while the lesser figure of 200 is cited by Brian Neve in his *Film and Politics in America* (London: Routledge, 1992), 271. Ceplair and Englund, *The Inquisition in Hollywood*, 387, put the number blacklisted at 212. However, Dalton Trumbo, in a 1957 TV program, identified 235 writers alone who were blacklisted and could not work under their real names. If Trumbo were correct, the blacklist would have had to exceed 250 names. See Dalton Trumbo papers, State Historical Society of Wisconsin (hereafter cited as SHSW).

24. Dan Georgakas, "Hollywood Blacklist" in *Encyclopedia of the American Left* (New York: Garland, 1990), 327–328.

25. Some of the organizations included: The Civil Rights Congress, National Federation for Constitutional Liberties, The Actors Laboratory, the Screenwriters Guild, and the Hollywood Writers Mobilization.

26. Herbert Biberman papers, SHSW. When called to testify, Ferrer swore under oath that he was not a communist.

27. Victor S. Navasky, *Naming Names* (New York: Penguin Books, 1981), 236. In his defense, Edward Dmytryk in his memoir, *Odd Man Out: A Memoir of the Hollywood Ten* (Carbondale: Southern Illinois University Press, 1996) reasons that he did not want to be punished further for a cause he no longer believed in; his flirtation with the CPUSA rested on antifascist grounds rather than ideological principle.

28. Dalton Trumbo papers, SHSW.

29. Neve, *Film and Politics in America*, 176–180.

30. Communist Party Headquarters in New York refused to provide any membership data to the author, thereby continuing the speculation as to its actual strength as opposed to government figures and academic estimates. Edward Schapsmeier and Frederick Schapsmeier in their book, *Political Parties and Civic Action Groups* (Westport, CT: Greenwood Press, 1981), pp. 110–112, present the votes garnered by Communist Party candidates in the presidential elections as follows: in 1932, 102,785 votes out of 40 million cast; in 1936, the number totaled 80,159; and in 1940, the votes for the party dropped to 46,251. Of course, these votes do not imply actual membership in the party. Another scholar, L. Sandy Maisel, in his book, *Political Parties and Elections in the United States* (New York: Garland Publishing, 1991), pp. 177–178 puts Communist Party membership at 75,000 based upon registration at the party's 1938 convention. Since party membership was on the decline after peaking in 1932, it is conceivable that membership dropped to 40,000–50,000 by World War II.

31. Georgakas, *Encyclopedia of the American Left*, 328.

32. See Joyce Milton, *Tramp: The Life of Charlie Chaplin* (New York: HarperCollins, 1996), a new biography that focuses on Chaplin's political life. Also consult Charles Chaplin, *My Autobiography* (New York: Simon and Schuster, 1964).

33. Nixon, of course, would make his political mark later during the Hiss-Chambers spy hearings. Of the other eight HUAC members, J. Parnell Thomas, committee chair, would end up in prison

for defrauding the government, Karl Mundt would be elected to the U.S. Senate, and the remaining members would fade from the political scene.

34. Richard A. Schwartz, "How the Hollywood Blacklist Worked" (paper presented at the annual meeting of the American Culture Association/Popular Culture Association (ACA/PCA), Orlando, April 1998), claims that the studios relied on a list of 300 names of alleged communists furnished by the American Legion. That list was converted into a *de facto* blacklist.

35. Pamphlet found in the Albert Bessie papers, SHSW. The pamphlet listed some of the biggest stars in Hollywood at the time, including Humphrey Bogart, Lauren Bacall, Charlie Chaplin, Melvyn Douglas, Gene Kelly, Frank Sinatra, Orson Welles, Danny Kaye, Katherine Hepburn, Gregory Peck, and Burt Lancaster, the majority of whom were never cited or named as communists or fellow travelers by any other source. True, nothing came of the mobilization efforts, but the fact that this unsubstantiated pamphlet was taken seriously by HUAC says plenty about the committee and the red scare hysteria.

36. Larry Ceplair, "Hollywood Left," in *Encyclopedia of the American Left*, 330–332.

37. See Ceplair and Englund, *The Inquisition in Hollywood*, 66–79.

38. Dorothy B. Jones, "Communism and the Movies: A Study of Film Content," in John Cogley, *Report on Blacklisting I: Movies* (New York: The Fund for the Republic, 1956), 197.

39. Dalton Trumbo papers, SHSW. The film scripts offered as evidence to the committee included: *A Guy Named Joe, Thirty Seconds Over Tokyo, Our Vines Have Tender Grapes,* and *Kitty Foyle.* Trumbo also had letters of praise from the military and juvenile court judges for several of his films. As a general rule, HUAC would not permit the reading of statements or the introduction of evidence during the hearings.

40. See Dorothy B. Jones, "Communism and the Movies: A Study in Film Content," Table 8, 272. The list includes only 150 films because nine were described as unclassified.

41. Quoted in Ring Lardner, Jr., papers, SHSW. Friendly HUAC witness, writer Ayn Rand, testified that the film was communist because it showed the Russian people in a better socioeconomic position than was actually true. Similarly, Lela Rogers testified that the film, *None But the Lonely Heart*, was communist propaganda because it was critical of the free enterprise system. See the Biberman-Sondegaard papers, SHSW. She also complained about *Tender Comrade* on grounds that five women sharing a house during wartime was socialism.

42. Georgakas, *Encyclopedia of the American Left*, 326–329.

43. Quoted in the Ned Young papers, SHSW. (cf. earlier footnote).

44. Larry Parks papers, SHSW. Parks made one film in England after the hearings, but Columbia Pictures refused to pick up his option after his HUAC testimony, an action that basically ended his film career.

45. Abraham Polonsky papers, SHSW. Polonsky also wrote screenplays; however, he went seventeen years before he received screen credit for his work.

46. Albert Maltz papers, SHSW. Maltz surmised that the Army pressured the government to deny assistance in the film's production. Maltz attributes other rejections directly to the HUAC hearings and the blacklist. Twentieth Century Fox purchased his novel, *The Journey of Simon McKeever,* but the screenplay was shelved due to pressure from the Motion Picture Alliance.

47. Ceplair and Englund, *The Inquisition in Hollywood*, 425.

48. The project was the collaborative effort of Shirley Clarke and Conrad Bromberg. The interviews produced eleven hours of tape. The staff at the University of Wisconsin Film Archives believes that the tapes have not been shown to the public.

49. Andy Mersler, "How Blacklisting Hurt Hollywood Children," *New York Times*, August 31, 1995, C13.

50. See Michael Wilson and Deborah Silverton Rosenfelt, *Salt of the Earth* (New York: Feminist Press, 1978) and James J. Lorence, *The Suppression of Salt of the Earth* (Albuquerque: University of New Mexico Press, 1999).

51. See Emma Horcombe, "Attitudes to Informing and the Informer" (Master's Degree, University of Nottingham, UK, 1994).

52. According to Fried, *McCarthyism: The Great American Red Scare*, 135–137, Kazan took out a one-page ad in the *New York Times* in the form of an open letter to the American people to explain his decision to cooperate with HUAC. His reasoning for informing on friends and colleagues came down to his disenchantment with the Communist Party because it had become authoritarian and manipulative. Of course, this is specious reasoning since Kazan could have preserved his honor, if not his career, by accepting the Miller-Hellman position of restricting his testimony to himself.

53. Letter to the *New York Times*, September 14, 1994, A18.

54. Was it coincidental that forty years had to pass before Miller's play reached the screen? When the film version of *The Crucible* opened in 1996, the critics found its story of witchcraft in seventeenth-century Salem powerful drama. But historians disputed its accuracy.

55. Kazan became a victim of contemporary Hollywood's unofficial blacklist since the film industry refused to honor him for his lifetime achievement until the Motion Picture Academy had a change of heart and awarded Kazan an honorary Oscar at the 1999 Academy Awards. For more on this issue, see Editorial, *New York Times*, January 19, 1997, 14 and the *New York Times*, January 13, 1999, B3.

56. Neve, *Film and Politics in America*, 171–210. As a rule, these films were financial flops as well as artistic disasters. Not one appeared on the top ten box office hits for the decade. Instead the list was populated by children's films, historical epics, and musicals.

57. See Lynne Arany, Tom Dyja, and Gary Goldsmith, *The Reel List* (New York: Dell Publishing, 1995), 283.

58. See Tom C. Williams, "*The Day the Earth Stood Still:* Cold War Parable or Messianic Metaphor?" (paper presented at the annual meeting of the American Culture Association/Popular Culture Association (ACA/PCA), Las Vegas, March 1996).

59. See Stuart Samuels, "The Age of Conspiracy and Conformity: *Invasion of the Body Snatchers*" (1956), in John O'Connor and Martin A. Jackson, *American History/American Film* (New York: Frederick Unger, 1979), 203–217.

60. See Arany, Dyja and Goldsmith, *The Reel List*, 284.

61. Ceplair and Englund, *The Inquisition in Hollywood*, 335–336.

62. Vivian Gornick, "The Left in the Fifties," *Lincoln Center Theatre Review*, no. 35 (spring/summer 2003): 12.

63. In his book, Peter Biskind, *Easy Riders, Raging Bulls: How the Sex-Drugs-and-Rock n' Roll Generation Saved Hollywood* (New York: Simon & Schuster, 1998) advances the thesis that the success of *Easy Rider* (1964) heralded a decade of rebellious young filmmakers whose films challenged (and saved the industry from) the old studio system.

Six: Reel Politicians: Idealists, Saviors and Villains

1. For the perspective on Nixon, see Irv Letofsky, "All the Presidents' Movies (And Not All PG)," *New York Times*, April 13, 1997, sec. 2, 29; for the view on Reagan, see Elizabeth Traube, *Dreaming Identities: Class, Gender and Generation in 1980s Hollywood Movies* (Boulder: Westview Press, 1992), 48.

2. See Sidney Wise, "Politicians: A Film Perspective," *News for Teachers of Political Science*, no. 32 (winter 1982): 1–3 and Robert Thompson, "American Politics on Film," *Journal of Popular Culture* 20 (summer 1986): 27–47.

3. See Richard Maltby and Jan Craven, *Hollywood Cinema* (Oxford: Blackwell Publishers, 1995), 361–411.

4. Ibid., 380–381.

5. See William L. Riordon, *Plunkitt of Tammany Hall* (New York: E. P. Dutton & Co., 1963).

6. *All the King's Men* was a critical success as it was nominated for eight Academy Awards, winning three Oscars for Best Picture, Actor, and Supporting Actress. When, forty years later, Hollywood decided to make a film about Huey's brother, Earl, three-time governor of Louisiana, the results were less gratifying. The film, *Blaze* (1989), proved a disappointment despite the casting of Paul Newman in the title role. Quite possibly the film's problem lay in the script since it was based on the memoirs of Earl's lover, stripper Blaze Starr. In this case, the combination of politics and sex failed to mesh.

7. In real life, Meade Esposito, Kings County political boss, was convicted of influence peddling and bribery while Donald Manes, his Queens counterpart, committed suicide just as Aiello does in the film. But not all deals end in prison or death. While the film crew was permitted to shoot inside most of City Hall, Mayor Giuliani put the mayor's office and the ceremonial blue room off limits. All was not lost, however. The studio struck a deal with the City Council Speaker. In return for the use of his large office to reconstruct a set to resemble the mayor's office and blue room, the Speaker had his office painted, carpeted and redecorated for free. No taxpayers objected to the deal, although rumor had it that some Council colleagues were envious.

8. Recall a similarity with the real life situation in the Democratic Party when Governor Mario Cuomo was picked to make the presidential nominating speech at the 1984 convention. Cuomo's stirring speech placed him high among Democratic presidential contenders for 1988, although he declined to be a candidate. Also, Franklin Roosevelt's nomination of Al Smith at the 1924 convention failed to win the nomination for Smith, but it did raise Roosevelt's stock among Democratic Party delegates and voters.

9. Newsletter #173 of the Political Film Society, July 15, 2003.

10. Oldman made the charge in *Premier* magazine, vol. 14, no. 3, Nov. 2000, 93–98. The charge was repeated on the Mr. Showbiz Web site and later reported in the *New York Times*, Oct. 16, 2000, C16.

11. Myron Levine, "The Transformed Presidency: The Real Presidency and Hollywood's Reel Presidency," in Peter C. Rollins and John E. O'Connor, eds., *Hollywood's White House: The American Presidency in Film and History* (Lexington: University of Kentucky Press, 2003), 358. This is the most comprehensive book on the subject.

12. Ibid., 353.

13. http://www.2.h-net.msu.edu/~filmhis/presidentialfilms/film.html.

14. Historian Ron Briley notes in "Hollywood and the American Presidency: A Nation Seeks to Define Itself" (paper presented at the annual meeting of the American Political Science Association, Washington, Aug. 1977), that the film was criticized because President Hammond used authoritarian methods to achieve his goals. It was no coincidence that William Randolph Hearst produced the film in conjunction with Metro-Goldwyn-Mayer, and that it opened in the early days of Roosevelt's New Deal administration.

15. For development of this view, see Deborah Carmichael, "*Gabriel Over the White House*," in Rollins and O'Connor, eds., *Hollywood's White House*, 159–179.

16. Kevan M. Yenerall and Christopher S. Kelley, "Shysters, Sycophants, and Sexual Deviants: The Hollywood Presidency in the 1990s" (paper presented at the Film & History Conference, Simi Valley, California, November 2000).

17. George McGovern, "Nixon and Historical Memory: Two Reviews," *Perspectives, AHA Newsletter* 34, no. 3 (March 1996): 3. A view of the Watergate scandal, rather than of Nixon himself, is presented in *All the President's Men* (1976), based on the story by Carl Bernstein and Bob Woodward, the two young reporters on the *Washington Post* whose investigations exposed the political corruption. *All the President's Men* became the top grossing film in 1976.

18. See Peter Rollins, "Hollywood's President 1944–1996: The Primacy of character," in Rollins and O'Connor, ed., *Hollywood's White House*, 251–261.

19. Historically, presidents did not have "doubles," but in crowded situations, the secret service is likely to use two limousines and one president to confuse would-be assassins. Reportedly, however, Presidents Bush and Clinton had Secret Service agents who closely resembled them in appearance. See Maureen Dowd, "Film View: Of Hems and Haws: The Insider's Guide to *Dave*," *New York Times*, May 16, 1993, sec. 2, 17.

20. Similarly, *The Manchurian Candidate* was withdrawn from theatrical circulation for twenty-five years after the Kennedy assassination.

21. Why is Barbara Jean, rather than Walker, assassinated? Political scientist G. Alan Tarr's review in *Notes for Teachers of Political Science*, no. 22 (Summer 1979): 21, believes that Altman's choice reflects his view that Americans are indifferent to politics, preferring instead the private lives of celebrities such as a country-western singer. Symbolically, therefore, her death is much more significant than the assassination of any political candidate.

22. Robert S. Robins and Jerrold M. Post, *Political Paranoia: The Psychopolitics of Hatred* (New Haven: Yale University Press, 1997).

23. Actually Robbins and Post, 240, counted eight different conspiracy loci in the film, e.g., the CIA, military, Dallas police, weapons manufacturers, establishment press, renegade anti-Castro Cubans, the White House, and the Mafia. Take your pick!

24. See Gerald Posner, "Garrison Guilty: Another Case Closed," *New York Times Magazine*, sec. 6, August 6, 1995, 40–41. Historian Stanley Karnow agrees with Posner and other Stone critics on the unsubstantiated notion that Kennedy intended to withdraw from Vietnam, one reason for his death. See his "*JFK*" in Mark C. Carnes, *Past Imperfect: History According to the Movies* (New York: Henry Holt & Co., 1995), 270–273.

25. See the advertisement for the *JFK* opening in the *New York Times*, Dec. 15, 1991, sec. 2, 10 with a large photo of Kevin Costner portraying D. A. Garrison in the film, with the blurb:
    He's a District Attorney,
    He will risk his life, the lives of his family,
    everything he holds dear
    for the one thing he holds sacred . . . the truth.
    Also see the ad for *JFK* in the *New York Times*, April 2, 1992, C17, where the text includes this dedication: "The truth is the most important value we have."

26. Michael Barkun, "Conspiracy Thinking in Contemporary America," *Maxwell Perspective* (Syracuse University) 8, no. 1 (fall 1997): 23.

27. Robert Alan Goldberg, *Enemies Within: The Culture of Conspiracy in Modern America* (New Haven: Yale University Press, 2001).

28. In a recent article, Allen Rostron, "Mr. Carter Goes to Washington," *Journal of Popular Film & Television* 25, no. 2 (summer 1997): 57–67, contends that Jimmy Carter came to Washington much

like Jefferson Smith—an innocent outsider from a small town who wanted to restore decency and morality to government. Carter failed in Washington whereas the fictional Smith succeeded, Rostron argues, because in real politics, Carter had to contend with external factors like the backlash from Vietnam and Watergate.

29. Michael Canning, "The Hill on Film: Hollywood's Take on the U.S. Congress and Its Members" (paper presented at the annual meeting of the American Political Science Association, Washington, August 1997).

30. William M. Jones, "Monumental Disasters: From *Mr. Smith Goes to Washington* to *Independence Day*" (paper presented at the annual meeting of the American Political Science Association, Washington, August 1997), concludes that the present trend in Hollywood to find national symbolic monuments and revered public buildings expendable and, therefore, subject to destruction, reflects the current cynicism on the part of American filmmakers. This attitude deviates considerably from Frank Capra's *Mr. Smith Goes to Washington* where the physical structures are treated as national shrines.

SEVEN: PICTURING JUSTICE: THE LAW AND LAWYERS IN HOLLYWOOD FILMS

1. Stewart Macaulay, "Images of Law in Everyday Life: The Lesson of School, Entertainment, and Spectator Sports," *Law & Society Review* 21, 2 (1987): 185–218.

2. Hearst Corporation, *The American Public, the Media and the Judicial System* (New York: Hearst Corporation, 1983).

3. Macaulay, 192–197.

4. John Denvir, ed., *Legal Reelism: Movies as Legal Texts* (Urbana: University of Illinois Press, 1996), introduction.

5. Timothy Lenz, *Changing Images of Law in Film & Television* (NY: Peter Lang, 2003), 8–14.

6. Ibid., 15–16.

7. "The Significance of the Frontier in American History," first presented to the American Historical Association in 1893 and later republished in his essays, *The Frontier in American History* (New York: Henry Holt & Co., 1920).

8. For a detailed discussion of 1930s westerns, see Francis M. Nevins, "Through the Great Depression on Horseback" in John Denvir, ed., *Legal Reelism*, 44–69.

9. For a discussion of film vigilantism, see Frankie Y. Bailey, "Getting Justice: Real Life Vigilantism and Vigilantism in Popular Films" (paper presented at the annual meeting of the Criminal Justice Sciences Association, Pittsburgh, March 1992).

10. Bruce Watson, "Hang 'em first, try 'em later," *Smithsonian* 29, 8 (June 1998): 96–107. Watson claims that the real Judge Bean was a paunchy fellow with a gray beard, hardly resembling actor Paul Newman. It is also dubious whether Bean actually hanged anybody. Nor did Bean die in a climactic shootout; rather his death took place in a bar after a drinking binge.

11. For data on Southern lynching, see W. Fitzhugh Brundage, *Lynching in the New South* (Urbana: University of Illinois Press, 1993) and Stewart E. Tolenay and E. M. Beck, *A Festival of Violence: An Analysis of Southern Lynching, 1882–1930* (Urbana: University of Illinois Press, 1995). For shocking photos of lynchings, see Leon F. Litwack, *Without Sanctuary: Lynching Photographs in America* (San Francisco: Twin Palms, 2000).

12. Quoted in Paul Bergmann and Michael Asimow, *Reel Justice: The Courtroom Goes to the Movies* (Kansas City, MO: Andrews and McMeel, 1996), 226. The authors note that there were sixty-six lynchings in the early years of the Depression, 1933–35. Moreover, it was rare for lynch mob participants to be apprehended and punished.

13. For a case study, see Leonard Dinnerstein, *The Leo Frank Case* (New York: Columbia University Press, 1968). Dinnerstein came to the conclusion that Frank was innocent but convicted of the murder of Mary Phagan, the thirteen-year-old girl who worked in his Atlanta, Georgia factory, on the basis of circumstantial evidence, the damaging testimony of the Negro janitor, which tarnished Frank's reputation, and the pervasive climate of anti-Semitism in the South. When Governor Slaton commuted Frank's sentence, Jewish businesses were told by vigilantes to close or suffer the consequences. Meanwhile, Christians were warned to avoid patronizing Jewish merchants.

14. Herbert Packer, *The Limits of the Criminal Sanction* (Stanford: Stanford University Press, 1968).

15. The Warren Court decisions included: *Mapp v. Ohio*, 367 U.S. 643 (1961) which extended the federal exclusionary rule as to illegally obtained evidence to the states; *Escobedo v. Illinois*, 378 U.S. 478 (1964) which expanded constitutional protections for the accused during police interrogation; and *Miranda v. Arizona*, 384 U.S. 436 (1966) which set down rules that the police had to follow before making an arrest, including the right to remain silent and to have an attorney present during questioning.

16. See Lenz, *Changing Images of Law*, chapter 2 for a thorough discussion of this point and an analysis of the *Dirty Harry* and *Death Wish* series.

17. *Goldman v. Weinberger*, 475 U.S. 503 (1985). The Congress reversed the military regulation two years later.

18. Bergmann and Asimow, *Reel Justice*, 76.

19. Alan M. Dershowitz, *The Best Defense* (New York: Vintage Books, 1983), xvi.

20. See Bergmann and Asimow, *Reel Justice*, 232–238.

21. Ibid., 14–20.

22. For a discussion of such films, see Roger Dooley, *From Scarface to Scarlett: American Films in the 1930s* (New York: Harcourt Brace Jovanovich, 1979), 310–318.

23. Leonard Maltin, *1997 Movie & Video Guide* (New York: Penguin Books, 1996).

24. According to Gerald Leonard Cohen, *Origin of the Term "Shyster"* (Frankfurt: Peter Lang, 1982), 1, lexicographers agree that the term originated in the 1840s in New York City newspapers to describe unscrupulous lawyers of that era. The word later was applied to other professions. There is some support, however, for the view that the term comes from the Shylock character in Shakespeare's *The Merchant of Venice*.

25. See Andrew Bergman, *We're in the Money* (New York: New York University Press, 1971), 18–29.

26. For a discussion of gangster films in the 1930s, see Dooley, *From Scarface to Scarlett: American Films in the 1930s*, 289–300.

27. Quoted in David Ray Papke, "Myth and Meaning: Francis Ford Coppola and Popular Response to the Godfather Trilogy," in John Denvir, ed., *Legal Reelism*, 3.

28. For the development of this argument, see Christine Noll Brinckmann, "The Politics of *Force of Evil*: An Analysis of Abraham Polonsky's Preblacklisted Film," *Prospects* 6 (1981): 357–386.

29. Bergmann and Asimow, *Reel Justice*, 306. The legal errors and unethical conduct depicted in the film include the following: (1) Gavin breaks into a mailbox to intercept a letter—a federal offense, (2) Gavin turns down a settlement without consulting his clients, (either act would get him disbarred) and (3) the trial judge conspires with the defense to protect the Boston Archdiocese.

30. For a discussion of these films, see Dooley, *From Scarface to Scarlett*, 317–318 and Ric Sheffield, "On Film: A Social History of Women Lawyers in Popular Culture 1930 to 1990," *Loyola of Los Angeles Entertainment Law Journal* 14 (1993): 73–114.

31. Sheffield, "On Film: A Social History of Women Lawyers in Popular Culture 1930 to 1990," 79.

32. For a contrary view that these early female lawyer films ultimately allowed the patriarchal power structure to win and dominate the action, see Cynthia Lucia, "Women on Trial: The Female Lawyer in the Hollywood Courtroom," *Cineaste* 19 (1993): 32–37.

33. "First Year Enrollment in ABA Approved Law Schools 1947–1996" [database online] (Chicago: American Bar Association) [cited 7 November 1997].

34. "Women in Law" [online] (Williamsburg, VA: National Center for State Courts) [cited 18 Nov. 1997] and "Goal IX Update" [online] (Chicago: American Bar Association) [cited 9 Feb. 1999].

35. See Lucia, "Women on Trial," 35.

36. See Bergman and Asimow, *Reel Justice*, 90–93.

37. http://www.Salon.com/ent/feature, April 14, 2000. Story by Kathleen Sharp.

38. Paul J. Mastrangelo, "Lawyers and the Law: A Filmography," *Legal Reference Services Quarterly* 3 (winter 1983): 31–72 put the number at 120, including twenty films that were produced outside the United States, primarily in the United Kingdom Writing almost twenty years later, Michael Asimow put the number at 284 in "Bad Lawyers in the Movies," *Nova Law Review*, 24, 2 (winter 2000): 533–591.

39. See Richard K. Sherwin, *When the Law Goes Pop: The Vanishing Line Between Law & Popular Culture* (Chicago: University of Chicago Press, 2002).

40. See Asimow, "Bad Lawyers in the Movies," 561.

41. http://w3.abanet.org/media, April 26, 2002.

42. http://www.gregbowes.org/commentary, December 9, 2002.

43. See Mark Tushnet, "Class Action: One View of Gender and Law in Popular Culture," in Denvir, ed., *Legal Reelism*, 244–260.

44. Sheffield, "On Film: A Social History of Women Lawyers in Popular Culture 1930 to 1990," 109–111.

45. See Lucia, "Women on Trial," 37.

EIGHT: HOLLYWOOD GOES TO WAR: FROM THE GREAT WAR TO THE GOOD WAR

1. *Corel All-Movie Guide 2*, 1996.

2. While *Saving Private Ryan* grossed more than $200 million in North America, *The Thin Red Line* struggled to recoup its costs, despite seven Academy Award nominations. Both the film critics and film historians meanwhile attacked the $135 million blockbuster, *Pearl Harbor*. It did moderate business at home but extremely well worldwide, especially in Japan.

3. Leo Cawley, "The War about the War: Vietnam Films and American Myth," 74, in Linda Dittmar and Gene Michaud, eds., *From Hanoi to Hollywood: The Vietnam War in American Film* (New Brunswick, NJ: Rutgers University Press, 1990), reports that the film cost the Pentagon over $1 million for supplies, facilities, etc. but that it billed Wayne only $18,623 for the assistance provided on the film.

4. *Home Building and Loan Association v. Blaisdell*, 290 U.S. 398 (1934).

5. Arthur Schlesinger, Jr., "The Rediscovery of World War II," AARP Newsletter, May 1999, 22.

6. See Tom Pollard, "The Hollywood War Machine," *New Political Science*, 24, no. 1 (March 2002), 122–124.

7. John Whiteclay Chambers II and David Culbert, eds. *World War II, Film, and History* (New York: Oxford University Press, 1996), Foreword.

8. John Keegan, *The First World War* (New York: Alfred A. Knopf, 1999).

9. According to Peter Rollins and John O'Connor, eds., *Hollywood's WWI: Motion Picture Images* (Bowling Green, OH: Popular Press, 1997), there is little footage of the First World War that is real. Much of the material was either censored or staged. The warring nations, for example, would not permit filming on the front lines or in the trenches.

10. Thomas Doherty, *Projections of War: Hollywood, American Culture and World War II* (New York: Columbia University Press, 1993), 88–91.

11. Ibid., 97.

12. Bernard F. Dick, *The Star-Spangled Screen: The American World War II Film*, rev. ed. (Lexington: University of Kentucky Press, 1996), 93–94.

13. See Sally E. Parry, "Confessions of an Interventionist: Did Hollywood Encourage the U.S. to Enter World War II?" (paper presented at the Popular Culture Association meeting, San Diego, March 1999).

14. Tom Wicker, "World War I," in Mark C. Carnes, ed., *Past Imperfect* (New York: Henry Holt & Co., 1995), 187.

15. Rudolph Chelminski, "The Maginot Line," *Smithsonian* 28, no. 3 (June 1997): 91.

16. U.S. Dept. of Commerce, Bureau of the Census, *Historical Statistics of the United States* (Washington, DC: Government Printing Office, 1975), 1140. Other estimates put the number of American soldiers dead and wounded at 350,000 to 400,000.

17. Estimates of losses vary and depend on sources and the timeframe utilized. Taking only the period from 1939 to 1945—from the invasion of Poland to the Japanese surrender—the total number of deaths due to the war has been estimated to be at least 30 million and as high as 60 million. American casualties, dead and wounded, is placed around 1 million, with 400,000 killed.

18. See Israel Gutman, editor in chief, *Encyclopedia of the Holocaust*, vol. 4 (New York: Macmillan Publishing Co., 1990); Richard C. Lukas, *The Forgotten Holocaust: The Poles Under German Occupation* (Lexington: University of Kentucky Press, 1986); and Betty Alt and Silvia Falts, *Weeping Violins: The Gypsy Tragedy in Europe* (Kirksville, MO: Thomas Jefferson University Press, 1996).

19. See James E. Wise, Jr. and Anne Collier Rehill, *Stars in Blue: Movie Actors in America's Sea Services* (Annapolis: Naval Institute Press, 1997).

20. By 1942 Lew Ayres was an established Hollywood star, best remembered as Dr. Kildare. When the war came, Ayres refused combat duty on religious grounds and served instead as a medic and chaplain's aide. The film studios shunned him until 1948. The plight of conscientious objectors (COs) has yet to be fully detailed, although their numbers are considerable. In World War I, 60,000 were classified as COs but only 4,000 served in that capacity. In World War II, 12,000 COs served in the Civilian Service Program (CSP) with another 6,000 imprisoned. About 5,000 men served as COs during the Korean conflict. The war in Vietnam saw over 171,000 eligible men declare themselves COs and war resistors and fled to Canada to avoid the draft. Philip Borkholder, Executive Director, National Interreligious Service Board for Conscientious Objectors, [email: July 9, 1997]. For the story of the CSP, see Albert N. Keim, *The CPS Story: An Illustrated History of Civilian Public Service* (Intercourse, PA: Good Books, 1990). For mistreatment of COs during the Vietnam period, see Stephen M. Kohn, *Jailed for Peace* (Westport, CT: Greenwood Press, 1986).

21. See William M. Tuttle, Jr., *Daddy's Gone to War* (New York: Oxford University Press, 1993), 148–154.

22. Clayton R. Koppes and Gregory D. Black, *Hollywood Goes to War* (Berkeley: University of California Press, 1987), 325. Recent research by Thomas Schatz, "World War II and the Hollywood War Film," in Nick Browne, ed., *Refiguring Genres* (Berkeley: University of California Press, 1998), 103–104, places the figure of World War II-related Hollywood features closer to 20 percent of the 1,636 films made between Pearl Harbor and the end of the war. Of these 340 war-related films, Schatz found that the most popular type were the combat films, followed by espionage and homefront movies.

23. Jeanine Basinger, *The World War II Combat Film* (New York: Columbia University Press, 1986).

24. James Bradley *Flags of our Fathers* (New York: Bantam Books, 2000).

25. See Ann Dorr, "The Women Who Flew—but Kept Silent," *New York Times Magazine*, May 7, 1995, sec. 6, 70–71 and Melissa Fay Greene, "The Flygirl" *Life*, June 1999, 80–86. These women were buried without military honors and those who survived received no benefits.

26. I am indebted to Dawn Letson, librarian at the Texas Woman's University for this information.

27. Sally E. Parry, "How Proudly Did We Serve? Popular Culture Images of Army Nurses in World War II" (paper presented at the Popular Culture Association meeting, Philadelphia, April 1995).

28. For the real-life story of seventy-two nurses trapped on Bataan and imprisoned for three years on Corregidor, read Elizabeth M. Norman, *We Band of Angels* (New York: Random House, 1999).

29. The $21 million Women's Memorial was dedicated in October 1997.

30. Although World War II was fought on a segregated basis, Hollywood has yet to tell the real story of Afro-American soldiers during the war. Most black soldiers were prohibited from combat and were assigned to do menial tasks like building roads, digging latrines, and loading ships. See Brent Staples, "Reliving WWII with a Captain America of a Different Color," *New York Times Magazine*, December 1, 2002, sec. 4, 8. For the story of black soldiers in combat, see David P. Colley, *Blood for Dignity: The Story of the First Integrated Combat Unit in the U.S. Army* (New York: St. Martin's Press, 2003).

31. See Basinger, *The World War II Combat Film*, 28, and Koppes and Black, *Hollywood Goes to War*, 248–277. In his unpublished paper, Ralph R. Donald, "Savages, Swine and Buffoons: Hollywood's Selected Stereotypical Characterizations of the Japanese, Germans and Italians in Films Produced During World War II" (paper presented at the Popular Culture Association meeting, Orlando, April 1998), advances the thesis that a descending order of brutality existed in Hollywood World War II movies. He maintains that the Italians received the most neutral characterization, usually portrayed as buffoons and hapless soldiers. The Nazis were despised and often depicted as military gangsters, but Hollywood distanced them from the German people. Donald argues that the most vicious attacks were saved for the Japanese, resulting in negative images "unmatched in American film propaganda," 7.

32. The entire episode is described in Koppes and Black, *Hollywood Goes to War*, 72–77.

33. Recent research by Iris Chang, *The Rape of Nanking: The Forgotten Holocaust of WWII* (New York: Basic Books, 1997), describes Japanese atrocities in the Chinese city of Nanking in 1937 where 200,000 to 350,000 civilians were slaughtered, almost half of the population. Yet American feeling toward the Japanese probably was influenced more by the "sneak attack" on Pearl Harbor.

34. Hollywood tried to redeem itself after the war when MGM released *Go for Broke* (1951), a film about the exploits of the 442nd Regimental Combat Team composed mainly of Japanese-American (Nisei) volunteers. The Nisei fought in seven major European campaigns and suffered 9,486 casualties. Their bravery and courage under fire earned them over 18,000 individual decorations and seven presidential citations. Two facts are interesting about the film version. First,

that Hollywood wisely focused on the Nisei rather than Van Johnson, the male star. Second, the film became a blatant piece of postwar propaganda. After the credits, the film displays President Roosevelt's message of support for the establishment of Nisei units, commenting that being American is a matter of heart and not race or ancestry. But it was Roosevelt who issued Executive Order 9066, which began the evacuation and internment of over 115,000 Japanese-Americans (three-quarters of whom were U.S. citizens) from the West Coast.

35. Kathryn Kane, "The World War II Combat Film, 1942–45," in Wes D. Gehring, ed., *Handbook of American Film Genres* (Westport, CT: Greenwood Press, 1988), 85–86.

36. On the other hand, not every World War II film is a commercial success. Terrence Malick's version of the James Jones novel *The Thin Red Line* (1998) flopped at the box office.

37. For an analysis of the film, see Sally E. Parry, "So Proudly They Serve: American Women in World War II Films" (paper presented at the annual meeting of the American Political Science Association, San Francisco, August/Sept. 1996).

38. The Harold Russell character (Homer) represented the more than 670,000 Americans who suffered war wounds, with 83,000 receiving treatment at VA hospitals. See Tuttle, *Daddy's Gone to War*, 216.

39. See Robert B. Westbrook, "I Want a Girl, Just Like the Girl that Married Harry James: American Women and the Problem of Political Obligation in World War II," *American Quarterly*, 42, no. 4 (December 1990), 587–614.

40. Tom Brokaw, *The Greatest Generation* (New York: Random House, 1998).

41. See Doherty, *Projections of War*, Appendix, 304–308.

42. Ibid., 229.

43. Bruce Shapiro, "Lugging the guts into the next room," [database online] (Salon Media Circus) [cited 30 July 1998]. The warrior myth perpetuated by the military is that combat soldiers fight and die heroically for God and country. Any combat soldier will tell you otherwise.

44. Basinger, *The World War II Combat Film*, 125–131. Ford's film, *December 7th*, has an interesting history. This government-funded film of the Japanese attack on Pearl Harbor alienated the U.S. Navy because it implied naval complacency before the assault. As a consequence, the government confiscated the film's negative and instead released an edited version of the film, which, nonetheless, won an Academy Award. The complete uncensored version was withheld from public view until the 1990s.

45. See Doherty, *Projections of War*, 237.

46. For a contrary view of the film by a military historian, see Roger J. Spiller, "War in the Dark," *American Heritage*, 50, no. 1 (February/March 1999), 41–51.

47. Peter Bart and Peter Guber, *Shoot Out* (New York: The Berkley Publishing Group, 2002), 82.

48. Basinger, *The World War II Combat Film*, 176–179.

49. Reported in Lewis H. Carlson, "*The Manchurian Candidate* and Other Korean War POW films," (paper presented at the Popular Culture Association meeting, New Orleans, April 2000).

50. President Roosevelt interned more than 115,000 Japanese-Americans during World War II on the basis of an executive order despite the fact that three-fourths were American citizens. In a series of cases, the U.S. Supreme Court upheld the internment order on national security grounds. Less known to the public is the treatment accorded Italian-Americans, mostly aliens, who were interned during the war in military camps in Montana, Minnesota, and Ellis Island and were forced to leave their homes on the West Coast, and branded "enemy aliens" by the U.S. government. The introduction of the Wartime Violation of Italian American Civil Liberties Act in 1997 was an attempt by Congress to force the Justice Department to document government mistreatment of Italian-Americans during the Second World War.

51. 374 U.S. 483 (1954).

52. Michael Walzer, *Just and Unjust Wars* 2d ed. (New York: Basic Books, 1992), 117–124.

53. See the reports in the *New York Times*, April 21, 2000, A6 and January 12, 2001, 1.

NINE: PICTURING VIETNAM ON FILM: LESSONS LEARNED AND FORGOTTEN

1. Charles Molir, "History and Hindsight: Lessons from Vietnam," *New York Times*, April 30, 1985, 6.

2. Transcript of lecture delivered at the Naval War College, December 10, 1964.

3. Quoted in Andrew Martin, *Receptions of War: Vietnam in American Culture* (Norman: University of Oklahoma Press, 1993), 107.

4. Michael Coyne, *The Crowded Prairie* (London: I. B. Tauris Publishers, 1997), 145, characterizes *The Green Berets* as "a John Wayne western set in Vietnam."

5. See Thomas Doherty, *Projections of War: Hollywood, American Culture, and World War II* (New York: Columbia University Press, 1993), 282–298 and Richard T. Jamesson, ed., *They Went Thataway: Redefining Film Genres* (San Francisco: Mercury House, 1994), 263–279.

6. Joseph Conrad, *Heart of Darkness*, ed. Robert Kimbrough, 2d ed. (New York: W. W. Norton & Company, 1971). According to Kimbrough, *Heart of Darkness* appeared in three different versions: a magazine version in 1899, a book edition in 1902, and a revised edition in 1921 considered by scholars to be Conrad's final text.

7. See Mark C. Carnes, *Past Imperfect: History According to the Movies* (New York: Henry Holt & Co., 1995).

8. According to Arnold R. Isaacs, *The War, Its Ghosts, and Its Legacy* (Baltimore: John Hopkins University Press, 1998), the idea that politicians, along with a hostile media and subversive demonstrators, prevented victory in Vietnam is a myth. Instead, Isaacs's thesis is that the country turned against the war when the military failed to win in the field.

9. Michael Rogin, *Ronald Reagan, the Movie* (Berkeley: University of California Press, 1988), 7, reports that after the American hostages in Lebanon, taken as part of the 1985 TWA skyjacking, were released, the president watched *First Blood, Part 2* and supposedly told aides, "Boy, I saw *Rambo* last night. Now I know what to do the next time this happens."

10. Marita Sturken, "Reenactment, Fantasy, and the Paranoia of History: Oliver Stone's Docudramas," *History and Theory* 36, no. 4 (December 1997), 66.

11. William J. Palmer, *The Films of the Eighties* (Carbondale: Southern Illinois University Press, 1993), 16–60.

12. Ibid., 18.

13. Ibid., 21.

14. See Frank P. Tomosulo, "The Politics of Ambivalence: Apocalypse Now as Prowar and Antiwar Film," in Linda Dittmar and Gene Michaud, eds., *From Hanoi to Hollywood* (New Brunswick: Rutgers University Press, 1990), 145–158.

15. See Palmer, *The Films of the Eighties*, 61–113.

16. See Leonard Quart, "The Deer Hunter: The Superman in Vietnam," in Dittmar and Michaud, *From Hanoi to Hollywood*, 159–168.

17. The interventionist analysis comes from Peter Huchthausen, *America's Splendid Little Wars* (New York: Viking, 2003). The author is a retired naval captain.

18. For an analysis that suggests more significance than normally accorded the film, see Pat Aufderheide, "Vietnam: Good Soldiers" in Mark Crispin Miller, ed., *Seeing Through Movies* (New York: Pantheon Books, 1990), 81–111.

19. Quoted in Maureen Dowd, "A Different Bush Conforms to a Nation's Mood," *New York Times*, March 2, 1991, A7.

20. Michael Norman, "Carnage and Glory, Legends and Lies," *New York Times*, sec. 2, July 7, 1996, 19.

21. See David Rieff, "Were Sanctions Right?" *New York Times Magazine*, sec. 6, July 27, 2003, 40–46. Also see *Paying the Price: Killing the Children of Iraq*, Bullfrog Films, 2000. In effect, the sanctions killed more people than the two atomic bombs dropped on Japan during World War II.

22. The idea comes from Bosah Ebo, "War as Popular Culture: the Gulf Conflict and the Technology of Illusionary Entertainment," *Journal of American Culture*, vol. 18, no. 3 (Fall 1995), 19–25.

23. See Neta C. Crawford, "Just War Theory and the U.S. Counterterror War," *Perspectives on Politics*, vol. I, no. 1 (March 2003), 5–25.

24. In *Just and Unjust Wars*, 97–101, Walzer concludes that the war was unjust because the United States could not justify its intervention for two reasons. First, the South Vietnamese government could not survive without external support. Therefore it lacked public support despite American aid. Second, when the United States intervened militarily, it did so to pursue its own policies. The war, then, became an American war fought in another country. In contrast, Korea was a just war because the North Korean aggression was undisputed and because the goal of counterintervention was to restore the status quo rather than win a military victory. Michael Ryan and Douglas Kellner, *Camera Politica* (Bloomington: Indiana University Press, 1990), 194–216 agree with Walzer that Vietnam was an unjust war but for a different reason. For Ryan and Kellner, the U.S. involvement was unjust because it lent support to a corrupt and undemocratic regime.

25. See Michael Anderegg, ed., *Inventing Vietnam: The War in Film and Television* (Philadelphia: Temple University Press, 1991) where he argues that, even though Vietnam was given life through film, the visual images remain subjective creations of the filmmakers.

26. Anthony Swofford, *Jarhead* (New York: Scribner & Sons, 2003), 114.

27. Reported in Norman, "Carnage and Glory, Legends and Lies," 19.

TEN: HOLLYWOOD CONFRONTS THE NUCLEAR HOLOCAUST

1. William J. Broad, "New Books Revive Old Talk of Spies," *New York Times*, May 11, 1999, D1.

2. Paul Boyer, *By the Bomb's Early Light* (Chapel Hill: University of North Carolina Press, 1994).

3. Quoted in ibid., *By the Bomb's Early Light*, 5.

4. "ShockWave," *Time*, July 31, 1995, 50. These are conservative figures because countless other deaths were likely caused by radioactivity. *The Catholic Light*, August 3, 1995, 2, put the Hiroshima deaths alone attributed to the atomic blast at 200,000 with another 39,000 dead in the Nagasaki blast. By any count, the numbers are considerable. However, estimates of the damage from the March 1945 air raids on Tokyo range from 100,000 to 200,000 deaths, while the total number of Japanese dead from conventional bombs and fire bombs was put at 500,000. On the other hand, estimates of the number of American casualties, had President Truman opted for an invasion of the Japanese islands, vary from 100,000 to 200,000. Revisionist historian Gar Alperovitz disputes these figures in his book, *The Decision to Use the Atomic Bomb* (New York: Alfred A. Knopf, 1995). Moreover, Alperovitz maintains that the number of American casualties was not the deciding factor in Truman's decision. Instead, he argues that Truman used the atom bomb as part of his postwar diplomacy to send a message to the Soviets to stay out of Asia.

5. Winston Churchill said that 1.5 million American and British lives would be saved. The president of the Japanese Medical Association believed that use of the atom bomb saved millions of Japanese lives because it broke the government's will to resist and prevented an invasion of the islands. See Harvard Nuclear Study Group, *Living with Nuclear Weapons* (New York: Bantam Books, 1983, 72–73 and John P. Roche, *The History and Impact of Marxist-Leninist Organizational Theory* (Cambridge, MA: Institute of Foreign Policy Analysis, 1984) 66–67.

6. Bill Gifford, "Bunker? What Bunker?" *New York Times Magazine*, December 3, 2000, sec. 6, 132–133.

7. James Barron, "Nuclear Winter of the Psyche Fading Away," *New York Times*, October 13, 1991, E3.

8. Boyer, *By the Bomb's Early Light*, 352. Similarly, the number of Americans who received significant amounts of radiation from atmospheric testing in New Mexico between 1951 and 1962 and who later developed cancer as a result remains unknown. A guess is that the number affected could be in the tens of thousands.

9. Ibid., 10–11.

10. Garth S. Jowett, "Hollywood, Propaganda and the Bomb: Nuclear Images in Post World War II Film," *Film and History* 18, no. 2 (May 1988): 27.

11. Boyer, *By the Bomb's Early Light*, 23.

12. Michael J. Strada, "Kaleidoscopic Nuclear Images of the Fifties," *Journal of Popular Culture* 20, no. 3 (1986): 191.

13. For a case study on the film, consult Nathan Reingold, "A Footnote to History: MGM Meets the Atomic Bomb," in Philip S. Cook, Douglas Goney, and Lawrence W. Lichty, *American Media* (Washington, DC: The Wilson Center Press, 1989). According to Jack Shaheen, ed., *Nuclear War Films* (Carbondale: Southern Illinois University Press, 1978), 8, the film was cut and reedited several times. One scene between an officer and a crew member that was mercifully left on the cutting room floor involved this verbal exchange:
    Crew Member: "Is it true that if you fool around with this stuff [atomic equipment] long enough, you don't like girls anymore?" To which the officer replied: "I hadn't noticed it."

14. History repeated itself when the Smithsonian Museum in Washington, D.C., ran into controversy when it planned to mark the fiftieth anniversary of the dropping of the A-bombs to end World War II. Originally, the museum intended a big exhibition to include material on the decision to use the bomb, the horror caused by the bomb, and the subsequent arms race that followed in the Cold War—all centered on the fuselage of the Enola Gay. But criticism from veterans groups and members of Congress that the planned exhibition exaggerated Japanese suffering and minimized Japanese aggression forced the museum to cut back. When the exhibition officially opened, what remained was the plane, a video, and a plaque. For the story, see the *New York Times*, February 5, 1995, E5.

15. See Michael Walzer, *Just and Unjust Wars* 2d ed. (New York: Basic Books, 1992).

16. See "How Hollywood Learned to Start Worrying and Hate the Bomb," *American Film* 8, no. 1 (October 1982): 57–63. Other film stars who were active in the antinuke campaign besides Newman included Ellen Burstyn, Jill Clayburgh, Sally Field, Meryl Streep, and Joanne Woodward.

17. See Mick Broderick, *Nuclear Movies* (Jefferson, NC: McFarland & Co., 1991), Filmography, 55–191.

18. The original *Godzilla* (1954) movie was a low-budget Japanese film that reflected the horrors of Hiroshima and Nagasaki. The film was edited and released in the United States in 1956 as *Godzilla, King of the Monsters*. Raymond Burr starred in a film that identified Godzilla as a radioactive monster that terrorizes Japan.

19. See Nora Sayre, *Running Time: Films of the Cold War* (New York: The Dial Press, 1982) chapter VII for a Cold War analysis of science fiction films of the fifties.

20. Jane Caputi has tried to establish a relationship between certain horror films such as *Night of the Living Dead* and the nuclear age. Her thesis is that although such films make no explicit references to nuclear technology, the ghouls are by-products of nuclear contamination. See her "Films of the Nuclear Age," *Journal of Popular Film and Television* 16, no. 3 (fall 1988): 100–107.

21. See Cyndy Hendershot, "The Atomic Scientist, Science Fiction Films, and Paranoia," *Journal of American Culture* 20, no. 1 (spring 1997): 31–41.

22. Reported in Lawrence Suid, "The Pentagon and Hollywood: Dr. Strangelove," in John O'Connor and Martin Jackson, eds, *American History/American Film*, 224. The same lack of cooperation was accorded the Stanley Kubrick film, *Dr. Strangelove*.

23. As an epilogue to *The War Game*, Watkins went into self-exile in Sweden. In the 1980s, one of Britain's two private television channels commissioned Watkins to begin work on another nuclear war film. This time Watkins intended to trace the effect of a nuclear strike on one family that would include a look at the government's measures before the strike and its response after the strike. But Watkins canceled the project amidst charges of overspending by the television station and censorship. For his comments on the television ban, see Peter Watkins, "The Fear of Commitment," *Literature/Film Quarterly* 11, no. 4 (1983): 221–233. For other articles on the subject, see ibid, 234–248. Also see James Welsh, "Banned in Britain," *American Film* 8, no. 1 (October 1982): 64, 69–71.

24. Richard Ostrom, "Re-Viewing *Dr. Stangelove*: The Funniest Things Were the Most Realistic" (paper presented at the annual meeting of the Far West Popular Culture Association, Las Vegas, January/February 2003. Political scientist Dan Lindley agrees the Doomsday device was unlikely yet mutual destruction was possible as a consequence of nuclear war, especially since there were 34,000 nuclear weapons in existence at the time.

25. See Bonnie Szumski, ed., *Nuclear War: Opposing Viewpoints* (St. Paul: Greenhaven Press, 1985), 15–42.

26. Ted Guy, "The Doomsday Blueprints," *Time* August 10, 1992, 32–34.

27. A number of incidents and mishaps have occurred in the United Kingdom involving American nuclear planes, dating as far back as the 1950s. But since they have an Official Secrets Act that allows the government of the day to operate in secret, information about such matters must be secured through utilization of the Freedom of Information Act in the United States. Finally, in 1996, the Ministry of Defense, after prodding by the Campaign for Freedom of Information in the United Kingdom, admitted to twenty nuclear incidents since 1960 but assured the public that none involved the release of radioactive material. Whether one should trust the credibility of a government that operates largely behind closed doors or believe journalist I. F. Stone's maxim that "All governments are run by liars" is the reader's choice.

28. Holly Stratts, "Chernobyl: Aftermath of a Catastrophe," *Villanova Magazine* 11, no. 4 (fall 1996): 26. Also see the book by Grigori Medvedev, the chief engineer at Chernobyl at the time of the explosion, *The Truth About Chernobyl* (New York: Basic Books, 1991) where Medvedev not only provides an insider's description and analysis of what happened, but also claims that there had been eleven accidents in the Soviet Union and twelve in the United States involving nuclear reactors that provided data that could have predicted the disaster at Chernobyl.

29. See Gregory A. Waller, "Re-placing the Day After," *Cinema Journal* 26, no. 3 (spring 1987): 3–20.

30. See Richard L. Zweigenhaft, "Students Surveyed About Nuclear War," *Bulletin of the Atomic Scientists* (February 1985): 26–27.

31. Quoted in Broderick, *Nuclear Movies*, 1.

32. Paul Boyer, *By the Bomb's Early Light* (Chapel Hill: University of North Carolina Press, 1994), 183. The poll participants were given four choices: (a) should not have used the bomb, (b) approved dropping both bombs, (c) should have dropped more bombs, and (d) should have dropped one somewhere (presumably over water) to impress Japanese and then use over land if Japanese fail to surrender.

33. Quoted in Strada, "Kaleidoscopic Nuclear Images of the Fifties," 182.

34. *New York Times*, September 11, 1996, A5.

35. See Bill Keller, "The Thinkable" *New York Times Magazine,* May 4, 2003, sec. 6, 48–53ff, and William Broad, "Facing a Second Nuclear Age," *New York Times*, August 3, 2003, sec. 4, 1, 12.

36. *U.S. News & World Report*, October 13, 2003, 48.

37. As reported in the *New York Times*, October 1, 1999, 1.

38. Eric Pooley, "Nuclear War," *Time*, March 4, 1996, 47–54.

39. Reported in the *U.S. News & World Report,* September 17, 2001, 44–46.

40. The story made headlines during the spring–summer of 2003, including the *New York Times*, May 20, 2003, A31, *The Journal News*, June 29, 2003, 1A & 16A, and the *Daily News*, July 26, 2003, 6.

ELEVEN: DOES POLITICAL FILM HAVE A FUTURE IN HOLLYWOOD?

1. The *New York Times,* July 2, 2004, C1.

2. Hollywood's early history is found in a number of publications, most recently in Neal Gabler's *An Empire of Their Own: How the Jews Invented Hollywood* (New York: Crown Publishers, 1988). This theme was reiterated in an exhibition at the Jewish Museum in New York, February 21–September 14, 2003 entitled, "*Entertaining America: Jews, Movies, and Broadcasting.* The curators were J. Hoberman and Jeffrey Shandler.

3. Peter Bart and Peter Guber do a commendable job in explaining contemporary Hollywood film-making in *Shoot Out: Surviving Fame and (Mis)Fortune in Hollywood* (New York: Berkley Publishing Group, 2002).

4. Figures are from the *New York Times*, March 12, 2001, C12.

5. Bart and Guber, *Shoot Out*, 130.

6. *The Wall Street Journal*, July 24, 2003, B1.

7. *New York Times,* January 18, 2004, sec. 3, B3.

8. Reported in the *New York Times*, September 2, 2002, C1, 4.

9. Peter Biskind, *Down and Dirty Pictures* (New York: Simon & Schuster, 2004).

10. Geoff Gilmore, "The State of Independent Film," *National Forum*, 77, no. 4 (fall 1997): 10.

11. This story of Redford, Sundance, Miramax and the indies movement is told in a rather unflattering way by Biskind in *Down and Dirty Pictures* and in a more positive fashion by Emanuel Levy in *Cinema of Outsiders: The Rise of American Independent Film* (New York: New York University Press, 1999).

12. See especially chapters 1 and 2 in Biskind, *Down and Dirty Pictures*.

13. Gilmore, "The State of Independent Film," 11.

14. The *New York Times,* January 22, 2001, C12.

15. The list is too long to repeat here but it is considerable. During the last decade, independents produced some of the best films and their actors gave some of the best performances on the big screen.

Check out Gail Kinn and Jim Piazza, *The Academy Awards: The Complete Unofficial History* (New York: Black Dog & Leventhal Productions, 2002).

16. Miramax did not always see the virtues in these films at first, though distributed them anyway with some reluctance. When these films were nominated and even won awards, naturally, the Miramax heads basked in the glory of their genius. Sometimes, the story behind the film is just as good—or better than the film itself. See Biskind, *Down and Dirty Pictures*, for all the details.

17. The debacle is reported in Bart & Guber, *Shoot Out*, 193–195. An insider's account is provided by one of the production executives, Steven Bach, in his book *Final Cut: Dreams and Disaster in the Making of Heaven's Gate* (London: Faber, 1986.)

18. *Premier*, vol. 15, no. 3 (November 2001), 48.

19. See Levy, *Cinema of Outsiders*, 282–284.

20. See the *New York Times,* January 26, 1998, B3 and January 22, 2004, B1. Even smaller is the number of films bought at Sundance that gross over $10 million.

21. Benjamin R. Barber, *Jihad vs. McWorld* (New York: Ballantine Books, 2001).

SELECT
BIBLIOGRAPHY

BOOKS

Alperovitz, Gar. *The Decision to Use the Atomic Bomb*. New York: Alfred A. Knopf, 1995.

Alt, Betty, and Silvia Falts. *Weeping Violins: The Gypsy Tragedy in Europe*. Kirksville, MO: Thomas Jefferson University Press, 1996.

Anderegg, Michael, ed. *Inventing Vietnam: The War in Film and Television*. Philadelphia: Temple University Press, 1991.

Arany, Lynne, Tom Dyja, and Gary Goldsmith. *The Reel List*. New York: Dell Publishing Co., 1995.

Bach, Steven. *Final Cut: Dreams and Disaster in the Making of Heaven's Gate*. London: Faber, 1986.

Barber, Benjamin R. *Jihad vs. McWorld*. New York: Ballantine Books, 2001.

Barsam, Richard M. *Non-Fiction Film*. Rev. ed. Bloomington: Indiana University Press, 1992.

Bart, Peter, and Peter Guber. *Shoot Out: Surviving Fame and (Mis)Fortune in Hollywood*. New York: Berkley Publishing Group, 2002.

Basinger, Jeanine. *The World War II Combat Film*. New York: Columbia University Press, 1986.

Benjamin, Walter. *Illuminations*. Edited with an introduction by Hannah Arendt. New York: Schocken Books, 1968.

Benson, Thomas W., and Carolyn Anderson. *Reality Fictions: The Films of Frederick Wiseman*, 2d ed. Carbondale: Southern Illinois University Press, 2002.

Bergman, Andrew. *We're in the Money*. New York: New York University Press, 1971.

Bergmann, Paul, and Michael Asimow. *Reel Justice: The Courtroom Goes to the Movies*. Kansas City, MD: Andrews and McMeel, 1996.

Bernstein, Walter. *Inside Out: A Memoir of the Blacklist*. Cambridge, MA: Da Capo Press, 2000.

Biberman, Herbert. *Salt of the Earth*. Boston: Beacon Press, 1965.

Biskind, Peter. *Down and Dirty Pictures*. New York: Simon & Schuster, 2004.

———. *Easy Riders, Raging Bulls*. New York: Simon & Schuster, 1998.

———. *Seeing Is Believing*. New York: Pantheon Books, 1983.

Black, Gregory D. *Hollywood Censored: Morality Codes, Catholics, and the Movies*. Cambridge, UK: Cambridge University Press, 1994.

Boyer, Paul. *By the Bomb's Early Light*. Chapel Hill: University of North Carolina Press, 1994.

Bradley, James. *Flags of our Fathers*. New York: Bantam Books, 2000.

British Board of Film Classification. *Annual Report for 1995–96*. London: BBFC, 1996.

Broderick, Mick. *Nuclear Movies*. Jefferson, NC: McFarland & Co., 1991.

Brokaw, Tom. *The Greatest Generation*. New York: Random House, 1998.

Browne, Nick, ed. *Refiguring Genres*. Berkeley: University of California Press, 1998.

Brownstein, Ronald. *The Power and the Glitter*. New York: Pantheon Books, 1990.

Brundage, W. Fitzhugh. *Lynching in the New South*. Urbana: University of Illinois Press, 1993.

Buhle, Paul, and Dave Wagner. *Radical Hollywood*. New York: The New Press, 2002.

Carnes, Mark C., ed. *Past Imperfect*. New York: Henry Holt, 1995.

Ceplair, Larry, and Steven Englund. *The Inquisition in Hollywood*. Garden City, NY: Anchor Press/Doubleday, 1980.

Chambers, II, John Whiteclay, and David Culbert, eds. *World War II, Film, and History*. New York: Oxford University Press, 1996.

Chang, Iris. *The Rape of Nanking*. New York: Basic Books, 1997.

Chaplin, Charles. *My Autobiography*. New York: Simon and Schuster, 1964.

Christensen, Terry. *Reel Politics*. New York: Blackwell Publishers, 1987.

Cogley, John. *Report on Blacklisting I: Movies*. New York: Fund for the Republic, 1956.

Colley, David P. *Blood for Dignity: The Story of the First Integrated Combat Unit in the U.S. Army*. New York: St. Martin's Press, 2003.

Combs, James, ed. *Movies and Politics*. New York: Garland Publishing Co., 1993.

Combs, James E., and Sara T. Combs. *Film Propaganda and American Politics*. New York: Garland Publishing Co., 1994.

Conrad, Joseph. *Heart of Darkness*. Edited by Robert Kimbrough, 2d ed. New York: W. W. Norton & Company, 1971.

Cook, Philip S., Douglas Goney, and Lawrence W. Lichty. *American Media*. Washington, DC: The Wilson Center Press, 1989.

Coyne, Michael. *The Crowded Prairie*. London: I. B. Tauris Publishers, 1997.

Crowdus, Gary, ed. *A Political Companion to American Film*. Chicago: Lake View Press, 1994.

Denvir, John, ed. *Legal Reelism: Movies as Legal Texts*. Urbana: University of Illinois Press, 1996.

Dershowitz, Alan M. *The Best Defense*. New York: Vintage Books, 1983.

Dick, Bernard F. *The Star-Spangled Screen: The American World War II Film*. Lexington: University of Kentucky Press, 1996.

Diggins, John Patrick. *The Proud Decades*. New York: Norton, 1989.

Dinnerstein, Leonard. *The Leo Frank Case*. New York: Columbia University Press, 1968.

Dittmar, Linda, and Gene Michaud, eds. *From Hanoi to Hollywood: The Vietnam War in American Film*. New Brunswick, NJ: Rutgers University Press, 1990.

Dmytryk, Edward. *Odd Man Out: A Memoir of the Hollywood Ten*. Carbondale: Southern Illinois University Press, 1996.

Doherty, Thomas. *Pre-Code Hollywood: Sex, Immorality, and Insurrection in American Cinema*. New York: Columbia University Press, 1999.

———. *Projections of War: Hollywood, American Culture and World War II*. New York: Columbia University Press, 1993.

Dooley, Roger. *From Scarface to Scarlett: American Films in the 1930s*. New York: Harcourt Brace Jovanovich, 1979.

Federal Trade Commission. *Report on Marketing Violent Entertainment to Children*. Washington, DC: Government Printing Office, 2000.

Fielding, Raymond. *The March of Time, 1945–51*. New York: Oxford University Press, 1978.

Fried, Albert. *McCarthyism: The Great American Red Scare*. New York: Oxford University Press, 1997.

Fried, Richard. *Nightmare in Red*. New York: Oxford University Press, 1990.

Gabler, Neal. *An Empire of Their Own*. New York: Crown Publishers, 1988.

———. *Life: the Movie: How Entertainment Conquered Reality*. New York: Alfred A. Knopf, 1998.

Geertz, Clifford. *The Interpretation of Cultures*. New York: Basic Books, 1973.

Gehring, Wes, ed. *Handbook of American Film Genres*. Westport, CT: Greenwood Press, 1988.

Genovese, Michael. *Politics and the Cinema*. Lexington, MA: Ginn Press, 1986.

Georgakas, Dan. *Encyclopedia of the American Left*. New York: Garland Publishing Co., 1990.

———, and Lenny Rubenstein, eds. *The Cineaste Interviews*. Chicago: Lake View Press, 1983.

Goldberg, Robert Alan. *Enemies Within: The Culture of Conspiracy in Modern America*. New Haven: Yale University Press, 2001.

Grant, Barry Keith. *Voyages of Discovery: The Cinema of Frederick Wiseman*. Urbana: University of Illinois Press, 1992.

———, and Jeannette Sloniowski, eds. *Documenting the Documentary*. Detroit: Wayne State University Press, 1998.

Gutman, Israel, ed. *Encyclopedia of the Holocaust*. Vol. 4. New York: Macmillan Publishing Co., 1990.

Halberstam, David. *The Fifties*. New York: Villard Books, 1993.

Hamilton, Marybeth. *When I'm Bad, I'm Better: Mae West, Sex, and American Entertainment*. Berkeley: University of California Press, 1997.

Harmetz, Aljean. *Round Up the Usual Suspects*. New York: Hyperion, 1992.

Hearst Corporation. *The American Public, the Media and the Judicial System*. New York: Hearst Corporation, 1983.

Huchthausen, Peter. *America's Splendid Little Wars*. New York: Viking Press, 2003.

Isaacs, Arnold R. *The War, Its Ghosts, and Its Legacy*. Baltimore: Johns Hopkins University Press, 1998.

Jamesson, Richard T., ed. *They Went Thataway: Redefining Film Genres*. San Francisco: Mercury House, 1994.

Jarvie, I. C., et al., eds. *Children and the Movies: Media Influences and the Payne Fund Controversy*. New York: Cambridge University Press, 1996.

Keegan, John. *The First World War*. New York: Alfred A. Knopf, 1999.

Keim, Albert N. *The CPS Story: An Illustrated History of Civilian Public Service*. Intercourse, PA: Good Books, 1990.

Keough, Peter, ed. *Flesh and Blood*. San Francisco: Mercury House, 1995.

Kinn, Gail and Jim Piazza. *The Complete Unofficial History of the Academy Awards*. New York: Black Dog & Leventhal Publishers, 2002.

Koch, Howard. *Casablanca: Script and Legend*. New York: Overlook Express, 1992.

Kohn, Stephen M. *Jailed for Peace*. Westport, CT: Greenwood Press, 1986.

Koppes, Clayton R., and Gregory D. Black. *Hollywood Goes to War*. Berkeley: University of California Press, 1993.

Leff, Leonard J., and Jerold L. Simmons. *The Dame in the Kimono: Hollywood, Censorship, and the Production Code from the 1920s to the 1960s*. New York: Grove Weidenfeld, 1990.

Lenz, Timothy. *Changing Images of Law in Film & Television*. New York: Peter Lang, 2003.

Levy, Emanuel. *Cinema of Outsiders: The Rise of American Independent Film*. New York: New York University Press, 1999.

Lewis, Jon. *Hollywood v. Hard Core: How the Struggle over Censorship Saved the Modern Film Industry.* New York: New York University Press, 2000.

Litwack, Leon F. *Without Sanctuary: Lynching Photographs in America.* San Francisco: Twin Palms, 2000.

Lorence, James J. *The Suppression of Salt of the Earth.* Albuquerque: University of New Mexico Press, 1999.

Lovell, Hugh, and Tasile Carter. *Collective Bargaining in the Motion Picture Industry.* Berkeley: University of California Press, 1955.

Lukas, Richard C. *The Forgotten Holocaust: The Poles Under German Occupation.* Lexington: University of Kentucky Press, 1986.

Lyons, Charles. *The New Censors.* Philadelphia: Temple University Press, 1997.

Maisel, L. Sandy. *Political Parties and Elections in the United States.* New York: Garland Publishing, 1991.

Maltby, Richard, and Ian Craven. *Hollywood Cinema.* Cambridge, MA: Blackwell Publishers, 1995.

Maltin, Leonard. *The Great Movie Shorts.* New York: Crown Publishers, 1972.

Martin, Andrew. *Receptions of War: Vietnam in American Culture.* Norman: University of Oklahoma Press, 1993.

Mast, Gerald, and Marshall Cohen, eds. *Film Theory and Criticism.* 3rd ed. New York: Oxford University Press, 1985.

Medved, Michael. *Hollywood v. America.* New York: HarperCollins, 1992.

Medvedev, Grigori. *The Truth About Chernobyl.* New York: Basic Books, 1991.

Miller, Mark Crispin, ed. *Seeing Through Movies.* New York: Pantheon Books, 1990.

Milton, Joyce. *Tramp: The Life of Charlie Chaplin.* New York: HarperCollins, 1996.

Mitchell, Greg. *The Campaign of the Century.* New York: Random House: 1992.

———. *Tricky Dick and the Pink Lady: Richard Nixon vs. Helen Gahagan Douglas–Sexual Politics and the Red Scare.* New York: Random House, 1950.

Morgan, Ted. *Reds: McCarthyism in Twentieth-Century America.* New York: Randon House, 2003.

Navasky, Victor S. *Naming Names.* New York: Penguin Books, 1981.

Neve, Brian. *Film and Politics in America.* London: Routledge, 1992.

Ness, Immanul, and James Ciment. *The Encyclopedia of Third Parties in America.* Vol. 1. New York: M. E. Sharpe, 2000.

Nichols, Bill. *Blurred Boundaries.* Bloomington: Indiana University Press, 1994.

Nielsen, Mike, and Gene Mailes. *Hollywood's Other Blacklist.* London: British Film Institute, 1995.

Norman, Elizabeth M. *We Band of Angels.* New York: Random House, 1999.

O'Connor, John, and Martin A. Jackson, eds. *American History/American Film.* Foreword by Arthur Schlesinger, Jr. New York: Frederick Unger, 1979.

Oshinsky, David M. *A Conspiracy So Immense.* New York: Free Press, 1983.

Packer, Herbert. *The Limits of the Criminal Sanction.* Stanford: Stanford University Press, 1968.

Palmer, William J. *The Films of the Eighties.* Carbondale: Southern Illinois University Press, 1993.

Perry, Richard, and Louis Perry. *A History of the Los Angeles Labor Movement.* Berkeley: University of California Press, 1963.

Powdermaker, Hortense. *Hollywood the Dream Factory: An Anthropologist Looks at the Movie-makers.* Boston: Little, Brown & Company, 1950.

Puttman, David, with Neil Watson. *Movies and Money.* New York: Alfred A. Knopf, 1997.

Reeves, Thomas C. *The Life and Times of Senator Joe McCarthy.* New York: Stein and Day, 1982.

Riordon, William L. *Plunkitt of Tammany Hall.* New York: E. P. Dutton & Co., 1963.

Roberts, Randy, and Robert E. May. *Learning to Think Critically: Film, Myth, and American History.* New York: HarperCollins, 1993.

Robins, Robert S., and Jerold M. Post. *Political Paranoia: The Psychopolitics of Hatred.* New Haven: Yale University Press, 1997.

Robinson, David. *Chaplin: His Life and Art.* New York: McGraw-Hill, 1985.

Rogin, Michael. *Ronald Reagan, the Movie.* Berkeley: University of California Press, 1988.

Rollins, Peter C., and John E. O'Connor, eds. *Hollywood's White House: The American Presidency in Film and History.* Lexington: University of Kentucky Press, 2003.

———. *Hollywood's World War I: Motion Picture Images.* Bowling Green: Popular Press, 1997.

Rosenthal, Alan, ed. *Why Docudrama?* Carbondale: Southern Illinois University Press, 1999.

Ross, Murray. *Stars and Strikes.* New York: Columbia University Press, 1941.

Ross, Steven J. *Working Class Hollywood: Silent Film and the Shaping of Class in America.* Princeton: Princeton University Press, 1998.

Rovere, Richard. *Senator Joe McCarthy.* New York: Harcourt, Brace, 1959.

Ryan, Michael, and Douglas Kellner. *Camera Politica: The Politics and Ideology of Contemporary Hollywood Film.* Bloomington: Indiana University Press, 1988.

Saunders, Frances Stoner. *The Cultural Cold War.* New York: The New Press, 1999.

Sayre, Nora. *Running Time: Films of the Cold War.* New York: The Dial Press, 1982.

Schapsmeier, Edward, and Frederick Schapsmeier. *Political Parties and Civic Action Groups.* Westport, CT: Greenwood Press, 1981.

Shaheen, Jack, ed. *Nuclear War Films.* Carbondale: Southern Illinois University Press, 1978.

Sherwin, Richard K. *When the Law Goes Pop: The Vanishing Line Between Law & Popular Culture.* Chicago: University of Chicago Press, 2002.

Sigmund, Anna Maria. *Women of the Third Reich.* Ontario, Canada: NDE Publishing, 2000.

Simon, John. *Movies Into Film.* New York: Dell Publishing Co., 1970.

Steffens, Lincoln. *The Shame of the Cities.* New York: Peter Smith, 1948.

Stinnett, Richard B. *Day of Deceit: The Truth About FDR & Pearl Harbor.* New York: Free Press, 1999.

Swofford, Anthony. *Jarhead.* New York: Scribner & Sons, 2003.

Szumski, Bonnie, ed. *Nuclear War: Opposing Viewpoints.* St. Paul, MN: Greenhaven Press, 1985.

Tolenay, Stewart E., and E. M. Beck. *A Festival of Violence: An Analysis of Southern Lynching, 1882–1930.* Urbana: University of Illinois Press, 1995.

Traube, Elizabeth. *Dreaming Identities: Class, Gender and Generation in 1980s Hollywood Movies.* Boulder, CO: Westview Press, 1992.

Turner, Frederick Jackson. "The Significance of the Frontier in American History." In *The Frontier in American History.* New York: Henry Holt & Co., 1920. First published in the *Annual Report of the American Historical Association for the Year 1883.* Washington, DC, 1894.

Tuttle, William M., Jr. *Daddy's Gone to War.* New York: Oxford University Press, 1993.

Valenti, Jack. *The Voluntary Movie Rating System.* Washington, DC: Motion Picture Association of America, 1996.

Vaughn, Stephen. *Ronald Reagan in Hollywood.* New York: Cambridge University Press, 1994.

Vieira, Mark. *Sin in Soft Focus: Pre-Code Hollywood.* New York: Harry N. Abrams, 1999.

Walzer, Michael. *Just and Unjust Wars.* 2d. ed. New York: Basic Books, 1992.

Welch, David. *Propaganda and the German Cinema.* New York: Oxford University Press, 1983.

Wilson, Michael, and Deborah Silverton Rosenfelt. *Salt of the Earth.* New York: Feminist Press, 1978.

Winston, Brian. *Claiming the Real: The Documentary Film Revisited.* London: British Film Institute, 1995.

Wise, James E., Jr., and Anne Collier Rehill. *Stars in Blue: Movie Actors in America's Sea Services.* Annapolis, MD: Naval Institute Press, 1997.

ARTICLES

Asimow, Michael. "Bad Lawyers in the Movies." *Nova Law Review* 24, no. 2 (winter 2000): 533–591.
———. "Divorce in the Movies: From the Hays Office to *Kramer v. Kramer*." *Legal Studies Forum* 24, no. 2 (2000): 221–267.

Barkun, Michael. "Conspiracy Thinking in Contemporary America." *Maxwell Perspective* (Syracuse University) 8, no. 1 (fall 1997): 23.

Bateman, Thomas S., Tomoaki Sakano, and Mokoto Fujita. "Roger, Me, and My Attitude: Film Propaganda and Cynicism toward Corporate Leadership." *Journal of Applied Psychology* 77, no. 5 (1992): 768–771.

Brinckmann, Christine Noll. "The Politics of *Force of Evil*: An Analysis of Abraham Polonsky's Preblacklisted Film." *Prospects* 6 (1981): 357–386.

Bruck, Connie. "The Personal Touch." *The New Yorker* (August 13, 2001): 42–59.

Caputi, Jane. "Films of the Nuclear Age." *Journal of Popular Film & Television* 16, no. 3 (fall 1988): 100–107.

Chelminski, Ralph. "The Maginot Line." *Smithsonian* 28, no. 3 (June 1997): 90–100.

Convents, Guido. "Documentaries and Propaganda Before 1914." *Framework*, no. 35 (1988): 107–108.

Crawford, Neta C. "Just War Theory and the U.S. Counterterror War." *Perspectives on Politics* 1, no. 1 (March 2003): 5–25.

DeVany, Arthur, and W. David Wells. "Does Hollywood Make Too Many R-rated Movies?: Risk, Stochastic Dominance, and the Illusion of Expectation." *Journal of Business* 75, no. 3 (July 2002): 425–452.

Ebo, Bosah. "War as Popular Culture: The Gulf Conflict and the Technology of Illusionary Entertainment." *Journal of American Culture* 18, no. 3 (fall 1995): 19–25.

Elliott, William R., and William J. Schenck-Hamlin. "Film, Politics and the Press: The Influence of *All the President's Men*." *Journalism Quarterly* 56, no. 3 (1979): 546–553.

Gans, Herbert J. "Hollywood Entertainment: Commerce or Ideology?" *Social Science Quarterly* 74, no. 1 (1993): 150–153.

Giglio, Ernest. "Using Film to Teach Political Concepts," *European Political Science* 1, no. 2 (spring 2002): 53–58.

Gilmore, Geoff. "The State of Independent Film." *National Forum* 77, no. 4 (fall 1997): 10.

Godmilow, Jill. "How Real Is the Reality in Documentary Film?" *History and Theory* 36, no. 4 (December 1997): 80–101.

Gornick, Vivian. "The Left in the Fifties." *Lincoln Center Theatre Review* no. 35 (spring/summer 2003): 12–13.

Hackett, David. "The Wonderful, Horrible Life of Leni Riefenstahl." *American Historical Review* 100, no. 4 (October 1995): 1227–1228.

Hendershot, Cyndy. "The Atomic Scientists, Science Fiction Films, and Paranoia." *Journal of American Culture* 20, no. 1 (spring 1997): 31–41.

Hoffer, Tom W., and Richard Alan Nelson. "Docudrama on American Television." *Journal of the University Film Association* 30, no. 2 (spring 1978): 22.

Huesmann, L. Rowell, Jessica Moise-Titus, Cheryl-Lynn Podolski, and Leonard D. Eron. "Longitudinal Relations Between Children's Exposure to TV Violence and Their Aggressive and Violent Behavior in Young Adulthood: 1977–1992." *Developmental Psychology* 39, no. 2 (2003): 201–221.

Jowett, Garth S. "Hollywood, Propaganda and the Bomb: Nuclear Images in Post World War II Film." *Film and History* 18, no. 2 (May 1988): 26–38.

———. "Propaganda and Communication: The Re-emergence of a Research Tradition." *Journal of Communication* 37, no. 1 (winter 1987): 113–114.

Keller, Laura Wittern. "Freedom of the Screen: Joseph Burstyn and *The Miracle*." *New York Archives*, 1, no. 4 (spring 2002): 23–25.

Lieberman, Robbie. "Communism, Peace Activism, and Civil Liberties: From the Waldorf Conference to the Peekskill Riot." *Journal of Popular Culture* 18, no. 3 (fall 1995): 59–65.

Lucia, Cynthia. "Women on Trial: The Female Lawyer in the Hollywood Courtroom." *Cineaste* 19 (1993): 32–37.

Macaulay, Stewart. "Images of Law in Everyday Life: The Lesson of School, Entertainment, and Spectator Sports." *Law & Society Review* 21, no. 2 (1987): 185–218.

Mastrangelo, Paul. "Lawyers and the Law: A Filmography." *Legal Reference Services Quarterly* 3 (winter 1983): 31–72.

May, Ernest R. "Thirteen Days in 145 Minutes." *National Forum* 81, no. 2 (spring 2001): 34–37.

McGovern, George. "Nixon and Historical Memory: Two Reviews." *Perspectives* (AHA Newsletter) 34, no. 3 (March 1996): 3.

Morlan, Don. "Slapstick Contributions to WWII Propaganda: The Three Stooges and Abbott & Costello." *Studies in Popular Culture* 17 (October 1994): 29–43.

Orwell, Miles. "Documentary and the Power of Interrogation: *American Dream* and *Roger & Me*." *Film Quarterly* 48 (winter 94/95): 10–18.

Rolo, Charles. "Camus at Stockholm." *The Atlantic Monthly* 201 (May 1958): 33–34.

Ross, Steven J. "Struggles for the Screen: Workers, Radicals, and the Political Uses of Silent Film." *American Historical Review* 96, no. 2 (April 1991): 333–367.

Rostron, Allen. "Mr. Carter Goes to Washington." *Journal of Popular Film & Television* 25, no. 2 (summer 1997): 57–67.

Sheffield, Ric. "On Film: A Social History of Women Lawyers in Popular Culture 1930 to 1990." *Loyola of Los Angeles Entertainment Law Journal* 14 (1993): 73–114.

Small, Melvin. "Buffoons and BraveHearts: Hollywood Portrays the Russians, 1939–1944." *California Historical Society* 52 (winter 1973): 326–337.

Spiller, Roger J. "War in the Dark." *American Heritage* 50, no. 1 (February/March 1999): 41–51.

Strada, Michael J. "Kaleidoscopic Nuclear Images of the Fifties." *Journal of Popular Culture* 20, no. 3 (1986): 179–198.

Stratts, Holly. "Chernobyl: Aftermath of a Catastrophe." *Villanova Magazine* 11, no. 4 (fall 1996): 26.

Sturken, Marita. "Reenactment, Fantasy, and the Paranoia of History: Oliver Stone's Docudramas." *History and Theory* 36, no.4 (December 1997): 66.

Sunstein, Cass. "Free Speech Now." *University of Chicago Law Review* 59 (1992): 255–316.

Tarr, Alan. Review of "Nashville." *Notes for Teachers of Political Science*, no. 22 (summer 1979): 21.

Thompson, Robert. "American Politics on Film." *Journal of Popular Culture* 20 (summer 1986): 27–47.

Waller, Gregory A. "Re-placing the Day After." *Cinema Journal* 26, no. 3 (spring 1987): 3–20.

Watkins, Peter. "The Fear of Commitment." *Literature/Film Quarterly* 11, no. 4 (1983): 221–233.

Watson, Bruce. "Hang 'em first, try 'em later." *Smithsonian* 29, no.8 (June 1998): 96–107.

Welsh, James. "Banned in Britain." *American Film* 8, no. 1 (October 1982): 64ff.

Westbrook, Robert B. "I Want a Girl, Just Like the Girl that Married Harry James: American Women and the Problem of Political Obligation in World War II." *American Quarterly* 42, no. 4 (December 1990): 587–614.

Wise, Sidney. "Politicians: A Film Perspective." *News for Teachers of Political Science* 32 (winter 1982): 1.

Zweigenhaft, Richard L. "Students surveyed about nuclear war." *Bulletin of the Atomic Scientists* (February 1985): 26–27.

CASES

Brandenburg v. Ohio, 395 U.S. 444 (1969)

Brown v. Board of Education, 374 U.S. 483 (1954)

Burstyn v. Wilson, 343 U.S. 495 (1952)

Escobedo v. Illinois, 378 U.S. 478 (1964)

Gitlow v. New York, 268 U.S. 652 (1925)

Goldman v. Weinberger, 475 U.S. 503 (1985)

Home Building and Loan Association v. Blaisdell, 290 U.S. 398 (1934)

Jacobellis v. Ohio, 378 U.S. 184 (1964)

Mapp v. Ohio, 367 U.S. 643 (1961)

Miranda v. Arizona, 384 U.S. 436 (1966)

Near v. Minnesota, 283 U.S. 697 (1931)

New York Times v. U.S., 403 U.S. 713 (1971)

New York Times Co. v. Sullivan, 376 U.S. 255 (1964)

Roe v. Wade, 410 U.S. 113 (1973)

Roth v. U.S., 354 U.S. 476 (1957)

Thornhill v. Alabama, 310 U.S. 88 (1940)

United States v. Paramount Pictures, 334 U.S. 131 (1947)

West Virginia State Board v. Barnette, 319 U.S. 624 (1943)

Whitney v. California, 274 U.S. 357 (1927)

SELECT FILMOGRAPHY

FEATURES

Abe Lincoln in Illinois (USA: 1940) Director: John Cromwell. Screenplay: Robert Sherwood. Cast: Raymond Massey, Gene Lockhart, Ruth Gordon. 110 min. (*)

About Schmidt (USA: 2002) Director: Alexander Payne. Screenplay: Alexander Payne. Cast: Jack Nicholson, Kathy Bates. 125 min. (*)

Above and Beyond (USA: 1952) Directors: Melvin Frank, Norman Panama. Screenplay: Norman Panama, Beirne Lay, Jr., Frank Panama. Cast: Robert Taylor, Eleanor Parker, James Whitmore. 122 min. (*)

Absolute Power (USA: 1996) Director: Clint Eastwood. Screenplay: William Goldman. Cast: Clint Eastwood, Gene Hackman, Ed Harris. 121 min. (*)

The Accused (USA: 1988) Director: Jonathan Kaplan. Screenplay: Tom Topor. Cast: Jodie Foster, Kelly McGillis. 101 min. (*)

Action in the North Atlantic (USA: 1944) Director: Lloyd Bacon. Screenplay: John Howard Lawson. Cast: Humphrey Bogart, Raymond Massey, Alan Hale, Julie Bishop. 126 min. (*)

Adam's Rib (USA: 1950) Director: George Cukor. Screenplay: Garson Kanin. Cast: Spencer Tracy, Katharine Hepburn, Judy Holliday, Tom Ewell. 101 min. (*)

Adventures of Pluto Nash (USA: 2002) Director: Ron Underwood. Screenplay: Neil Cuthbert. Cast: Eddie Murphy. 95 min. (*)

Advise and Consent (USA: 1962) Director: Otto Preminger. Screenplay: Wendell Mayes. Cast: Don Murray, Charles Laughton, Henry Fonda, Walter Pidgeon, Lew Ayres. 139 min. (*)

Air Force One (USA: 1997) Director: Wolfgang Peterson. Screenplay: Andrew W. Marlowe. Cast: Harrison Ford, Glenn Close, Gary Oldman. 124 min. (*)

The Alamo (USA: 2004) Director: John Lee Hancock. Screenplay: Leslie Bohem and Stephen Gaghan. Cast: Dennis Quaid, Billy Bob Thornton, Jason Patric. 137 min. (*)

Alamo Bay (USA: 1985) Director: Louis Malle. Screenplay: Alice Arlan. Cast: Ed Harris, Ho Nguyen, Amy Madigan. 99 min. (*)

All Quiet on the Western Front (USA: 1930) Director: Lewis Milestone. Screenplay: Lewis Milestone, Maxwell Anderson, Del Andrews, George Abbott. Cast: Louis Wolheim, Lew Ayres. 140 min. (*)

All the King's Men (USA: 1949) Director: Robert Rossen. Screenplay: Robert Rossen. Cast: Broderick Crawford, John Ireland, Mercedes McCambridge, Joanne Dru. 109 min. (*)

All the President's Men (USA: 1976) Director: Alan J. Pakula. Screenplay: William Goldman. Cast: Robert Redford, Dustin Hoffman, Jason Robards, Jr. 135 min. (*)

American Beauty (USA: 1999) Director: Sam Mendes. Screenplay: Alan Ball. Cast: Kevin Spacey, Annette Bening, Chris Cooper. 122 min. (*)

American Pie (USA: 1999) Director: Paul Weitz. Screenplay: Adam Herz. Cast: Jason Biggs, Chris Klein. 95 min. (*)

The American President (USA: 1995) Director: Rob Reiner. Screenplay: Aaron Sorkin. Cast: Michael Douglas, Annette Bening, Martin Sheen, Michael J. Fox. 115 min. (*)

American Psycho (USA: 2000) Director: Mary Harron. Screenplay: Mary Harron. Cast: Christian Bale, Reese Witherspoon. 101 min. (*)

Amistad (USA: 1997) Director: Steven Spielberg. Screenplay: David H. Franzoni. Cast: Anthony Hopkins, Matthew McConaughey, Djimon Hounsou. 150 min. (*)

Anatomy of Murder (USA: 1959) Director: Otto Preminger. Screenplay: Wendell Mayes. Cast: James Stewart, George C. Scott, Lee Remick, Arthur O'Connell. 161 min. (*)

And Justice for All (USA: 1979) Director: Norman Jewison. Screenplay: Barry Levinson, Valerie Curtin. Cast: Al Pacino, Jack Warden, Christine Lahti. 120 min. (*)

Angels From Hell (USA: 1968) Director: Bruce Kessler. Screenplay: Jerome Wish. Cast: Tom Stern, Arlene Martel, Ted Markland, Stephen Oliver. 86 min. (*)

Angels With Dirty Faces (USA: 1938) Director: Michael Curtiz. Screenplay: John Wexley, Warren Duff. Cast: James Cagney, Pat O'Brien, Humphrey Bogart, Ann Sheridan. 97 min. (*)

Ann Carver's Profession (USA: 1933) Director: Edward Buzzell. Screenplay: Robert Riskin. Cast: Fay Wray, Gene Raymond. 68 min.

Apocalypse Now (USA: 1979) Director: Francis Ford Coppola. Screenplay: Francis Ford Coppola, John Milius. Cast: Marlon Brando, Martin Sheen, Robert Duvall. 153 min. (*)

Apollo 13 (USA: 1995) Director: Director: Ron Howard. Screenplay: William Broyles, Jr. and Al Reinert. Cast: Tom Hanks, Ed harris, Bill Paxton, Gary Sinise. 140 min. (*)

Armageddon (USA: 1998) Director: Michael Bay. Screenplay: Tony Gilroy, Shane Salerno, Jonathan Hensleigh, Jeffrey Abrams. Cast: Bruce Willis, Billy Bob Thornton, Ben Affleck. 144 min. (*)

Baby Doll (USA: 1956) Director: Elia Kazan. Screenplay: Tennessee Williams. Cast: Eli Wallach, Carroll Baker, Karl Malden. 115 min. (*)

Back to Bataan (USA: 1985) Director: Edward Dmytryk. Screenplay: Ben Barzman, Richard Landau. Cast: John Wayne, Anthony Quinn. 95 min. (*)

Bad Company (USA: 2002) Director: Joel Schumacher. Screenplay: Gary Goodman and David Himmelstein. Cast: Anthony Hopkins, Chris Rock. 116 min. (*)

Bad Lieutenant (USA: 1992) Director: Abel Ferrara. Screenplay: Zoe Tamerlaine Lund, Abel Ferrara. Cast: Harvey Keitel. 98 min. (*)

Basic Instinct (USA: 1992) Director: Paul Verhoeven. Screenplay: Joe Eszterhas. Cast: Michael Douglas, Sharon Stone, George Dzundza, Jeanne Tripplehorn. 123 min. (*)

Bataan (USA: 1943) Director: Tay Garnett. Screenplay: Robert D. Andrews. Cast: Robert Taylor, George Murphy, Thomas Mitchell. 115 min. (*)

Battle Cry of Peace (USA: 1915) Directors: J. Stuart Blackton, Wilfred North. Screenplay: J. Stuart Blackton. Cast: Charles Richman, L. Rogers Lytton, Charles Kent. Nine reels.

Battle of the Bulge (USA: 1965) Director: Ken Annakin. Screenplay: Philip Yordan, Milton Sperling, John Melson. Cast: Henry Fonda, Robert Shaw, Robert Ryan, Dana Andrews. 167 min. (*)

The Beast from 20,000 Fathoms (USA: 1953) Director: Eugene Lourie. Cast: Paul Christian, Paula Raymond, Cecil Kellaway, Kenneth Tobey. 80 min. (*)

The Beginning or the End (USA: 1947) Director: Norman Taurog. Screenplay: Robert Considine. Cast: Brian Donlevy, Robert Walker, Tom Drake, Beverly Tyler. 112 min.

Behind Enemy Lines (USA: 2001) Director: John Moore. Screenplay: John Thomas. Cast: Owen Wilson, Gene Hackman. 106 min. (*)

Behind the Rising Sun (USA: 1943) Director: Edward Dmytryk. Screenplay: Emmet Lavery. Cast: Tom Neal, J. Carrol Naish. 88 min. (*)

The Best Man (USA: 1964) Director: Franklin J. Schaffner. Screenplay: Gore Vidal. Cast: Henry Fonda, Cliff Robertson, Lee Tracy, Margaret Leighton. 104 min. (*)

The Best Years of Our Lives (USA: 1946) Director: Willian Wyler. Screenplay: Robert Sherwood. Cast: Frederic March, Myrna Loy, Dana Andrews, Harold Russell, Teresa Wright. 170 min. (*)

Big Jim McLain (USA: 1952) Director: Edward Ludwig. Screenplay: James Edward Grant, Richard English, Eric Taylor. Cast: John Wayne, Nancy Olson, James Arness. 90 min. (*)

The Big Parade (USA: 1925) Director: King Vidor. Screenplay: Lawrence Stallings, Harry Behn. Cast: John Gilbert, Renee Adoree, Hobart Bosworth. 141 min. (*)

The Big Red One (USA: 1980) Director: Samuel Fuller. Screenplay: Samuel Fuller. Cast: Lee Marvin, Robert Carradine, Mark Hamill. 113 min. (*)

The Birth of a Nation (USA: 1915) Director: D. W. Griffith. Screenplay: D.W. Griffith, Frank Woods. Cast: Henry B. Walthall, Mae Marsh, Miriam Cooper, Lillian Gish. 100 min. (*)

Black Hawk Down (USA: 2001) Director: Ridley Scott. Screenplay: Ken Nolan. Cast: Josh Hartnett, Ewan McGregor. 144 min. (*)

Black Legion (USA: 1937) Director: Archie Mayo. Screenplay: Robert Lord, Abem Finkel, William Wister Haines. Cast: Humphrey Bogart, Erin O'Brien Moore, Dick Foran, Ann Sheridan. 83 min. (*)

The Blair Witch Project (USA: 1999) Director: Daniel Myrick and Eduardo Sanchez. Screenplay: Daniel Myrick and Eduardo Sanchez. Cast: Heather Donahue, Joshua Leonard. 86 min. (*)

Blockade (USA: 1938) Director: William Dierterle. Screenplay: John Howard Wilson. Cast: Madeleine Carroll, Henry Fonda, Leo Carrillo, John Halliday. 85 min. (*)

Blow-Up (Great Britain & Italy: 1966) Director: Michelangelo Antonioni. Screenplay: Tonino Guerra, Michelangelo Antonioni. Cast: David Hemmings, Vanessa Redgrave, Sarah Miles. 111 min. (*)

Bob Roberts (USA: 1992) Director: Tim Robbins. Screenplay: Tim Robbins. Cast: Tim Robbins, Giancarlo Esposito, Alan Rickman. 105 min. (*)

Bolshevism on Trial (USA: 1919) Director: Harley Knoles. Screenplay: Thomas Dixon, Harry Chandler. Cast: Robert Frazer, Leslie Stowe. 85 min.

Born on the Fourth of July (USA: 1989) Director: Oliver Stone. Screenplay: Oliver Stone, Ron Kovic. Cast: Tom Cruise, William Dafoe, Tom Berenger. 144 min. (*)

Bound (USA: 1996) Directors: Andy and Larry Wachowski. Screenplay: Andy and Larry Wachowski. Cast: Jennifer Tilly, Gina Gershon. 107 min. (*)

A Boy and His Dog (USA: 1975) Director: L.Q. Jones. Screenplay: Harlan Ellison, L.Q. Jones. Cast: Don Johnson, Suzanne Benton, Jason Robards, Jr., Charles McGraw. 87 min. (*)

The Boys in Company C (USA: 1977) Director: Sidney J. Furie. Screenplay: Sidney J. Furie. Cast: Stan Shaw, Andrew Stevens, James Canning. 127 min. (*)

Braddock: Missing in Action III (USA: 1988) Director: Aaron Norris. Screenplay: James Bruner, Chuck Norris. Cast: Chuck Norris. 101 min. (*)

Braveheart (USA: 1995) Director: Mel Gibson. Screenplay: Randall Wallace. Cast: Mel Gibson, Sophie Marceau. 177 min. (*)

Brian's Song (USA: 1971) Director: Buzz Kulik. TV script: William Blinn. Cast: James Caan, Billy Dee Williams. 73 min. (*)

The Bridge on the River Kwai (Great Britain: 1957) Director: David Lean. Screenplay: Michael Wilson, Carl Foreman. Cast: William Holden, Alec Guinness, Jack Hawkins, Sessue Hayakawa. 161 min. (*)

The Brothers MacMullen (USA: 1995) Director: Edward Burns. Screenplay: Edward Burns. Cast: Edward Burns, Mike McGlone, Jack Mulcahy. 98 min. (*)

Buffalo Soldiers (UK/Germany: 2001) Director: Gregor Jordan. Screenplay: Eric Weiss. Cast: Joaquin Phoenix, Ed Harris, Scott Glenn. 98 min. (*)

Bulworth (USA: 1998) Director: Warren Beatty. Screenplay: Warren Beatty, Jeremy Pikser. Cast: Warren Beatty, Halle Berry. 108 min. (*)

Butch Cassidy and the Sundance Kid (USA: 1969) Director: George Roy Hill. Screenplay: William Goldman. Cast: Paul Newman, Robert Redford. 110 min. (*)

The Caine Mutiny (USA: 1954) Director: Edward Dmytryk. Screenplay: Stanley Roberts. Cast: Humphrey Bogart, Jose Ferrer, Van Johnson, Fred MacMurray. 125 min. (*)

Canadian Bacon (USA: 1994) Director: Michael Moore. Screenplay: Michael Moore. Cast: Alan Alda, Kevin Pollak, John Candy, Rhea Perlman. 91 min. (*)

The Candidate (USA: 1972) Director: Michael Ritchie. Screenplay: Jeremy Larner. Cast: Robert Redford, Peter Boyle, Don Porter, Allan Garfield. 105 min. (*)

Cape Fear (USA: 1962) Director: J. Lee Thompson. Screenplay: James Webb. Cast: Gregory Peck, Robert Mitchum. 105 min. (*)

Cape Fear (USA: 1991) Director: Martin Scorsese. Screenplay: Wesley Strick. Cast: Robert DeNiro, Nick Nolte, Jessica Lange. 128 min. (*)

Career Woman (USA: 1936) Director: Lewis Seiler. Screenplay: Lamar Trotti. Cast: Erville Alderson, Edward S. Brophy. 75 min.

Casablanca (USA: 1942) Director: Michael Curtiz. Screenplay: Julius J. Epstein, Philip C. Epstein, Howard Koch. Cast: Humphrey Bogart, Ingrid Bergman, Paul Henreid, Claude Rains. 102 min. (*)

Casino (USA: 1995) Director: Martin Scorsese. Screenplay: Nicholas Pileggi, Martin Scorsese. Cast: Robert DeNiro, Sharon Stone, Joe Pesci, James Woods. 182 min. (*)

Casualties of War (USA: 1989) Director: Brian DePalma. Screenplay: David Rabe. Cast: Sean Penn, Michael J. Fox, Thuy Thu Le. 120 min. (*)

The China Syndrome (USA: 1979) Director: James Bridges. Screenplay: Mike Gray, T. S. Cook, James Bridges. Cast: Jane Fonda, Jack Lemmon, Michael Douglas. 123 min. (*)

Chrome and Hot Leather (USA: 1971) Director: Lee Frost. Screenplay: Michael Haynes, David Neibel, Don Tait. Cast: William Smith, Tony Young, Michael Haynes, Peter Brown. 91 min. (*)

Citizen Kane (USA: 1941) Director: Orson Welles. Screenplay: Herman Mankiewicz and Orson Welles. Cast: Orson Welles, Joseph Cotton. 119 min. (*)

City Hall (USA: 1996) Director: Harold Becker. Screenplay: Bo Goldman, Paul Schrader, Nicholas Pileggi. Cast: Al Pacino, John Cusack, Bridget Fonda, Danny Aiello. 111 min. (*)

A Civil Action (USA: 1998) Director: Steven Zaillian. Screenplay: Steven Zaillian. Cast: John Travolta, Robert Duvall. 113 min. (*)

Civilization (USA: 1916) Director: Thomas Ince. Screenplay: C. Gardner Sullivan. Cast: Howard Hickman, Enid Markey, Lola May. 80 min. (*)

Class Action (USA: 1991) Director: Michael Apted. Screenplay: Samantha Shad. Cast: Mary Elizabeth Mastrantonio, Gene Hackman, Larry Fishburne, Donald Moffat. 110 min. (*)

Clerks (USA: 1994) Director: Kevin Smith. Screenplay: Kevin Smith. Cast: Brian O'Halloran, Darryl Anderson. 92 min. (*)

The Client (USA: 1994) Director: Joel Schumacher. Screenplay: Akiva Goldsman. Cast: Susan Sarandon, Tommy Lee Jones. 119 min. (*)

A Clockwork Orange (Great Britain: 1971) Director: Stanley Kubrick. Screenplay: Stanley Kubrick. Cast: Malcolm McDowell, Patrick MaGee. 137 min. (*)

Cold Mountain (USA: 2003) Director: Anthony Minghella. Screenplay: Anthony Minghella. Cast: Jude Law, Nicole Kidman, Renee Zellweger. 152 min. (*)

Collateral Damage (USA: 2002) Director: Andrew Davis. Screenplay: Ronald Roose and David Griffiths. Cast: Arnold Schwarzenegger. 108 min. (*)

Coming Home (USA: 1978) Director: Hal Ashby. Screenplay: Robert C. Jones. Cast: Jane Fonda, Jon Voight, Bruce Dern. 130 min. (*)

Commandos Strike at Dawn (USA: 1943) Director: John Farrow. Screenplay: Irwin Shaw. Cast: Paul Muni, Lillian Gish, Cedric Hardwick, Anna Lee. 100 min. (*)

Compulsion (USA: 1959) Director: Richard Fleischer. Screenplay: Richard Murphy. Cast: Orson Welles, Diane Varsi, Dean Stockwell, Bradford Dillman. 103 min. (*)

Comrade X (USA: 1940) Director: King Vidor. Screenplay: Ben Hecht. Cast: Clark Gable, Hedy Lamarr, Oscar Homolka. 87 min. (*)

Conan the Barbarian (USA: 1982) Director: John Milius. Screenplay: John Milius. Cast: Arnold Schwarzenegger. 129 min. (*)

Confession of a Nazi Spy (USA: 1939) Director: Anatole Litvak. Screenplay: Milton Krims, John Wexley. Cast: Edward G. Robinson, Paul Lucas, George Sanders. 110 min.

Conspiracy Theory (USA: 1996) Director: Richard Donner. Screenplay: Brian Hegeland. Cast: Mel Gibson, Julia Roberts. 135 min. (*)

The Contender (USA/Germany/UK: 2000) Director: Rod Lurie. Screenplay: Rod Lurie. Cast: Jeff Bridges, Joan Allen, Gary Oldman. 126 min. (*)

Counselor-At-Law (USA: 1933) Director: William Wyler. Screenplay: Elmer Rice. Cast: John Barrymore, Beebe Daniels, Melvyn Douglas, Doris Kenton. 78 min. (*)

Country (USA: 1984) Director: Richard Pearce. Screenplay: Bill Wittliff. Cast: Jessica Lange, Sam Shepard, Wilford Brimley. 109 min. (*)

Courage of the Commonplace (USA: 1917) Director: Ben Turbett. Five reels.

Courage Under Fire (USA: 1996) Director: Edward Zwick. Screenplay: Patrick Sheane Duncan. Cast: Denzel Washington, Meg Ryan. 115 min. (*)

The Court Martial of Billy Mitchell (USA: 1955) Director: Otto Preminger. Screenplay: Emmet Lavery, Milton Sperling & (uncredited: Ben Hecht, Dalton Trumbo, Michael Wilson). Cast: Gary Cooper, Charles Bickford, Ralph Bellamy, Rod Steiger. 100 min. (*)

Crash (USA: 1996) Director: David Cronenberg. Screenplay: David Cronenberg. Cast: James Spader, Holly Hunter. 100 min. (*)

Crash Dive (USA: 1943) Director: Archie Mayo. Screenplay: Jo Swerling. Cast: Tyrone Power, Ann Baxter, Dana Andrews. 105 min. (*)

Crime School (USA: 1938) Director: Lewis Seiler. Screenplay: Vincent Sherman, Crane Wilbur. Cast: Humphrey Bogart, Gale Page. 85 min. (*)

Crossfire (USA: 1947) Director: Edward Dmytryk. Screenplay: John Paxton. Cast: Robert Young, Robert Mitchum, Robert Ryan. 86 min. (*)

The Crucible (USA: 1996) Director: Nicholas Hytner. Screenplay: Arthur Miller. Cast: Daniel Day-Lewis, Winona Ryder, Paul Scofield. 123 min. (*)

Cry Havoc (USA: 1944) Director: Richard Thorpe. Screenplay: Paul Osborn. Cast: Margaret Sullivan, Ann Sothern, Joan Blondell. 97 min. (*)

Damage (France & Great Britain: 1992) Director: Louis Malle. Screenplay: David Hare. Cast: Jeremy Irons, Juliette Binoche, Rupert Graves, Miranda Richardson. 111 min. (*)

Dances with Wolves (USA: 1990) Director: Kevin Costner. Screenplay: Michael Blake. Cast: Kevin Costner, Mary McDonnell, Graham Greene. 181 min. (*)

Dangerous Hours (USA: 1919) Director: Fred Niblo. Cast: Lloyd Hughes. 88 min. (*)

Dante's Peak (USA: 1997) Director: Roger Donaldson. Screenplay: Leslie Bohem. Cast: Pierce Brosnan, Linda Hamilton. 109 min. (*)

The Dark Horse (USA: 1946) Director: Will Jason. Cast: Jane Darwell, Dick Elliott, Donald MacBride, Phillip Terry. 59 min. (*)

Dave (USA: 1993) Director: Ivan Reitman. Screenplay: Gary Ross. Cast: Kevin Kline, Sigourney Weaver, Frank Langella. 110 min. (*)

The Day After (USA: 1983) Director: Nicholas Meyer. Screenplay: Edward Hume. Cast: Jason Robards, Jr., JoBeth Williams, John Lithgow, Steve Guttenberg. 126 min. (*)

The Day the Earth Stood Still (USA: 1951) Director: Robert Wise. Screenplay: Edmund North. Cast: Michael Rennie, Patricia Neal, Hugh Marlowe, Sam Jaffe. 92 min. (*)

Days of Glory (USA: 1943) Director: Jacques Tourneur. Screenplay: Casey Robinson, Melchior Lengyel. Cast: Tamara Tourmanova, Gregory Peck, Alan Reed, Maria Palmer. 86 min. (*)

D.C. Sniper: 23 Days of Fear (USA: 2003) Director: Tom McLoughlin. TV Script: Dave Erickson. Cast: Charles Dutton, Jay O. Sanders. 120 min. (*)

Dead End (USA: 1937) Director: William Wyler. Screenplay: Lillian Hellman. Cast: Sylvia Sydney, Joel McCrea, Humphrey Bogart. 92 min. (*)

The Deadly Mantis (USA: 1957) Director: Nathan Juran. Screenplay: Martin Berkeley. Cast: Craig Stevens, William Hopper, Pat Conway. 79 min. (*)

Death Wish (USA: 1974) Director: Michael Winner. Screenplay: Wendell Mayes. Cast: Charles Bronson, Vincent Gardenia, William Redfield, Hope Lange. 93 min. (*)

Death Wish II (USA: 1982) Director: Michael Winner. Screenplay: David Engelbach and Brian Garfield. Cast: Charles Bronson, Jill Ireland. 89 min. (*)

Deep Impact (USA: 1998) Director: Mimi Leder. Screenplay: Bruce Joel Rubin and Michael Tolkin. Cast: Robert Duvall, Morgan Freeman. 120 min. (*)

The Deer Hunter (USA: 1978) Director: Michael Cimino. Screenplay: Deric Washburn, Michael Cimino. Cast: Robert DeNiro, Christopher Walken, Meryl Streep, John Savage. 183 min. (*)

The Defense Rests (USA: 1934) Director: Lambert Hillyer. Screenplay: Jo Swerling. Cast: Jack Holt, Jean Arthur. 70 min. (*)

Defenseless (USA: 1991) Director: Martin Campbell. Screenplay: James Hicks, Jeff Burkhart. Cast: Barbara Hershey, Sam Shepard, Mary Beth Hurt, J. T. Walsh. 106 min. (*)

Desperate Journey (USA: 1942) Director: Raoul Walsh. Screenplay: Arthur T. Horman. Cast: Errol Flynn, Ronald Reagan, Raymond Massey, Nancy Coleman. 108 min. (*)

Destination Tokyo (USA: 1943) Director: Delmer Daves. Screenplay: Delmar Daves, Albert Maltz, Steve Fisher. Cast: Cary Grant, John Garfield, Alan Hale, Dane Clark. 135 min. (*)

Deterrence (USA: 1999) Director: Rod Lurie. Screenplay: Rod Lurie. Cast: Kevin Pollak, Timothy Hutton. 101 min. (*)

The Devil's Advocate (USA: 1997) Director: Taylor Hackford. Screenplay: Jonathan Lemkin, Tony Gilroy. Cast: Al Pacino, Keanu Reeves. 144 min. (*)

Dick (USA: 1999) Director: Andrew Fleming. Screenplay: Andrew Fleming and Sheryl Longin. Cast: Dan Hedaya, Kirsten Dunst, Michelle Williams. 94 min. (*)

Dirty Harry (USA: 1971) Director: Don Siegel. Screenplay: Harry Julian Fink and Rita Fink. Cast: Clint Eastwood, Harry Guardino. 102 min. (*)

Dive Bomber (USA: 1941) Director: Michael Curtiz. Screenplay: Frank Wead, Robert Buckner. Cast: Errol Flynn, Fred MacMurray, Ralph Bellamy, Alexis Smith. 130 min. (*)

Do the Right Thing (USA: 1989) Director: Spike Lee. Screenplay: Spike Lee. Cast: Danny Aiello, Spike Lee, John Turturro. 120 min. (*)

Dogma (USA: 1999) Director: Kevin Smith. Screenplay: Kevin Smith. Cast: Matt Damon, Ben Affleck. 130 min. (*)

The Door in the Floor (USA: 2004) Director: Tod Williams. Screenplay: Tod Williams. Cast: Jeff Bridges, Kim Basinger, Jon Foster. 111 min. (*)

Dr. Strangelove, or: How I Learned to Stop Worrying and Love the Bomb (Great Britain: 1964) Director: Stanley Kubrick. Screenplay: Terry Southern, Peter George, Stanley Kubrick. Cast: Peter Sellers, George C. Scott, Sterling Hayden, Keenan Wynn. 93 min. (*)

Dressed to Kill (USA: 1980) Director: Brian DePalma. Screenplay: Brian DePalma. Cast: Michael Caine, Angie Dickinson. 105 min. (*)

The Eagle and the Hawk (USA: 1933) Director: Stuart Walker. Screenplay: Seton I. Miller, Bogart Rogers, John Monk Saunders. Cast: Fredric March, Cary Grant, Dennis O'Keefe. 68 min. (*)

Easy Rider (USA: 1964) Director: Dennis Hopper. Screenplay: Dennis Hopper, Peter Fonda, Terry Southern. Cast: Peter Fonda, Dennis Hopper, Jack Nicholson. 94 min. (*)

Edge of Darkness (USA: 1943) Director: Lewis Milestone. Screenplay: Robert Rossen. Cast: Errol Flynn, Ann Sheridan, Walter Huston, Nancy Coleman. 120 min. (*)

The English Patient (USA: 1996) Director: Anthony Minghella. Screenplay: Anthony Minghella. Cast: Ralph Fiennes, Juliette Binoche, Kristin Scott Thomas. 160 min. (*)

Erin Brockovich (USA: 2000) Director: Steven Soderbergh. Screenplay: Susannah Grant. Cast: Julia Roberts, Albert Finney. 130 min. (*)

The Execution of Eddie Slovak (USA: 1974) Director: Lamont Johnson. Screenplay: Richard Levinson, William Link. Cast: Martin Sheen, Ned Beatty, Gary Busey. 122 min. (*)

Executive Action (USA: 1973) Director: David Miller. Screenplay: Dalton Trumbo. Cast: Burt Lancaster, Robert Ryan, Will Geer. 91 min. (*)

Executive Power (USA: 1997) Director: David Corley. Screenplay: David Corley. Cast: Craig Sheffer, Andrea Roth. 105 min. (*)

Eyes Wide Shut (USA/UK: 1999) Director: Stanley Kubrick. Screenplay: Stanley Kubrick. Cast: Tom Cruise, Nicole Kidman. 159 min. (*)

Fail Safe (USA: 1964) Director: Sidney Lumet. Screenplay: Walter Bernstein. Cast: Henry Fonda, Dan O'Herlihy, Walter Matthau, Larry Hagman. 111 min. (*)

Far from Heaven (France/USA: 2002) Director: Todd Haynes. Screenplay: Todd Haynes. Cast: Julianne Moore, Dennis Quaid. 107 min. (*)

The Farmer's Daughter (USA: 1947) Director: H.C. Potter. Screenplay: Hella Wvolijoki (Juhni Tervataa), Larry Rivkin, Laura Kerr. Cast: Loretta Young, Joseph Cotten, Ethel Barrymore. 97 min. (*)

Fat Man and Little Boy (USA: 1989) Director: Roland Joffe. Screenplay: Bruce Robinson, Tony Garnett, Roland Joffe. Cast: Paul Newman, Dwight Schultz, Bonnie Bedelia, John Cusack. 127 min. (*)

Fellow Traveler (USA: 1989) Director: Philip Savile. Screenplay: Michael Eaton. Cast: Ron Silver, Imogen Stubbs, Hart Bochner, Daniel J. Travanti. 97 min. (*)

A Few Good Men (USA: 1992) Director: Rob Reiner. Screenplay: Aaron Sorkin. Cast: Tom Cruise, Jack Nicholson, Demi Moore, Kevin Bacon. 138 min. (*)

The Fighting Seabees (USA: 1944) Director: Edward Ludwig. Screenplay: Bordon Chase, Aeneas MacKenzie. Cast: John Wayne, Susan Hayward, Dennis O'Keefe, William Frawley. 100 min. (*)

The Fighting 69th (USA: 1940) Director: William Keighley. Screenplay: Fred Niblo, Norman Reilly Raine, Dean Franklin. Cast: James Cagney, Pat O'Brien, George Brent. 90 min. (*)

Finding Nemo (USA: 2003) Director: Andrew Stanton and Lee Unkrich. Screenplay: Andrew Stanton. Cast: Animation. 100 min. (*)

The Finest Hour (USA: 1991) Director: Shimon Dotan. Screenplay: Shimon Dotan. Cast: Rob Lowe, Gale Hansen, Tracy Griffith. 105 min. (*)

The Firm (USA: 1993) Director: Sydney Pollack. Screenplay: David Rabe. Cast: Tom Cruise, Jeanne Tripplehorn, Gene Hackman. 154 min. (*)

First Blood (USA: 1982) Director: Ted Kotcheff. Screenplay: Sylvester Stallone. Cast: Sylvester Stallone, Richard Crenna, Brian Dennehy. 96 min. (*)

Five (USA: 1951) Director: Arch Oboler. Screenplay: Arch Oboler. Cast: Susan Douglas, William Phipps. 93 min. (*)

Fixed Bayonets (USA: 1951) Director: Samuel Fuller. Screenplay: Samuel Fuller. Cast: Richard Basehart, Gene Evans. 92 min. (*)

Flight Command (USA: 1940) Director: Frank Borzage. Screenplay: Wells Root. Cast: Robert Taylor, Ruth Hussey, Walter Pidgeon. 110 min. (*)

Flying Tigers (USA: 1942) Director: David Miller. Screenplay: Kenneth Gamet, Barry Trivers. Cast: John Wayne, Paul Kelly, John Carroll, Anna Lee. 101 min. (*)

For Whom the Bell Tolls (USA: 1943) Director: Sam Wood. Screenplay: Dudley Nichols. Cast: Gary Cooper, Ingrid Bergman, Akim Tamiroff. 168 min. (*)

Force of Evil (USA: 1948) Director: Abraham Polonsky. Screenplay: Abraham Polonsky. Cast: John Garfield, Thomas Gomez, Marie Windsor, Sheldon Leonard. 78 min. (*)

Foreign Correspondent (USA: 1940) Director: Alfred Hitchcock. Screenplay: Robert Benchley, Charles Bennett, Joan Harrison, James Hilton. Cast: Joel McCrea, Laraine Day, Herbert Marshall, George Sanders. 120 min. (*)

Forrest Gump (USA: 1994) Director: Robert Zemeckis. Screenplay: Eric Roth. Cast: Tom Hanks, Robin Wright, Sally Field, Gary Sinise. 142 min. (*)

The Fortune Cookie (USA: 1966) Director: Billy Wilder. Screenplay: Billy Wilder, I. A. L. Diamond. Cast: Jack Lemmon, Walter Matthau, Ron Rich, Cliff Osmond. 125 min. (*)

The Fourth Protocol (USA: 1987) Director: John MacKenzie. Screenplay: Frederick Forsythe, Richard Burridge, George Axelrod. Cast: Michael Caine, Pierce Brosnan, Ned Beatty, Joanna Cassidy. 119 min. (*)

From Dusk to Dawn (USA: 1913) Director: Frank E. Wolfe. Screenplay: Frank E. Wolfe. Cast: Clarence Darrow. Five reels.

From Here to Eternity (USA: 1953) Director: Fred Zinneman. Screenplay: Daniel Taradash. Cast: Burt Lancaster, Montgomery Clift, Frank Sinatra, Deborah Kerr. 118 min. (*)

The Front (USA: 1976) Director: Martin Ritt. Screenplay: Walter Bernstein. Cast: Woody Allen, Zero Mostel, Herschel Bernardi, Michael Murphy. 95 min. (*)

Full Metal Jacket (USA: 1987) Director: Stanley Kubrick. Screenplay: Michael Herr, Gustav Hasford, Stanley Kubrick. Cast: Matthew Modine, R. Lee Ermey, Vincent D'Onofrio, Adam Baldwin. 116 min. (*)

The Full Monty (Great Britain: 1997) Director: Peter Cattaneo. Screenplay: Simon Beaufoy. Cast: Robert Carlyle, Tom Wilkinson. 91 min. (*)

Fury (USA: 1936) Director: Fritz Lang. Screenplay: Fritz Lang, Bartlett Cormack. Cast: Spencer Tracy, Sylvia Sidney, Walter Abel. 96 min. (*)

Gabriel Over the White House (USA: 1933) Director: Gregory LaVaca. Screenplay: Carey Wilson, Bertram Bloch. Cast: Walter Huston, Karen Morley, Franchot Tone. 87 min. (*)

Gandhi (Great Britian: 1982) Director: Richard Attenborough. Screenplay: John Briley. Cast: Ben Kingsley, Candice Bergen, Edward Fox. 188 min. (*)

Gangs of New York (USA: 2002) Director: Martin Scorsese. Jay Cocks. Cast: Leonardo DiCaprio, Daniel Day-Lewis. 166 min. (*)

Gentleman's Agreement (USA: 1947) Director: Elia Kazan. Screenplay: Moss Hart. Cast: Gregory Peck, Dorothy McGuire, John Garfield. 118 min. (*)

Giant (USA: 1956) Director: George Stevens. Screenplay: Fred Guiol and Ivan Moffat. Cast: Rock Hudson, Elizabeth Taylor, James Dean. 201 min. (*)

Gladiator (UK/USA: 2000) Director: Ridley Scott. Screenplay: David Franzoni. Cast: Russell Crowe, Joaquin Phoenix. 155 min. (*)

The Glass Key (USA: 1942) Director: Stuart Heisler. Screenplay: Jonathan Latimer. Cast: Alan Ladd, Veronica Lake, Brian Donlevy, William Bendix. 85 min. (*)

Go For Broke (USA: 1951) Director: Robert Pirosh. Screenplay: Robert Pirosh. Cast: Van Johnson. 92 min. (*)

Go Tell the Spartans (USA: 1978) Director: Ted Post. Screenplay: Wendell Mayes. Cast: Burt Lancaster, Craig Wasson. 114 min. (*)

The Godfather (USA: 1972) Director: Francis Ford Coppola. Screenplay: Mario Puzo, Francis Ford Coppola. Cast: Marlon Brando, Al Pacino, Robert Duvall, James Caan. 171 min. (*)

The Godfather, Part 2 (USA: 1974) Director: Francis Ford Coppola. Screenplay: Mario Puzo, Francis Ford Coppola. Cast: Al Pacino, Robert DeNiro, Diane Keaton, Robert Duvall. 200 min. (*)

The Godfather, Part 3 (USA: 1990) Director: Francis Ford Coppola. Screenplay: Mario Puzo, Francis Ford Coppola. Cast: Al Pacino, Diane Keaton, Andy Garcia, Joe Mantegna. 170 min. (*)

Godzilla (USA: 1998) Director: Roland Emmerich. Screenplay: Dean Devlin, Roland Emmerich. Cast: Matthew Broderick, Jean Reno. 140 min. (*)

Gone With the Wind (USA: 1939) Director: Victor Fleming. Screenplay: Sidney Howard. Cast: Clark Gable, Vivien Leigh, Olivia de Havilland, Leslie Howard. 231 min. (*)

Good Morning, Vietnam (USA: 1987) Director: Barry Levinson. Screenplay: Mitch Markowitz. Cast: Robin Williams, Forest Whitaker, Bruno Kirby, Richard Edson. 121 min. (*)

Good Will Hunting (USA: 1997) Director: Gus Van Sant. Screenplay: Matt Damon and Ben Affleck. Cast: Robin Williams, Matt Damon, Ben Affleck. 126 min. (*)

Goodfellas (USA: 1990) Director: Martin Scorsese. Screenplay: Nicholas Pileggi. Cast: Robert DeNiro, Ray Liotta, Joe Pesci. 145 min. (*)

The Grapes of Wrath (USA: 1940) Director: John Ford. Screenplay: Nunnally Johnson. Cast: Henry Fonda, Jane Darwell, John Carradine, Charley Grapewin. 129 min. (*)

The Great Dictator (USA: 1940) Director: Charles Chaplin. Screenplay: Charles Chaplin. Cast: Charles Chaplin, Paulette Goddard, Jack Oakie. 127 min. (*)

The Great Escape (USA: 1963) Director: John Sturges. Screenplay: James Clavell, W. R. Burnett. Cast: Steve McQueen, James Garner, Richard Attenborough. 168 min. (*)

The Great McGinty (USA: 1940) Director: Preston Sturges. Screenplay: Preston Sturges. Cast: Brian Donlevy, Akim Tamiroff. 82 min. (*)

The Great Train Robbery (USA: 1903) Director: Edwin S. Porter. Screenplay: Edwin S. Porter. Cast: Marie Murray, Broncho Billy Anderson, George Barnes. 10 min. (*)

The Green Berets (USA: 1968) Directors: John Wayne, Ray Kellogg. Screenplay: James Lee Barrett. Cast: John Wayne, David Janssen, Jim Hutton. 141 min. (*)

Guadalcanal Diary (USA: 1943) Director: Lewis Seiler. Screenplay: Jerome Cady, Richard Tregaskis, Lamar Trotti. Cast: Preston Foster, Lloyd Nolan, William Bendix, Richard Conte. 93 min. (*)

Guess Who's Coming to Dinner (USA: 1967) Director: Stanley Kramer. Screenplay: William Rose. Cast: Katherine Hepburn, Spencer Tracy, Sidney Poitier, Katherine Houghton. 108 min. (*)

Guilty as Sin (USA: 1993) Director: Sidney Lumet. Screenplay: Larry Cohen. Cast: Don Johnson, Rebecca DeMornay, Jack Warden, Stephen Lang. 120 min. (*)

Guilty by Suspicion (USA: 1991) Director: Irwin Winkler. Screenplay: Irwin Winkler. Cast: Robert DeNiro, Annette Bening. 105 min. (*)

Gung Ho! (USA: 1943) Director: Ray Enright. Screenplay: Joseph Hoffman, Lucien Hubbard, W.S. LeFrancois. Cast: Robert Mitchum, Randolph Scott, Noah Beery, Jr., Alan Curtis. 88 min. (*)

Hamburger Hill (USA: 1987) Director: John Irvin. Screenplay: Jim Carabatsos. Cast: Michael Dolan, Daniel O'Shea, Dylan McDermott, Tommy Swerdlow. 104 min. (*)

Heartbreak Ridge (USA: 1986) Director: Clint Eastwood. Screenplay: Jim Carabatsos. Cast: Clint Eastwood, Marsha Mason. 130 min. (*)

Heaven's Gate (USA: 1980) Director: Michael Cimino. Screenplay: Michael Cimino. Cast: Kris Kristofferson, Christopher Walken, John Hurt. 219 min. (*)

Hell's Kitchen (USA: 1963) Directors: Lewis Seiler, E. A. Dupont. Screenplay: Fred Niblo, Jr., Crane Wilbur. Cast: Ronald Reagan, Stanley Fields, Grant Mitchell, Margaret Lindsay. 81 min. (*)

Henry and June (USA: 1990) Director: Philip Kaufman. Screenplay: Philip Kaufman. Cast: Fred Ward, Uma Thurman, Maria de Medeiros, Richard E. Grant. 136 min. (*)

The Heroes of Desert Storm (USA: 1991) Director: Don Ohlmeyer. Screenplay: Lionel Chetwynd. Cast: Daniel Baldwin, Angela Bassett. 93 min. (*)

High Noon (USA: 1952) Director: Fred Zinneman. Screenplay: Carl Foreman. Cast: Gary Cooper, Grace Kelly, Lloyd Bridges, Lon Chaney, Jr. 85 min. (*)

Home of the Brave (USA: 1949) Director: Mark Robson. Screenplay: Carl Foreman. Cast: Lloyd Bridges, James Edwards, Frank Lovejoy. 86 min. (*)

The House on 92nd Street (USA: 1945) Director: Henry Hathaway. Screenplay: Charles G. Booth. Cast: Lloyd Nolan, Signe Hasso. 89 min. (*)

I Am a Fugitive from a Chain Gang (USA: 1932) Director: Mervyn LeRoy. Screenplay: Howard J. Green. Cast: Paul Muni, Glenda Farrell, Preston Foster. 93 min. (*)

I'm No Angel (USA: 1933) Director: Wesley Ruggles. Screenplay: Mae West. Cast: Mae West, Cary Grant, Edward Arnold. 88 min. (*)

I Married a Communist (USA: 1950) Director: Robert Stevenson. Screenplay: Charles Grayson, Robert Hardy Andrews. Cast: Laraine Day, Robert Ryan, John Agar. 73 min.

I Want You (USA: 1951) Director: Mark Robson. Screenplay: Irwin Shaw. Cast: Dana Andrews, Dorothy McQuire, Farley Granger. 101 min. (*)

I Was a Communist for the FBI (USA: 1951) Director: Gordon Douglas. Screenplay: Crane Wilbur, Matt Cvetic. Cast: Frank Lovejoy, Dorothy Hart, Phil Carey. 83 min.

The Ice Storm (USA: 1997) Director: Ang Lee. Screenplay: James Schamus. Cast: Joan Allen, Kevin Kline, Sigourney Weaver. 112 min. (*)

In the Bedroom (USA: 2001) Director: Todd Field. Screenplay: Robert Festinger and Todd Field. Cast: Tom Wilkinson, Sissy Spacek. 130 min. (*)

Independence Day (USA: 1996) Director: Roland Emmerich. Screenplay: Dean Devlin, Roland Emmerich. Cast: Will Smith, Bill Pullman, Jeff Goldblum. 145 min. (*)

Inherit the Wind (USA: 1960) Director: Stanley Kramer. Screenplay: Nathan E. Douglas (aka Ned Young), Harold Jacob Smith. Cast: Spencer Tracy, Fredric March, Gene Kelly. 128 min. (*)

Intruder in the Dust (USA: 1949) Director: Clarence Brown. Screenplay: Ben Maddow. Cast: David Brian, Claude Jarman, Jr., Juano Hernandez. 87 min. (*)

Invasion of the Body Snatchers (USA: 1956) Director: Don Siegel. Screenplay: Daniel Mainwaring. Cast: Kevin McCarthy, Dana Wynter, Larry Gates, King Donovan. 80 min. (*)

It Came from Beneath the Sea (USA: 1955) Director: Robert Gordon. Screenplay: Hal Smith, George Worthing Yates. Cast: Kenneth Tobey, Faith Domergue, Ian Keith, Donald Curtis. 80 min. (*)

It Came from Outer Space (USA: 1953) Director: Jack Arnold. Screenplay: Ray Bradbury. Cast: Richard Carlson, Barbara Rush, Charles Drake, Russell Johnson. 81 min. (*)

Jagged Edge (USA: 1985) Director: Richard Marquand. Screenplay: Joe Eszterhas. Cast: Jeff Bridges, Glenn Close, Robert Loggia. 108 min. (*)

Jaws (USA: 1975) Director: Steven Spielberg. Screenplay: Peter Benchley, Carl Gottlieb. Cast: Richard Dreyfuss, Roy Scheider, Robert Shaw. 124 min. (*)

JFK (USA: 1991) Director: Oliver Stone. Screenplay: Oliver Stone, Zachary Skiar. Cast: Kevin Costner, Sissy Spacek, Kevin Bacon, Tommy Lee Jones. 189 min. (*)

Johnny Guitar (USA: 1953) Director: Nicholas Ray. Screenplay: Philip Yordan. Cast: Joan Crawford, Ernest Borgnine, Sterling Hayden, Mercedes McCambridge. 110 min. (*)

Judge Priest (USA: 1934) Director: John Ford. Screenplay: Dudley Nichols, Lamar Trotti. Cast: Will Rogers, Stepin Fetchit, Anita Louise, Henry B. Walthall. 80 min. (*)

Jungle Fever (USA: 1991) Director: Spike Lee. Screenplay: Spike Lee. Cast: Anabella Sciorra, Wesley Snipes. 131 min. (*)

Jurassic Park (USA: 1993) Director: Steven Spielberg. Screenplay: Michael Crichton. Cast: Sam Neill, Laura Dern, Richard Attenborough. 127 min. (*)

Kill Bill: Vol. 1 (USA: 2003) Director: Quentin Tarantino. Screenplay: Quentin Tarantino and Uma Thurman. Cast: Uma Thurman. Lucy Liu. 111 min. (*)

Kill Bill: Vol. 2 (USA: 2004) Director: Quentin Tarantino. Screenplay: Quentin Tarantino and Uma Thurman. Cast: Uma Thurman, David Carradine. 136 min. (*)

A King in New York (USA: 1957) Director: Charlie Chaplin. Screenplay: Charles Chaplin. Cast: Charlie Chaplin, Dawn Addams, Michael Chaplin. 105 min. (*)

King of the Pecos (USA: 1936) Director: Joseph Kane. Screenplay: Bernard McConville, Dorrell McGowan, Stuart E. McGowan. Cast: John Wayne, Muriel Evans, Cy Kendall, Jack Clifford. 54 min. (*)

Knock on Any Door (USA: 1949) Director: Nicholas Ray. Screenplay: Daniel Taradash, John Monks, Jr. Cast: Humphrey Bogart, John Derek, George MacCready. 100 min. (*)

Kundun (USA: 1997) Director: Martin Scorsese. Screenplay: Melissa Mathison. Cast: Tenzin Thuthob Tsarong, Gyurme Tethog, Robert Lin (II). 135 min. (*)

Ladies Courageous (USA: 1944) Director: John Rawlins. Screenplay: Doris Gilbert. Cast: Loretta Young, Geraldine Fitzgerald. 88 min. (*)

Ladybug, Ladybug (USA: 1963) Director: Frank Perry. Screenplay: Eleanor Perry. Cast: Estelle Parsons, Jane Connell. 81 min.

The Last Hurrah (USA: 1958) Director: John Ford. Screenplay: Frank Nugent. Cast: Spencer Tracy, Jeffrey Hunter, Diane Foster, Pat O'Brien. 121 min. (*)

The Last Letter (USA: 2002) Director: Frederick Wiseman. Screenplay: Veronique Aubouy. Cast: Catherine Samie. 61 min.

The Last Woman on Earth (USA: 1961) Director: Roger Corman. Screenplay: Robert Towne. Cast: Antony Carbone, Edward Waine, Betsy Jones-Moreland. 71 min. (*)

The Last Temptation of Christ (USA: 1988) Director: Martin Scorsese. Screenplay: Paul Schrader. Cast: Willem Dafoe, Harvey Keitel, Barbara Hershey, Harry Dean Stanton. 164 min. (*)

Lawyer Man (USA: 1932) Director: William Dieterle. Screenplay: Riam James, James Seymour. Cast: William Powell, Joan Blondell. 70 min. (*)

Legal Eagles (USA: 1986) Director: Ivan Reitman. Screenplay: Jim Cash, Jack Epps, Jr. Cast: Robert Redford, Debra Winger, Daryl Hannah, Brian Dennehy. 116 min. (*)

Legally Blonde 2: Red, White & Blonde (USA: 2003) Director: Charles Herman-Wurmfeld. Screenplay: Amanda Brown and Eve Ahlert. Cast: Reese Witherspoon, Sally Field. 95 min. (*)

The Life and Times of Judge Roy Bean (USA: 1972) Director: John Huston. Screenplay: John Milius. Cast: Paul Newman, Stacy Keach, Ava Gardner, Jacqueline Bisset. 124 min. (*)

A Lion Is in the Streets (USA: 1953) Director: Raoul Walsh. Screenplay: Luther Davis. Cast: James Cagney, Barbara Hale, Anne Francis. 88 min. (*)

Little Caesar (USA: 1930) Director: Mervyn LeRoy. Screenplay: Francis Faragoh, Robert E. Lee. Cast: Edward G. Robinson, Glenda Farrell, Sidney Blackmer, Douglas Fairbanks, Jr. 80 min. (*)

A Little Princess (USA: 1995) Director: Alfonso Cuaron. Screenplay: Elizabeth Chandler, Richard LaGravenese. Cast: Eleanor Bron, Liesel Matthews. 97 min. (*)

Little Tokyo, U.S.A. (USA: 1942) Director: Otto Brower. Screenplay: George Bricker. Cast: Preston Foster, Brenda Joyce. 64 min.

Lolita (USA: 1997) Director: Adrian Lyne. Screenplay: Stephen Schiff. Cast: Jeremy Irons, Dominique Swain, Melanie Griffith, Frank Langella. 137 min. (*)

Lone Star (USA: 1996) Director: John Sayles. Screenplay: John Sayles. Cast: Chris Cooper, Kris Kristofferson, Matthew McConaughey. 135 min. (*)

The Longest Day (USA: 1962) Director: Ken Annakin. Screenplay: Bernhard Wicki. Cast: John Wayne, Richard Burton, Red Buttons, Robert Mitchum. 179 min. (*)

Lord of the Rings: The Fellowship of the Ring (New Zealand/USA: 2001) Director: Peter Jackson. Screenplay: Frances Walsh. Cast: Ian McKellen, Cate Blanchett, Sean Astin. 178 min. (*)

Lost Boundaries (USA: 1949) Director: Alfred L. Werker. Screenplay: Eugene Ling, Charles Palmer, Virginia Shaler. Cast: Mel Ferrer, Susan Douglas, Beatrice Pearson, Canada Lee. 99 min. (*)

Mad Max (USA: 1980) Director: George Miller. Screenplay: George Miller. Cast: Mel Gibson, Joanne Samuel. 93 min. (*)

Mad Max: Beyond Thunderdome (USA: 1985) Directors: George Miller, George Olgilvie. Screenplay: George Miller, Terry Hayes. Cast: Mel Gibson, Tina Turner. 107 min. (*)

The Majestic (USA: 2001) Director: Frank Darabont. Screenplay: Michael Sloane. Cast: Jim Carrey. 152 min. (*)

Malcolm X (USA: 1992) Director: Spike Lee. Screenplay: Spike Lee, Arnold Perl, James Baldwin. Cast: Denzel Washington, Angela Bassett, Albert Hall, Al Freeman, Jr. 201 min. (*)

The Man in the Gray Flannel Suit (USA: 1956) Director: Nunnally Johnson. Screenplay: Nunnally Johnson. Cast: Gregory Peck, Frederic March, Jennifer Jones, Ann Harding. 152 min. (*)

The Man with the Golden Arm (USA: 1955) Director: Otto Preminger. Screenplay: Walter Newman. Cast: Frank Sinatra, Eleanor Parker, Kim Novak. 119 min. (*)

The Man Who Shot Liberty Valance (USA: 1962) Director: John Ford. Screenplay: Willis Goldbeck, James Warner Bellah. Cast: James Stewart, John Wayne, Vera Miles, Lee Marvin. 123 min. (*)

The Manchurian Candidate (USA: 1962) Director: John Frankenheimer. Screenplay: George Axelrod, John Frankenheimer. Cast: Frank Sinatra, Laurence Harvey, Janet Leigh, James Gregory, Angela Lansbury. 126 min. (*)

The Manchurian Candidate (USA: 2004) Director: Jonathan Demme. Screenplay: Daniel Pyne and Dean Georgaris. Cast: Denzel Washington, Meryl Streep, Liev Schreiber. 130 min. (*)

Manhattan Project (USA: 1986) Director: Marshall Brickman. Screenplay: Marshall Brickman. Cast: John Lithgow, Christopher Collet, Cynthia Nixon, Jill Eikenberry. 112 min. (*)

Man Hunt (USA: 1941) Director: Fritz Lang. Screenplay: Dudley Nichols. Cast: Walter Pidgeon, Joan Bennett, George Sanders. 105 min. (*)

Mars Attacks (USA: 1996) Director: Tim Burton. Screenplay: Jonathan Gems. Cast: Jack Nicholson, Glenn Close, Annette Bening, Pierce Bronson. 106 min. (*)

A Martyr to His Cause (USA: 1911) Produced by the AFL's McNamara Legal Defense Committee. Two reels.

M*A*S*H (USA: 1970) Director: Robert Altman. Screenplay: Ring Lardner, Jr. Cast: Donald Sutherland, Elliott Gould, Robert Duvall. 116 min. (*)

Matewan (USA: 1987) Director: John Sayles. Screenplay: John Sayles. Cast: Chris Cooper, James Earl Jones, Mary McDonnell, William Oldham. 130 min. (*)

The Matrix (USA: 1999) Director: Andy and Larry Wachowski. Screenplay: Andy and Larry Wachowski. Cast: Keanu Reeves, Laurence Fishburne. 136 min. (*)

Meet John Doe (USA: 1941) Director: Frank Capra. Screenplay: Robert Riskin, Richard Connell, Robert Presnell. Cast: Gary Cooper, Barbara Stanwyck, Edward Arnold. 135 min. (*)

Men in Black (USA: 1997) Director: Barry Sonnenfeld. Screenplay: Lowell Cunningham, Ed Solomon. Cast: Tommy Lee Jones, Will Smith. 98 min. (*)

Michael Collins (UK/Ireland/USA: 1996) Director: Neil Jordan. Screenplay: Neil Jordan. Cast: Liam Neeson, Aidan Quinn, Stephen Rea, Alan Rickman, Julia Roberts. 133 min. (*)

Missing (USA: 1982) Director: Costa-Gavras. Screenplay: Costa-Gavras, Donald Stewart. Cast: Jack Lemmon, Sissy Spacek, John Shea. 122 min. (*)

Missing in Action (USA: 1984) Director: Joseph Zito. Screenplay: James Bruner. Cast: Chuck Norris, M. Emmet Walsh. 101 min. (*)

Missing in Action 2: The Beginning (USA: 1985) Director: Lance Hool. Screenplay: Steve Bing. Cast: Chuck Norris, Soon-Teck Oh. 96 min. (*)

Mission to Moscow (USA: 1943) Director: Michael Curtiz. Screenplay: Howard Koch. Cast: Walter Huston, Ann Harding, Oscar Homolka. 123 min.

Mississippi Burning (USA: 1988) Director: Alan Parker. Screenplay: Chris Gerolmo. Cast: Gene Hackman, Willem Dafoe, Frances McDormand, Brad Dourif. 127 min. (*)

Mr. Smith Goes to Washington (USA: 1939) Director: Frank Capra. Screenplay: Sidney Buchman. Cast: James Stewart, Jean Arthur, Edward Arnold, Claude Rains. 130 min. (*)

Modern Times (USA: 1936) Director: Charles Chaplin. Screenplay: Charles Chaplin. Cast: Charles Chaplin, Paulette Goddard. 85 min. (*)

Money Train (USA: 1995) Director: Joseph Ruben. Screenplay: David Richardson, David Loughery. Cast: Wesley Snipes, Woody Harrelson, Jennifer Lopez, Robert Blake. 110 min. (*)

Monster's Ball (USA: 2001) Director: Marc Forster. Screenplay: Milo Addica and Will Rokos. Cast: Billy Bob Thornton, Halle Berry. 111 min. (*)

The Moon is Blue (USA: 1953) Director: Otto Preminger. Screenplay: F. Hugh Herbert. Cast: William Holden, David Niven, Maggie McNamara. 99 min. (*)

The Moon Is Down (USA: 1943) Director: Irving Pichel. Screenplay: Nunnally Johnson. Cast: Cedric Hardwicke, Henry Travers, Lee J. Cobb. 90 min.

The Mortal Storm (USA: 1940) Director: Frank Borzage. Screenplay: Claudine West, George Froeschel, Anderson Ellis. Cast: Margaret Sullavan, James Stewart, Robert Young. 100 min. (*)

The Mouthpiece (USA: 1932) Directors: Elliott Nugent, James Flood. Screenplay: Joseph Jackson, Earl Baldwin. Cast: Warren William, Sidney Fox, Mae Madison, Aline MacMahon. 90 min.

Music Box (USA: 1989) Director: Constantin Costa-Gavras. Screenplay: Joe Eszterhas. Cast: Jessica Lange, Frederic Forrest, Lukas Haas, Armin Mueller-Stahl. 126 min. (*)

Mutiny on the Bounty (USA: 1935) Director: Frank Lloyd. Screenplay: Talbot Jennings, Jules Furthman, Carey Wilson. Cast: Charles Laughton, Clark Gable, Franchot Tone. 132 min. (*)

My Big Fat Greek Wedding (USA: 2002) Director: Joel Zwick. Screenplay: Nia Vardalos. Cast: Nia Vardalos, John Corbett. 95 min. (*)

My Cousin Vinny (USA: 1992) Director: Jonathan Lynn. Screenplay: Dale Launer. Cast: Joe Pesci, Ralph Macchio, Marisa Tomei. 120 min. (*)

My Fellow Americans (USA: 1996) Director: Peter Segal. Screenplay: Jack Kaplan. Cast: Jack Lemmon, James Garner, Dan Akroyd. 101 min. (*)

My Son John (USA: 1952) Director: Leo McCarey. Screenplay: Myles Connolly, Leo McCarey, John Mahin. Cast: Helen Hayes, Robert Walker, Dean Jagger, Van Heflin. 122 min.

Mystic River (USA: 2003) Director: Clint Eastwood. Screenplay: Brian Helgeland. Cast: Sean Penn, Tim Robbins, Kevin Bacon. 137 min. (*)

Nashville (USA: 1975) Director: Robert Altman. Screenplay: Joan Tewkesbury. Cast: Keith Carradine, Lily Tomlin, Henry Gibson, Ronee Blakely, Barbara Harris. 159 min. (*)

Natural Born Killers (USA: 1994) Director: Oliver Stone. Screenplay: Quentin Tarantino, Oliver Stone. Cast: Woody Harrelson, Juliette Lewis, Robert Downey, Jr., Tommy Lee Jones. 119 min. (*)

Network (USA: 1976) Director: Sidney Lumet. Screenplay: Paddy Chayefsky. Cast: Faye Dunaway, William Holden, Peter Finch. 120 min. (*)

Next Stop Wonderland (USA: 1998) Director: Brad Anderson. Screenplay: Brad Anderson, Lyn Vaus. Cast: Hope Davis, Alan Gelfant. 104 min. (*)

Ninotchka (USA: 1939) Director: Ernst Lubitsch. Screenplay: Billy Wilder. Cast: Greta Garbo, Melvyn Douglas. 110 min. (*)

Nixon (USA: 1995) Director: Oliver Stone. Screenplay: Oliver Stone. Cast: Anthony Hopkins, Joan Allen, Powers Boothe, Ed Harris. 190 min. (*)

No Way Out (USA: 1987) Director: Roger Donaldson. Screenplay: Robert Garland. Cast: Kevin Costner, Sean Young, Gene Hackman, Will Patton. 114 min. (*)

Norma Rae (USA: 1979) Director: Martin Ritt. Screenplay: Harriet Frank, Jr., Irving Ravetch. Cast: Sally Field, Ron Leibman, Beau Bridges, Pat Hingle. 114 min. (*)

The North Star (USA: 1943) Director: Lewis Milestone. Screenplay: Lillian Hellman. Cast: Anne Baxter, Dana Andrews, Walter Huston, Farley Granger. 105 min. (*)

The Nuisance (USA: 1933) Director: Jack Conway. Cast: Lee Tracy, Madge Evans, Charles Butterworth. 80 min.

Objective, Burma! (USA: 1945) Director: Raoul Walsh. Screenplay: Ranald MacDougall, Lester Cole. Cast: Errol Flynn, James Brown, William Prince, George Tobias. 142 min. (*)

On the Beach (USA: 1959) Director: Stanley Kramer. Screenplay: John Paxon, James Lee Barrett. Cast: Gregory Peck, Ava Gardner, Fred Astaire, Anthony Perkins. 133 min. (*)

On the Waterfront (USA: 1954) Director: Elia Kazan. Screenplay: Budd Schulberg. Cast: Marlon Brando, Rod Steiger, Eva Marie Saint, Lee J. Cobb. 108 min. (*)

The Ox-Bow Incident (USA: 1943) Director: William A. Wellman. Screenplay: Lamar Trotti. Cast: Henry Fonda, Harry Morgan, Dana Andrews, Anthony Quinn. 75 min. (*)

The Package (USA: 1989) Director: Andrew Davis. Screenplay: John Bishop. Cast: Gene Hackman, Tommy Lee Jones, Joanna Cassidy, Dennis Franz. 108 min. (*)

Panic in Year Zero! (USA: 1962) Director: Ray Milland. Screenplay: John Morton (II), Jay Simms. Cast: Ray Milland, Jean Hagen, Frankie Avalon, Mary Mitchell. 92 min. (*)

The Parallax View (USA: 1974) Director: Alan J. Pakula. Screenplay: David Giler, Lorenzo Semple, Jr., Loren Singer. Cast: Warren Beatty, Hume Cronyn, William Daniels, Paula Prentiss. 102 min. (*)

The Passion of the Christ (USA: 2004) Director: Mel Gibson. Screenplay: Benedict Fitzgerald and Mel Gibson. Cast: James Caviezel. 127 min. (*)

The Patriot (Germany/USA: 2000) Director: Roland Emmerich. Screenplay: Robert Rodat. Cast: Mel Gibson, Jason Isaacs. 164 min. (*)

Patton (USA: 1970) Director: Franklin J. Schaffner. Screenplay: Francis Ford Coppola, Edmund H. North. Cast: George C. Scott, Karl Malden. 171 min. (*)

Pearl Harbor (USA: 2001) Director: Michael Bay. Screenplay: Randall Wallace. Cast: Ben Affleck, Josh Hartnett. 183 min. (*)

The Pelican Brief (USA: 1993) Director: Alan J. Pakula. Screenplay: Alan J. Pakula. Cast: Julia Roberts, Denzel Washington. 141 min. (*)

The People Against O'Hara (USA: 1951) Director: John Sturges. Screenplay: John Monk, Jr. Cast: Spencer Tracy, Diana Lynn, Pat O'Brien. 102 min.

The Perfect Husband: The Laci Peterson Story (USA: 2004) Director: Roger Young. TV Script: Dave Erickson. Cast: Dean Cain. 120 min.

Personal Velocity: Three Portraits (USA: 2002) Director: Rebecca Miller. Screenplay: Rebecca Miller. Cast: Kyra Sedgwick, Parker Posey, Fairuza Balk. 86 min. (*)

Pinky (USA: 1949) Director: Elia Kazan. Screenplay: Philip Dunne, Dudley Nichols. Cast: Jeanne Crain, Ethel Waters, Ethel Barrymore. 102 min. (*)

Platoon (USA: 1986) Director: Oliver Stone. Screenplay: Oliver Stone. Cast: Charlie Sheen, William Dafoe, Tom Berenger. 113 min. (*)

Pork Chop Hill (USA: 1959) Director: Lewis Milestone. Screenplay: James R. Webb. Cast: Gregory Peck, Harry Guardino, Rip Torn, George Peppard. 97 min. (*)

The Postman (USA: 1997) Director: Kevin Costner. Screenplay: Eric Roth, Brian Helgeland. Cast: Kevin Costner, Will Patton, Olivia Williams. 177 min. (*)

Presumed Innocent (USA: 1990) Director: Alan J. Pakula. Screenplay: Frank Pierson. Cast: Harrison Ford, Brian Dennehy, Bonnie Bedelia, Greta Scacchi. 127 min. (*)

Primary Colors (USA: 1998) Director: Mike Nichols. Screenplay: Elaine May. Cast: John Travolta, Emma Thompson. 140 min. (*)

Prisoner of War (USA: 1954) Director: Andrew Marton. Screenplay: Allen Rivkin. Cast: Ronald Reagan, Steve Forrest. 80 min.

The Public Enemy (USA: 1931) Director: William Wellman. Screenplay: Kubec Glasmon, John Bright. Cast: James Cagney, Edward Woods, Jean Harlow, Jean Blondell. 83 min. (*)

Pulp Fiction (USA: 1994) Director: Quentin Tarantino. Screenplay: Quentin Tarantino, Roger Roberts Avary. Cast: John Travolta, Samuel L. Jackson, Uma Thurman, Harvey Keitel. 153 min. (*)

The Quiet American (USA/Germany/Australia: 2002) Director: Phillip Noyce. Screenplay: Christopher Hampton. Cast: Michael Caine, Brendan Fraser. 101 min. (*)

The Racket (USA: 1928) Director: Lewis Milestone. Screenplay: Del Andrews, Harry Behn. Cast: Helen Hayes, Louis Wolheim. 8 reels.

The Rainmaker (USA: 1997) Director: Francis Ford Coppola. Screenplay: Francis Ford Coppola. Cast: Matt Damon, Danny DeVito. 135 min. (*)

Rambo: First Blood Part II (USA: 1985) Director: George Pan Cosmatos. Screenplay: James Cameron, Kevin Jarre, Michael Kozoll, Phil Alden Robinson, Sylvester Stallone. Cast: Sylvester Stallone, Richard Crenna. 93 min. (*)

The Reagans (USA: 2003) Director: Robert Allan Ackerman. TV Script: Jane Marchwood. Cast: Judy Davis, James Brolin. 180 min.

Red Corner (USA: 1997) Director: Jon Avnet. Screenplay: Robert King. Cast: Richard Gere, Bai Ling. 119 min. (*)

Red Dawn (USA: 1984) Director: John Milius. Screenplay: Kevin Reynolds. Cast: Powers Boothe, Ron O'Neal, Patrick Swayze. 114 min. (*)

The Red Menace (USA: 1944) Director: R. G. Springsteen. Screenplay: Albert Demond, Gerald Geraghty. Cast: Robert Rockwell, Hanna Axman. 81 min. (*)

Red Nightmare (USA: 1962) Director: George Waggner. Produced for the Department of Defense. Cast: Peter Brown, Jeanne Cooper, Jack Kelly. 30 min.

Red River (USA: 1948) Director: Howard Hawkes. Screenplay: Borden Chase, Charles Schnee. Cast: John Wayne, Montgomery Clift, Walter Brennen, Joanna Dru. 133 min. (*)

Reservoir Dogs (USA: 1992) Director: Quentin Tarantino. Screenplay: Quentin Tarantino. Cast: Harvey Keitel, Tim Roth, Michael Madsen, Steve Buscemi. 100 min. (*)

Reversal of Fortune (USA: 1990) Director: Barbet Schroeder. Screenplay: Nicholas Kazan. Cast: Jeremy Irons, Glenn Close, Ron Silver, Annabella Sciorra. 112 min. (*)

The Right Stuff (USA: 1993) Director: Philip Kaufman. Screenplay: Philip Kaufman. Cast: Sam Shepard, Scott Glenn, Ed Harris. 193 min. (*)

The Road Warrior (Mad Max 2) (USA: 1982) Director: George Miller. Screenplay: George Miller. Cast: Mel Gibson, Bruce Spence, Emil Minty. 95 min. (*)

Rolling Thunder (USA: 1977) Director: John Flynn. Screenplay: Paul Schrader. Cast: William Devane, Tommy Lee Jones. 99 min. (*)

Romero (USA: 1989) Director: John Duigan. Screenplay: John Sacret Young. Cast: Raul Julia, Richard Jordan, Ana Alicia. 102 min. (*)

Roots (USA: 1977) Director: Marvin Chomsky and John Erman. TV Script: William Blinn and M. Charles Cohen. Cast: Le Var Burton, Edward Asner. 573 min. (*)

Runaway Jury (USA: 2003) Director: Gary Fleder. Screenplay: Brian Koppelman. Cast: John Cusack, Gene Hackman, Dustin Hoffman. 127 min. (*)

Salt of the Earth (USA: 1954) Director: Herbert Biberman. Screenplay: Michael Wilson. Cast: Rosaura Revueltas, Juan Chacon, Will Geer. 94 min. (*)

Salvador (USA: 1986) Director: Oliver Stone. Screenplay: Oliver Stone. Cast: James Woods, James Belushi, John Savage, Michael Murphy. 123 min. (*)

Sands of Iwo Jima (USA: 1949) Director: Allan Dwan. Screenplay: Harry Brown, James Edward Grant. Cast: John Wayne, Forrest Tucker, John Agar, Richard Jaeckel. 109 min. (*)

Saving Jessica Lynch (USA: 2003) Director: Peter Markle. TV Script: John Fasano. Cast: Laura Regan, Nicholas Guilak. 120 min.

Saving Private Ryan (USA: 1998) Director: Steven Spielberg. Screenplay: Robert Rodat. Cast: Tom Hanks, Edward Burns, Matt Damon, Tom Sizemore. 170 min. (*)

Savior (USA: 1998) Director: Predrag Antonijevic. Screenplay: Robert Orr. Cast: Dennis Quaid. 103 min. (*)

Scarface (USA: 1931) Director: Howard Hawkes. Screenplay: Ben Hecht, W. R. Burnett. Cast: Paul Muni, Ann Dvorak, Karen Morley. 93 min. (*)

Scarlet Pages (USA: 1930) Director: Ray Enright. Cast: Elsie Ferguson, John Halliday. 65 min.

Schindler's List (USA: 1993) Director: Steven Spielberg. Screenplay: Steven Zallian. Cast: Liam Neeson, Ben Kingsley, Ralph Fiennes. 195 min. (*)

Seabiscuit (USA: 2003) Director: Gary Ross. Screenplay: Gary Ross. Cast: Jeff Bridges, Chris Cooper, Tobey Maguire. 141 min. (*)

Secret Honor (USA: 1985) Director: Robert Altman. Screenplay: Donald Freen, Arnold Stone. Cast: Philip Baker Hall. 90 min. (*)

The Seduction of Joe Tynan (USA: 1979) Director: Jerry Schatzberg. Screenplay: Alan Alda. Cast: Alan Alda, Barbara Harris, Meryl Streep, Melvyn Douglas. 107 min. (*)

The Senator (USA: 1915) Director: Joseph Golden. Five reels.

Seraphita's Diary (USA: 1980) Director: Frederick Wiseman. Cast: Apollonia van Ravenstein. 90 min.

Sergeant York (USA: 1941) Director: Howard Hawks. Screenplay: Abe Finkel, Harry Chandler, Howard Koch, John Huston. Cast: Gary Cooper, Joan Leslie, Walter Brennan. 134 min. (*)

Seven Days in May (USA: 1964) Director: John Frankenheimer. Screenplay: Rod Sterling. Cast: Burt Lancaster, Kirk Douglas, Edmond O'Brien, Fredric March. 117 min. (*)

Seven Years in Tibet (USA: 1997) Director: Jean-Jacques Annaud. Screenplay: Becky Johnston. Cast: Brad Pitt, David Thewlis, B. D. Wong. 139 min. (*)

sex, lies, and videotape (USA: 1989) Director: Steven Soderberg. Screenplay: Steven Soderberg. Cast: James Spader, Andie MacDowell, Peter Gallagher. 101 min. (*)

Shakespeare in Love (UK/USA: 1998) Director: John Madden. Screenplay: Marc Norman and Tom Stoppard. Cast: Joseph Fiennes, Gwyneth Paltrow. 122 min. (*)

She Done Him Wrong (USA: 193) Director: Lowell Sherman. Screenplay: Harvey Theu, John Bright. Cast: Mae West, Cary Grant. 65 min. (*)

Showgirls (USA: 1995) Director: Paul Verhoeven. Screenplay: Joe Eszterhas. Cast: Elizabeth Berkley, Kyle MacLachlan, Gina Gershon. 131 min. (*)

Silkwood (USA: 1983) Director: Mike Nichols. Screenplay: Nora Ephron, Alice Arlen. Cast: Meryl Streep, Kurt Russell, Cher. 131 min. (*)

Since You Went Away (USA: 1944) Director: John Cromwell. Screenplay: David O. Selznick. Cast: Claudette Colbert, Jennifer Jones, Shirley Temple, Joseph Cotton. 172 min. (*)

So Proudly We Hail (USA: 1943) Director: Mark Sandrich. Screenplay: Alan Scott. Cast: Claudette Colbert, Paulette Goddard, Veronica Lake. 126 min. (*)

Song of Russia (USA: 1943) Director: Gregory Ratoff. Screenplay: Paul Jarrico, Richard Collins. Cast: Robert Taylor, Susan Peters. 107 min.

Speechless (USA: 1994) Director: Ron Underwood. Screenplay: Robert King. Cast: Michael Keaton, Geena Davis, Christopher Reeve. 98 min. (*)

Spiderman (USA: 2002) Director: Sam Raimi. Screenplay: David Koepp. Cast: Tobey Maguire, William Dafoe, Kirsten Dunst. 121 min. (*)

Stalag 17 (USA: 1953) Director: Billy Wilder. Screenplay: Billy Wilder, Edwin Blum. Cast: William Holden, Don Taylor, Otto Preminger. 120 min. (*)

Star Wars (USA: 1977) Director: George Lukas. Screenplay: George Lukas. Cast: Mark Hamill, Carrie Fisher, Harrison Ford, Alec Guinness. 121 min. (*)

State of the Union (USA: 1948) Director: Frank Capra. Screenplay: Myles Connolly, Anthony Veiller, Russell Crouse, Howard Lindsay. Cast: Spencer Tracy, Katherine Hepburn, Angela Lansbury, Van Johnson. 124 min. (*)

The Steel Helmet (USA: 1951) Director: Samuel Fuller. Screenplay: Samuel Fuller. Cast: Gene Evans, Robert Hutton, Richard Loo. 84 min. (*)

The Story of GI Joe (USA: 1945) Director: William A. Wellman. Screenplay: Leopold Atlas, Guy Endore, Philip Stevenson. Cast: Burgess Meredith, Robert Mitchum, Freddie Steele. 108 min.

A Streetcar Named Desire (USA: 1951) Director: Elia Kazan. Screenplay: Tennessee Williams. Cast: Vivien Leigh, Marlon Brando, Kim Hunter. 122 min. (*)

Stuart Little 2 (USA: 2002) Director: Rob Minkoff. Screenplay: Bruce Joel Rubin. Cast: Actors and Animation. 78 min. (*)

Sudden Death (USA: 1995) Director: Peter Hyams. Screenplay: Gene Quintano, Karen Baldwin. Cast: Jean-Claude Van Damme, Powers Boothe. 110 min. (*)

Suddenly (USA: 1954) Director: Lewis Allen. Screenplay: Richard Sale. Cast: Frank Sinatra, Sterling Hayden, James Gleason, Nancy Gates. 75 min. (*)

Summertree (USA: 1971) Director: Anthony Newley. Screenplay: Edward Hume, Stephen Yafa. Cast: Michael Douglas, Brenda Vaccaro, Jack Warden. 89 min. (*)

Sunrise at Campobello (USA: 1960) Director: Vincent J. Donehue. Screenplay: Dore Schary. Cast: Ralph Bellamy, Greer Garson, Hume Cronyn, Jean Hagen. 143 min. (*)

Suspect (USA: 1987) Director: Peter Yates. Screenplay: Eric Roth. Cast: Dennis Quaid, Cher, Liam Neeson. 101 min. (*)

Tanner '88 (USA: 1988) Director: Robert Altman. Screenplay: Gary Trudeau. Cast: Michael Murphy, Pamela Reed, Cynthia Nixon. 120 min. (*)

Tarantula (USA: 1955) Director: Jack Arnold. Screenplay: Robert M. Fresco, Martin Berkeley. Cast: Leo G. Carroll, John Agar, Mara Corday. 81 min. (*)

Taxi Driver (USA: 1976) Director: Martin Scorsese. Screenplay: Paul Schrader. Cast: Robert DeNiro, Jodie Foster, Harvey Keitel. 112 min. (*)

Tender Comrade (USA: 1943) Director: Edward Dmytryk. Screenplay: Dalton Trumbo. Cast: Ginger Rogers, Robert Ryan, Ruth Hussey, Patricia Collinge. 101 min. (*)

The Terminator (USA: 1984) Director: James Cameron. Screenplay: James Cameron, Gale Anne Hurd. Cast: Arnold Schwarzenegger, Michael Biehn, Linda Hamilton, Paul Winfield. 108 min. (*)

The Terror from the Year 5000 (USA: 1958) Director: Robert J. Gurney, Jr. Screenplay: Robert J. Gurney, Jr. Cast: Joyce Holden, Ward Costello. 74 min. (*)

Testament (USA: 1983) Director: Lynne Littman. Screenplay: John Sacret Young, Carol Amen. Cast: Jane Alexander, William Devane, Ross Harris, Roxana Zal. 90 min. (*)

Them! (USA: 1954) Director: Gordon Douglas. Screenplay: Ted Sherdeman, Russell Hughes. Cast: James Whitmore. Edmund Gwenn, Joan Weldon, James Arness. 93 min. (*)

They Were Expendable (USA: 1945) Directors: John Ford, Robert Montgomery (uncredited). Screenplay: Frank W. Weed. Cast: John Wayne, Robert Montgomery, Donna Reed. 135 min. (*)

They Won't Forget (USA: 1937) Director: Mervyn LeRoy. Screenplay: Robert Rossen, Aben Kandel. Cast: Claude Rains, Otto Kruger, Lana Turner, Alan Joslyn, Edward Norris. 95 min. (*)

The Thin Red Line (USA: 1998) Director: Terrence Malick. Screenplay: Terrence Malick. Cast: Sean Penn, Nick Nolte, John Cusack, Woody Harrelson, George Clooney. 166 min. (*)

The Thing (USA: 1951) Director: Christian Nyby. Screenplay: Charles Lederer. Cast: Kenneth Tobay, James Arness, Margaret Sheridan. 87 min. (*)

Thirteen Days (USA: 2000) Director: Roger Donaldson. Screenplay: David Self. Cast: Kevin Costner, Bruce Greenwood, Steven Culp. 147 min. (*)

Three Kings (USA: 1999) Director: David O. Russell. Screenplay: David O. Russell. Cast: George Clooney, Mark Wahlberg. 114 min. (*)

Three Seasons (Vietnam/USA: 1999) Director: Tony Bui. Screenplay: Tony Bui, Timothy Linh. Cast: Harvey Keitel. 113 min. (*)

A Time to Kill (USA: 1996) Director: Joel Schumacher. Screenplay: Akiva Goldsman. Cast: Matthew McConaughey, Sandra Bullock, Samuel L. Jackson. 149 min. (*)

Titanic (USA: 1997) Director: James Cameron. Screenplay: James Cameron. Cast: Leonardo DiCaprio, Kate Winslet, Billy Zane, Kathy Bates. 195 min. (*)

To Kill a Mockingbird (USA: 1962) Director: Robert Mulligan. Screenplay: Horton Foote. Cast: Gregory Peck, Brock Peters, Robert Duvall, Philip Alford, Mary Badham. 129 min. (*)

To the Shores of Hell (USA: 1965) Director: Will Zens. Screenplay: Will Zens, Robert McFadden. Cast: Marshall Thompson, Kiva Lawrence. 82 min. (*)

Traffic (Germany/USA: 2000) Director: Steven Soderbergh. Screenplay: Stephen Gaghan. Cast: Michael Douglas, Benicio Del Toro, Don Cheadle. 147 min. (*)

Trial (USA: 1955) Director: Mark Robson. Screenplay: Don Mankiewicz. Cast: Glenn Ford, Dorothy McGuire, Arthur Kennedy. 105 min.

True Believer (USA: 1989) Director: Joseph Ruben. Screenplay: Wesley Strick. Cast: James Woods, Robert Downey, Jr. 103 min. (*)

True Colors (USA: 1991) Director: Herbert Ross. Screenplay: Kevin Wade. Cast: John Cusack, James Spader, Imogen Stubbs, Mandy Patinkin. 111 min. (*)

Truman (USA: 1995) Director: Frank Pierson. Screenplay: Tom Rickman. Cast: Gary Sinise, Diana Scarwid, Richard Dysart. 135 min. (*)

Twelve Monkeys (USA: 1995) Director: Terry Gilliam. Screenplay: Chris Marker, David Peoples, Janet Peoples. Cast: Bruce Willis, Madeleine Stowe, Brad Pitt, Christopher Plummer. 131 min. (*)

Twister (USA: 1996) Director: Jan De Bont. Screenplay: Michael Crighton. Cast: Helen Hunt, Bill Paxton. 113 min. (*)

U-571 (France/USA: 2000) Director: Jonathan Mostow. Screenplay: Jonathan Mostow. Cast: Matthew McConaughey, Bill Paxton, Harvey Keitel. 116 min. (*)

Uncommon Valor (USA: 1983) Director: Ted Kotcheff. Screenplay: Joe Gayton. Cast: Gene Hackman, Fred Ward, Patrick Swayze, Randall Cobb. 105 min. (*)

Unfaithful (USA/Germany: 2002) Director: Adrian Lyne. Screenplay: Alvin Sargent. Cast: Diane Lane, Richard Gere. 124 min. (*)

The Verdict (USA: 1982) Director: Sidney Lumet. Screenplay: David Mamet. Cast: Paul Newman, James Mason, Charlotte Rampling, Jack Warden. 122 min. (*)

A View from the Bridge (France: 1961) Director: Sidney Lumet. Screenplay: Norman Rosten. Cast: Raf Vallone, Maureen Stapleton, Jean Sorel, Carol Lawrence. 110 min.

Wag the Dog (USA: 1997) Director: Barry Levinson. Screenplay: David Mamet, Hilary Henkin. Cast: Dustin Hoffman, Robert DeNiro. 120 min. (*)

Wake Island (USA: 1942) Director: John Farrow. Screenplay: W. R. Burnett, Frank Butler. Cast: Robert Preston, Brian Donlevy, William Bendix, MacDonald Carey. 88 min. (*)

A Walk in the Sun (USA: 1946) Director: Lewis Milestone. Screenplay: Robert Rossen. Cast: Dana Andrews, Richard Conte, John Ireland, Lloyd Bridges. 117 min. (*)

War Games (USA: 1983) Director: John Badham. Screenplay: Lawrence Lasker, Walter Parkes. Cast: Matthew Broderick, Dabney Coleman, John Wood, Ally Sheedy. 113 min. (*)

The Way We Were (USA: 1973) Director: Sydney Pollack. Screenplay: Arthur Laurents. Cast: Barbra Streisand, Robert Redford. 118 min. (*)

We Were Soldiers (USA/Germany: 2002) Director: Randall Wallace. Screenplay: Randall Wallace. Cast: Mel Gibson, Madeleine Stowe. 138 min. (*)

Welcome to Sarajevo (Great Britain/USA: 1997) Director: Michael Winterbottom. Screenplay: Frank Cottrell Boyce. Cast: Woody Harrelson, Marisa Tomei, Stephen Dillane. 102 min. (*)

What Price Glory? (USA: 1926) Director: Raoul Walsh. Screenplay: James T. O'Donohoe. Cast: Edmund Lowe, Victor McLaglen. 120 min. (*)

Who's Afraid of Virginia Woolf (USA: 1966) Director: Mike Nicholas. Screenplay: Ernest Lehman. Cast: Richard Burton, Elizabeth Taylor, George Segal, Sandy Dennis. 127 min. (*)

The Wild One (USA: 1953) Director: Laszlo Benedek. Screenplay: John Paxton. Cast; Marlon Brando, Mary Murphy. 79 min. (*)

Wilson (USA: 1944) Director: Henry King. Screenplay: Lamar Trotti. Cast: Alexander Knox, Charles Coburn, Geraldine Fiztgerald, Thomas Mitchell. 154 min. (*)

Wings (USA: 1927) Director: William Wellman. Screenplay: Hope Loring, Louis D. Lighton. Cast: Charles (Buddy) Rogers, Clara Bow, Richard Arlen. 139 min. (*)

Winter Kills (USA: 1979) Director: William Richert. Screenplay: William Richert. Cast: Jeff Bridges, John Huston, Anthony Perkins, Richard Boone. 97 min. (*)

The Wizard of Oz (USA: 1939) Director: Victor Fleming. Screenplay: Noel Langley. Cast: Judy Garland, Margaret Hamilton, Ray Bolger, Jack Haley, Bert Lahr. 101 min. (*)

A Woman Under the Influence (USA: 1974) Director: John Cassavetes. Screenplay: John Cassavetes. Cast: Peter Falk, Gena Rowlands. 155 min. (*)

The World, the Flesh, and the Devil (USA: 1959) Director: Ranald MacDougall. Screenplay: Ferdinand Reyher, Ranald MacDougall. Cast: Harry Belefonte, Inger Stevens, Mel Ferrer. 95 min. (*)

Xiu Xiu: The Sent Down Girl (China: 1998) Director: Joan Chen. Screenplay: Joan Chen and Geling Yan. Cast: Lu Lu. 99 min. (*)

A Yank in the R.A.F. (USA: 1941) Director: Henry King. Screenplay: Karl Tunberg, Darrell Ware, Darryl F. Zanuck. Cast: Tyrone Power, Betty Grable, John Sutton. 98 min. (*)

Year of the Dragon (USA: 1985) Director: Michael Cimino. Screenplay: Oliver Stone. Cast: Mickey Rourke, John Lone. 134 min. (*)

You Can Count on Me (USA: 2000) Director: Kenneth Lonergan. Screenplay: Kenneth Lonergan. Cast: Laura Linney, Mark Ruffalo. 111 min. (*)

Young Mr. Lincoln (USA: 1939) Director: John Ford. Screenplay: Lamar Trotti. Cast: Henry Fonda, Alice Brady, Marjorie Weaver, Arleen Whelan. 100 min. (*)

DOCUMENTARIES

America's Answer (USA: 1918) Produced by the U.S. Signal Corps and the Committee on Public Information.

American Dream (USA: 1989) Director: Barbara Kopple. 100 min. (*)

Baptism of Fire (Germany: 1940) Director: Fritz Hippler. 50 min.

The Battle of San Pietro (USA: 1944) Director: John Huston. 43 min. (*)

The Battle of Midway (USA: 1942) Director: John Ford. 28 min.

Belfast, Maine (USA: 2000) Director: Frederick Wiseman. 245 min.

The Big One (USA: 1998) Director: Michael Moore. 96 min. (*)

Bowling for Columbine (USA: 2002) Director: Michael Moore. 120 min. (*)

Britain Prepared (Great Britain: 1915) Produced by the British War Propaganda Bureau.

Dark Days (USA: 2000) Director: Marc Singer. 94 min. (*)

Dear America: Letters Home from Vietnam (USA: 1988) Director: Bill Couturie. 85 min. (*)

December 7th: The Movie (USA: 1943) Director: John Ford, Gregg Toland. Narrators: Walter Huston, Harry Davenport, Dana Andrews, Paul Hurst. 82 min. (*)

The External/Wandering Jew (Germany: 1940). Director: Fritz Hippler.

Fahrenheit 9/11 (USA: 2004) Director: Michael Moore. 122 min. (*)

Harlan County, U.S.A. (USA: 1976) Director: Barbara Kopple. 103 min. (*)

High School (USA: 1968) Director: Frederick Wiseman. 75 min.

High School II (USA: 1994) Director: Frederick Wiseman. 220 min.

Hospital (USA: 1970) Director: Frederick Wiseman. 84 min.

Juvenile Court (USA: 1973) Director: Frederick Wiseman. 144 min.

Law and Order (USA: 1969) Director: Frederick Wiseman. 81 min.

Let There Be Light (USA: 1946) Director: John Huston. 58 min.

Live Nude Girls Unite! (USA: 2000) Director: Vicky Funari and Julia Query. 75 min. (*)

Meat (USA: 1976) Director: Frederick Wiseman. 113 min.

The Memphis Belle (USA: 1943) Director: William Wyler. 45 min. (*)

Nanook of the North (USA: 1922) Director: Robert Flaherty. 55 min.

Near Death (USA: 1989) Director: Frederick Wiseman. 358 min.

A Perfect Candidate (USA: 1996) Directors: R. J. Cutler, David Van Taylor. 105 min. (*)

Pershing's Crusaders (USA: 1918) Produced by the Committee on Public Information.

The Plow That Broke the Plains (USA: 1934) Director: Pare Lorentz. 49 min. (*) [listed under New Deal
    documentaries].

Public Housing (USA: 1997) Director: Frederick Wiseman. 200 min.

Pumping Iron (USA: 1977) Director: George Butler and Robert Fiore. 85 min. (*)

The Ramparts We Watch (USA: 1940) Director: Louis de Rochemont. Screenplay: Robert L. Richards,
    Cedric R. Worth. Cast: Non-professional actors. 90 min.

Report from the Aleutians (USA: 1943) Director: John Huston. U.S. Signal Corps. 47 min.

The River (USA: 1937) Director: Pare Lorentz. Produced by the Farm Security Administration. 31 min.
    (*) [listed under New Deal documentaries].

Roger and Me (USA: 1989) Director: Michael Moore. 91 min. (*)

Rush to Judgment (USA: 1967) Director: Emile de Antonio. 122 min. (*)

The Store (USA: 1983) Director: Frederick Wiseman. 89 min.

Titicut Follies (USA: 1967) Director: Frederick Wiseman. 89 min.

Triumph of the Will (Germany: 1934) Director: Leni Riefenstahl. 115 min. (*)

Under Four Flags (USA: 1918) Director: S. L. Rothafel. Produced by the U.S. Army Signal Corp.

The War Game (Great Britain: 1967) Director: Peter Watkins. 47 min. (*)

The War Room (USA: 1993) Director: Chris Hegedus, D. A. Pennebaker. 93 min. (*)

The Weather Underground (USA: 2002) Director: Sam Green and Bill Siegel. 92 min. (*)

Why We Fight series (USA: 1943–45) Director: Frank Capra. U.S. War Department Productions.

Wild Man Blues (USA: 1997) Director: Barbara Kopple. 105 min. (*)

(*) denotes film is available on video

INDEX

-A-

Abe Lincoln in Illinois, 22
About Schmidt, 249
Above and Beyond, 225
Absolute Power, 121, 136, 143
Accused, 168, 169
Acheson, D., 23
Action in the North Atlantic, 184
Adam's Rib, 167
Adventures of Pluto Nash, 246
Advise and Consent, 129
Affleck, B., 9, 247
Aideed, M., 213
Aiello, D., 128
Air Force One, 34, 41, 120, 121, 131, 137, 143
Alamo, 23
Alamo Bay, 33
Albee, E., 75
Albert, E., 181
Alda, A., 22, 129, 142
Alexander, J., 237
Allen, J., 130
Allen, W., 96
All Quiet on the Western Front, 178, 197
All the King's Men, 127

All the President's Men, 26
Al Qaeda, 218
Al-Rehaief, M., 58
Altman, R., 125, 126, 136, 139, 198
A Martyr to His Cause, 45
Ambrose, S., 252
AMC, 77
American Bar Association, 171
American Beauty, 29
American Communist Party, 100, 102
American Dream, 47, 53
American Federation of Labor, 45, 251
American Film Institute, 81
American Pie, 79, 82, 83, 85, 86, 89, 92, 93
American Political Science Association, 28
American President, 41, 121, 137
American Psycho, 69, 86
America's Answer, 178
Amet, E., 45
Anatomy of a Murder, 159
And Justice for All, 158, 159, 169
Andrews, D., 185, 190, 197
Angels from Hell, 210
Angels with Dirty Faces, 22
Ann Carter's Profession, 167
Antonioni, M., 76
AOL/Time Warner, 244, 249

A Perfect Candidate, 126
Apocalypse Now, 177, 205, 206, 208, 209
Apollo 13, 13
Arbuckle, F., 71
Aristotle, 173
Armageddon, 131
Arness, J., 227
Arnold, E., 128
Arthur, J., 167
Ashby, H., 206
Asimow, M., 171
A Time to Kill, 160
Atom Man versus Superman, 226
Attenborough, R., 37
A Walk in the Sun, 185
A Yank in the RAF, 63
Ayers, L., 181

-B-

Babbitt, B., 125
Baby Doll, 73, 74, 75
Baby Face, 71
Back to Bataan, 184, 204
Bad Company, 13, 92, 246
Bad Lieutenant, 84
Baldwin, A., 11
Band of Brothers, 252
Baptism of Fire, 61
Barber, B., 252
Barkun, M., 141
Barrymore, J., 163
Barsam, R., 44
Basic Instinct, 78, 79, 82, 84, 87
Basinger, J., 183
Basinger, K., 11
Bataan, 183, 196
Battle Cry of Peace, 177
Battle of Midway, 192
Battle of San Pietro, 192
Battle of the Bulge, 189
Bay, M., 23, 176
Beast from 20,000 Fathoms, 227
Beatty, W., 9, 11, 29, 125, 140, 143
Beginning or the End?, 224

Behind Enemy Lines, 214
Behind the Rising Sun, 189
Belfast, Maine, 50
Benjamin, W. 21
Benning, A., 137
Bergman, I., 38, 59, 179
Bertolucci, B., 31
Bessie, A., 106
Best Man, 121, 123
Best Years of Our Lives, 190, 197
Biberman, H., 106, 111, 112
Big Jim McLain, 116
Big One, 44, 53, 56
Big Parade, 178
Big Red One, 220
Bing, S., 11
bin Laden, O., 218
Birth of a Nation, 7, 21, 24, 30, 67
Biskind, P., 36, 247
Black, G., 73
Black Hawk Down, 213
blacklist. *See* HUAC (House Committee on Un-American Activities)
Blacklist Company, 111, 112
Blackton, J. S., 177
Blair, T., 217
Blair Witch Project, 248
Blockade, 63
Blow Up, 76
Bob Roberts, 124, 125
Bogart, H., 27, 38, 59, 75, 155, 157, 179
Bolshevism on Trial, 46
Bond, W., 105
Bono, S., 8
Born on the Fourth of July, 207
Bosnia, 214
Bound, 85
Bowling for Columbine, 44, 51, 53, 56
Boy and His Dog, 237
Boyer, P., 222, 223, 224
Boys in Company C, 205, 206
Braddock: Missing in Action III, 207
Bradley, J., 183, 191
Brady, M., 177
Brando, M., 16, 75, 114, 205
Braveheart, 82

breakpoint.com, 92
Brecht, B., 104, 106
Breen, J., 71, 72, 75
Brian's Song, 57
Bridge on the River Kwai, 189, 195
Bridges, J., 130, 140, 168
Britain Prepared, 45
British Board of Film Classification, 83, 90
Brockovich, E., 170
Broderick, M., 232
Brokaw, T., 176, 191
Bromberg, E., 111
Bromberg, J., 112
Bronson, C., 151
Bruckheimer, J., 213
Bryant, W. J., 160
Buffalo Soldiers, 14
Buhle, P., 12
Bulow, C. von, 159
Bulworth, 28, 29, 30, 40, 125
Bundy, M., 23
Bureau of Motion Pictures, 180, 191
Burstyn v. Wilson, 70, 75, 87
Bush, G. H. W., 4, 17, 51, 55, 132, 213–214, 215, 217
Bush, G. W., 215, 218, 239, 240, 251
Bush, J., 8
Bustamante, C., 4
Butch Cassidy and the Sundance Kid, 248
Buttafuoco, J., 57
By the Bomb's Early Light, 222

-C-

Cagney, J., 70, 180
Caine Mutiny, 154
Canadian Bacon, 47
Candidate, 34, 119, 123
Cape Fear, 146, 147
Capra, F., 20, 22, 35, 47, 51, 66, 127, 128, 142, 192
Carabatsos, J., 211, 213
Career Woman, 167
Carey, M., 4
Carrey, J., 96
Carter, J., 212

Casablanca, 27, 28, 33, 38, 59, 60, 75, 179
Cassavetes, J., 18, 22
Castle Rock, 247
Casualites of War, 207, 211
CatholicDigest.com, 92
Catholic League of Decency, 73
CBS, 58
censorship, 87–90
Chaplin, C., 13, 20, 38, 39, 108, 179
Chen, J., 87
Cher, 8, 168, 169
China Syndrome, 19, 32, 233
Christiansen, T., 31, 33, 35
Chrome and Hot Leather, 210
Churchill, W., 132, 186
Cimino, M., 78, 206, 249
Cineast Group, 31, 32
cinema vérité, 48, 50
Cineplex Odeon, 77
Citizen Kane, 27
City Hall, 41, 127, 128
Civil Action, 166
Civilization, 177
Clansman, 67
Clarke, M., 70
Class Action, 168, 169, 172
Client, 161
Clift, M., 67
Clinton, B., 6, 7, 8, 10, 11, 15, 68, 81, 142, 204, 214, 243
Clockwork Orange, 87, 88
Clooney, G., 11, 17, 216
Close, G., 168
Cobb, L. J., 115
Code and Rating Administration (CARA), 77–79, 82–85
Cochran, J., 187
Cohen, W., 14
Colbert, C., 190
Cold Mountain, 245
Cold War, 97–98
Cole, L., 106
Coleman, G., 4
Collateral Damage, 13, 82, 92
Collins, R., 107
Colson, C., 92
Columbia Pictures, 39, 244

combat films, 183–88
Coming Home, 205, 206, 208, 210
Commandos Strike at Dawn, 186
Committee on Public Information (CPI), 45, 178
communism, 107–110
Compulsion, 160
Comrade X, 64
Conan the Barbarian, 3
Condon, R., 140
Confessions of a Nazi Spy, 63, 179
Conrad, J., 205
Conspiracy Theory, 141
Contender, 30, 40, 121, 130, 250
Coolidge, C., 178
Cool World, 48
Cooper, G., 22, 104, 110, 154
Copland, A., 99, 185
Coppola, F. F., 34, 163, 177, 206
Corman, R., 235
Corridon, J., 115
Costas Gavras, 18, 31
Costner, K., 20, 22, 41, 130, 140
cost sharing, 245–246
Cotton, J., 122
Coughlin, C., 179
Counsellor at Law, 163, 165
Country, 28
Courage of the Commonplace, 46
Courage under Fire, 215, 216
Court Martial of Billy Mitchell, 154
Crane, S., 208
Crash, 84, 90
Crash Dive, 183, 185
Crawford, B., 127
Crawford, J., 117
Creel Committee, 180
Creel, G., 178
Crime School, 22
Cronenberg, D., 84
Crossfire, 37
Crucible, 115
Cruise, T., 155
Crusades, 57
Cry Havoc, 187, 188
Cuban Missile Crisis, 22, 196
Culbert, D., 59

Curtiz, M., 59
Cusack, J., 128, 130, 142

-D-

Damage, 84
Damon, M., 161, 247
Dances with Wolves, 20
Dangerous Hours, 46
Dante's Peak, 237
Dark Days, 47
Dark Horse, 122
Darrow, C., 160
Dassin, J., 111
Dave, 121, 136
Davies, J., 64
Davis, E., 43
Davis, G., 4, 5, 6, 40, 41
Day After, 236, 237
Day, D., 117
Days of Glory, 64, 185, 185
Day the Earth Stood Still, 116, 228
Deadly Mantis, 227
Dear America: Letters Home from Vietnam
Death Wish, 19, 151, 152
Death Wish II, 152
D.C. Sniper, 58
December 7th: The Movie, 192
Deep Impact, 131
Deer Hunter, 205, 206, 208, 209, 249
Defenseless, 168
Defense Rests, 167
De Mille, C B., 57
DeMornay, R., 169
DeNiro, R., 6, 95, 97, 104, 206, 210
Denvir, J., 146
DePalma, B., 78, 80, 207
Derek, J., 157
Der Fuehrer's Face, 64
Dershowitz, A., 159
Desert Storm: Cockpit Videos of Bomb Runs, 215
Desert Storm: Eagles over the Gulf, 215
Desert Triumph, 215
Desperate Journey, 188
Destination Tokyo, 38
Deterrence, 131, 143

Devil's Advocate, 166
DiCaprio, L., 247
Dick, 121, 137
Dirty Harry, 19, 151, 152
Disney Company, 14, 54
Dive Bomber, 63
Dmytryk, E., 104–106, 190
docudrama, 57–59
documentary films, 48–56
Dogma, 249
Dole, B., 25, 125
Door in the Floor, 249
Do the Right Thing, 19
Douglas, M., 41, 120, 129, 137, 201, 202
Down and Dirty Pictures, 247
Downsize This!, 51, 53
DreamWorks, 131, 244, 250
Dressed to Kill, 78, 80
Dr. Strangelove, 121, 134, 230, *231*
Drury, A., 129
Dude, Where's My Country?, 51
Duvall, R., 163, 209

- E -

Eagle and the Hawk, 178
Eagleton, T., 123
Eastman, C., 136, 151
Eastwood, C., 213
Edge of Darkness, 186
Einstein, A., 239
Eisenhower, D. D., 99, 223, 238, 239
Eliot, T. S., 237
Enfield, C., 107, 108
Enterprise Productions, 164
Erin Brockovich, 169
Execution of Eddie Slovak, 111
Executive Action, 139, 140
Executive Power, 121
External/Wandering Jew, 60
Eyes Wide Shut, 78, 83

- F -

Fahrenheit 9/11, 19, 44, 54, 55, 56, 251
Fail Safe, 121, 229, 230

Fairbanks, D., 13
Fairbanks, D., Jr., 181
Far from Heaven, 249
Farmer's Daughter, 122
Fate of the Earth, 238
Fat Man and Little Boy, 225
Faulkner, W., 74
Federal Trade Commission, 91
Federated Film Corporation, 46
Ferguson, E., 167
Fermi, E., 221
Ferrer, J., 105, 155
Ferrigno, L., 3
Few Good Men, 155
Fighting 69ᵗʰ, 179, 180
film
    average cost of producing, 245
    business of, 244–47
    censorship and, 70–74, 87–90
    content of, 18–26
    cost sharing and, 245, 246
    docudrama, 57–59
    documentary, 48–56, 191–92
    as history, 21–24
    as ideology, 18–20
    law and lawyers portrayed in, 145–73
    locations, 245
    nonfiction, 43–47
    nuclear holocaust, 221–33, 235–41
    political, 1–6, 6–18, 27–34, 35–42, 119–44, 243, 248–53
    as politicizing agent, 24–26
    propaganda, 20–21, 59–68
    rating system for, 77–82, 85–90
    regulation of, 70–74, 76–77
    sex and violence in, 69–70
    war, 175–99, 201–20
filmvalues. com, 93
Finding Nemo, 246
Finest Hour, 215
Firm, 161
First Blood, 207
Five, 235
Fixed Bayonets, 196
Flags of Our Fathers, 183, 191
Flaherty, R., 43, 44, 51
Flight Command, 63

Flynn, E., 185, 186, 188
Flynt, L., 4
Fonda, H., 123, 129, 149, 157, 181, 229
Fonda, J., 11, 16, 17, 210
Force of Evil, 36, 164, 165, 173, 251
Ford, G., 157, 158
Ford, H., 34, 120, 131, 137, 143, 169
Ford, J., 37, 121–23, 127, 170, 184, 192
Foreign Correspondent, 179
Foreman, C., 35, 111
Forsythe, J., 158
Forrest Gump, 37
Fortune Cookie, 162, 173
For Whom the Bell Tolls, 110
Foster, J., 169
Fourth Protocol, 226
Fox-Searchlight, 249
Francis, R., 155
Frank, L., 150, 151
Frankenheimer, J., 138
Freeman, M., 131
Fried, A., 99, 100
From Dusk to Dawn, 45
From Here to Eternity, 75, 195
Front, 96
Fuchs, K., 222, 225
Fuller, S., 196, 213, 220
Full Metal Jacket, 177, 207, 208, 211
Fury, 37, 150, 151

-G-

Gable, C., 181
Gabriel over the White House, 133, 142
Gandhi, 37
Gangs of New York, 82
Gardner, A., 229
Garfield, J., 111, 164, 251
Garrett, B., 111
Gazzara, B., 159
Geer, W., 112
Geertz, C., 28
Genovese, M., 31, 32, 35
Gentlemans' Agreement, 37
Gere, R., 15, 16
Gershwin, I., 185
Giant, 13

Gibson, M., 19, 80, 141, 176, 219, 237, 245
Gilbert, J., 178
GKC Theatres, 86
Gladiator, 82
Glass Key, 127
Glickman, D., 243
Godfather, 16, 34, 81, 146, 162, 163
Goebbels, J., 20, 60
Goetz, B., 153
Goldberg, R. A., 141
Goldwyn, S., 7, 11, 244, 249
Gomez, T., 164
Gone with the Wind, 34, 75, 181
Goodfellas, 82
Good Morning, Vietnam, 219
Good Will Hunting, 247, 248
Gore, A., 10, 11
Gornick, V., 117
Go Tell the Spartans, 205, 219
Grant, L., 111
Grapes of Wrath, 19, 33, 37
Great Dictator, 20, 30, 33, 38–40, 179
Great Escape, 189
Great McGinty, 127
Great Train Robbery, 148
Green Berets, 13, 19, 176, 185, 203, 204, 209
Greenglass, D., 222, 225
Grenada, 212
Grierson, J., 44
Griffith, D. W., 7, 67
Grisham, J., 147, 160, 161
Groves, L., 222
Guadalcanal Diary, 184, 189
Guess Who's Coming to Dinner?, 37, 38
Guilt by Suspicion, 95–97, 104
Guilty as Sin, 169
Gung Ho!, 185

-H-

Haas, P., 33, 34, 35
Hackman, G., 130, 136, 172, 210
Hall, P. B., 136
Hamburger Hill, 207, 208, 211, 213
Hamilton, G., 163
Hammett, D., 99, 127

Hammond, J., 142
Hanks, T., 11, 23, 245, 252
Harding, W. G., 178
Harlan County, USA, 47, 56
Harlow, J., 71
Harris, E., 17
Hart, G., 11, 125
Harvey, L., 138
Hawks, H., 67
Hayden, S., 116
Hayden, T., 203
Hayes, H., 65
Haynes, T., 249
Hays, W., 18, 71
HBO, 252
Hearst, W. R., 12
Heartbreak Ridge, 213
Heart of Darkness (Conrad), 205
Heaven's Gate, 78, 249
Hellman, L., 110, 113, 185
Hell's Kitchen, 22
Henry and June, 84
Hentschel, I., 103
Hepburn, K., 37, 41, 122, 167
Hercules in New York, 3
Heroes of Desert Storm, 215
Hershey, B., 168
Heston, C., 56
H-film, 88
High Noon, 22, 35, 36, 66, 67, 96
High School I, 49
High School II, 49
Hitchcock, A., 179
Hitler, A., 20, 21, 60–64
Hollywood
    blacklist and, 101–05, 110–18
    communism and, 13, 107–110
    criminal behavior and, 25
    European Union and, 16
    film content and, 18–26
    indies and, 247–49
    political films and, 243, 249–253
    Production Code and, 69–76
    social responsibility of, 90–93
Hollywood Ten, 104, 105–107, 109, 110, 165
Home of the Brave, 37

Hoover, H., 12, 133
Hoover, J. E., 98, 107
Hopkins, A., 246
Hospital, 49
House on 92nd Street, 224
Houston, W., 133
Howard, L., 181
HUAC (House Committee on Un-American
    Activities), 95–97, 100, 101–105, 109, 110,
    122, 165, 191
    blacklist and, 110–18
    Hollywood Ten and, 105–107
Hudson, R., 117
Huffington, A., 4
Hughes, Justice, 176
Hussein, S., 6, 16, 17, 205, 212, 215, 216,
    218
Huston, J., 176, 192

-|-

I Am a Soldier Too, 59
Ice Storm, 29
ICON, 245
IFC Films, 54
I Married a Communist, 116
I'm No Angel, 73
Ince, T., 177
Independence Day, 34, 120, 121, 131, 137, 143,
    232, 237
Independent Production Corporation, 112
indies, 247–49
Inherit the Wind, 160
International Alliance of Theatrical and Stage
    Employees, 102
In the Bedroom, 249
Intruder in the Dust, 37
Invasion of the Body Snatchers, 116, 227, 228
Iraq, 217, 218
Irving, J., 207
It Came from Beneath the Sea, 227
It Came from Outer Space, 228
It Can't Happen Here, 74
I Want You, 197, 198
I Was a Communist for the FBI, 116

- J -

Jagged Edge, 168
Janssen, D., 204
Jarrico, P., 112
JFK, 19, 20, 35, 66, 140, 141
Jobs, S., 246
Johnny Guitar, 96, 116
Johnson, D., 169
Johnson, L. B., 15, 75, 100, 203
Johnson, V., 155
Jones, D. B., 109
Jones, J., 75
Jones, P., 6, 11
Jones, T. L., 140
Jordan, M., 53
Jordan, N., 37
Juarez, B., 57
Judge Priest, 121
Jungle, 49
Jungle Fever, 19
Jurassic Park, 30
Just and Unjust Wars (Walzer), 198
Juvenile Court, 49

- K -

Kael, P., 65, 113
Kahn, G., 107
Kahn, H., 232
Kaltenborn, H. V., 222
Kazan, E., 46, 73, 113, 114
Keystone theaters, 86
Keaton, M., 40, 41
Kelly, G., 181, *182*
Kennedy, A., 158
Kennedy, B., 125
Kennedy, E., 3
Kennedy, J. F., 57, 100, 139
Keough, P., 81
Kill Bill, 249
King of the Pecos, 148, 149
King in New York, 38, 39
King, M. L., 22
Kissinger, H., 15

Kline, K., 41, 136
Kmart, 54
Knock on Any Door, 157
Koch, E., 128
Koch, H., 107
Kopple, B., 47, 53, 56
Korean War movies, 192–99
Kosovo, 214
Kovich, R., 207
Kramer, S., 37, 38, 228
Kubrick, S., 78, 83, 87, 88, 134, 177, 207, 208, 230, 232
Kundun, 14
Kuwait, 215

- L -

Labor Film Services, 46
Ladies Courageous, 187
Ladybug, Ladybug, 223
Lafollette, R., 99
Lahti, C., 169
Lancaster, B., 205
Lane, M., 139
Lang, F., 150
Lange, J., 168
Lardner, R., 95, 106, 117
Last Hurrah, 127
Last Letter, 48
Last Temptation of Christ, 80
Last Woman on Earth, 235
law and lawyer films, 145–73
Lawson, J. H., 46, 106, 111
Lawyer Man, 162
League of Women Voters, 104
Lee, C., 111
Lee, H., 157
Lee, S., 18
Legal Eagles, 168
Legally Blond II, 129
Legion of Decency, 72
Lemmon, J., 162, 233, 251
Leno, J., 4, 8
Lenz, T., 146, 147, 152
Let There Be Light, 176
Levinson, B., 136

Levy, E., 250
Lewinsky, M., 6, 142
Lewis, S., 74
Lichter, R., 1
Life and Times of Judge Roy Bean, 149
Lincoln, A., 133
Lipper, K., 128
Lions Gate Films, 54
Little Caesar, 70, 72
Littlefeather, S., 16
Little Tokyo, U.S.A, 188
Live Nude Girls, 47
Lolita, 87, 252
Lombard, C., 181
Long, H., 127, 128
Longest Day, 189
Lord of the Rings, 30
Lorentz, P., 46, 63
Losey, J., 111
Lost Boundaries, 37
Lost City of the Jungle, 226
Lumet, S., 229
Lurie, R., 130
Lynch, J., 59
Lyne, A., 87
Lyons, C., 79

-M-

Macauley, S., 146, 147
Mad Max, 237
Madonna, 17
Mailes, G, 101
Majestic, 96
Malden, C., 114
Malick, T., 175, 184
Malle, L., 83, 84
Maltz, A., 46, 105, 106, 111
Manchurian Candidate, 138, 141, 195
Manhattan Project, 221, 222
Manhattan Project, 225
Man Hunt, 63
Man in the Gray Flannel Suit, 33
Man Who Shot Liberty Valence, 122, 148, 170
Man With the Golden Arm, 75

March, F., 178, 190
March of Time, 51
Mars Attacks, 232
Marshall, S. L. A., 197
Marvin, L., 123
Marx, G., 16
M*A*S*H, 14, 198
Mastrantonio, M. E., 168, 169, 172
Matrix, 245
Matthau, W., 173
Matusow, H., 104
Mayer, L., 11, 12, 110, 244
MCA-Universal, 16
McCambridge, M., 117
McCarthy, J., 98–101, 107, 123
McClintock, T., 4
McGillis, K., 168, 169
McGovern, G., 9, 125, 135
McNamara, G., 23
Meat, 49, 50
Medved, M., 89
Meet John Doe, 127
Memphis Belle, 192
Menjou, A., 104
MGM, 64, 76, 110, 117, 179, 187, 188, 191, 224, 225, 249
Michael Collins, 37, 83
Milestone, L., 107, 185, 197
Milland, R., 235, 236
Miller, A., 113, 115
Miller, R., 250
Milosevic, S., 214
Minnesota Moratorium, 176
Miramax, 14, 54, 247, 248, 249
Missing, 19, 57
Missing in Action, 207
Missing in Action 2: The Beginning, 207
Mission to Moscow, 64–67, 110
Mississippi Burning, 22
Modern Times, 19
Money Train, 25, 90
Monroe, M., 194
Monster's Ball, 82
Montgomery, R., 181
Moon Is Blue, 75
Moore, D., 155

Moore, H., 219
Moore, M., 17, 19, 26, 44, 47, 51–56, 251, 252
Morgan, H., 149
Morgan, T., 101
Morlan, D., 39, 63
Mortal Storm, 63, 179
Mostel, J., 112
Mostel, Z., 112
Mothers and Others, 16
Motion Picture Alliance for the Preservation of
     American Ideals, 103, 105, 110, 111
Motion Picture Association of America, 14,
     15, 75, 77, 78, 79, 82, 86, 243
Mouthpiece, 162
moviemom.com, 93
Movietone News, 192
MoveOn, 4
Mr. Smith Goes to Washington, 20, 22, 34, 128,
     142, 166
Muni, P., 70
Murphy, E., 246
Murphy, G., 8
Murrow, E. R., 179
Music Box, 168
Mussolini, B., 20
Mutiny on the Bounty, 67
My Big Fat Greek Wedding, 245, 246
My Cousin Vinny, 162
Myers, H., 71
My Fellow Americans, 41, 121
My Son John, 116
Mystic River, 18

- N -

Nanook of the North, 44
Nashville, 125, 139
national amusements, 77
National Association of Theater Owners, 85
National Legion of Decency, *71*
National Resources Defense Council, 16
Natural Born Killers, 82, 84, 85, 87, 90
NBC, 58
Near Death, 49
Network, 151

New Line Cinema, *249*
Newman, P., 149, 165, 169, 173, 225, 251
news of the day, 192
New York Film Festival, 237
Nichols, M., 125, 233
Nicholson, J., 155
Nicomachean Ethics, 173
Nielsen, M., 101
Nike, 53
Nimmo, D., 22, 66, 67
Ninotchka, 64
Nitti, F., 102
Nixon, 19, 20, 22, 66, 121, 135
Nixon, R., 19, 57, 76, 108, 120, 135–37
nonfiction film, 43–44
     development of, 44–47, 191–92
     docudrama, 57–59
     documentary, 48–56
     propaganda, 59–68
Noriega, M., 213
Norma Rae, 19
Norris, C., 207
Norris, F., 55
North, O., 68
North Star, 64, 110, 185
No Way Out, 37, 41, 130
nuclear holocaust movies, 221–41
Nuisance, 161

- O -

Objective Burma, 185
Obler, A., 235
O'Connor, E., 127
O'Connor, H., 56
O'Connor, R., 14
October, 249
O'Donnell, K., 22
Office of War Information, 47, 110, 180, 189,
     191
Oldman, G., 131
On the Beach, 228, 229, 241
On the Waterfront, 114
Oppenheimer, J. R., 222, 225, 238
Ornitz, S., 106, 111
Ostrom, R., 231

Oswald, L. H., 139
Outer Limits, 224
Ox-Bow Incident, 149

-P-

Pacino, A., 41, 128, 158, 166, 169
Package, 226
Packer, H., 151
Palmer, A. G., 98
Palmer, W., 207, 208
Panama, 213
Panic in Year Zero!, 235
Parallax View, 140
Paramount, 187, 188, 192, 237, 244
Parker, A., 22
Parks, L., 104, 107, 111
Passion of the Christ, 19, 80, 245
Pasteur, L., 57
Pataki, G., 241
Patriot, 176
Patton, 120, 189
Payne, A., 249
Payne Fund Studies, 24
PBS, 237
Pearl Harbor, 23, 176
Peck, G., 157, 185, 197, 228
Pelican Brief, 161
Penn, S., 17, 18
People Against O'Hara, 165
Perfect Candidate, 68
Perfect Husband, 58
Perry, F., 223
Pershing's Crusaders, 178
Persian Gulf War, 215
Persian Gulf: The Images of a Conflict, 215
Personal Velocity, 250
Pesci, J., 162
Peters, S., 64
Peterson, L., 58
Peterson, S., 58
phase analysis, 207–209
Pichel, I., 107
Pickford, M., 13
Pinky, 37
Pitt, B., 247

Platoon, 19, 81, 177, 207–09, 211
Plow That Broke the Plains, 46
Plunkitt, G. W., 126
Poitier, S., 37
political expediency factor, 209–211
political films, 1–18, 27–31, 119–21, 128–32, 141–44, 243
    definition of, 32
    effect of, 36–42
    future of, 248–53
    identifying, 31–34
    intent of, 35–36
    portrayal of assassinations in, 137–41
    portrayal of campaigns, 121–26
    portrayal of political machines, 126–28
    portrayal of presidents in, 132–37
    redefining, 35–42
    typology, 34
Political Film Society, 33
Pollack, K., 131
Polonsky, R., 36, 97, 111, 164, 165, 251
Pope Gregory XV, 60
Popular Front, 108
Pork Chop Hill, 196, 197
Powdermaker, H., 80
Powell, C., 215
Power, T., 181, 185
Presumed Innocent, 169
Primary Colors, 6, 7, 29, 40, 125, 136
Prisoner of War, 196
Production Code, 69, 70, 71, 72–74, 74–76, 76–77, 89, 244
Production Code Administration, 72, 74
propaganda films, 59–68
Public Enemy, 70, 72
Public Housing, 49
Pullman, B., 34, 120, 131, 137, 143
Pulp Fiction, 31, 81, 82, 248
Pumping Iron, 3
Puzo, M., 163
Pyle, E., 185

-Q-

Quaid, D., 169, 214
Quiet American, 249

-R-

Rabe, D., 211
Racket, 142
Radar Men from the Moon, 226
Radical Hollywood, 12
Rainmaker, 161
Rains, C., 27
Rambo: First Blood, 207
Rambo: First Blood Part II, 28, 120
Ramparts We Watch, 47
Rampling, C., 165, 169
Randolph, M., 112
Ray, N., 116
Reagan, R., 8, 22, 24, 28, 52, 58, 89, 103, 110, 120, 124, 131, 134, 196, 210, 212
Reagans, 58
reality fictions, 48–51
Red Alert, 230
Red Badge of Courage, 208
Red Corner, 15
Red Dawn, 28
Red-Headed Woman, 71
Red Menace, 65, 116
Red Nightmare, 65
Red River, 66, 67
Red Stars and Fellow Travelers in Hollywood, 108
Redford, R., 16, 96, 119, 123, 143, 248, 252
Reedy, G., 95
Reel Politics, 31
Reeves, K., 166
Reiner, R., 137
Reno, J., 8
Report from the Aleutians, 192
Republic Pictures, 148
Reservoir Dogs, 31, 82, 84
Reversal of Fortune, 159
Revueltas, R., 112, 113
Rice, E., 163
Riefenstahl, L., 20, 35, 43, 59, 61–64
Right Stuff, 13
River, 46
RKO Pictures, 189, 192
Robbins, T., 17, 18, 124, 143
Roberts, J., 79, 161, 169, 245

Robeson, P., 104
Robertson, C., 123
Robertson, P., 125
Robinson, E. G., 70
Rochemont, L. de, 47
Rock, C., 246
Roe v. Wade, 57
Roger and Me, 26, 44, 47, 52, 56, 252
Rogers, G., 190
Rogers, W., 121
Rolling Thunder, 210
Romero, 42
Roosevelt, F. D., 23, 132, 133, 180, 221
Roots, 57
Rosenberg, J., 225
Rossen, R., 107
Runaway Jury, 147
Rush to Judgment, 139
Russell, D. O., 18, 216, 249
Russell, H., 190
Ryan, M., 215

-S-

Saint, E. M., 114
Salt of the Earth, 33, 65, 66, 111–*114*,
Salt, W., 107
Salvador, 19, 35
Sands of Iwo Jima, 183, 189, 208
Sandstorm in the Gulf: Digging Out, 215
Sarandon, S., 17, 161
Saunders, F., 13
Savage, J., 206
Saving Jessica Lynch, 58
Saving Private Ryan, 23, 175, 189, 192, 219
Savior, 214
Sawyer, D., 215
Scarface, 70, 72
Scarlet Pages, 167
Schell, J., 237
Schindler's List, 188, 189
Schlesinger, A., Jr., 176
Schreiber, L., 138
Schulberg, B., 115
Schwartz, L., 112
Schwarzenegger, A., 3, 5, 6, 8, 124, 237

Schwarzkopf, N., 215

Scopes, J. T., 160

Scorsese, M., 80, 147

Scott, A., 106, 111

Scott, R., 185, 213

Screen Actors Guild, 110

screenit.com, 93

Seabiscuit, 39, 245

Secret Honor, 136

Seduction of Joe Tynan, 22, 129, 143

Selznick, D. O., 75

Senator, 121

Seraphita's Diary, 48

Sergeant York, 63, 179, 180, 208

Seven Days in May, 121

Seven Years in Tibet, 14

Sex, Lies, and Videotape, 31, 248

Shakespeare in Love, 249

Shaw, R., 138

She Done Him Wrong, 73

Sheen, C., 209

Sheen, M., 17, 205

Showtime, 252

Shriver, M., 3

Shriver, S., 3

Showgirls, 82, 83, 84

Shute, N., 228

Shultz, G., 4

Siegel, D., 228

Sign of the Cross, 57

Silkwood, 57, 233, 234

Silkwood, K., 234

Silver, R., 159

Simon, B., 4

Simon, J., 30

Sinatra, F., 111, 138, 139, 196

Since You Went Away, 190

Sinclair, U., 12, 49, 55

Sinese, G., 134

Slaton, J., 151

Smith, K., 13, 249

Smith, R., 26, 52, 56

Soderbergh, S., 31, 169, 248, 249

Sondergaard, G., 111

Song of Russia, 64, 110

Sony, 77, 244

So Proudly We Hail, 187, 188

Southern Christian Leadership Conference, 22

Spader, J., 130

Speechless, 40, 41

Spencer, H., 236

Spiderman, 30

Spielberg, S., 23, 79, 131, 175, 189, 192

Stalag 17, 189, 195

Stalin, J., 64, 67

Stallone, S., 207, 208

Stanwyck, B., 70

State of the Union, 122

Steel Helmet, 196, 220

Stevens, G., 192

Stewart, J., 122, 128, 148, 159, 181, 251

Stewart, P., 42

Stone, O., 18, 19, 20, 35, 66, 84, 90, 135, 136, 138, 140, 177, 207, 209, 211, 214

Store, 50

Story of GI Joe, 185

Streep, M., 16, 22, 129, 138

Streetcar Named Desire, 75

Streisand, B., 9, 10, 96

Stuart Little II, 246

Students for a Democratic Society, 203

Studio Basic Agreement, 102

Stupid White Men, 51

Sturges, P., 127

Sudden Death, 85

Suddenly, 139

Summertree, 201, 202

Sundance Film Festival, 248, 252

Sunrise at Campobello, 22, 133

Sunstein, C., 35

Suspect, 168, 169

Swofford, A., 220

- T -

Tanner 88, 125, 126

Tarantino, Q., 31, 249

Tarantula, 227

Tarleton, B., 176

Tavernier, B., 31

Taxi Driver, 81, 210

Taylor, E., 65

Taylor, R., 64, 65, 181

Teller, E., 222, 232, 238
Temple, S., 8
Tender Comrade, 190
Terminator 3, 237
Terror from the Year 5000, 228
Testament, 236, 237
Thatcher, M., 213
Them!, 227
They Were Expendable, 184
They Won't Forget, 37, 150, 151
Thing, 116, 227
Thin Red Line, 176, 184
Thirteen Days, 22, 34, 121
Three Kings, 216, 249
Three Stooges, 39, 40
Tibbets, P., 225
Titanic, 15, 30
Titicut Follies, 48, 49, 50, 56
To Kill a Mockingbird, 157, 170
Tolstoy, L., 74
Tone, F., 129
To the Shores of Hell, 203, 204
Townsend, L., 105
Tracy, S., 37, 41, 122, 127, 150, 165, 167, 173
Tradeau, G., 125
Traffic, 249
Travolta, J., 7, 11, 136, 166
Trevor, C., 167
Trial, 158
TriStar, 78
Triumph of the Will, 20, 21, 35, 43, 59, 61, 62, 64
True Believer, 165, 171
True Colors, 130, 142
Truman, 133
Truman, H., 133, 134, 144, 238
Trumbo, D., 102, 106, 109, 111, 117, 139, 190
Turner, F. J., 148
Torow, S., 169
12 Monkeys, 85
Twentieth Century Fox, 117, 192, 244, 249
Twilight Zone, 224
Twister, 237

- U -

U-571, 23

Ueberroth, P., 4
Uncommon Valor, 28, 210
Under Four Flags, 178
Unfaithful, 72
Union of Russian Workers, 98
United Artists, 77, 244, 249
United Service Organization, 181
Universal, 226, 244, 249
Universal Newsreel, 192
USA Network, 58
U. S. Catholic Conference, 92
U. S. Film Festival, 248
U. S. Film Service, 46

- V -

Valenti, J., 14, 15, 75, 76, 82, 86, 89, 203, 241
Van Sant, G., 247
Vaughn, S., 24
Ventura, J., 4, 124
Verdict, 165, 169, 171
Verhoeven, P., 78
Viacom, 244
Vidal, G., 123
Vietnam movies, 201–211
View from the Bridge, 115
Vivendi, 244
Voight, J., 210
Von Braun, W., 232

- W -

Wagner, D., 12
Wag the Dog, 6, 7, 29, 40, 136, 141
Wajda, A., 31
Wake Island, 183, 184, 188, 189, 196
Walken, C., 206
Walt Disney, 63, 104, 244, 249, 251
Walters, D., 215
Walzer, M., 198, 219
war films, 175–20
War Games, 229, 232, 233
Warner Brothers, 22, 27, 38, 52, 57, 63, 65, 102, 110, 141, 150, 179, 180, 186, 244

Warner, H., 11
Warner, J., 11, 95
War Relocation Authority, 189
Warren Report, 35
Warren, R. P., 127
War Room, 47, 68, 126
Washington, D., 138, 161, 215
Wasserman, L., 16
Watkins, P., 229
wave theory, 204–207
Wayne, J., 13, 23, 65–67, 105, 116, 122, 148, 176, 184, 185, 203, 204, 209
Way We Were, 96
Weather Underground, 47
Weinstein, H., 247, 248
Welch, J., 95
Welcome to Sarajevo, 37, 214
Welles, O., 160
Wertmuller, L., 31
West, M., 72
West Wing, 17
We Were Soldiers, 219
What Price Glory?, 178
White, J., 39
Who's Afraid of Virginia Woolf?, 75
Why We Fight, 20, 22, 35, 47, 51, 66
Widmer, R., 130
Wild One, 75
Wilder, B., 173
Williams, R., 219, 247
Williams, T., 75
Wilson, 22, 133
Wilson, M., 111, 112
Wilson, P., 4
Wilson, W., 21, 45, 67, 132, 133, 178, 180
Winger, D., 168
Wings, 178
Winkler, I., 95, 97
Winter Kills, 140
Wiseman, F., 43, 47, 48, 49, 50, 56
Witherspoon, R., 129
Woman Under the Influence, 19
Women Airforce Service Pilots (WASP), 186, 187
Wood, S., 110
Woods, J., 165, 173
World, the Flesh, and the Devil, 235

World War I movies, 177–80
World War II movies, 180–82
Wouk, H., 155
Wray, F., 167
Wyler, W., 192

- X -

X-Files, 141
Xiu Xiu: the Sent Down Girl, 87, 89

- Y-

Yari, B., 246
Year of the Dragon, 79
York, A., 180
You Can Count on Me, 250
You Nazty Spy, 39, 63
Young, L., 122, 142, 187
Young Mr. Lincoln, 157, 171
Young, N., 111

- Z -

Zemen, J., 15
Zola, E., 57
Zombies of the Stratosphere, 226

Politics,
Media &
Popular Culture

David A. Schultz, *General Editor*

This series is devoted to both scholarly and teaching materials that examine the ways politics, the media, and popular culture interact and influence social and political behavior. Subject matters to be addressed in this series include, but will not be limited to: media and politics; political communication; television, politics, and mass culture; mass media and political behavior; and politics and alternative media and telecommunications such as computers. Submission of single-author and collaborative studies, as well as collections of essays are invited.

Authors wishing to have works considered for this series should contact:

Peter Lang Publishing
Acquisitions Department
275 Seventh Avenue, 28th floor
New York, New York 10001

To order other books in this series, please contact our Customer Service Department at:

800-770-LANG (within the U.S.)
(212) 647-7706 (outside the U.S.)
(212) 647-7707 FAX

or browse online by series at:

WWW.PETERLANGUSA.COM